Story and Art by
Rumiko Takahashi

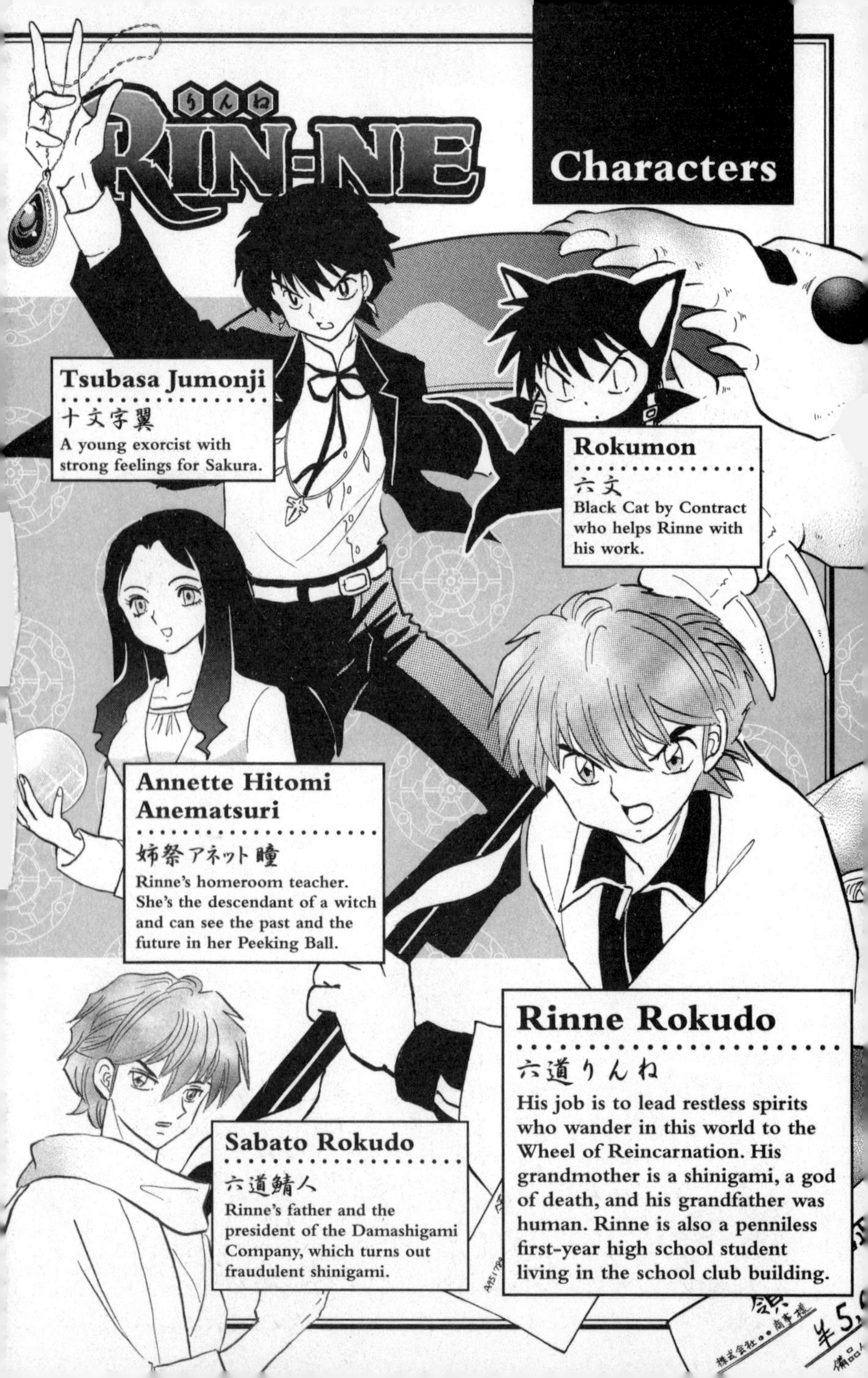
りんね
RIN-NE
Characters
Tsubasa Jumonji
十文字翼
A young exorcist with strong feelings for Sakura.
Rokumon
六文
Black Cat by Contract who helps Rinne with his work.
Annette Hitomi Anematsuri
姉祭アネット瞳
Rinne's homeroom teacher. She's the descendant of a witch and can see the past and the future in her Peeking Ball.
Rinne Rokudo
六道りんね
His job is to lead restless spirits who wander in this world to the Wheel of Reincarnation. His grandmother is a shinigami, a god of death, and his grandfather was human. Rinne is also a penniless first-year high school student living in the school club building.
Sabato Rokudo
六道鯖人
Rinne's father and the president of the Damashigami Company, which turns out fraudulent shinigami.

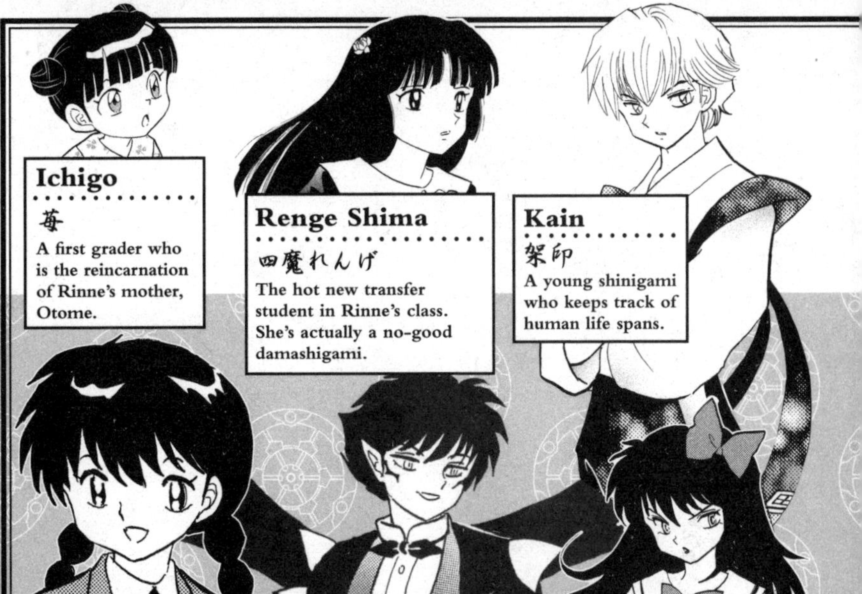
Ichigo
苺
A first grader who is the reincarnation of Rinne's mother, Otome.
Renge Shima
四魔れんげ
The hot new transfer student in Rinne's class. She's actually a no-good damashigami.
Kain
架印
A young shinigami who keeps track of human life spans.
Sakura Mamiya
真宮 桜
When she was a child, Sakura gained the ability to see ghosts after getting lost in the Afterlife. Calm and collected, she stays cool no matter what happens.
Masato
魔狭人
Holds a grudge against Rinne and is a terribly narrow-minded devil.
Ageha
鳳
A devoted shinigami who has a crush on Rinne.

The Story So Far

Sakura, the girl who can see ghosts, and Rinne, the shinigami (sort of), spend their days together helping spirits that can't pass on reach the Afterlife and dealing with all kinds of strange phenomena at their school.

Anju becomes BFFs with Matsugo, but her true aim is romance, so she works with Rinne—who's stressed out by Matsugo's intense feelings for him—to lure Matsugo to a powerful love spot known as the Red Bride Church! Between trying to keep Crescent Moon Hall from going out of business and dealing with young Shoma's exorcism ambitions at the local pool, Rinne's summer vacation is anything but restful!

Contents

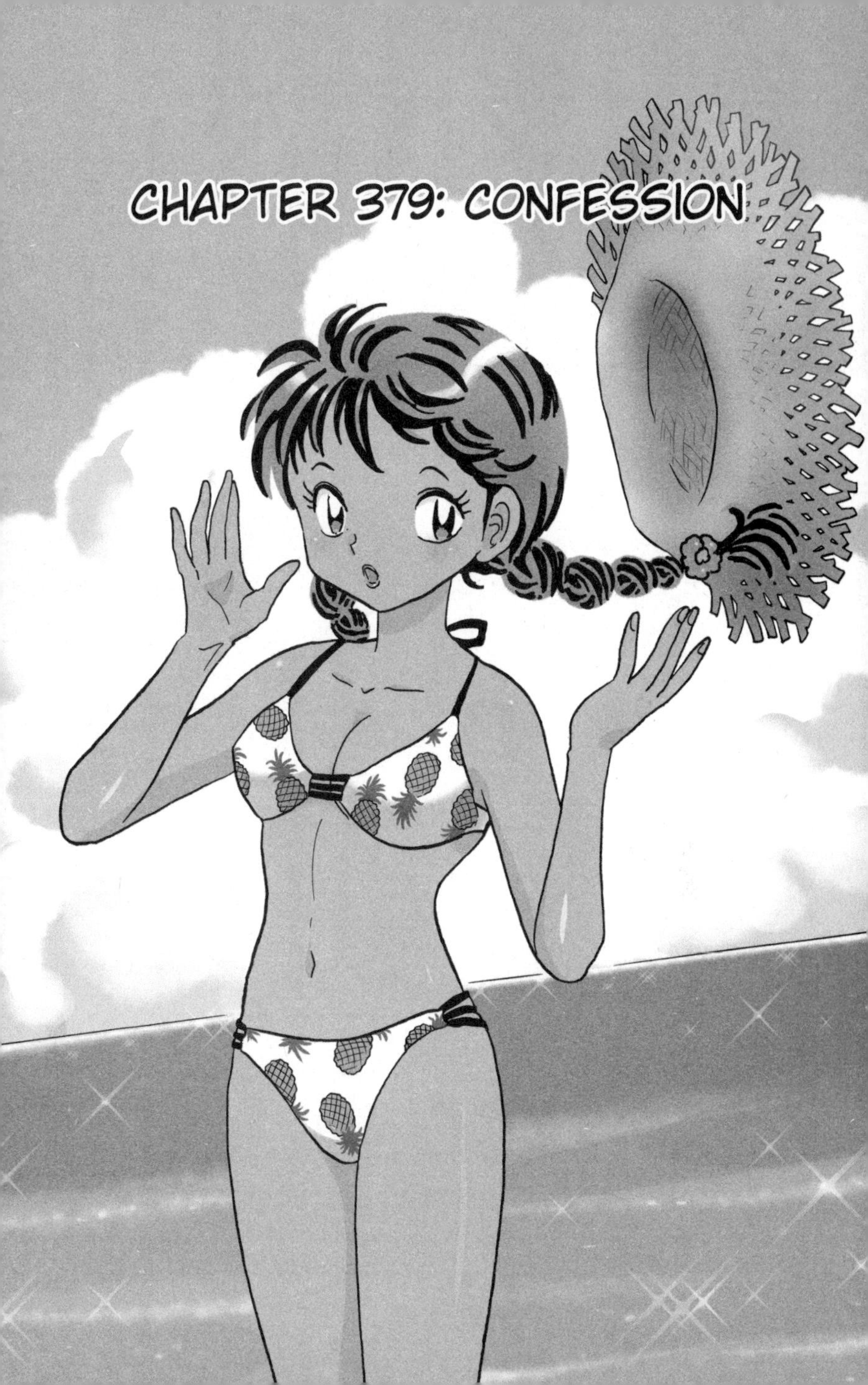
CHAPTER 379: CONFESSION

りんね

RIN-NE

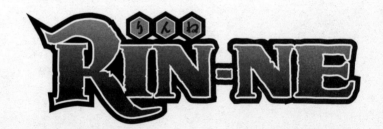

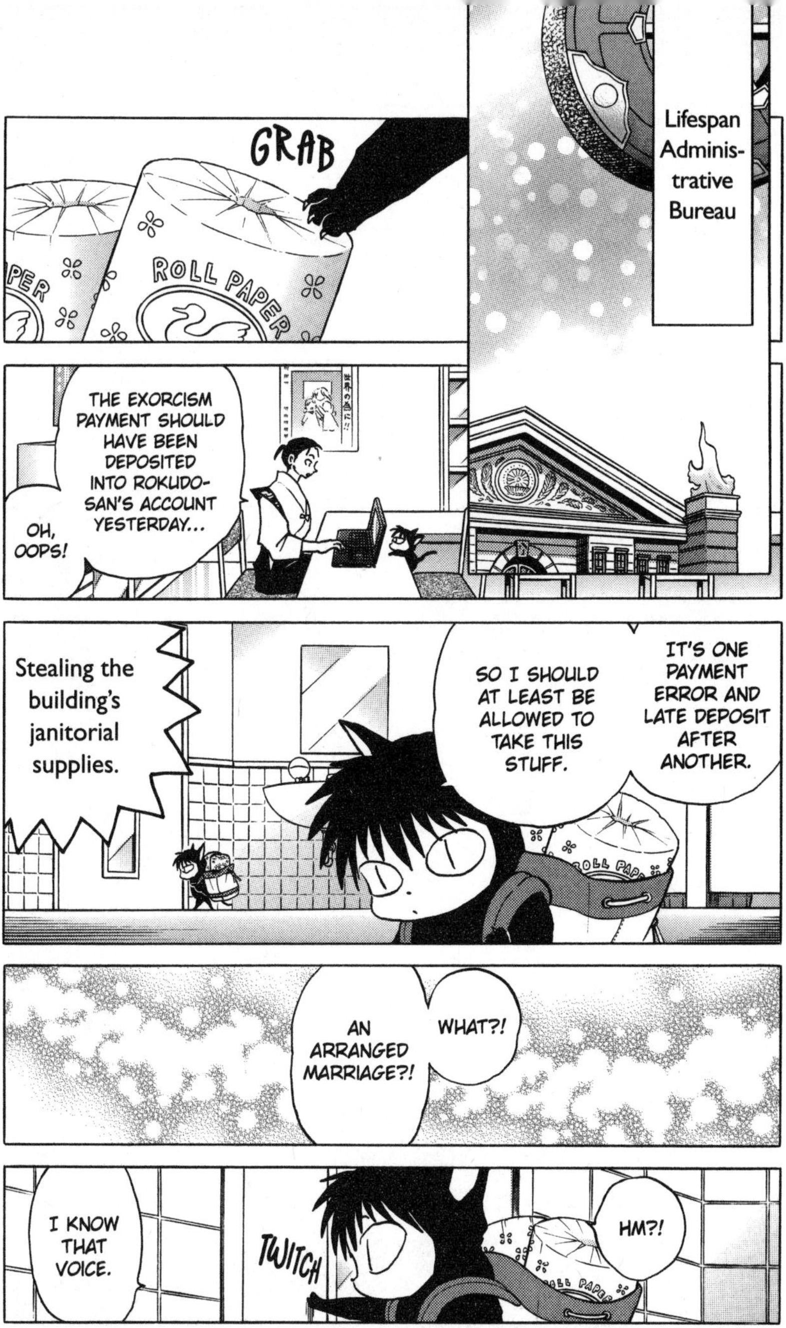
Lifespan Administrative Bureau
GRAB
ROLL PAPER
THE EXORCISM PAYMENT SHOULD HAVE BEEN DEPOSITED INTO ROKUDO-SAN'S ACCOUNT YESTERDAY...
OH, OOPS!
IT'S ONE PAYMENT ERROR AND LATE DEPOSIT AFTER ANOTHER.
SO I SHOULD AT LEAST BE ALLOWED TO TAKE THIS STUFF.
Stealing the building's janitorial supplies.
ROLL PAPER
WHAT?!
AN ARRANGED MARRIAGE?!
HM?!
TWITCH
I KNOW THAT VOICE.

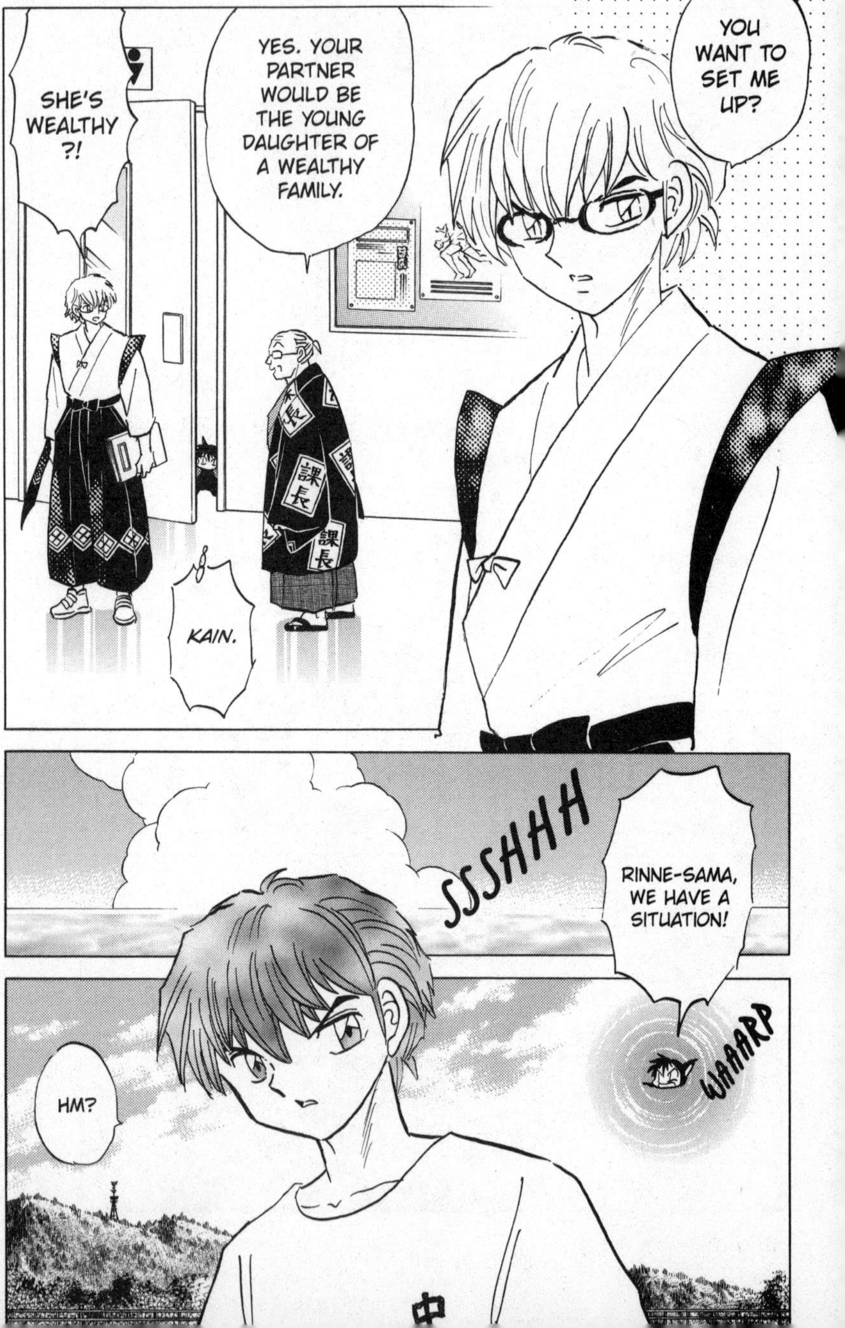
YOU WANT TO SET ME UP?
YES. YOUR PARTNER WOULD BE THE YOUNG DAUGHTER OF A WEALTHY FAMILY.
SHE'S WEALTHY ?!
KAIN.
SSSHHH
RINNE-SAMA, WE HAVE A SITUATION!
WAAARP
HM?

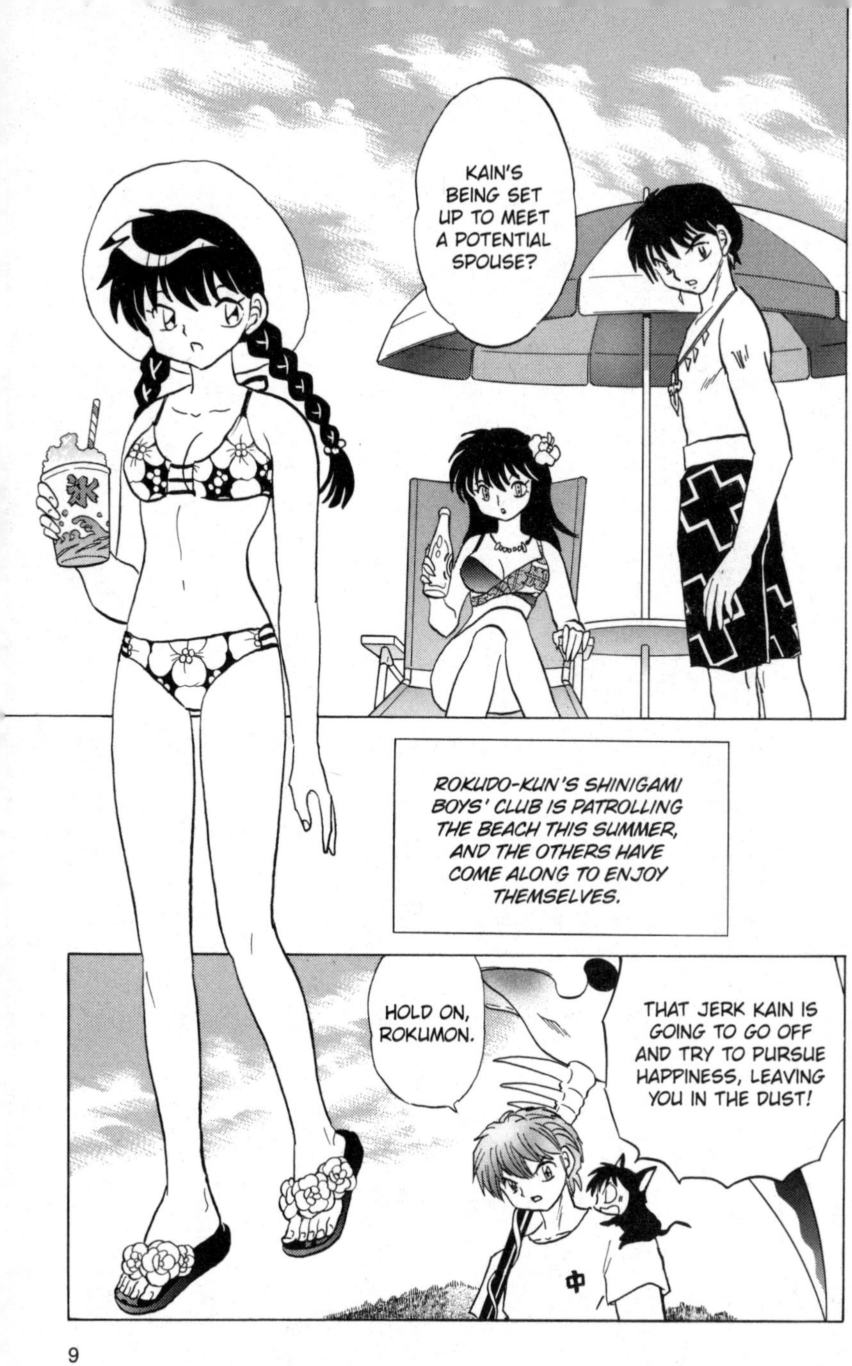
KAIN'S BEING SET UP TO MEET A POTENTIAL SPOUSE?
ROKUDO-KUN'S SHINIGAMI BOYS' CLUB IS PATROLLING THE BEACH THIS SUMMER, AND THE OTHERS HAVE COME ALONG TO ENJOY THEMSELVES.
THAT JERK KAIN IS GOING TO GO OFF AND TRY TO PURSUE HAPPINESS, LEAVING YOU IN THE DUST!
HOLD ON, ROKUMON.

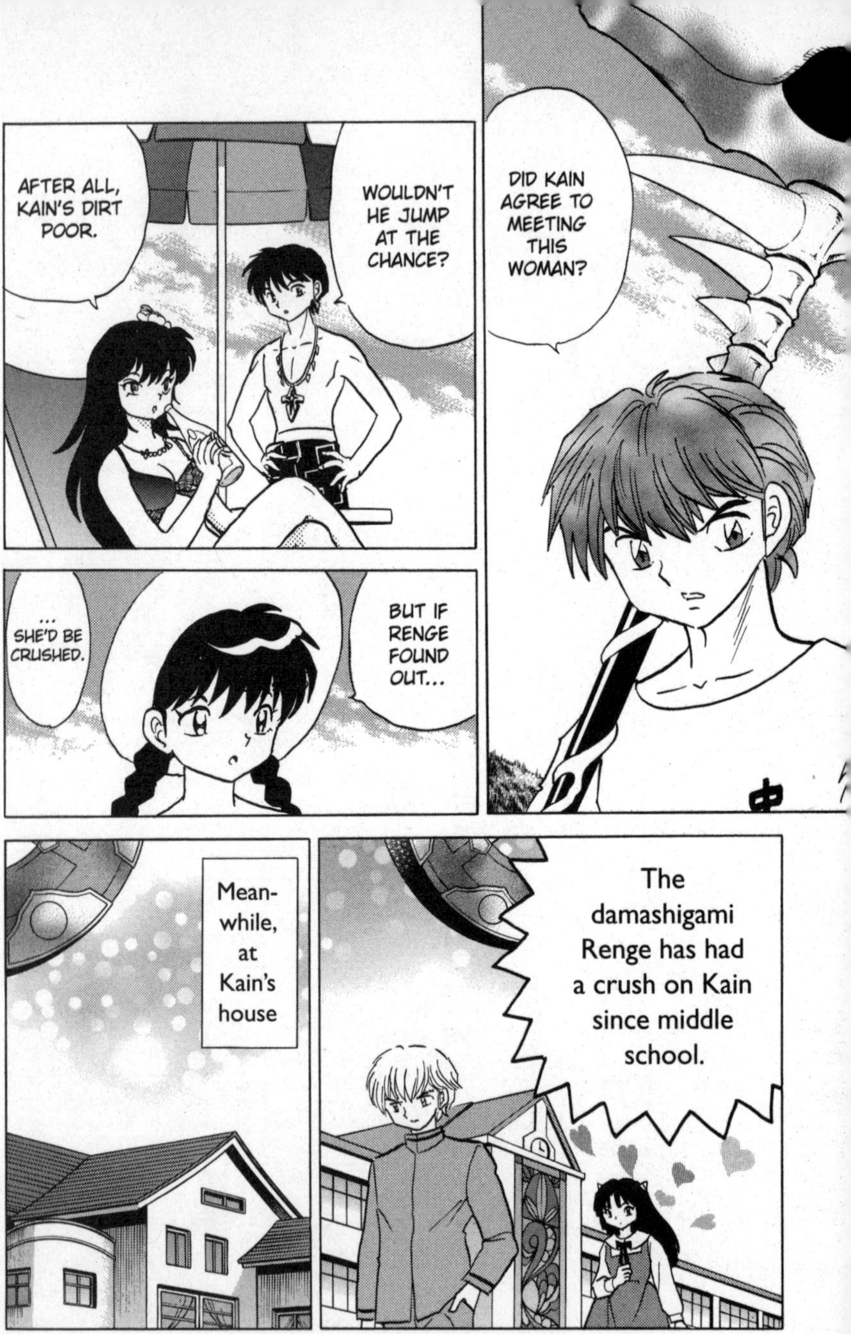
DID KAIN AGREE TO MEETING THIS WOMAN?
WOULDN'T HE JUMP AT THE CHANCE?
AFTER ALL, KAIN'S DIRT POOR.
BUT IF RENGE FOUND OUT...
... SHE'D BE CRUSHED.
The damashigami Renge has had a crush on Kain since middle school.
Mean-while, at Kain's house

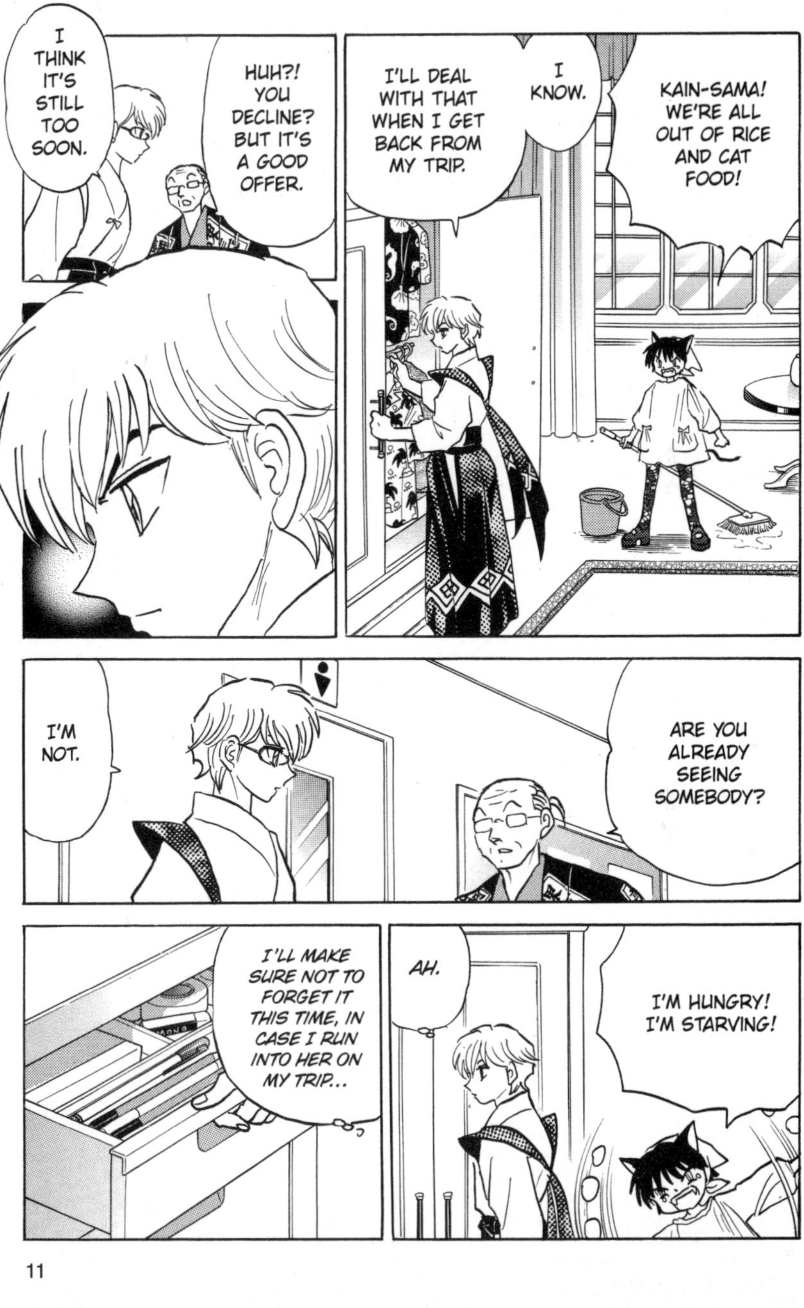
KAIN-SAMA! WE'RE ALL OUT OF RICE AND CAT FOOD!
I KNOW.
I'LL DEAL WITH THAT WHEN I GET BACK FROM MY TRIP.
HUH?! YOU DECLINE? BUT IT'S A GOOD OFFER.
I THINK IT'S STILL TOO SOON.
ARE YOU ALREADY SEEING SOMEBODY?
I'M NOT.
I'M HUNGRY! I'M STARVING!
AH.
I'LL MAKE SURE NOT TO FORGET IT THIS TIME, IN CASE I RUN INTO HER ON MY TRIP...

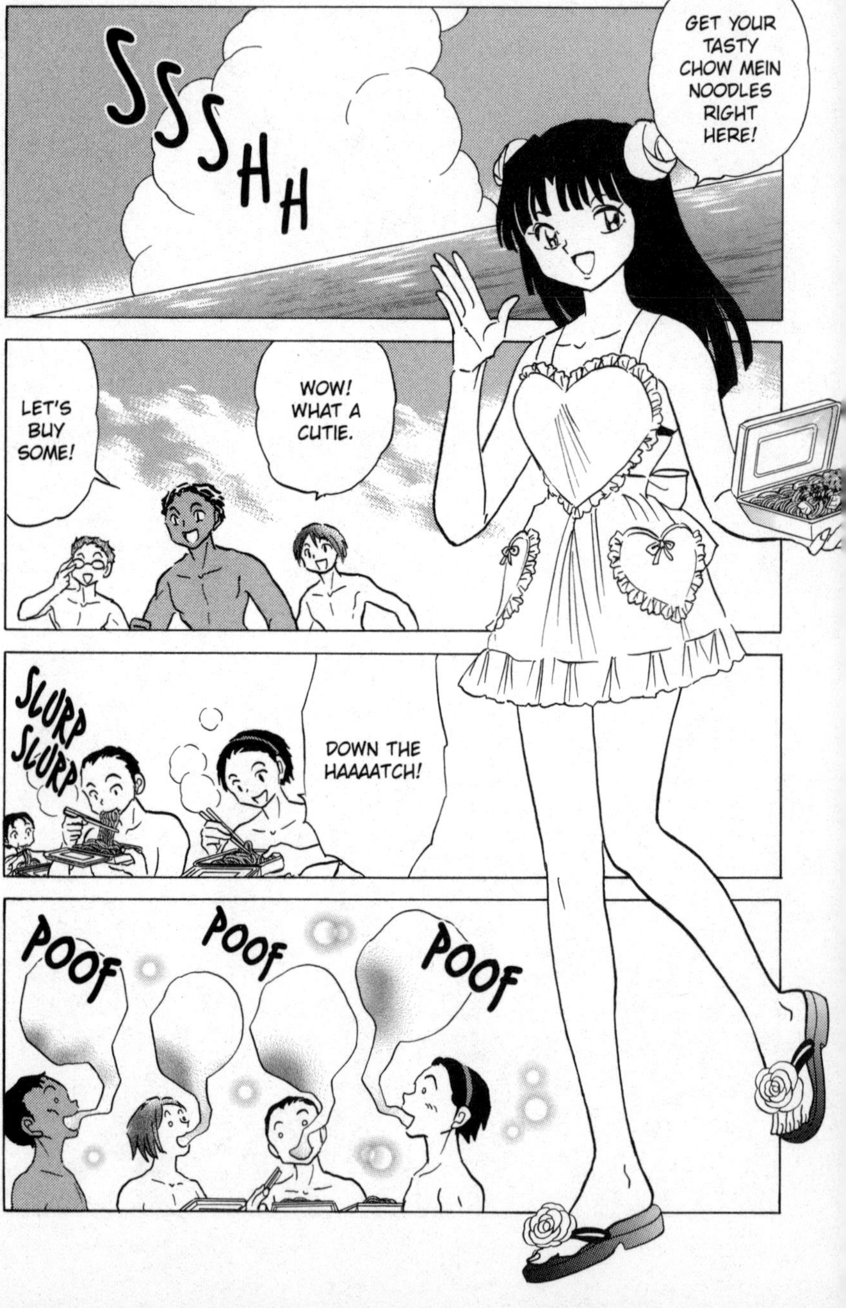
GET YOUR TASTY CHOW MEIN NOODLES RIGHT HERE!
SSSHH
WOW! WHAT A CUTIE.
LET'S BUY SOME!
DOWN THE HAAAATCH!
SLURP SLURP
POOF
POOF
POOF

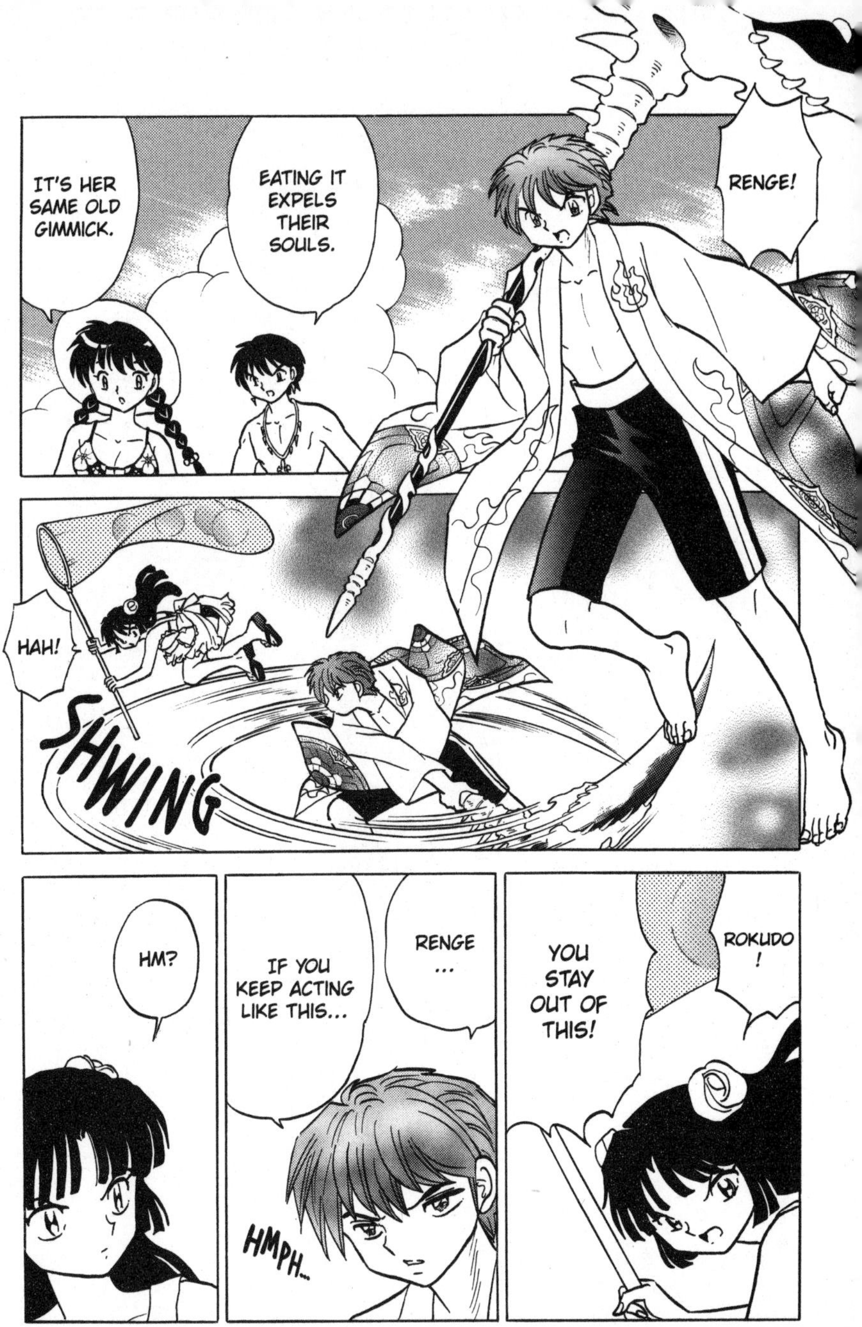
RENGE!
EATING IT EXPELS THEIR SOULS.
IT'S HER SAME OLD GIMMICK.
HAH!
SHWING
ROKUDO!
YOU STAY OUT OF THIS!
RENGE...
IF YOU KEEP ACTING LIKE THIS...
HMPH...
HM?

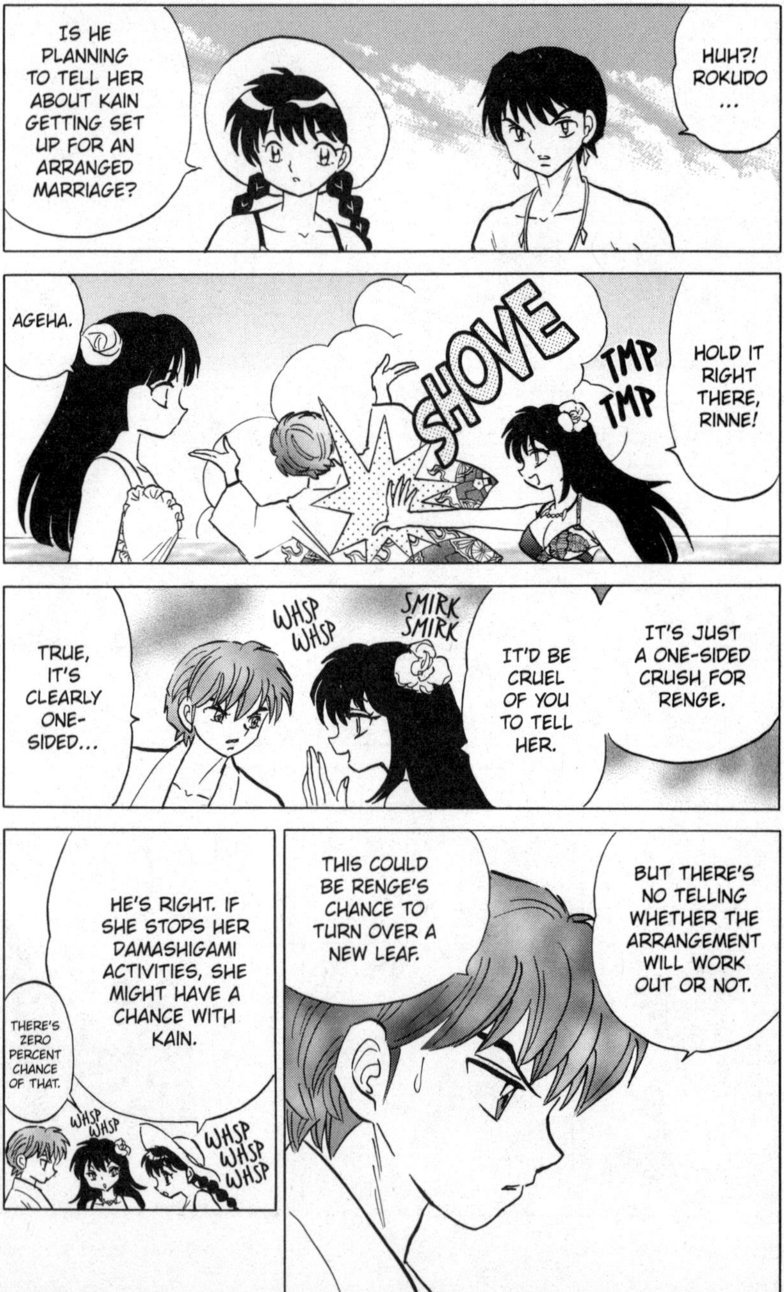
HUH?! ROKUDO ...
IS HE PLANNING TO TELL HER ABOUT KAIN GETTING SET UP FOR AN ARRANGED MARRIAGE?
HOLD IT RIGHT THERE, RINNE!
TMP TMP
SHOVE
AGEHA.
IT'S JUST A ONE-SIDED CRUSH FOR RENGE.
IT'D BE CRUEL OF YOU TO TELL HER.
SMIRK SMIRK
WHSP WHSP
TRUE, IT'S CLEARLY ONE-SIDED...
BUT THERE'S NO TELLING WHETHER THE ARRANGEMENT WILL WORK OUT OR NOT.
THIS COULD BE RENGE'S CHANCE TO TURN OVER A NEW LEAF.
HE'S RIGHT. IF SHE STOPS HER DAMASHIGAMI ACTIVITIES, SHE MIGHT HAVE A CHANCE WITH KAIN.
WHSP WHSP WHSP
THERE'S ZERO PERCENT CHANCE OF THAT.
WHSP WHSP

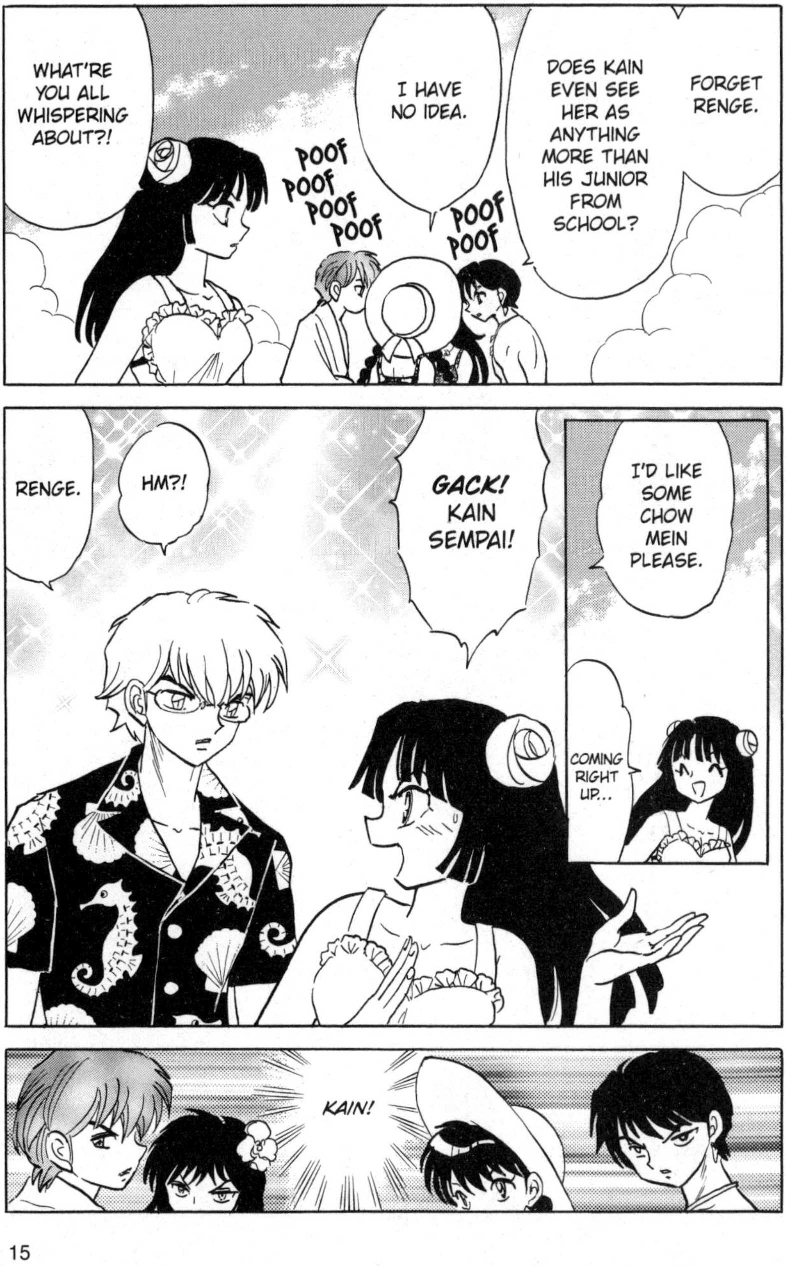
FORGET RENGE.
DOES KAIN EVEN SEE HER AS ANYTHING MORE THAN HIS JUNIOR FROM SCHOOL?
POOF POOF
I HAVE NO IDEA.
POOF POOF POOF POOF
WHAT'RE YOU ALL WHISPERING ABOUT?!
I'D LIKE SOME CHOW MEIN PLEASE.
COMING RIGHT UP...
GACK! KAIN SEMPAI!
HM?!
RENGE.
KAIN!

POOF
POOF
焼そば
SEMPAI, BEHIND YOU!
HM?!
CRAAASH
ZWOOOP
WHA
WHA
FWIP
THEIR SOULS RETURNED TO THEM.
I WAS JUST IMAGINING THINGS.
OKAY.
RENGE, ARE YOU PATROLLING WITH THE SHINIGAMI BOYS' CLUB TOO?
YES!
Renge absolutely doesn't want Kain to know that she's a damashigami.
Sign: Chow Mein

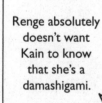

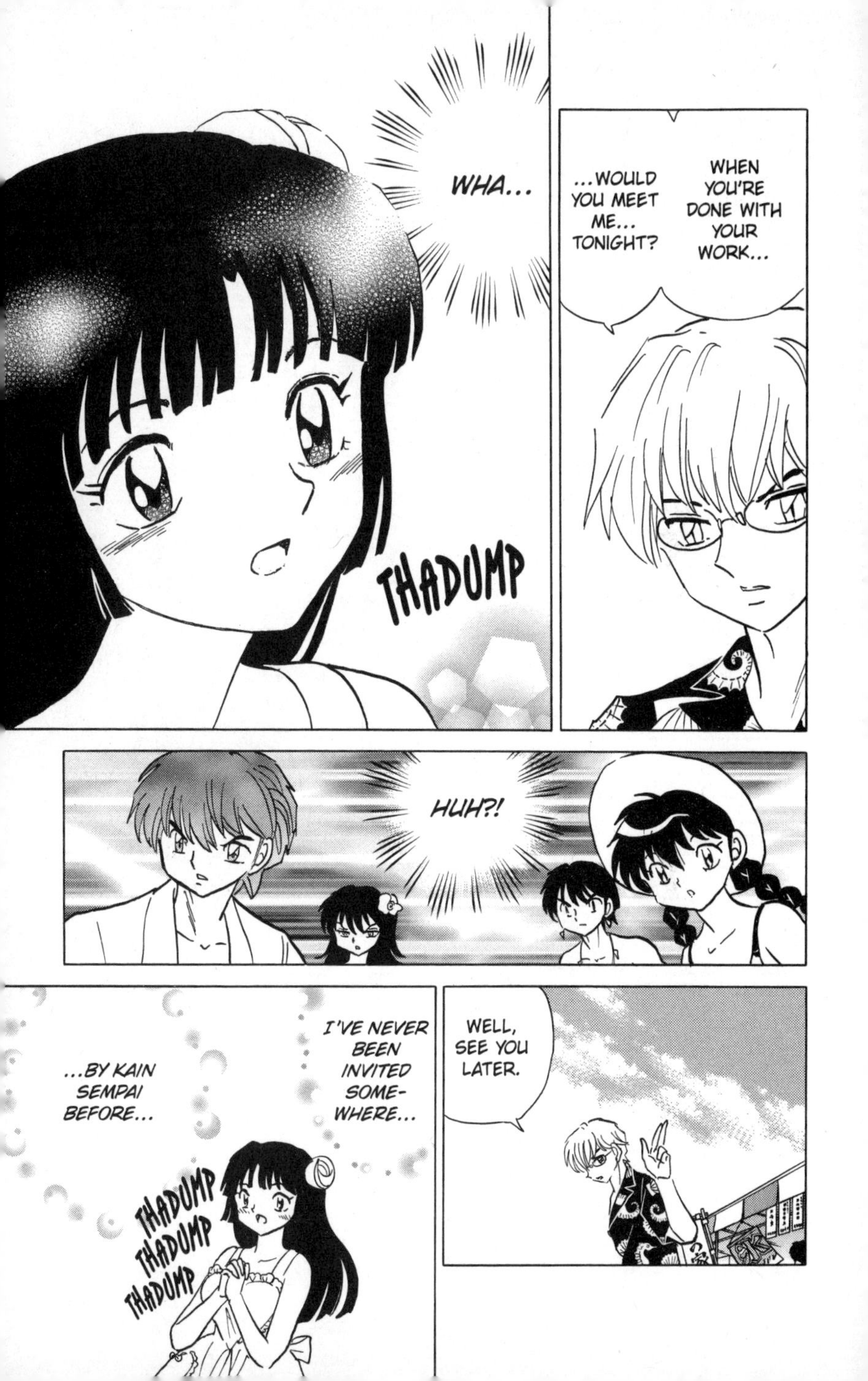
WHEN YOU'RE DONE WITH YOUR WORK...
...WOULD YOU MEET ME... TONIGHT?
WHA...
THADUMP
HUH?!
WELL, SEE YOU LATER.
I'VE NEVER BEEN INVITED SOME-WHERE...
...BY KAIN SEMPAI BEFORE...
THADUMP THADUMP THADUMP

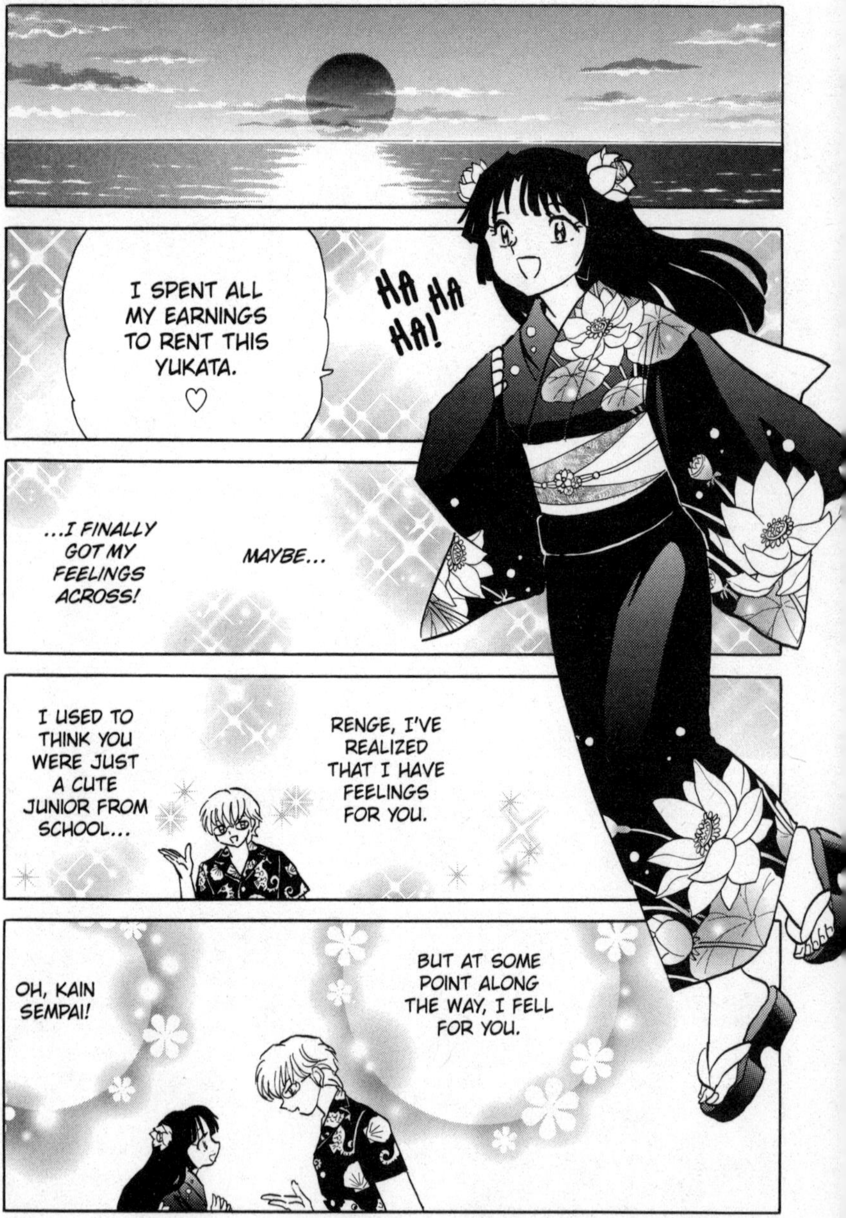
HA HA HA!
I SPENT ALL MY EARNINGS TO RENT THIS YUKATA. ♡
MAYBE...
...I FINALLY GOT MY FEELINGS ACROSS!
RENGE, I'VE REALIZED THAT I HAVE FEELINGS FOR YOU.
I USED TO THINK YOU WERE JUST A CUTE JUNIOR FROM SCHOOL...
BUT AT SOME POINT ALONG THE WAY, I FELL FOR YOU.
OH, KAIN SEMPAI!

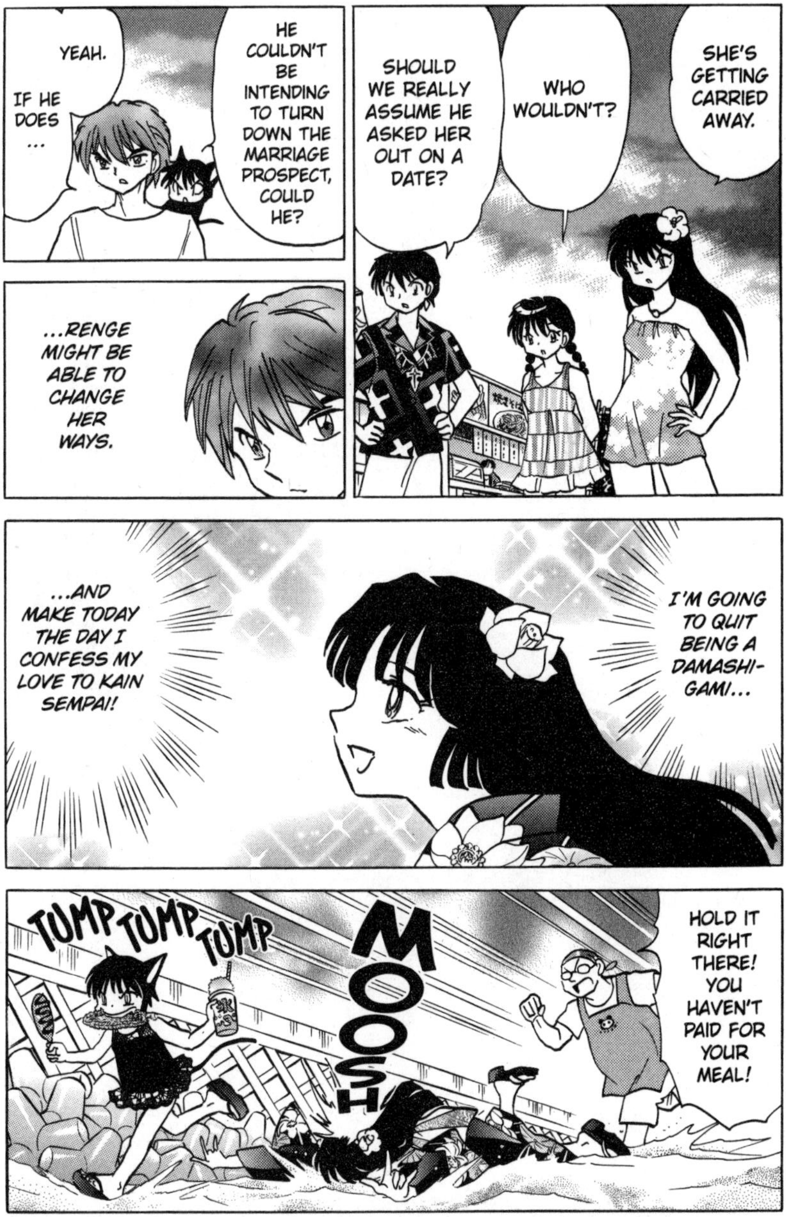
SHE'S GETTING CARRIED AWAY.
WHO WOULDN'T?
SHOULD WE REALLY ASSUME HE ASKED HER OUT ON A DATE?
HE COULDN'T BE INTENDING TO TURN DOWN THE MARRIAGE PROSPECT, COULD HE?
YEAH.
IF HE DOES ...
...RENGE MIGHT BE ABLE TO CHANGE HER WAYS.
I'M GOING TO QUIT BEING A DAMASHI-GAMI...
...AND MAKE TODAY THE DAY I CONFESS MY LOVE TO KAIN SEMPAI!
HOLD IT RIGHT THERE! YOU HAVEN'T PAID FOR YOUR MEAL!
MOOOSH
TUMP TUMP TUMP

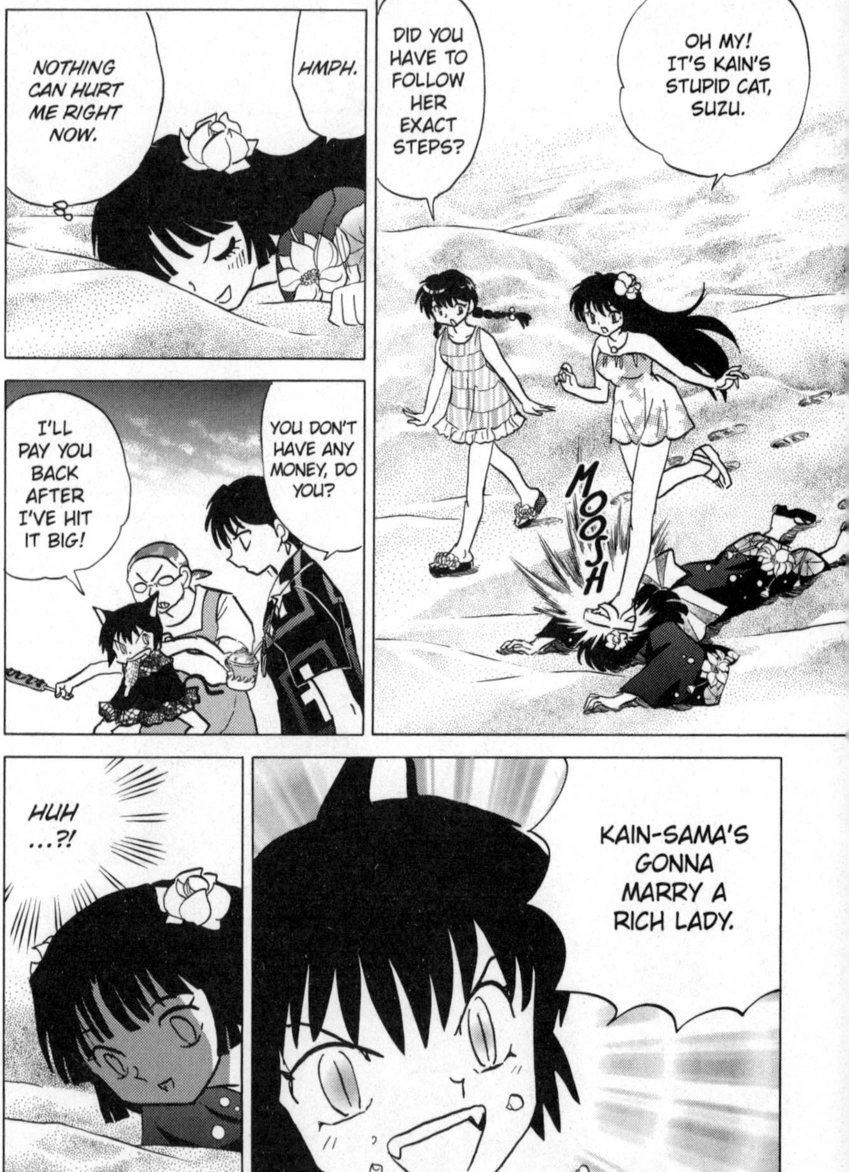
OH MY! IT'S KAIN'S STUPID CAT, SUZU.
DID YOU HAVE TO FOLLOW HER EXACT STEPS?
MOOSH
HMPH.
NOTHING CAN HURT ME RIGHT NOW.
YOU DON'T HAVE ANY MONEY, DO YOU?
I'LL PAY YOU BACK AFTER I'VE HIT IT BIG!
KAIN-SAMA'S GONNA MARRY A RICH LADY.
HUH ...?!

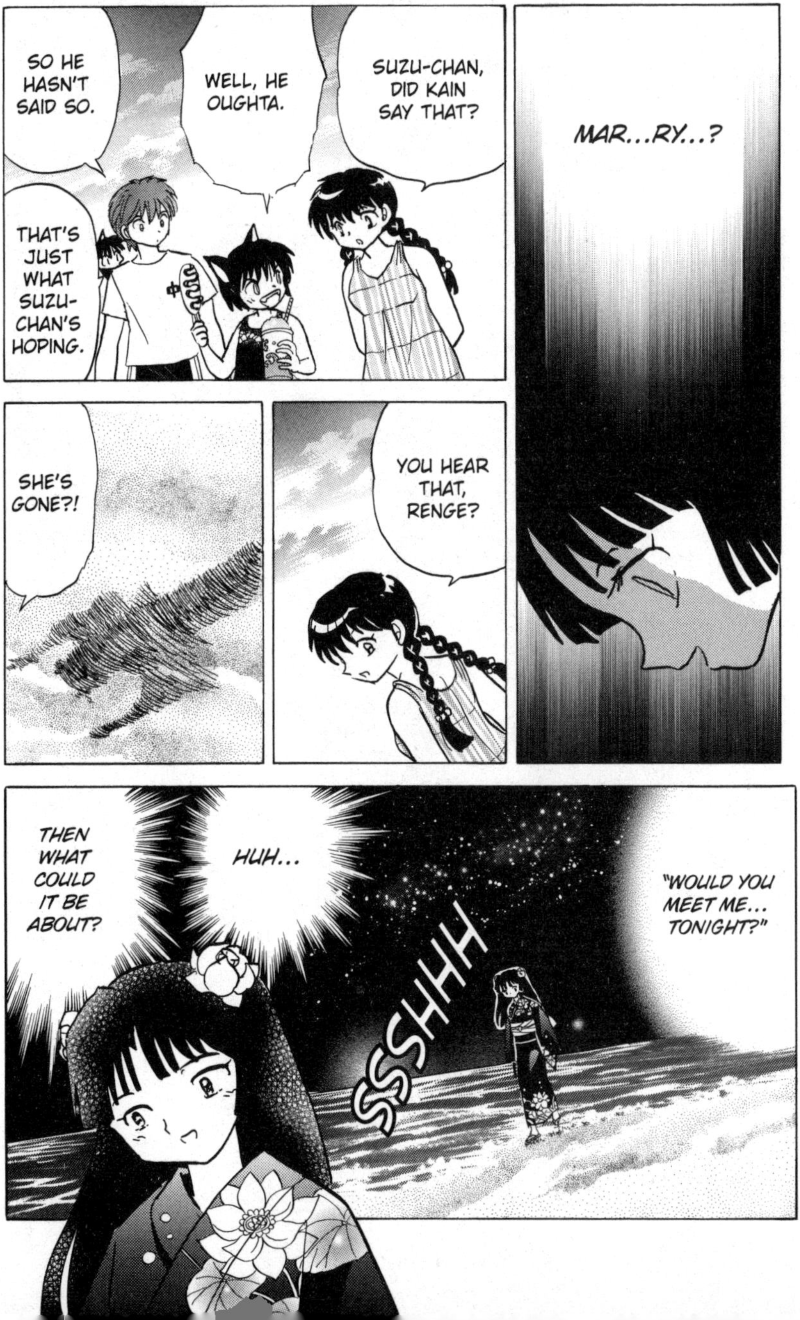
MAR...RY...?
SUZU-CHAN, DID KAIN SAY THAT?
WELL, HE OUGHTA.
SO HE HASN'T SAID SO.
THAT'S JUST WHAT SUZU-CHAN'S HOPING.
YOU HEAR THAT, RENGE?
SHE'S GONE?!
"WOULD YOU MEET ME... TONIGHT?"
SSSHHH
HUH...
THEN WHAT COULD IT BE ABOUT?

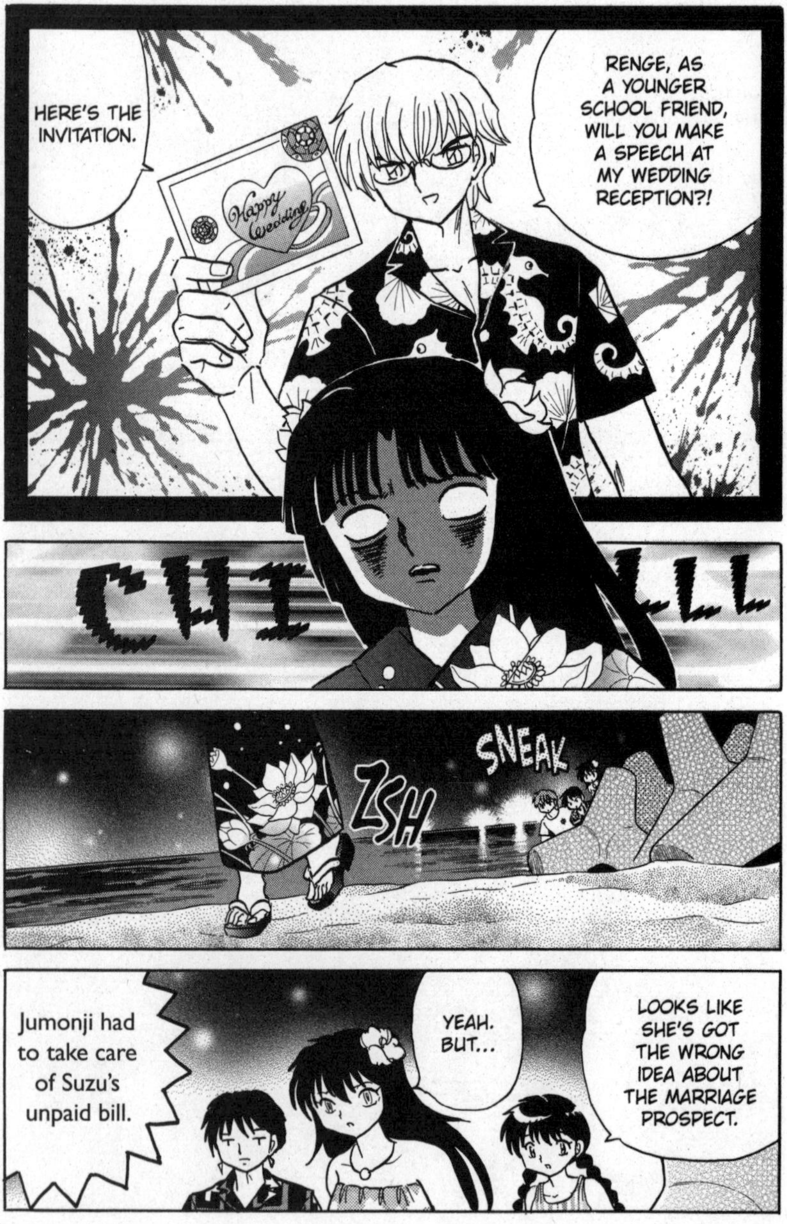
RENGE, AS A YOUNGER SCHOOL FRIEND, WILL YOU MAKE A SPEECH AT MY WEDDING RECEPTION?!
HERE'S THE INVITATION.
Happy Wedding
CHILLL
SNEAK
ZSH
LOOKS LIKE SHE'S GOT THE WRONG IDEA ABOUT THE MARRIAGE PROSPECT.
YEAH. BUT...
Jumonji had to take care of Suzu's unpaid bill.

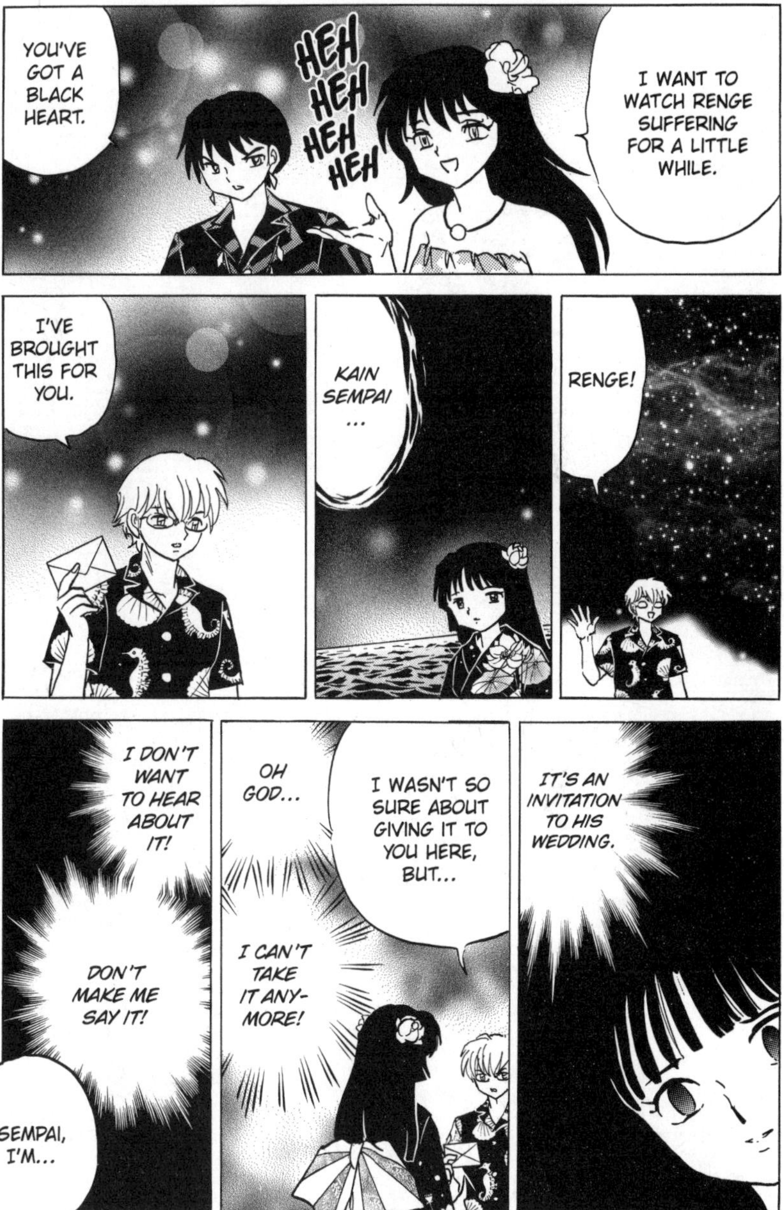
I WANT TO WATCH RENGE SUFFERING FOR A LITTLE WHILE.
HEH HEH HEH HEH
YOU'VE GOT A BLACK HEART.
RENGE!
KAIN SEMPAI ...
I'VE BROUGHT THIS FOR YOU.
IT'S AN INVITATION TO HIS WEDDING.
I WASN'T SO SURE ABOUT GIVING IT TO YOU HERE, BUT...
OH GOD...
I CAN'T TAKE IT ANY-MORE!
I DON'T WANT TO HEAR ABOUT IT!
DON'T MAKE ME SAY IT!
SEMPAI, I'M...

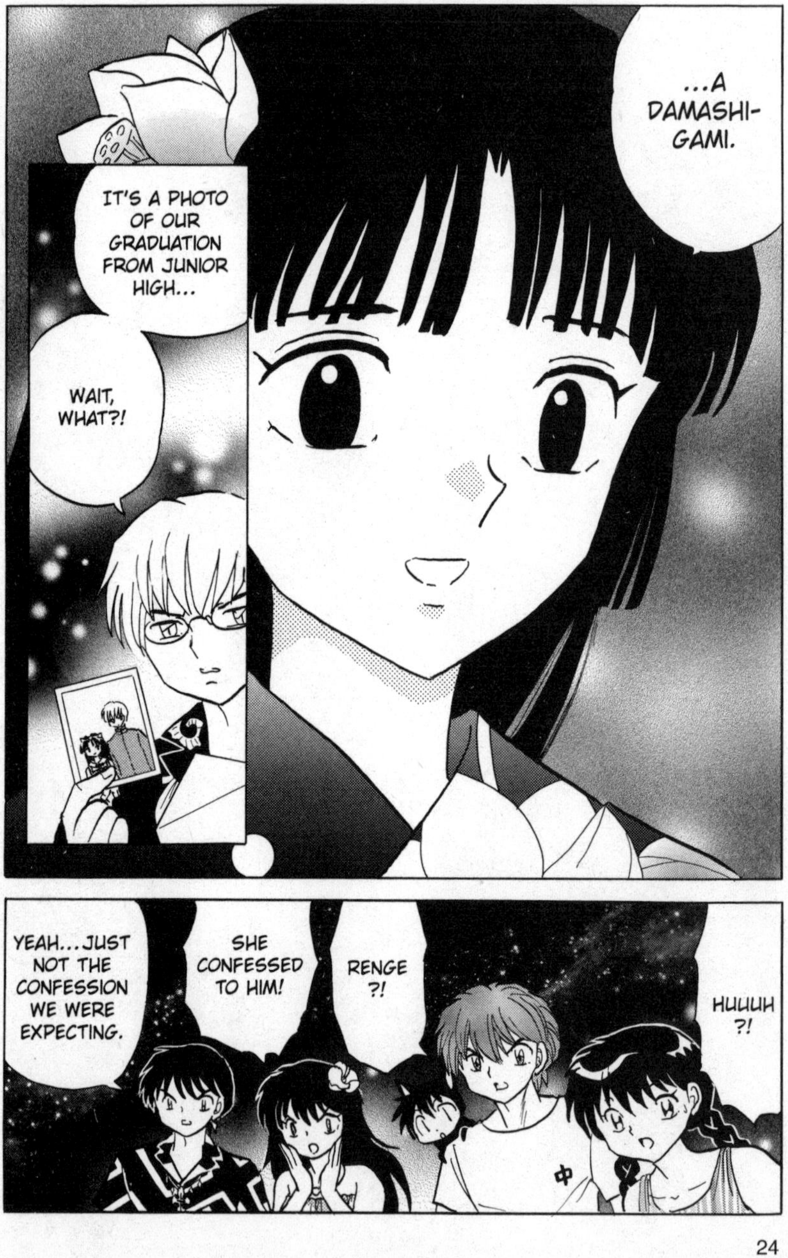
...A DAMASHI-GAMI.
IT'S A PHOTO OF OUR GRADUATION FROM JUNIOR HIGH...
WAIT, WHAT?!
HUUUH ?!
RENGE ?!
SHE CONFESSED TO HIM!
YEAH...JUST NOT THE CONFESSION WE WERE EXPECTING.

CHAPTER 380: REVERSAL OF FORTUNE

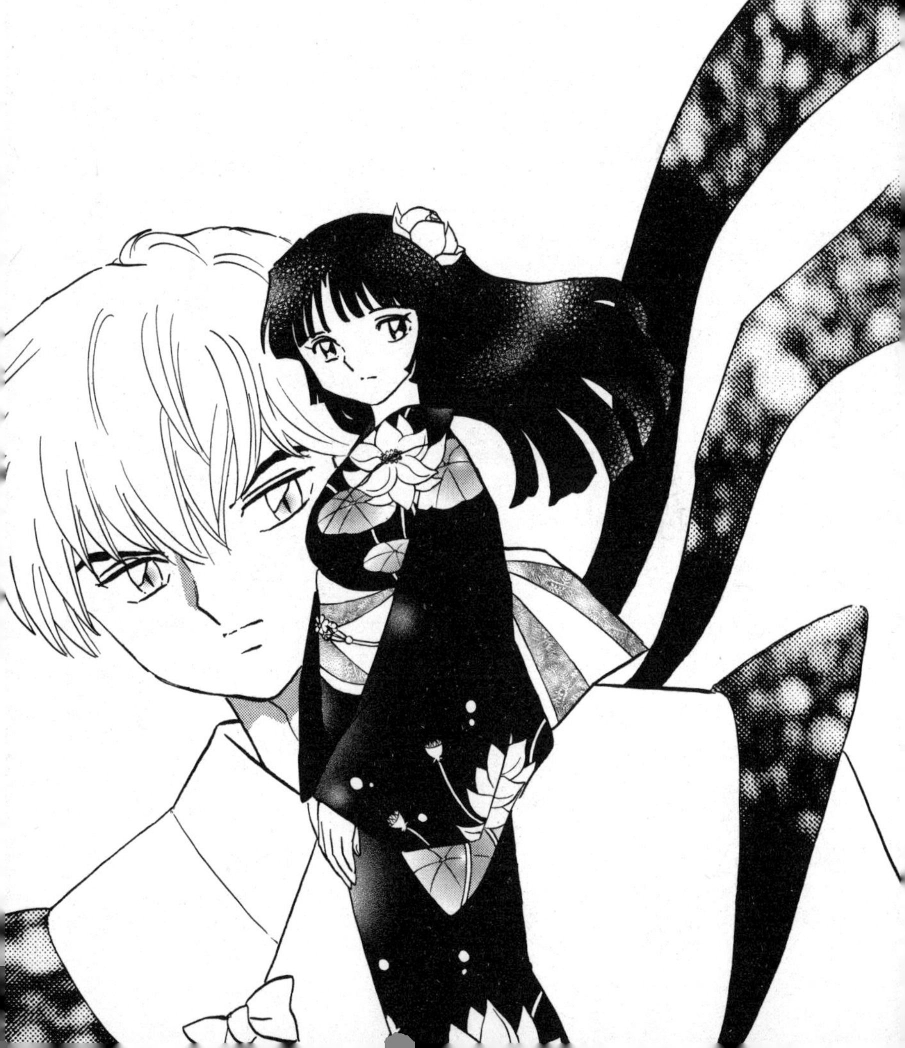

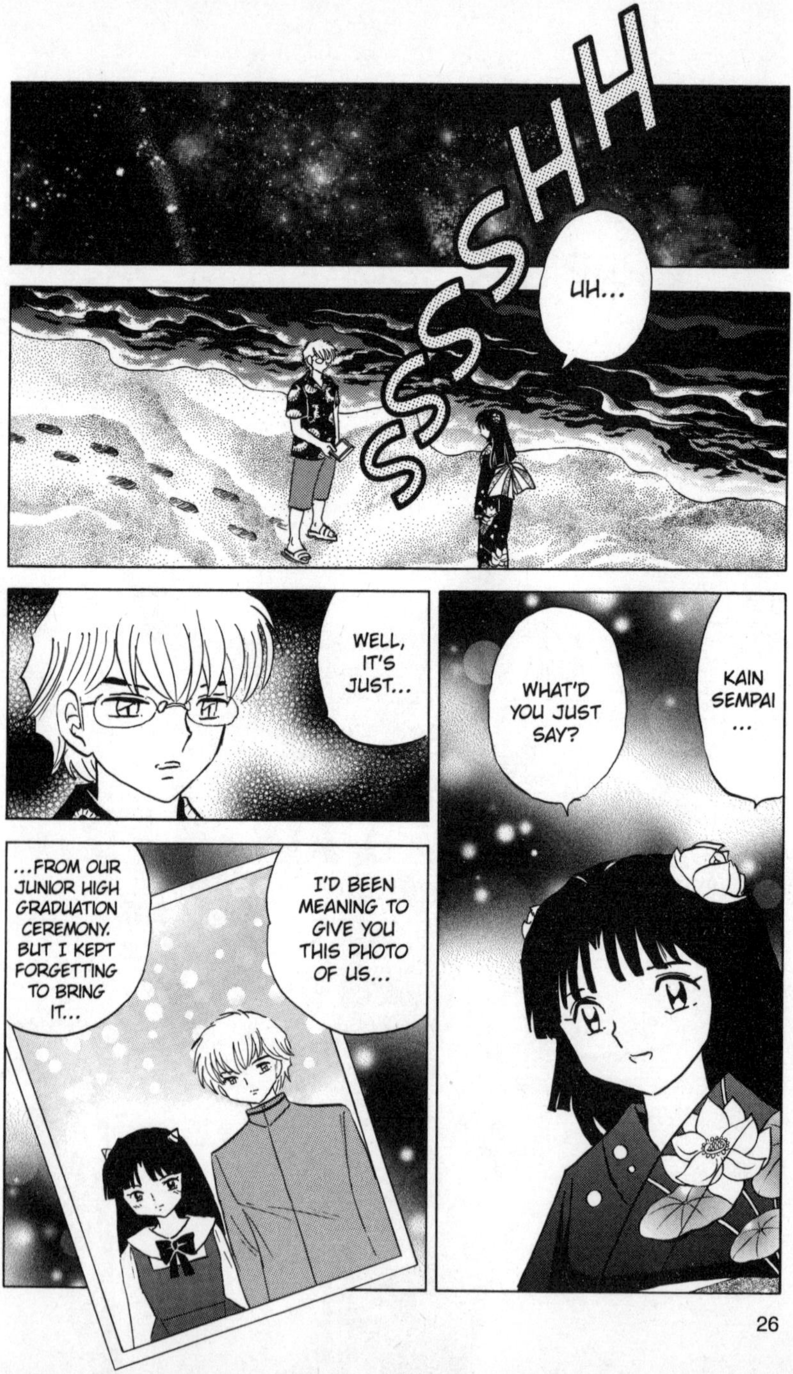
SSSHH
UH...
KAIN SEMPAI ...
WHAT'D YOU JUST SAY?
WELL, IT'S JUST...
I'D BEEN MEANING TO GIVE YOU THIS PHOTO OF US...
...FROM OUR JUNIOR HIGH GRADUATION CEREMONY. BUT I KEPT FORGETTING TO BRING IT...

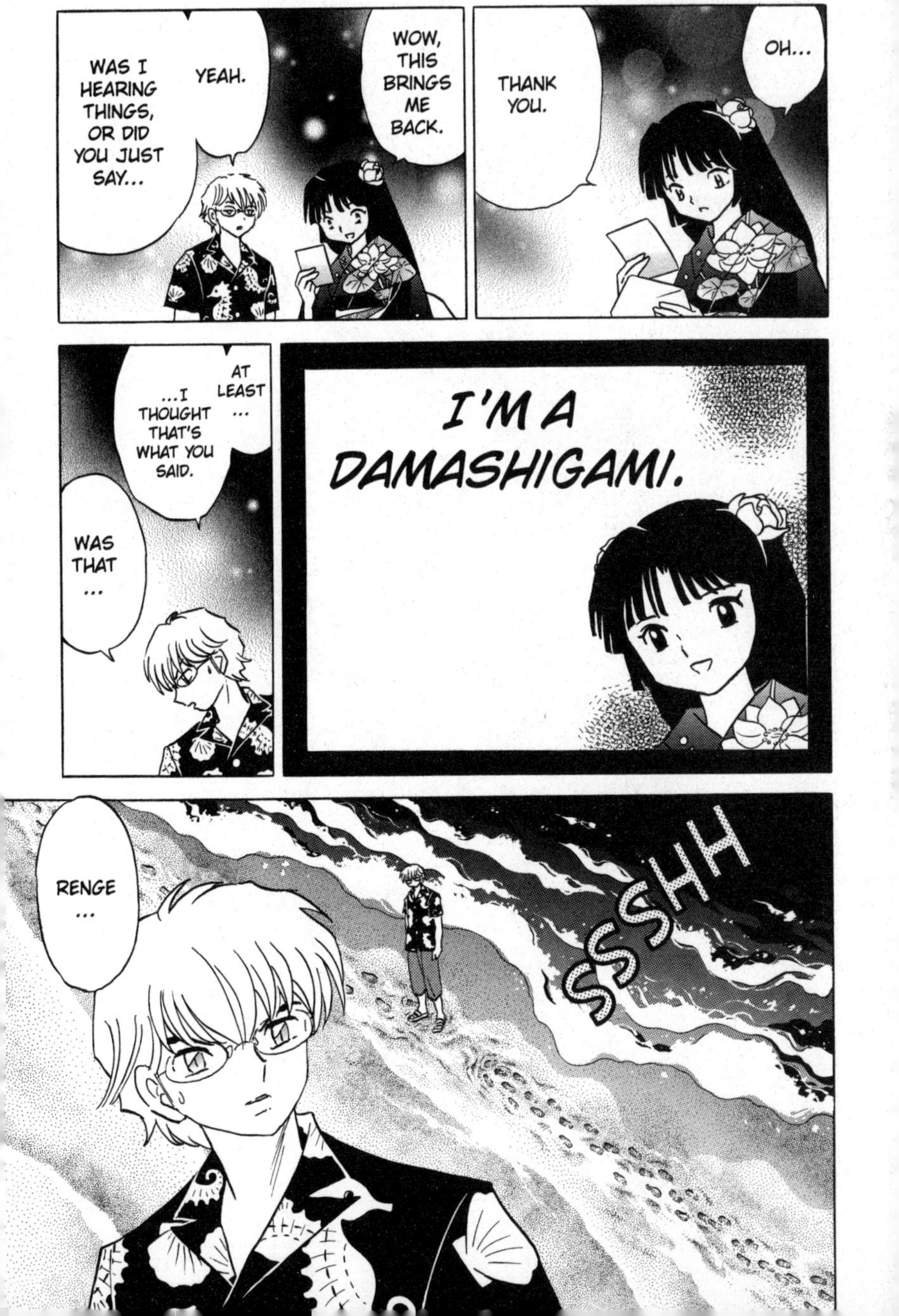
OH...
THANK YOU.
WOW, THIS BRINGS ME BACK.
YEAH.
WAS I HEARING THINGS, OR DID YOU JUST SAY...
I'M A DAMASHIGAMI.
AT LEAST...
...I THOUGHT THAT'S WHAT YOU SAID.
WAS THAT...
SSSHH
RENGE...

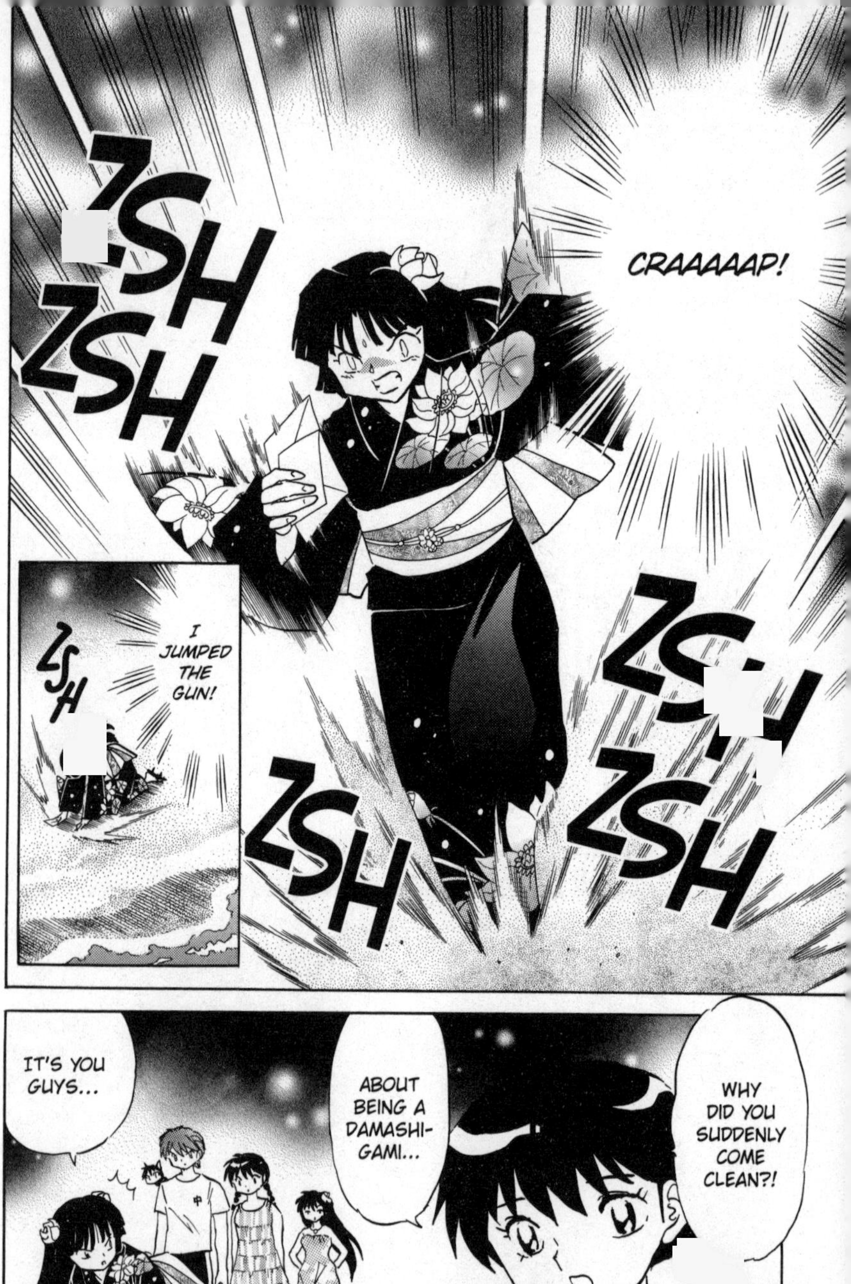
CRAAAAAP!
ZSH
ZSH
ZSH
ZSH
ZSH
ZSH
I JUMPED THE GUN!
WHY DID YOU SUDDENLY COME CLEAN?!
ABOUT BEING A DAMASHI-GAMI...
IT'S YOU GUYS...

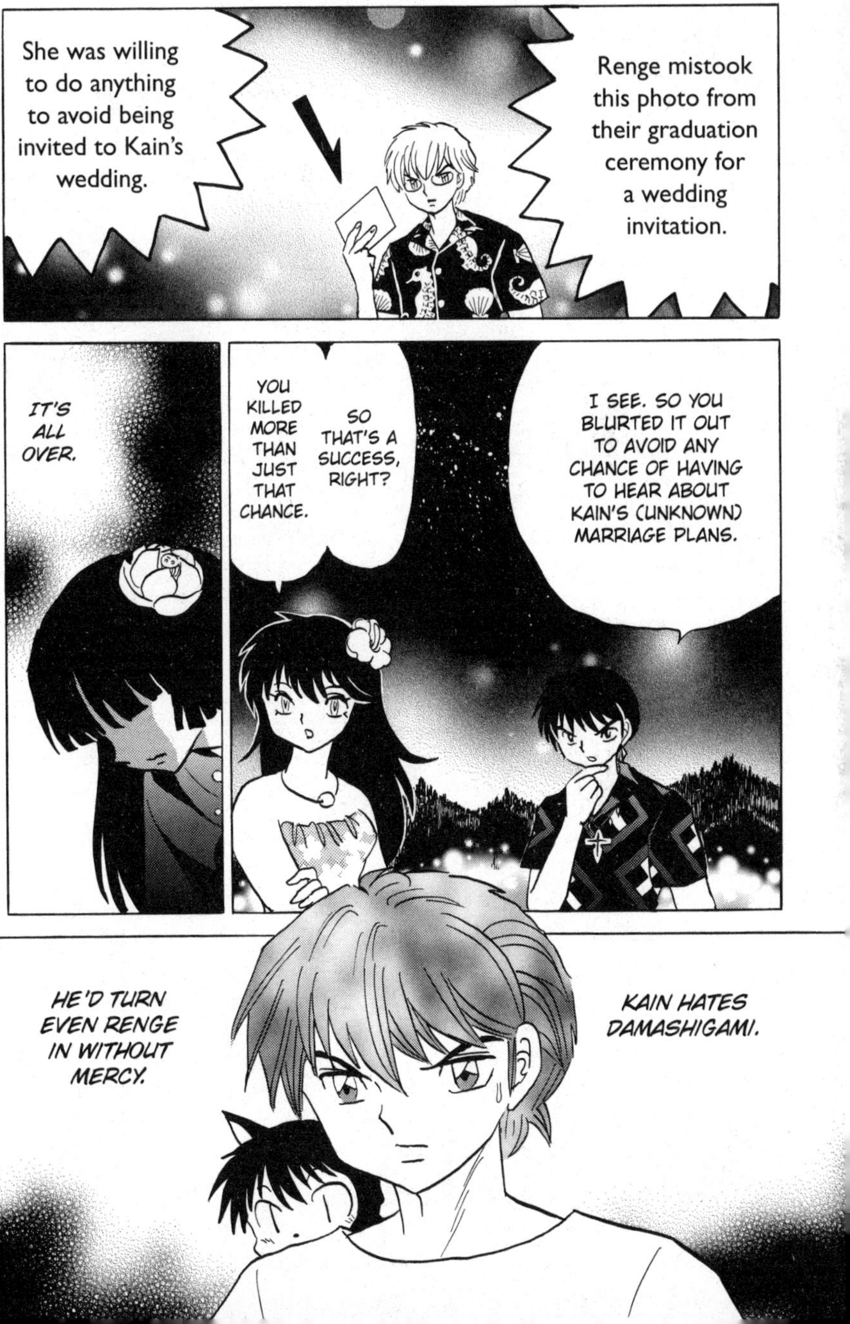
Renge mistook this photo from their graduation ceremony for a wedding invitation.
She was willing to do anything to avoid being invited to Kain's wedding.
I SEE. SO YOU BLURTED IT OUT TO AVOID ANY CHANCE OF HAVING TO HEAR ABOUT KAIN'S (UNKNOWN) MARRIAGE PLANS.
SO THAT'S A SUCCESS, RIGHT?
YOU KILLED MORE THAN JUST THAT CHANCE.
IT'S ALL OVER.
KAIN HATES DAMASHIGAMI.
HE'D TURN EVEN RENGE IN WITHOUT MERCY.

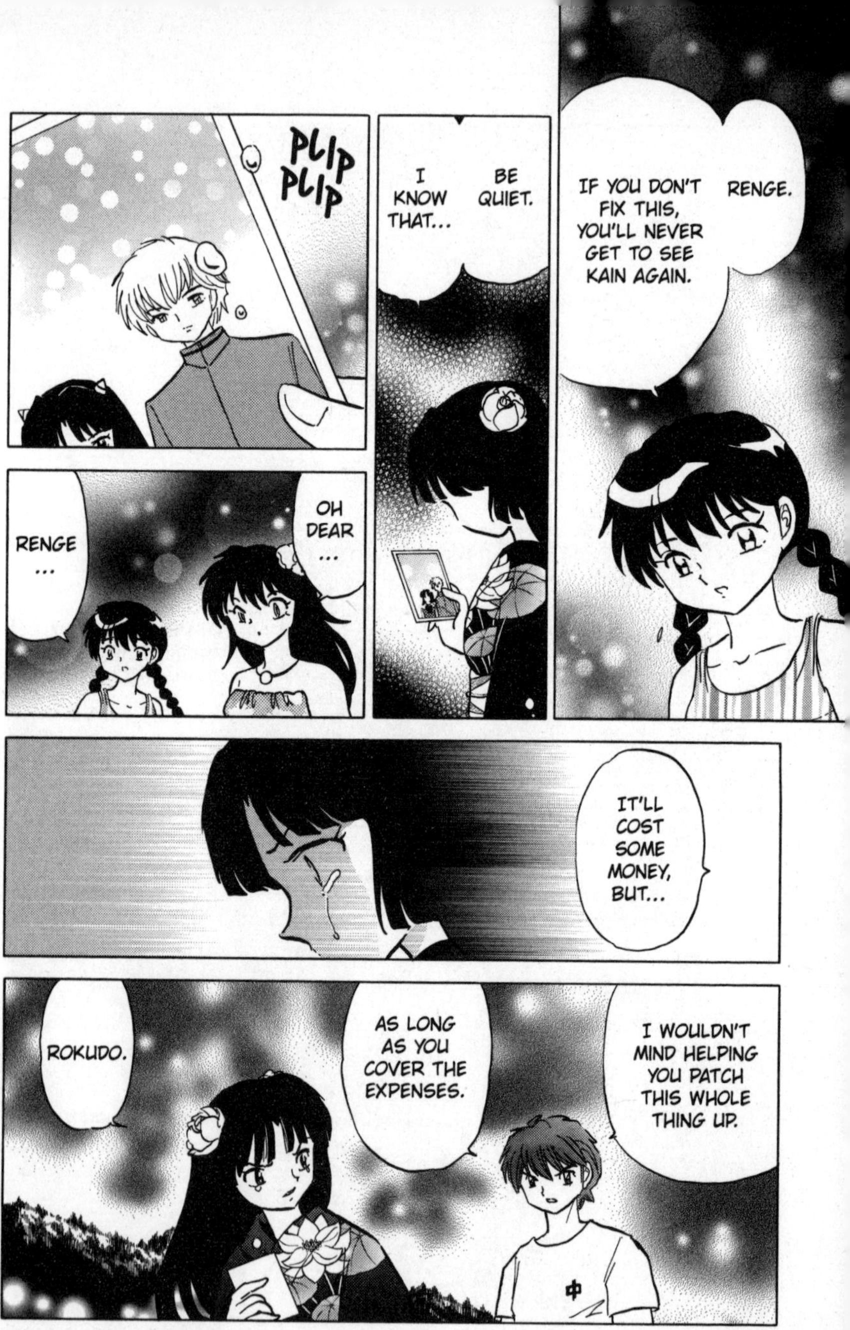
RENGE.
IF YOU DON'T FIX THIS, YOU'LL NEVER GET TO SEE KAIN AGAIN.
BE QUIET.
I KNOW THAT...
PLIP PLIP
OH DEAR...
RENGE...
IT'LL COST SOME MONEY, BUT...
I WOULDN'T MIND HELPING YOU PATCH THIS WHOLE THING UP.
AS LONG AS YOU COVER THE EXPENSES.
ROKUDO.

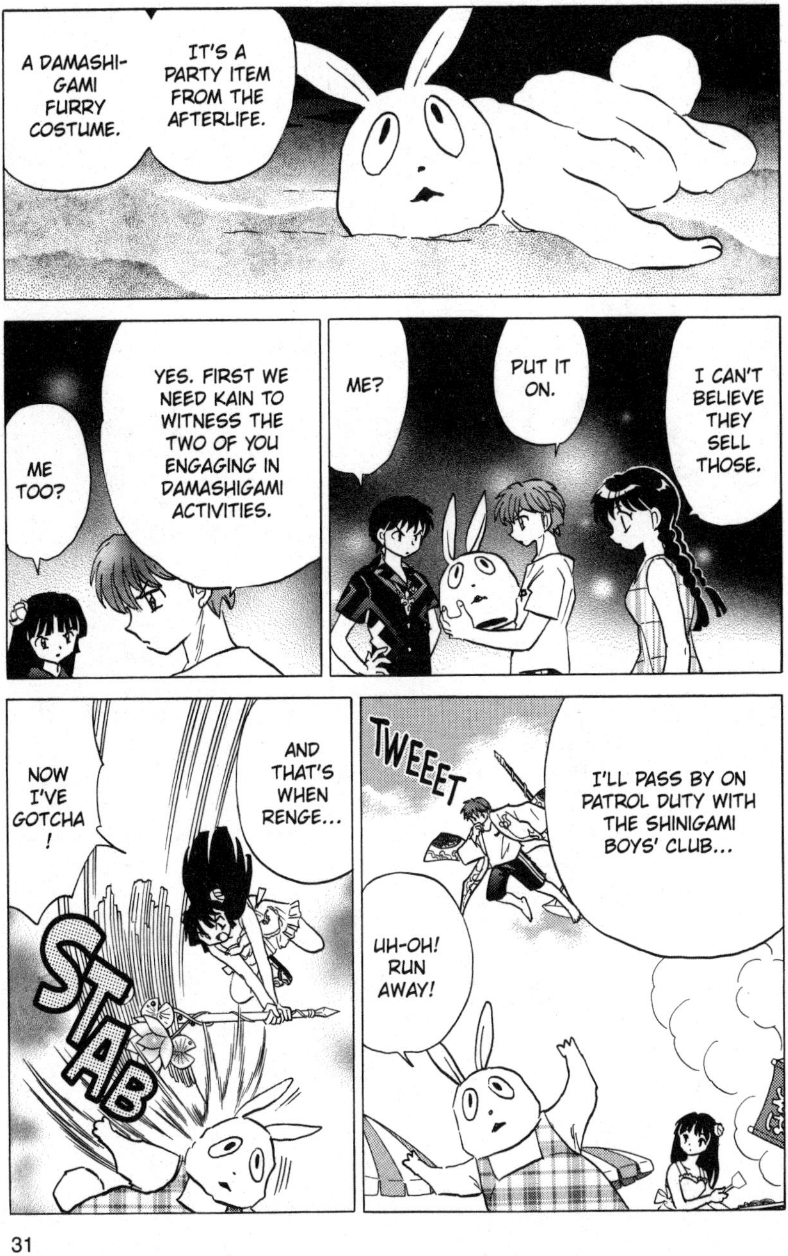
IT'S A PARTY ITEM FROM THE AFTERLIFE.
A DAMASHIGAMI FURRY COSTUME.
I CAN'T BELIEVE THEY SELL THOSE.
PUT IT ON.
ME?
YES. FIRST WE NEED KAIN TO WITNESS THE TWO OF YOU ENGAGING IN DAMASHIGAMI ACTIVITIES.
ME TOO?
I'LL PASS BY ON PATROL DUTY WITH THE SHINIGAMI BOYS' CLUB...
TWEEEET
UH-OH! RUN AWAY!
AND THAT'S WHEN RENGE...
NOW I'VE GOTCHA!
STAB

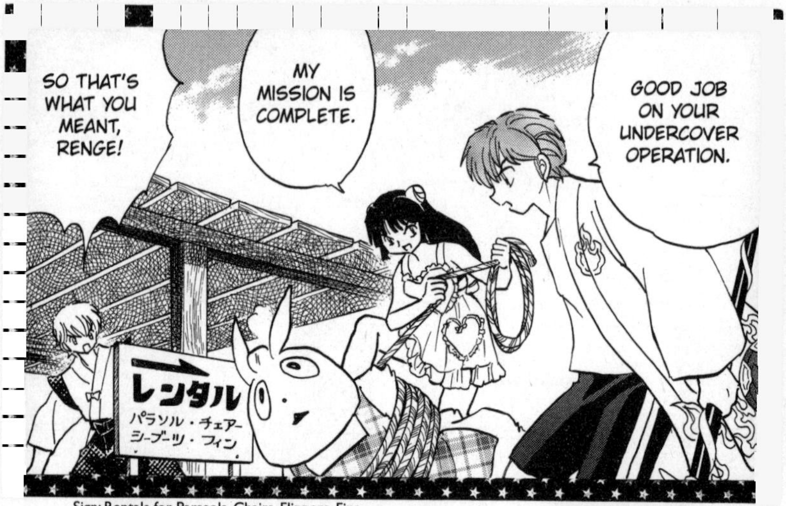
GOOD JOB ON YOUR UNDERCOVER OPERATION.
MY MISSION IS COMPLETE.
SO THAT'S WHAT YOU MEANT, RENGE!
レンタル
パラソル・チェアー
シーブーツ・フィン
Sign: Rentals for Parasols, Chairs, Flippers, Fins

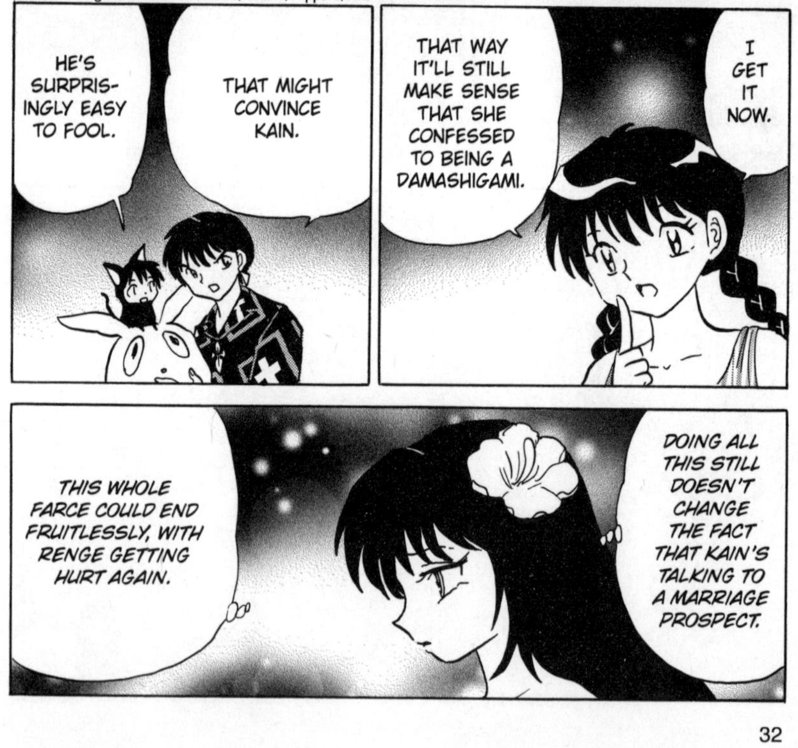
I GET IT NOW.
THAT WAY IT'LL STILL MAKE SENSE THAT SHE CONFESSED TO BEING A DAMASHIGAMI.
THAT MIGHT CONVINCE KAIN.
HE'S SURPRIS-INGLY EASY TO FOOL.
DOING ALL THIS STILL DOESN'T CHANGE THE FACT THAT KAIN'S TALKING TO A MARRIAGE PROSPECT.
THIS WHOLE FARCE COULD END FRUITLESSLY, WITH RENGE GETTING HURT AGAIN.

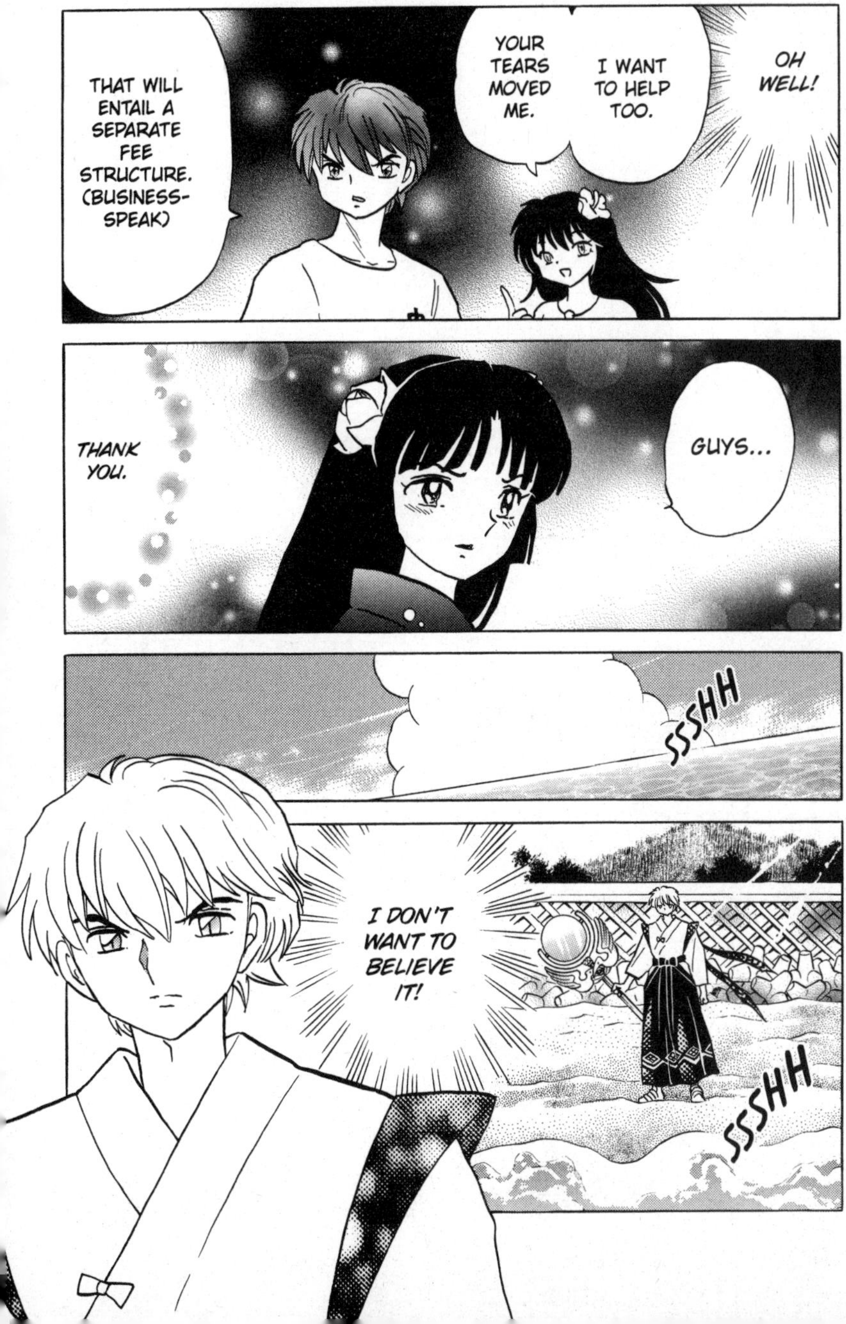
OH WELL!
I WANT TO HELP TOO.
YOUR TEARS MOVED ME.
THAT WILL ENTAIL A SEPARATE FEE STRUCTURE. (BUSINESS-SPEAK)
GUYS...
THANK YOU.
SSSHH
SSSHH
I DON'T WANT TO BELIEVE IT!

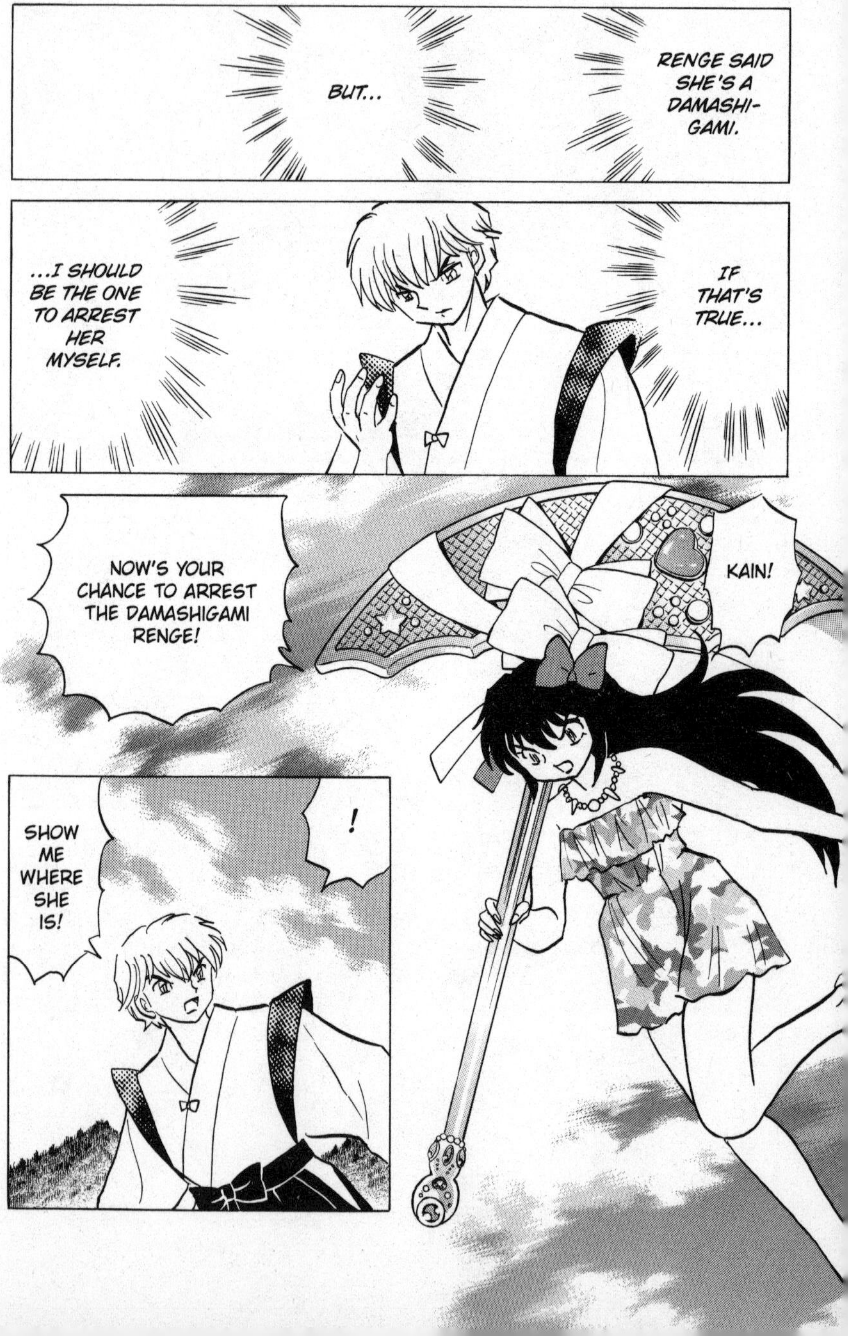
RENGE SAID SHE'S A DAMASHI-GAMI.
BUT...
IF THAT'S TRUE...
...I SHOULD BE THE ONE TO ARREST HER MYSELF.
KAIN!
NOW'S YOUR CHANCE TO ARREST THE DAMASHIGAMI RENGE!
!
SHOW ME WHERE SHE IS!

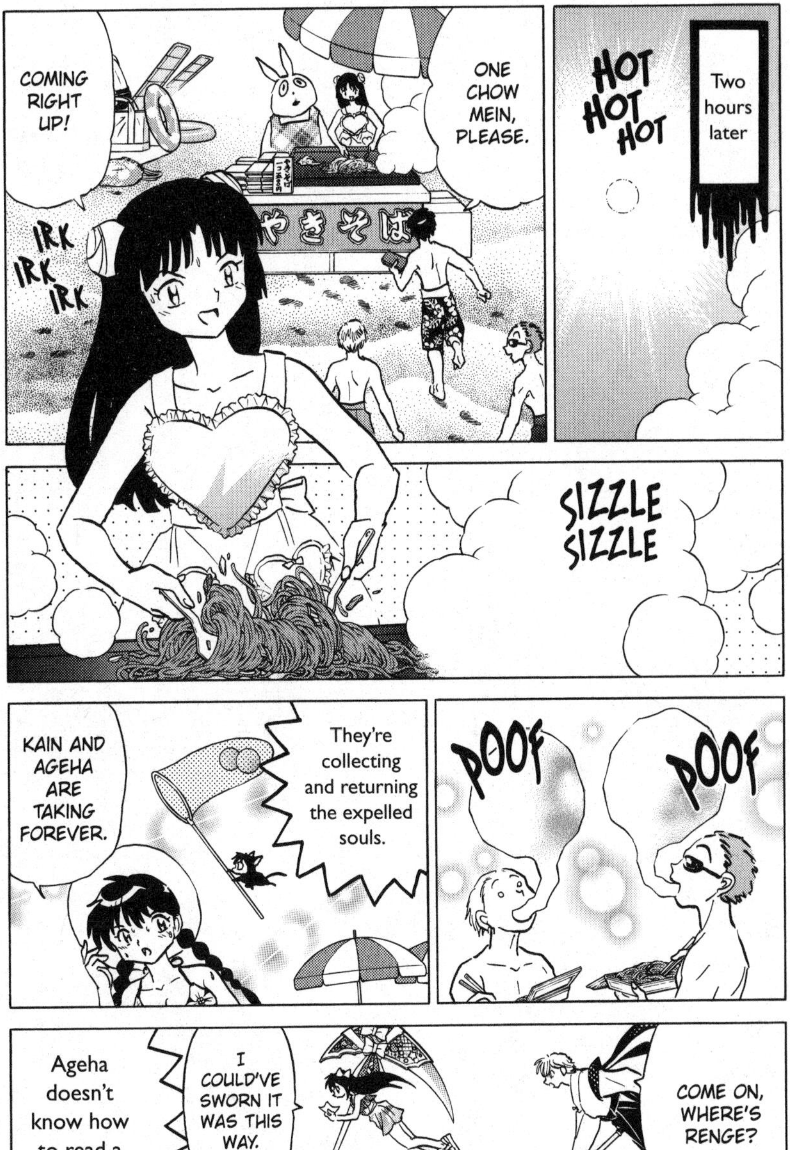
Two hours later
HOT HOT HOT
ONE CHOW MEIN, PLEASE.
COMING RIGHT UP!
IRK IRK IRK
SIZZLE SIZZLE
POOF
POOF
They're collecting and returning the expelled souls.
KAIN AND AGEHA ARE TAKING FOREVER.
COME ON, WHERE'S RENGE?
I COULD'VE SWORN IT WAS THIS WAY.
Ageha doesn't know how to read a map.

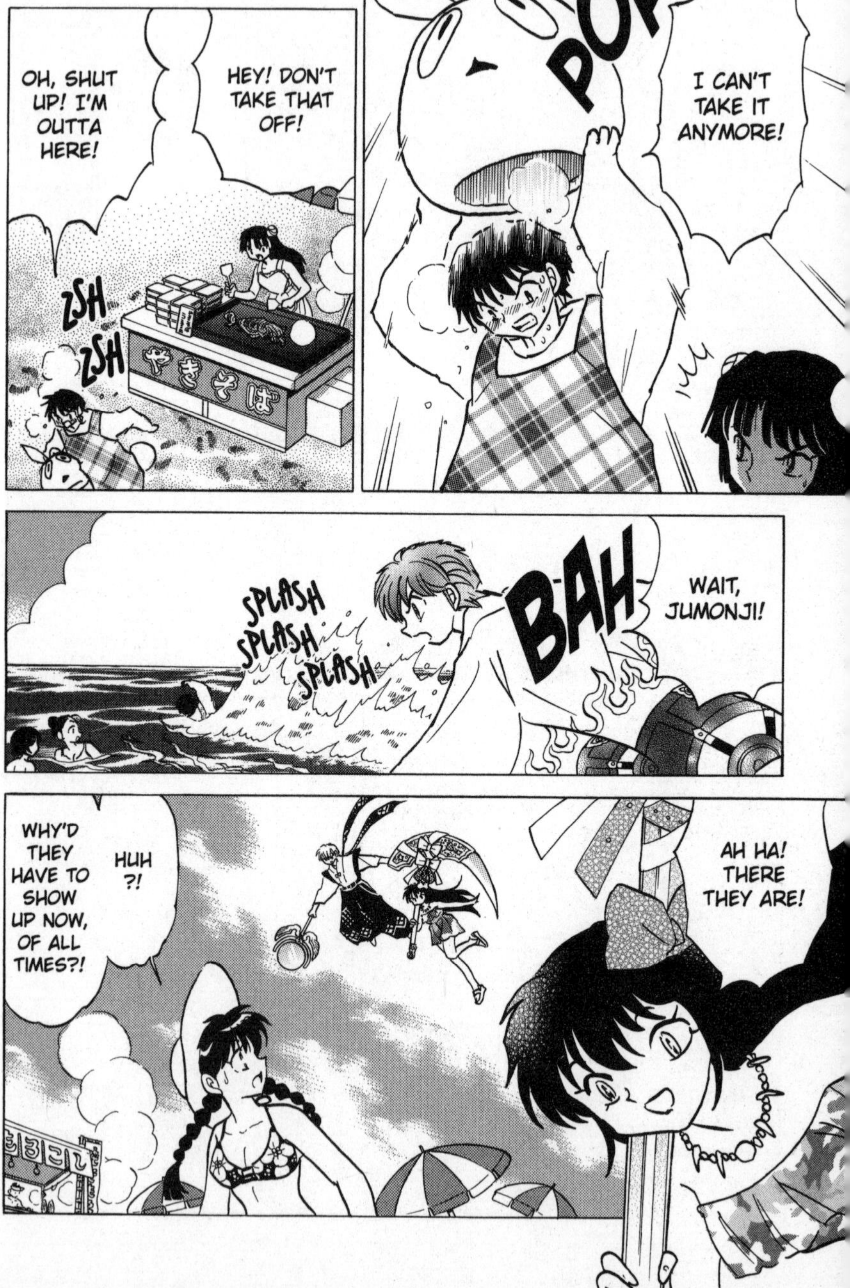
POP
I CAN'T TAKE IT ANYMORE!
HEY! DON'T TAKE THAT OFF!
OH, SHUT UP! I'M OUTTA HERE!
ZSH
ZSH
やきそは
WAIT, JUMONJI!
BAH
SPLASH
SPLASH
SPLASH
AH HA! THERE THEY ARE!
HUH ?!
WHY'D THEY HAVE TO SHOW UP NOW, OF ALL TIMES?!

WAAARP

I'LL RETREAT FOR THE TIME BEING!

KUH!

TUMBL TUMBL

CRASH

AH...!

AH...

JUMONJI ?!

OH DEAR! OH NO!

SMASH

CLATTER

Boxes: Soul-Sucking Noodles

37

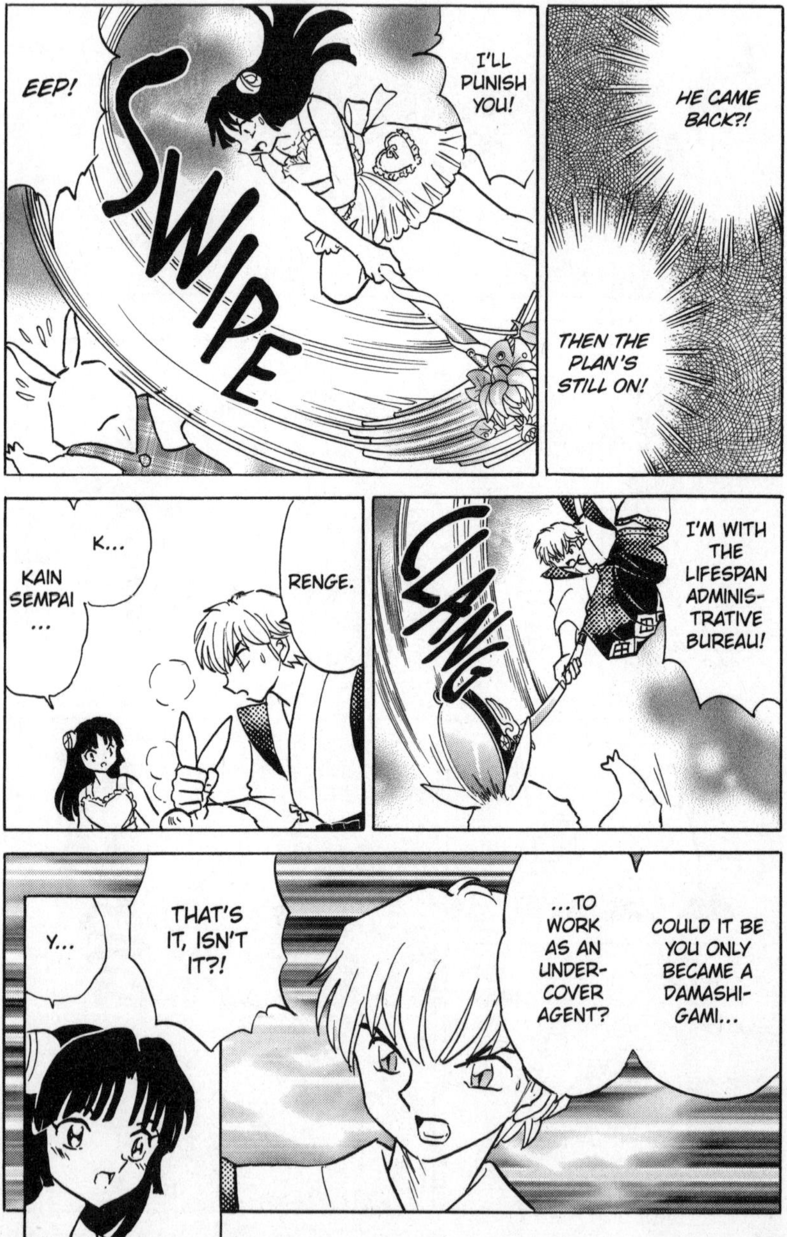
HE CAME BACK?!
THEN THE PLAN'S STILL ON!
I'LL PUNISH YOU!
EEP!
SWIPE
I'M WITH THE LIFESPAN ADMINIS-TRATIVE BUREAU!
CLANG
RENGE.
K... KAIN SEMPAI ...
COULD IT BE YOU ONLY BECAME A DAMASHI-GAMI...
...TO WORK AS AN UNDER-COVER AGENT?
THAT'S IT, ISN'T IT?!
Y...

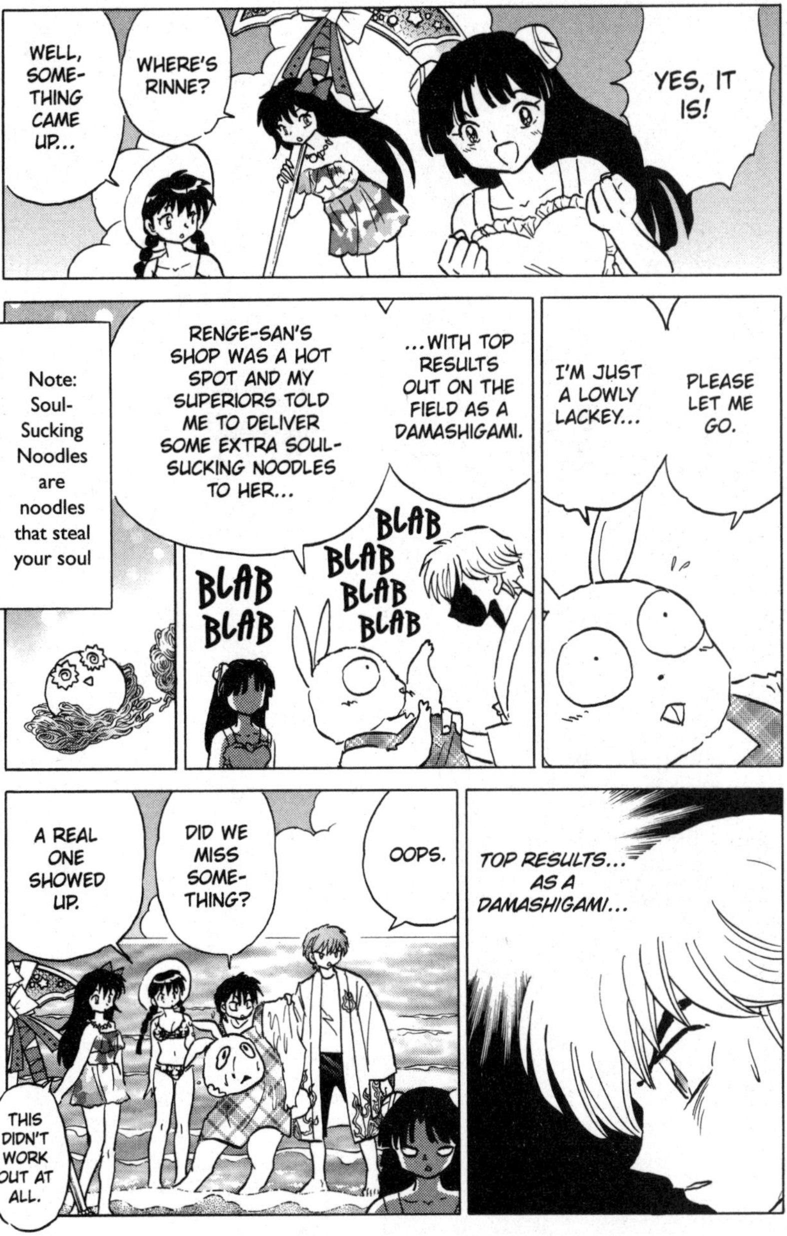
YES, IT IS!
WHERE'S RINNE?
WELL, SOMETHING CAME UP...
PLEASE LET ME GO.
I'M JUST A LOWLY LACKEY...
...WITH TOP RESULTS OUT ON THE FIELD AS A DAMASHIGAMI.
RENGE-SAN'S SHOP WAS A HOT SPOT AND MY SUPERIORS TOLD ME TO DELIVER SOME EXTRA SOUL-SUCKING NOODLES TO HER...
BLAB BLAB BLAB BLAB
BLAB BLAB
Note: Soul-Sucking Noodles are noodles that steal your soul
TOP RESULTS... AS A DAMASHIGAMI...
OOPS.
DID WE MISS SOMETHING?
A REAL ONE SHOWED UP.
THIS DIDN'T WORK OUT AT ALL.

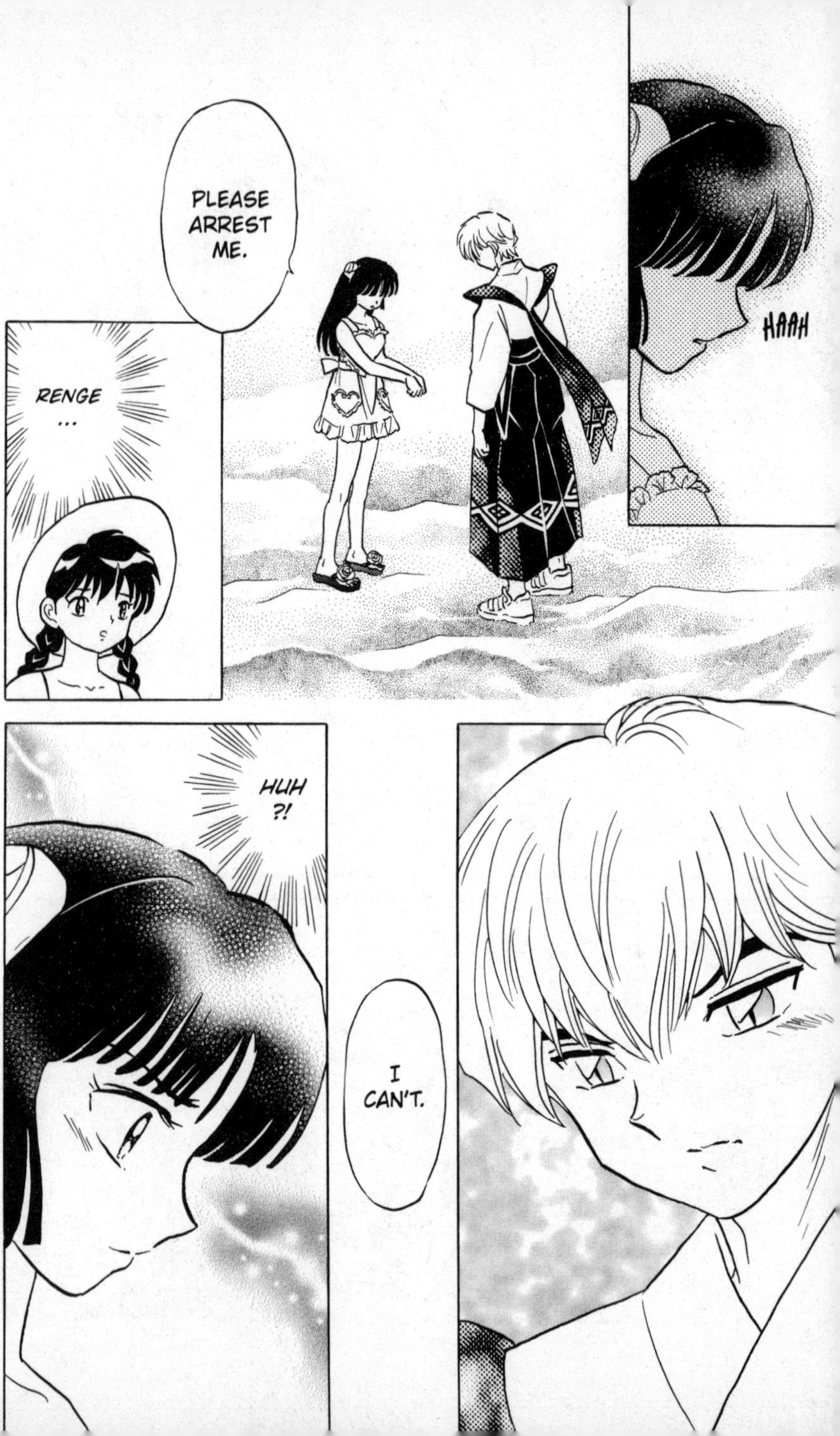
HAAH
PLEASE ARREST ME.
RENGE ...
I CAN'T.
HUH ?!

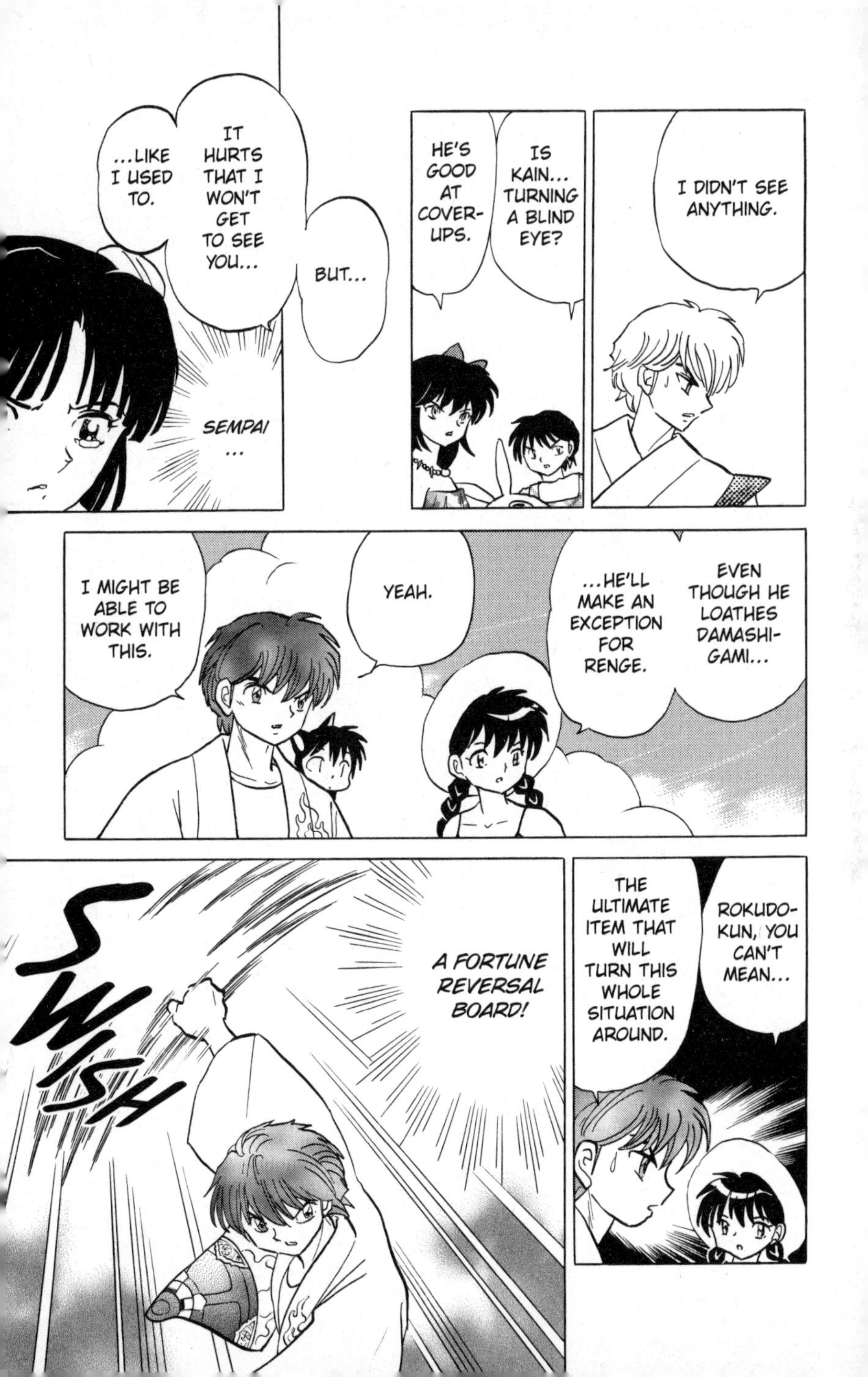
I DIDN'T SEE ANYTHING.
IS KAIN... TURNING A BLIND EYE?
HE'S GOOD AT COVER-UPS.
IT HURTS THAT I WON'T GET TO SEE YOU...
...LIKE I USED TO.
BUT...
SEMPAI ...
EVEN THOUGH HE LOATHES DAMASHI-GAMI...
...HE'LL MAKE AN EXCEPTION FOR RENGE.
YEAH.
I MIGHT BE ABLE TO WORK WITH THIS.
ROKUDO-KUN, YOU CAN'T MEAN...
THE ULTIMATE ITEM THAT WILL TURN THIS WHOLE SITUATION AROUND.
A FORTUNE REVERSAL BOARD!
SWISH

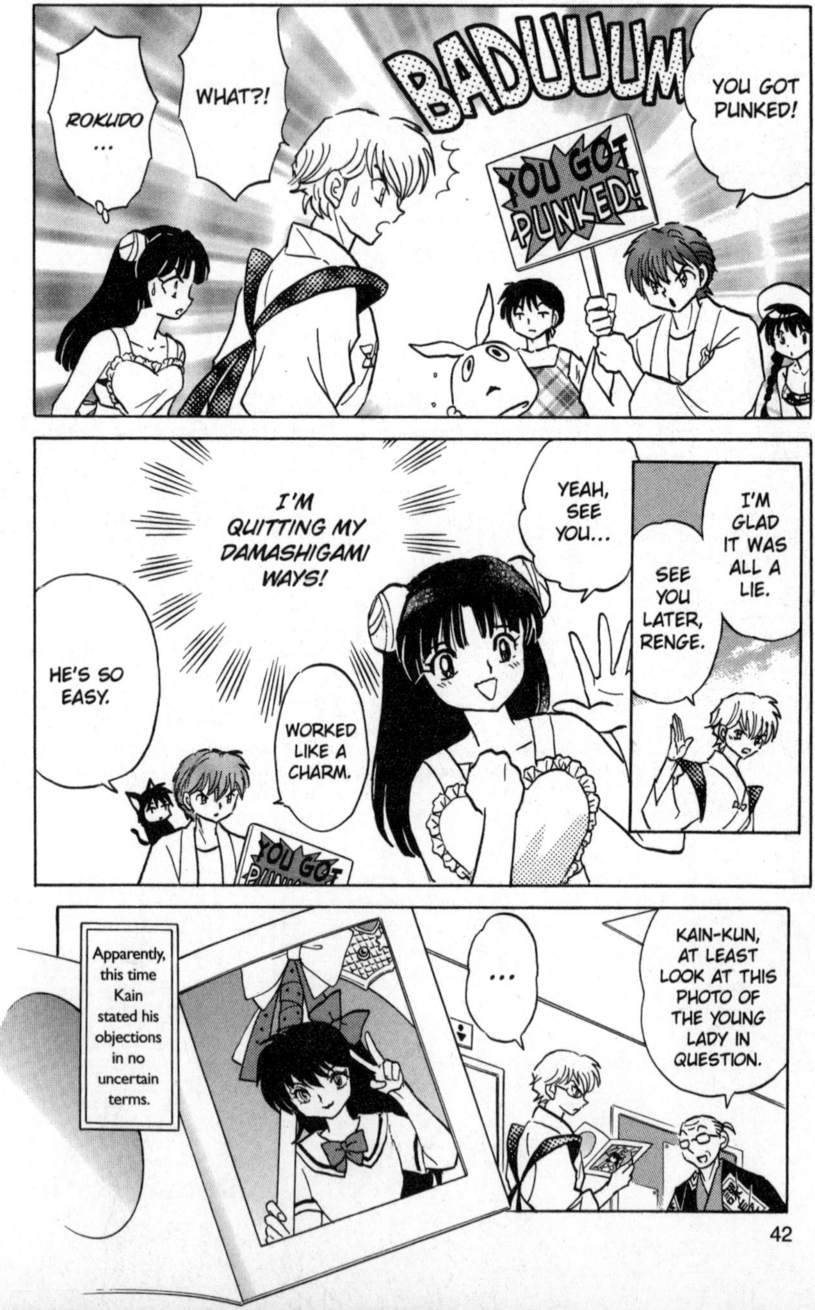
YOU GOT PUNKED!
BADUUUM
YOU GOT PUNKED!
WHAT?!
ROKUDO ...
I'M GLAD IT WAS ALL A LIE.
SEE YOU LATER, RENGE.
YEAH, SEE YOU...
I'M QUITTING MY DAMASHIGAMI WAYS!
WORKED LIKE A CHARM.
HE'S SO EASY.
YOU GOT
KAIN-KUN, AT LEAST LOOK AT THIS PHOTO OF THE YOUNG LADY IN QUESTION.
...
Apparently, this time Kain stated his objections in no uncertain terms.

CHAPTER 381: THE WITCH'S SUMMER VACATION

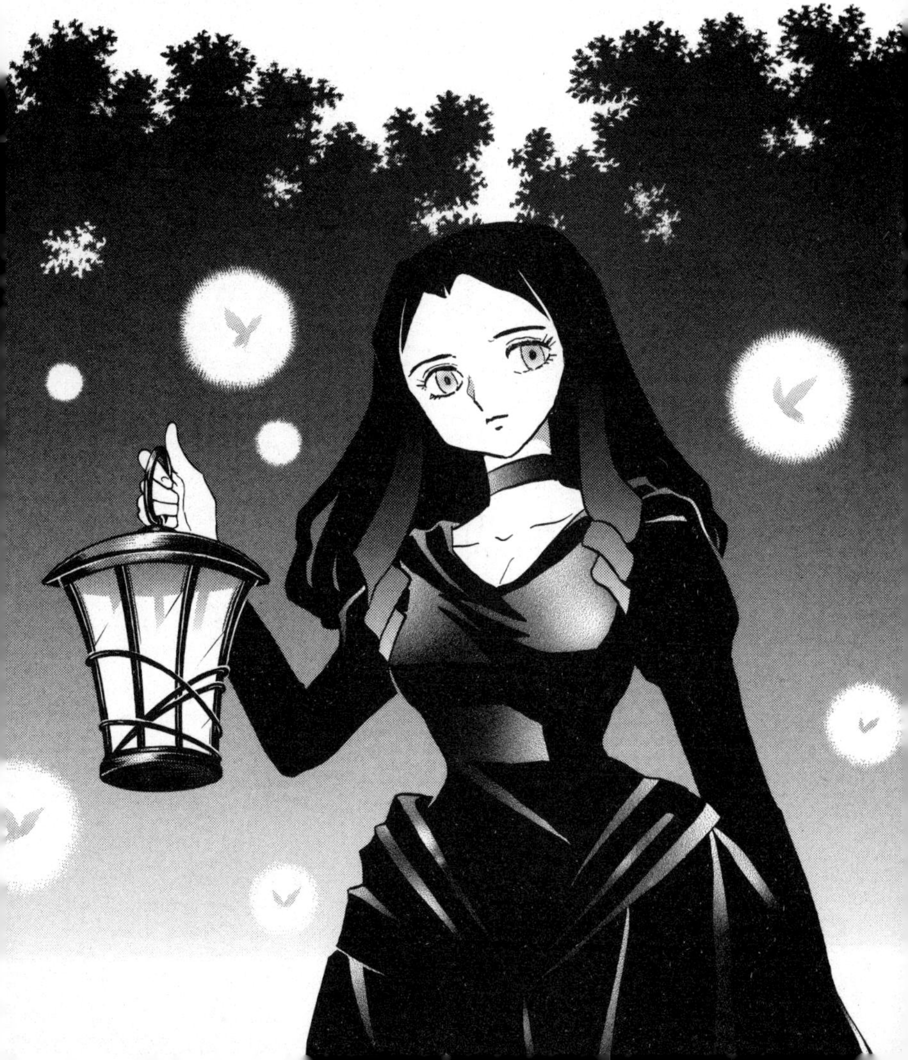

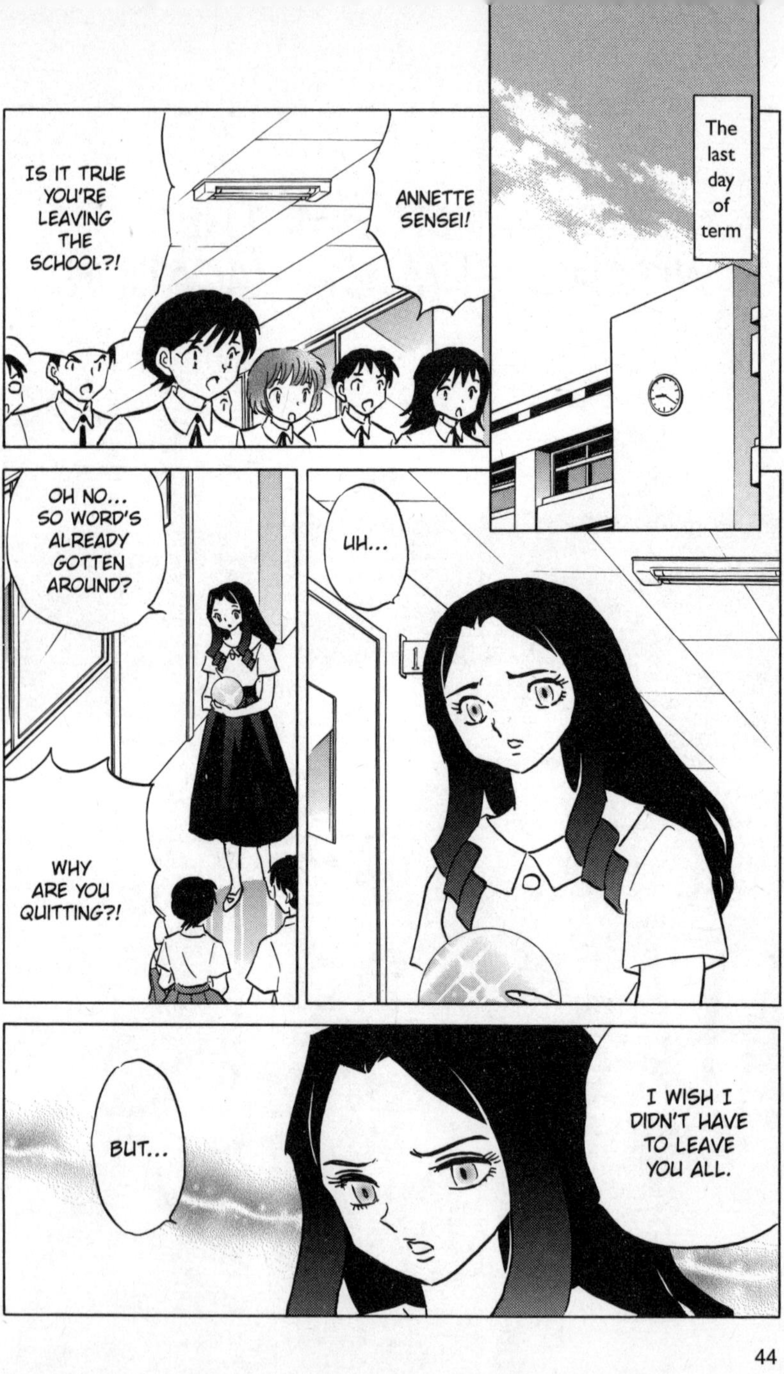
The last day of term
ANNETTE SENSEI!
IS IT TRUE YOU'RE LEAVING THE SCHOOL?!
UH...
OH NO... SO WORD'S ALREADY GOTTEN AROUND?
WHY ARE YOU QUITTING?!
I WISH I DIDN'T HAVE TO LEAVE YOU ALL.
BUT...

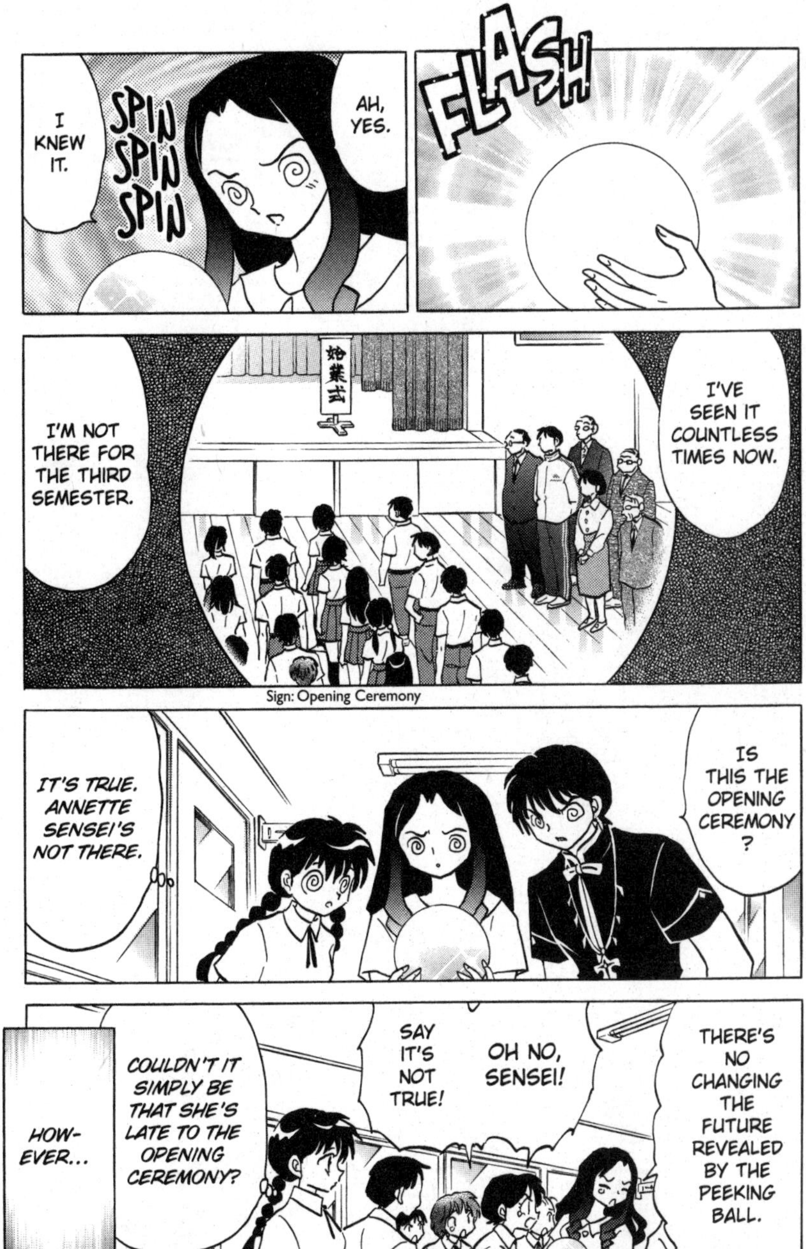
FLASH
AH, YES.
SPIN SPIN SPIN
I KNEW IT.
I'VE SEEN IT COUNTLESS TIMES NOW.
I'M NOT THERE FOR THE THIRD SEMESTER.
IS THIS THE OPENING CEREMONY?
IT'S TRUE. ANNETTE SENSEI'S NOT THERE.
THERE'S NO CHANGING THE FUTURE REVEALED BY THE PEEKING BALL.
OH NO, SENSEI!
SAY IT'S NOT TRUE!
COULDN'T IT SIMPLY BE THAT SHE'S LATE TO THE OPENING CEREMONY?
HOW-EVER...
Sign: Opening Ceremony

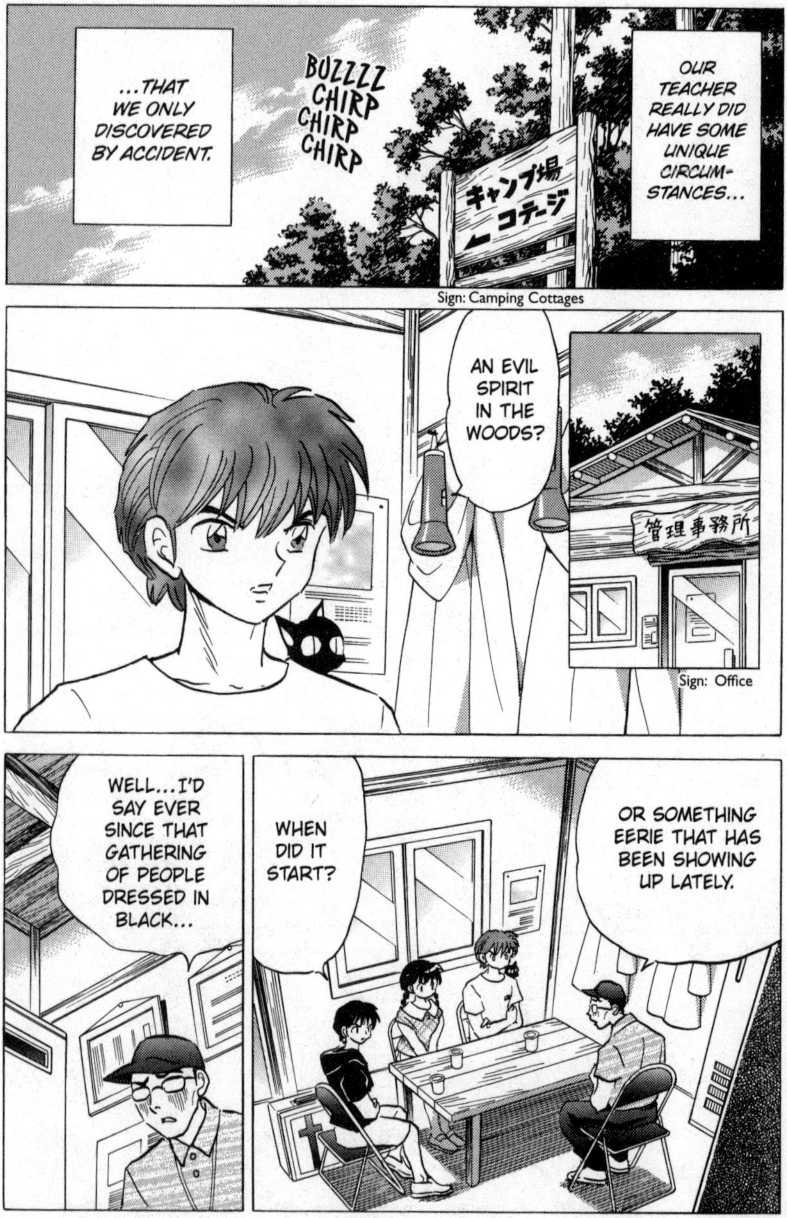
OUR TEACHER REALLY DID HAVE SOME UNIQUE CIRCUM-STANCES...
BUZZZZ CHIRP CHIRP CHIRP
キャンプ場 コテージ
...THAT WE ONLY DISCOVERED BY ACCIDENT.
管理事務所
AN EVIL SPIRIT IN THE WOODS?
OR SOMETHING EERIE THAT HAS BEEN SHOWING UP LATELY.
WHEN DID IT START?
WELL...I'D SAY EVER SINCE THAT GATHERING OF PEOPLE DRESSED IN BLACK...
Sign: Camping Cottages
Sign: Office

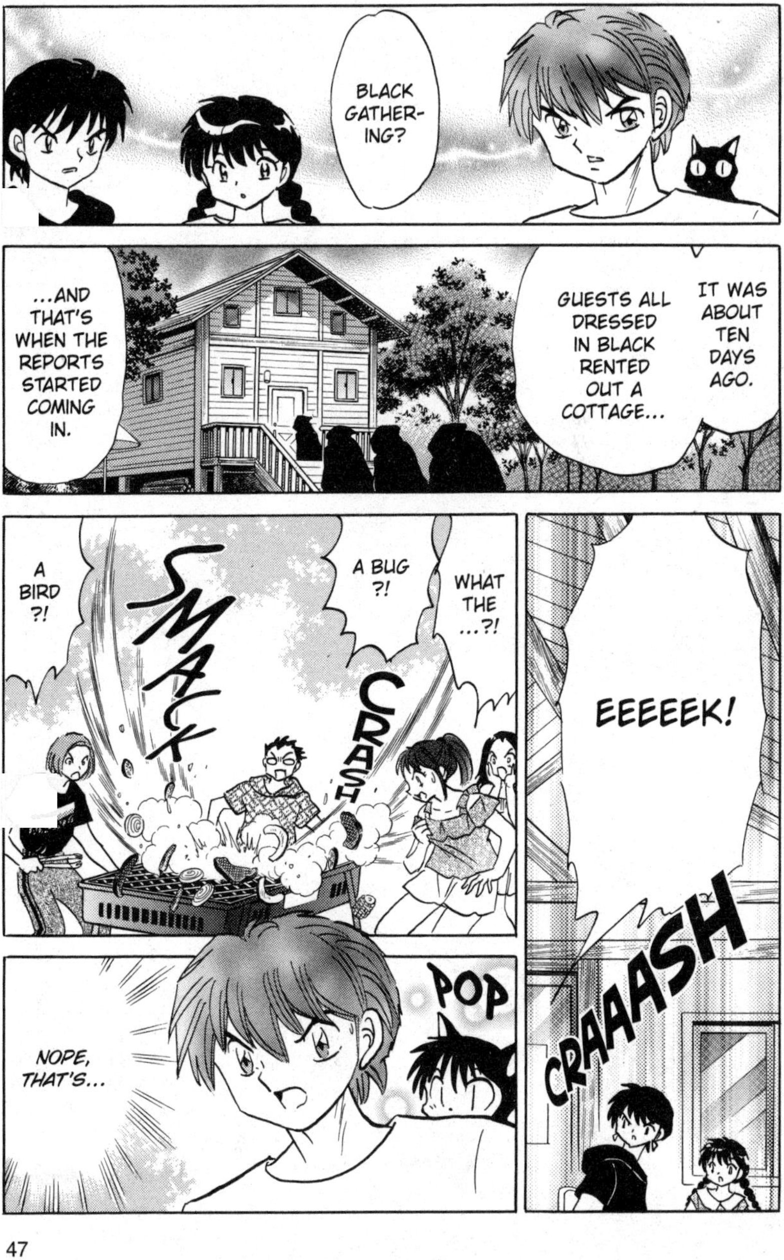
BLACK GATHERING?
IT WAS ABOUT TEN DAYS AGO.
GUESTS ALL DRESSED IN BLACK RENTED OUT A COTTAGE...
...AND THAT'S WHEN THE REPORTS STARTED COMING IN.
EEEEEK!
CRAAASH
WHAT THE ...?!
A BUG ?!
A BIRD ?!
SMACK
CRASH
POP
NOPE, THAT'S...

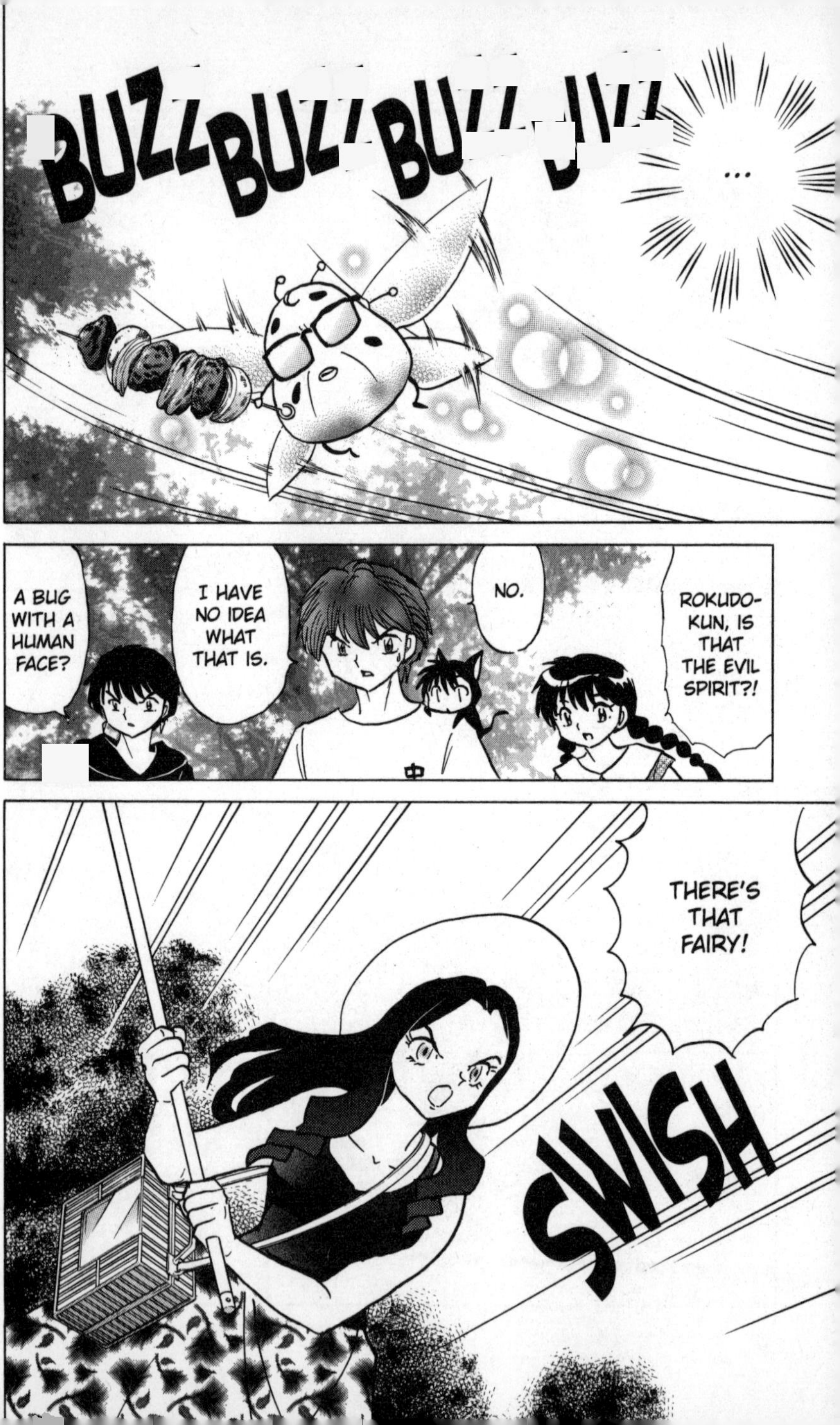
BUZZ BUZZ BU
...
ROKUDO-KUN, IS THAT THE EVIL SPIRIT?!
NO.
I HAVE NO IDEA WHAT THAT IS.
A BUG WITH A HUMAN FACE?
THERE'S THAT FAIRY!
SWISH

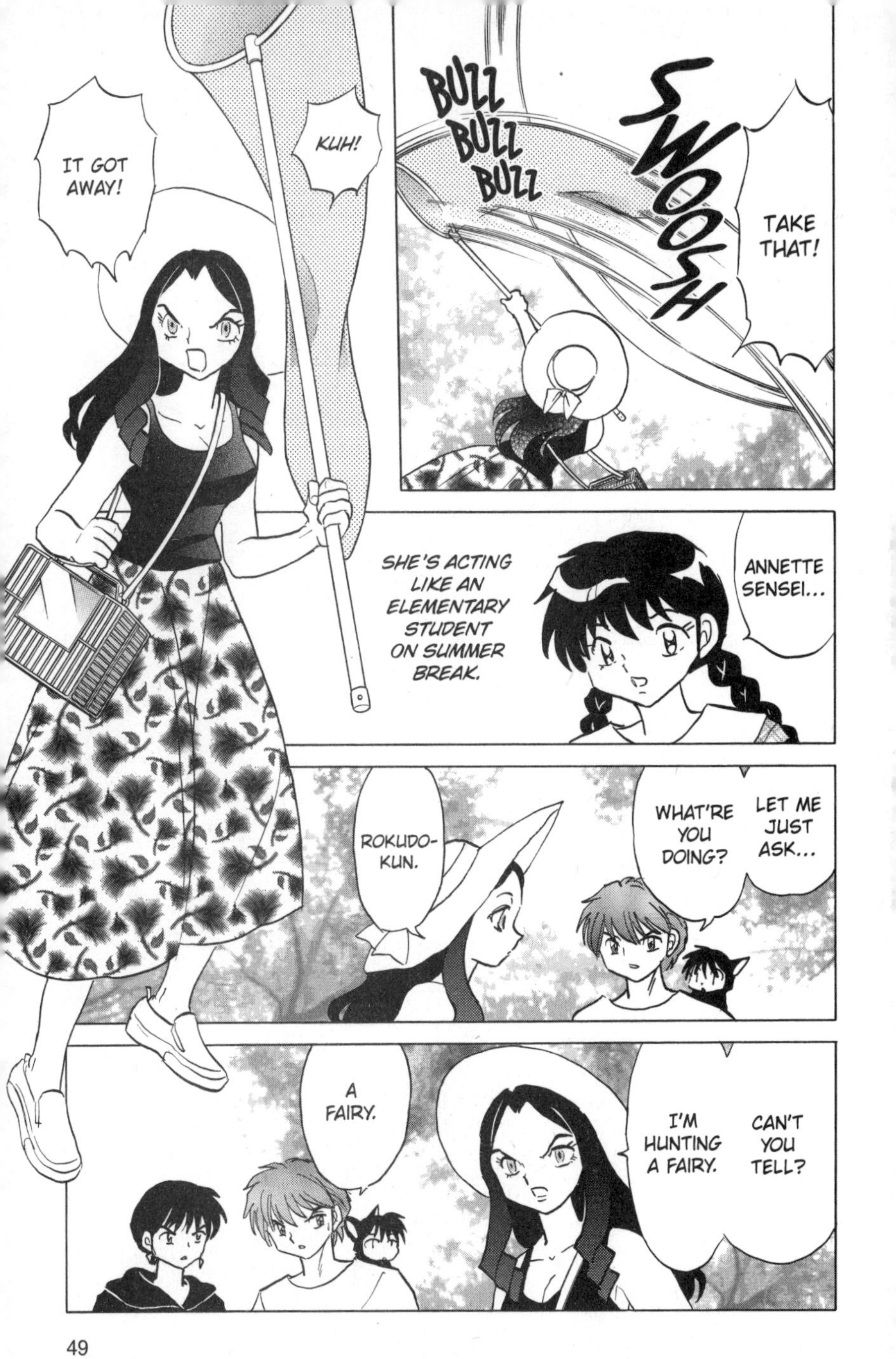
TAKE THAT!
SWOOSH
BUZZ BUZZ BUZZ
KUH!
IT GOT AWAY!
ANNETTE SENSEI...
SHE'S ACTING LIKE AN ELEMENTARY STUDENT ON SUMMER BREAK.
LET ME JUST ASK...
WHAT'RE YOU DOING?
ROKUDO-KUN.
CAN'T YOU TELL?
I'M HUNTING A FAIRY.
A FAIRY.

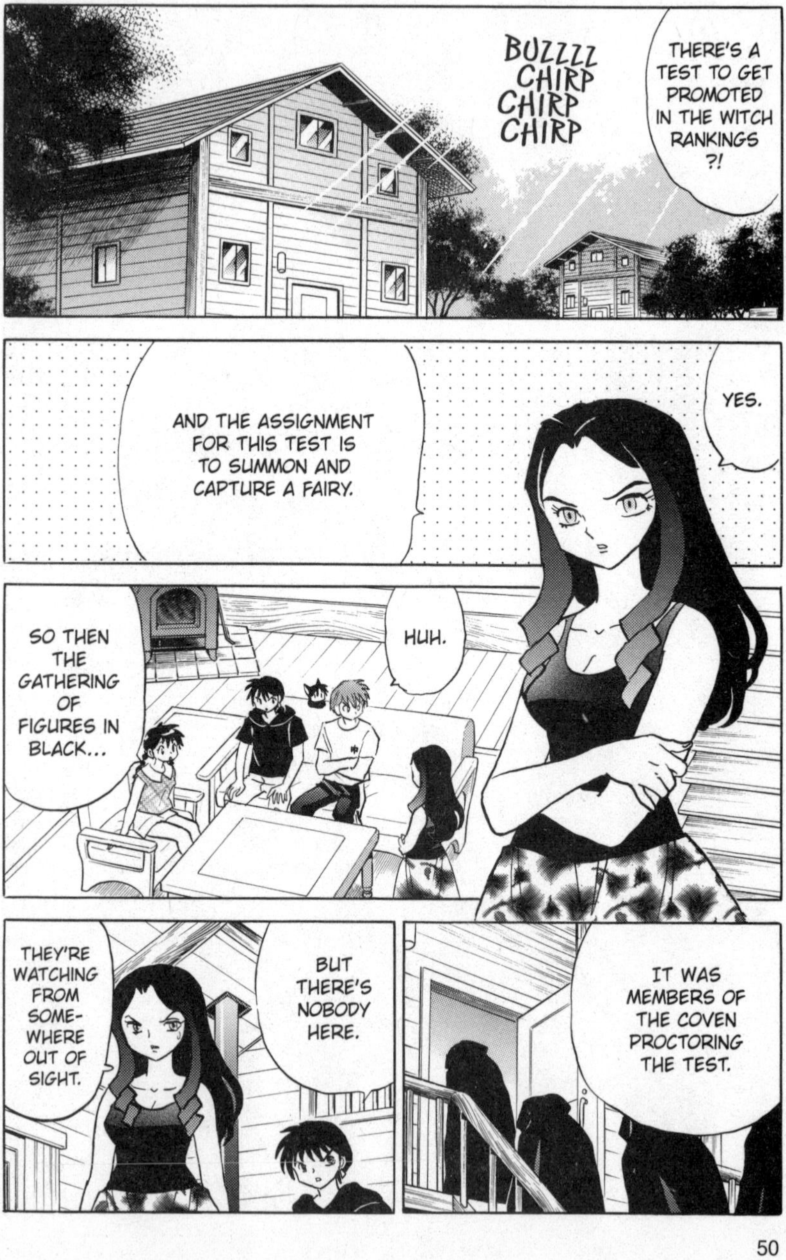
THERE'S A TEST TO GET PROMOTED IN THE WITCH RANKINGS ?!
BUZZZZ CHIRP CHIRP CHIRP
YES.
AND THE ASSIGNMENT FOR THIS TEST IS TO SUMMON AND CAPTURE A FAIRY.
HUH.
SO THEN THE GATHERING OF FIGURES IN BLACK...
IT WAS MEMBERS OF THE COVEN PROCTORING THE TEST.
BUT THERE'S NOBODY HERE.
THEY'RE WATCHING FROM SOME-WHERE OUT OF SIGHT.

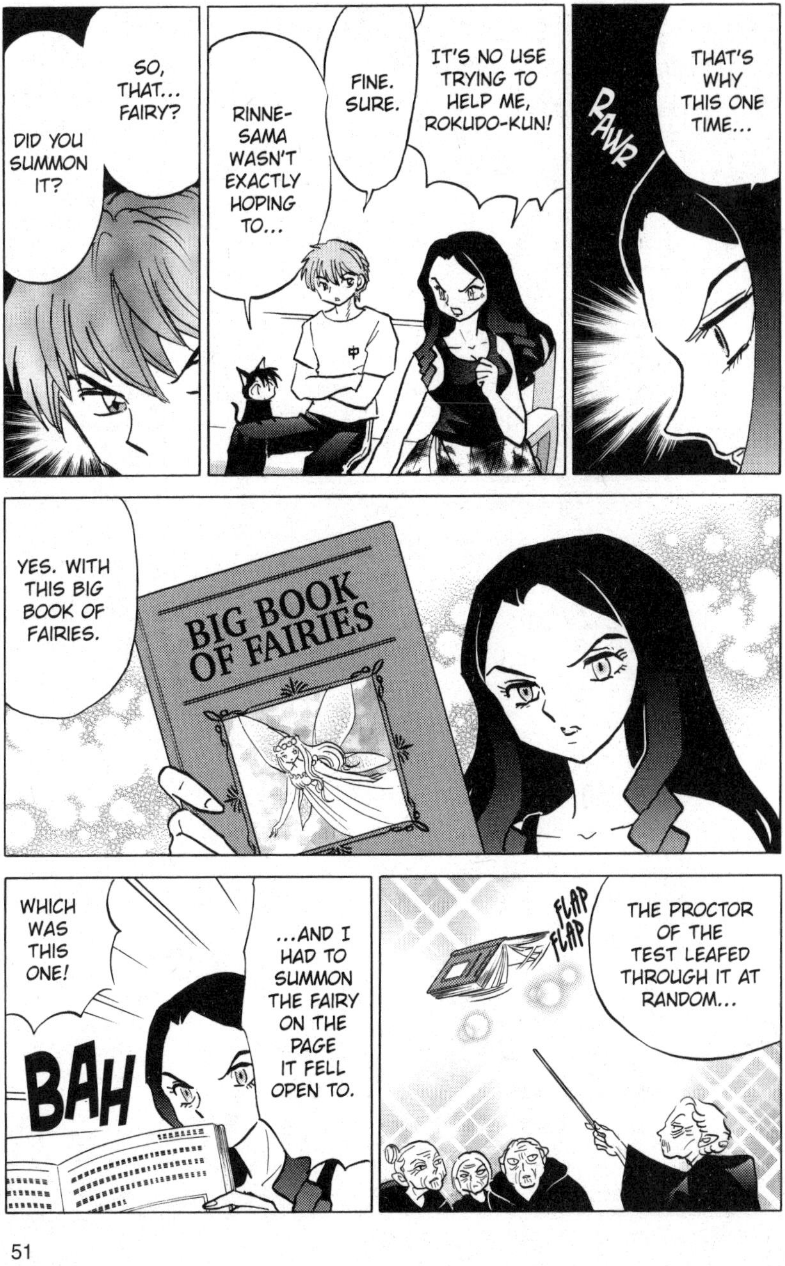
THAT'S WHY THIS ONE TIME...
RAWR
IT'S NO USE TRYING TO HELP ME, ROKUDO-KUN!
FINE. SURE.
RINNE-SAMA WASN'T EXACTLY HOPING TO...
SO, THAT... FAIRY?
DID YOU SUMMON IT?
YES. WITH THIS BIG BOOK OF FAIRIES.
BIG BOOK OF FAIRIES
FLAP FLAP
THE PROCTOR OF THE TEST LEAFED THROUGH IT AT RANDOM...
...AND I HAD TO SUMMON THE FAIRY ON THE PAGE IT FELL OPEN TO.
WHICH WAS THIS ONE!
BAH

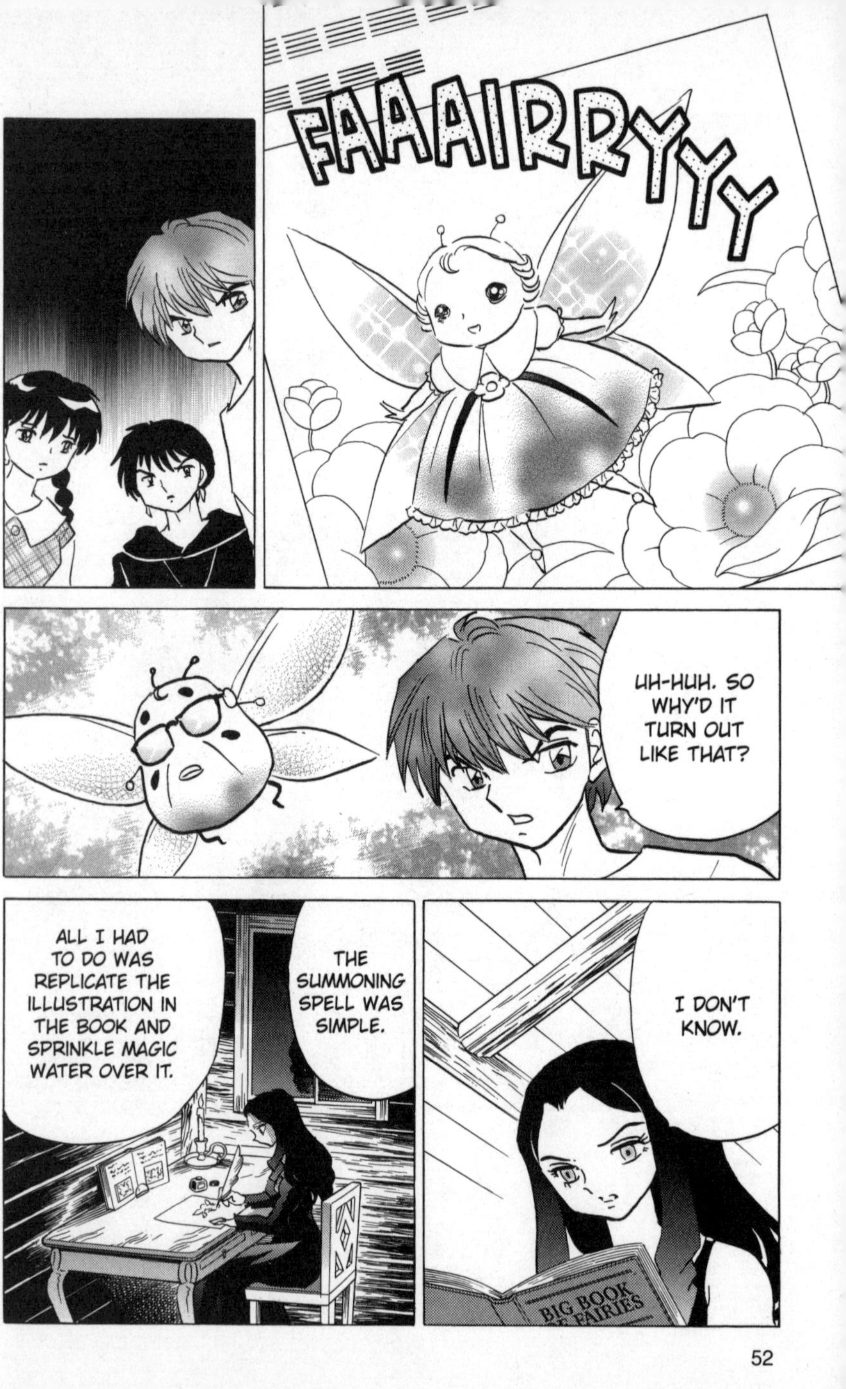
FAAAIRRYYY
UH-HUH. SO WHY'D IT TURN OUT LIKE THAT?
I DON'T KNOW.
BIG BOOK
FAIRIES
THE SUMMONING SPELL WAS SIMPLE.
ALL I HAD TO DO WAS REPLICATE THE ILLUSTRATION IN THE BOOK AND SPRINKLE MAGIC WATER OVER IT.

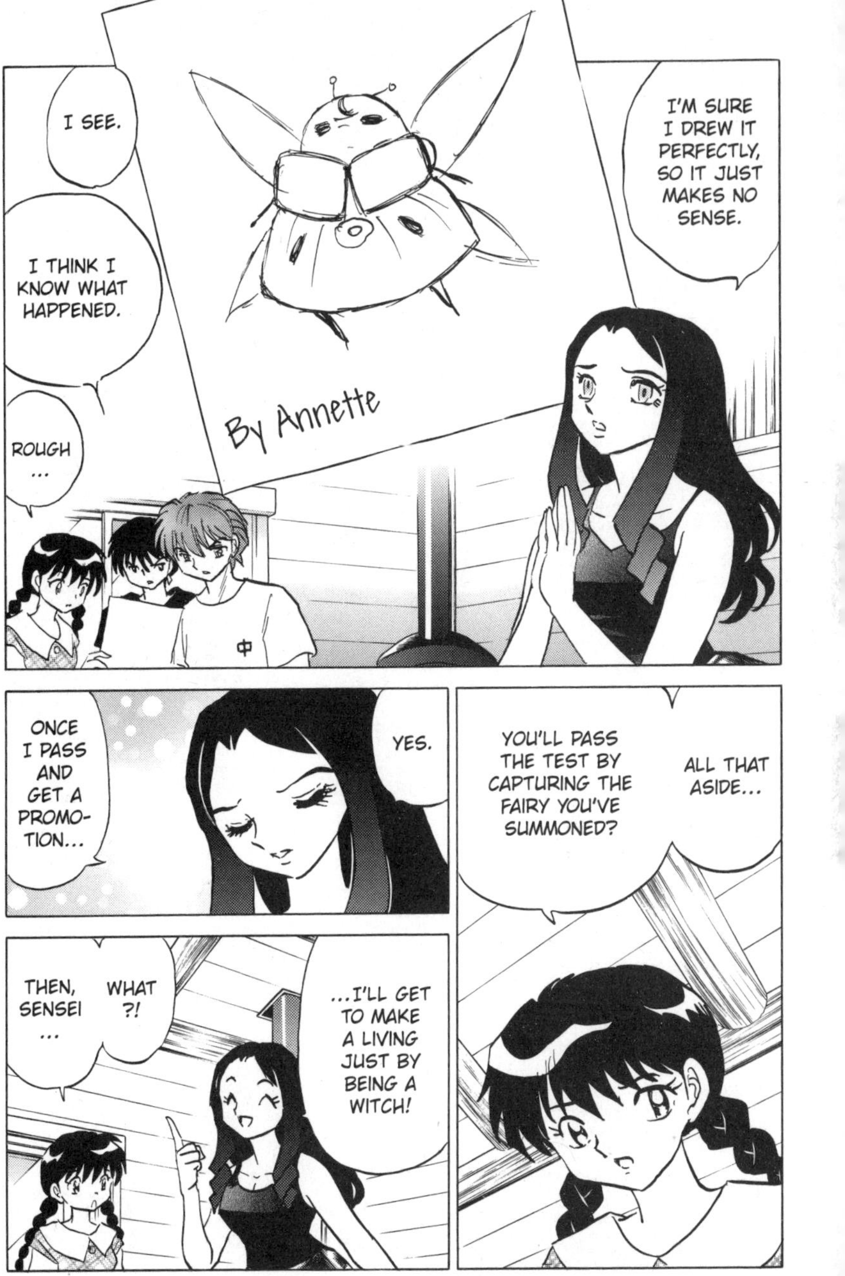
I'M SURE I DREW IT PERFECTLY, SO IT JUST MAKES NO SENSE.
By Annette
I SEE.
I THINK I KNOW WHAT HAPPENED.
ROUGH ...
ALL THAT ASIDE...
YOU'LL PASS THE TEST BY CAPTURING THE FAIRY YOU'VE SUMMONED?
YES.
ONCE I PASS AND GET A PROMOTION...
...I'LL GET TO MAKE A LIVING JUST BY BEING A WITCH!
WHAT ?!
THEN, SENSEI ...

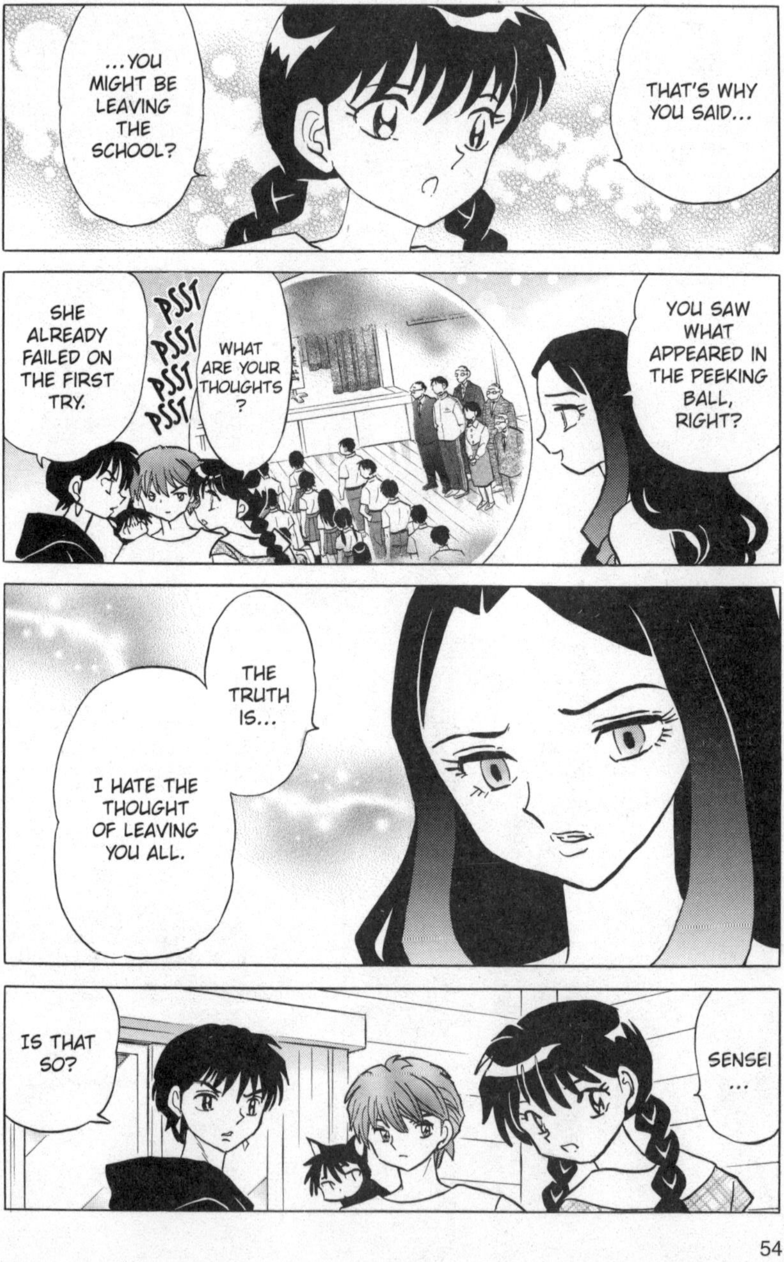
THAT'S WHY YOU SAID...
...YOU MIGHT BE LEAVING THE SCHOOL?
YOU SAW WHAT APPEARED IN THE PEEKING BALL, RIGHT?
WHAT ARE YOUR THOUGHTS?
PSST PSST PSST PSST
SHE ALREADY FAILED ON THE FIRST TRY.
THE TRUTH IS...
I HATE THE THOUGHT OF LEAVING YOU ALL.
SENSEI...
IS THAT SO?

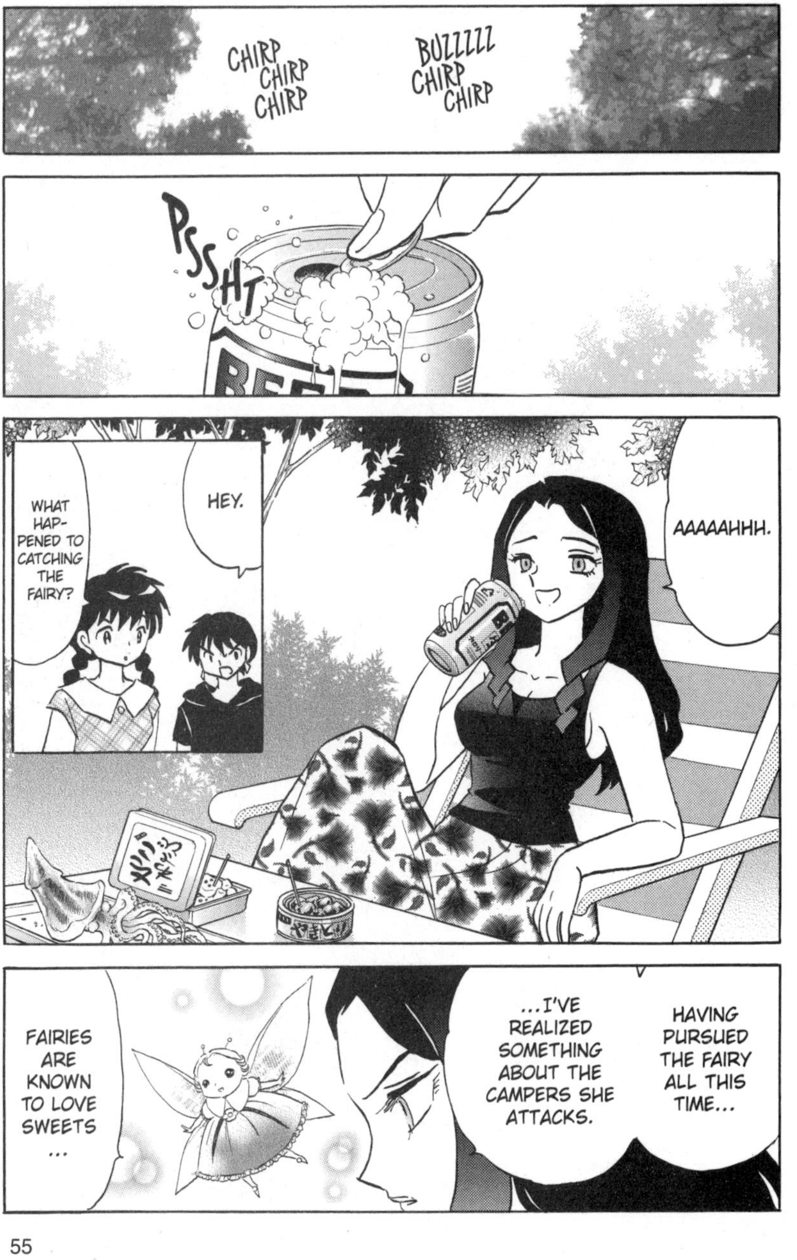
BUZZZZZ CHIRP CHIRP
CHIRP CHIRP CHIRP
PSSHT
AAAAAHHH.
HEY.
WHAT HAP-PENED TO CATCHING THE FAIRY?
HAVING PURSUED THE FAIRY ALL THIS TIME...
...I'VE REALIZED SOMETHING ABOUT THE CAMPERS SHE ATTACKS.
FAIRIES ARE KNOWN TO LOVE SWEETS ...

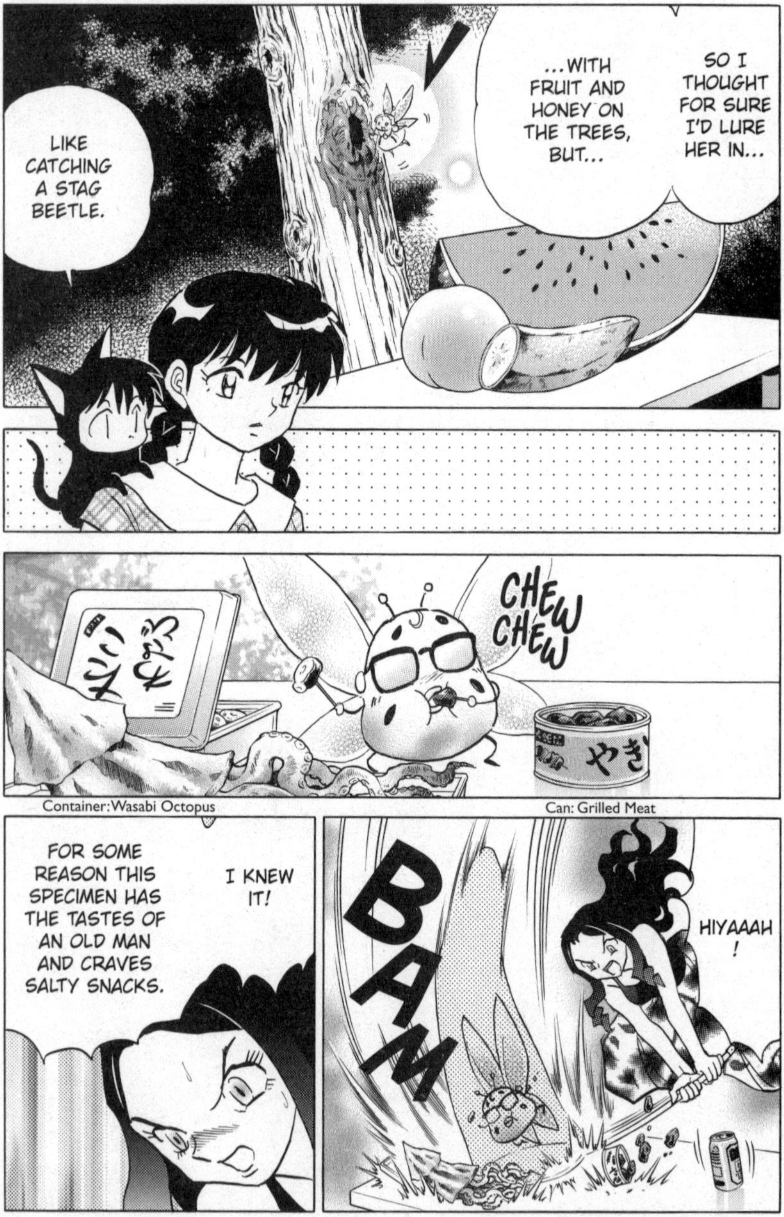
SO I THOUGHT FOR SURE I'D LURE HER IN...
...WITH FRUIT AND HONEY ON THE TREES, BUT...
LIKE CATCHING A STAG BEETLE.
CHEW CHEW
やき
Container: Wasabi Octopus
Can: Grilled Meat
BAM
HIYAAAH!
I KNEW IT!
FOR SOME REASON THIS SPECIMEN HAS THE TASTES OF AN OLD MAN AND CRAVES SALTY SNACKS.

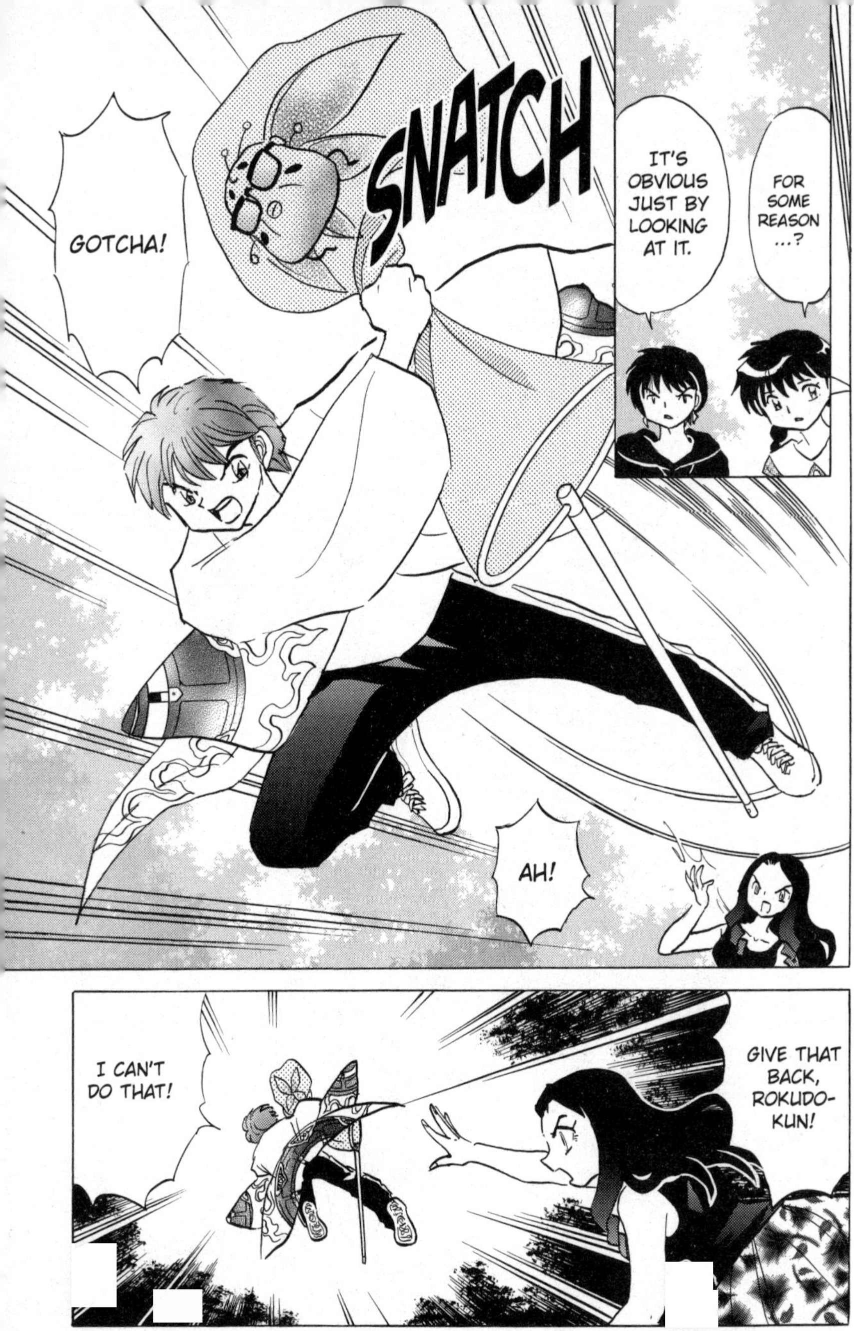
FOR SOME REASON ...?
IT'S OBVIOUS JUST BY LOOKING AT IT.
SNATCH
GOTCHA!
AH!
GIVE THAT BACK, ROKUDO-KUN!
I CAN'T DO THAT!

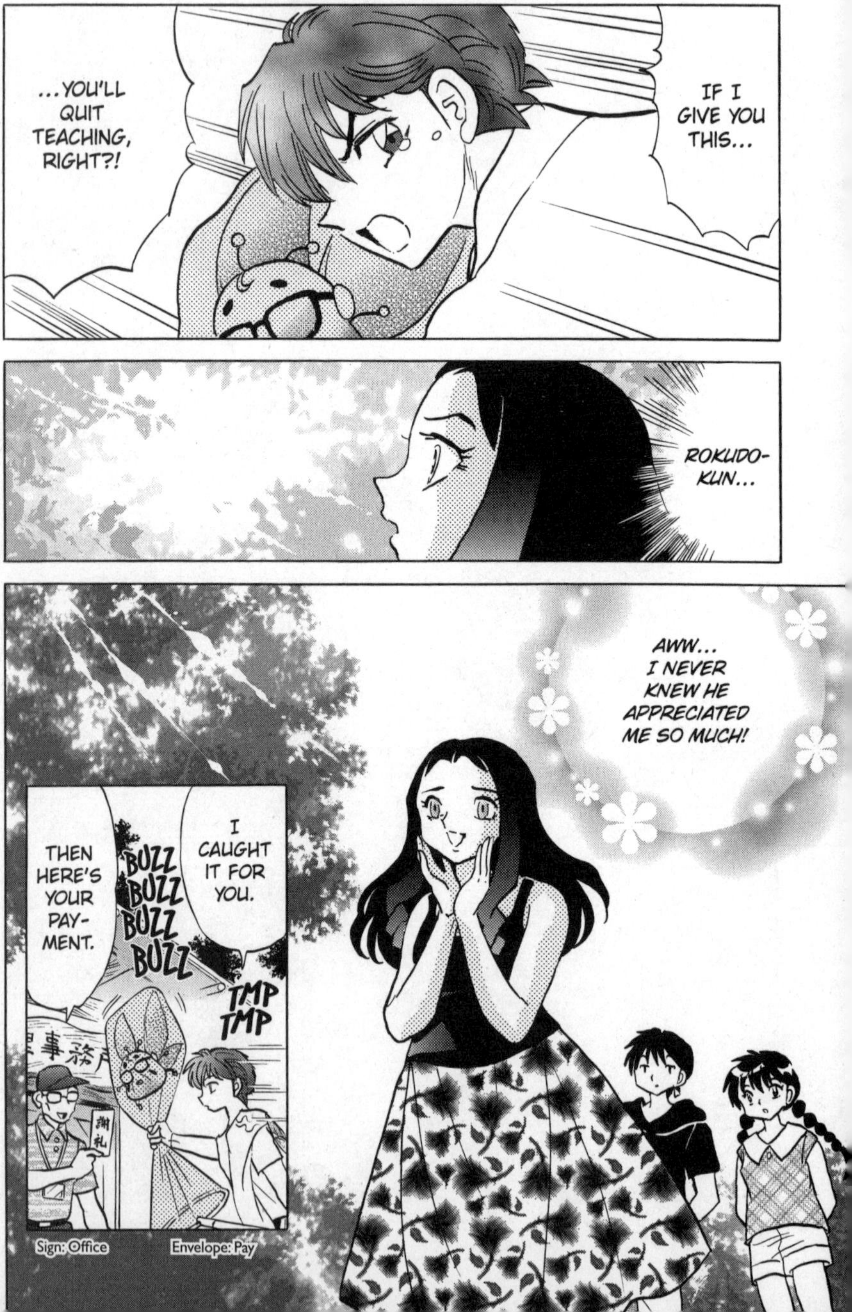
IF I GIVE YOU THIS...
...YOU'LL QUIT TEACHING, RIGHT?!
ROKUDO-KUN...
AWW... I NEVER KNEW HE APPRECIATED ME SO MUCH!
I CAUGHT IT FOR YOU.
TMP TMP
BUZZ BUZZ BUZZ BUZZ
THEN HERE'S YOUR PAY-MENT.
Sign: Office
Envelope: Pay

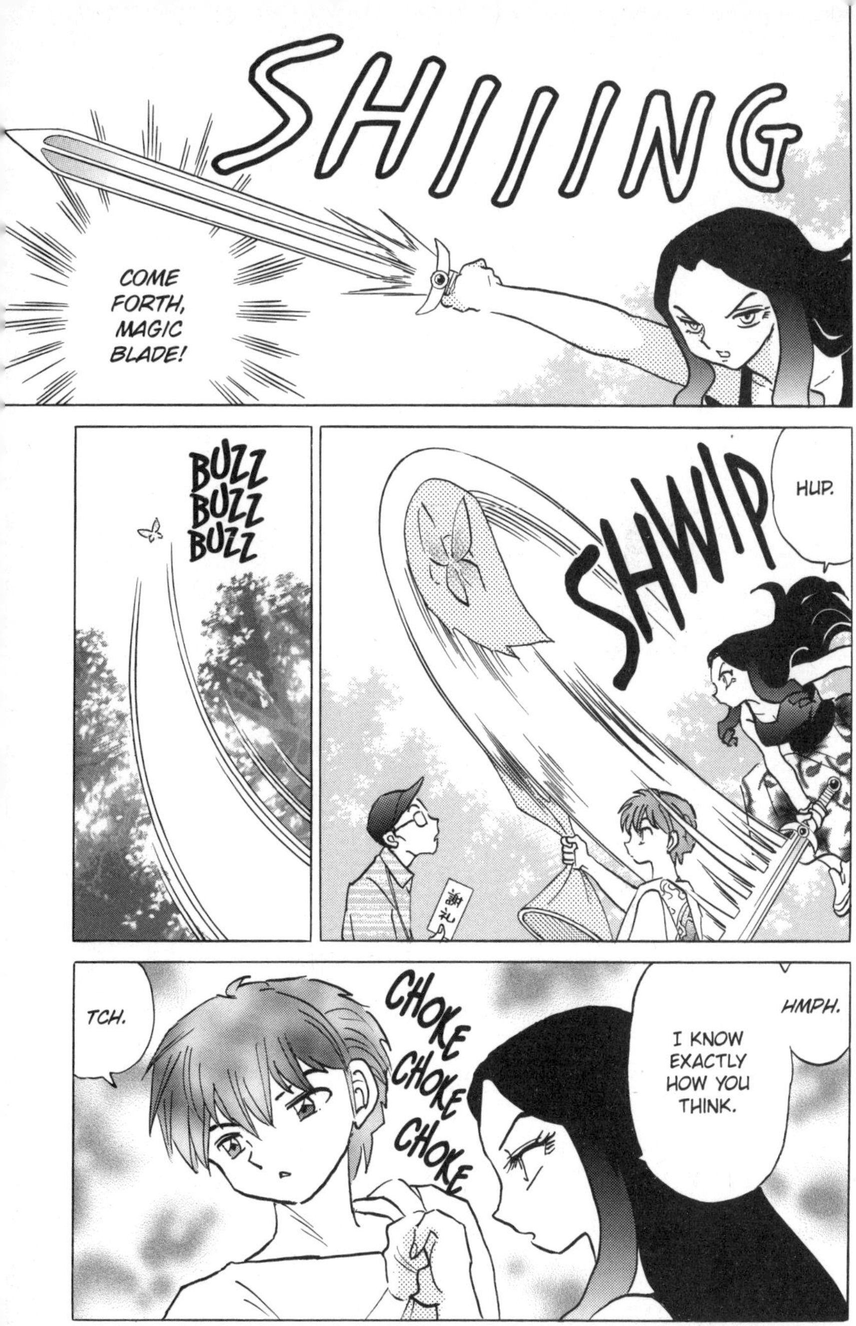
SHIIING
COME FORTH, MAGIC BLADE!
HUP.
SHWIP
謝礼
BUZZ BUZZ BUZZ
HMPH.
I KNOW EXACTLY HOW YOU THINK.
CHOKE CHOKE CHOKE
TCH.

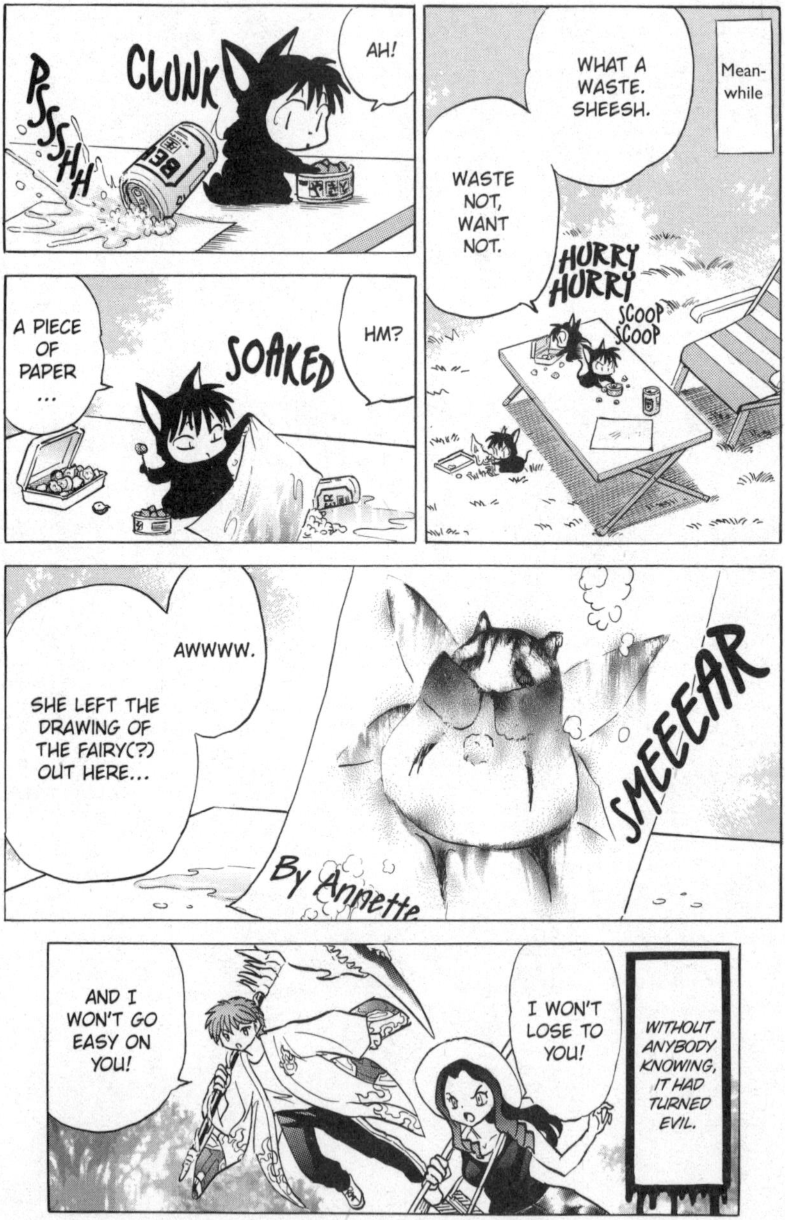
Mean-while
WHAT A WASTE. SHEESH.
WASTE NOT, WANT NOT.
HURRY HURRY
SCOOP SCOOP
AH!
CLUNK
PSSSHH
HM?
SOAKED
A PIECE OF PAPER ...
SMEEEAR
AWWWW.
SHE LEFT THE DRAWING OF THE FAIRY(?) OUT HERE...
By Annette
WITHOUT ANYBODY KNOWING, IT HAD TURNED EVIL.
I WON'T LOSE TO YOU!
AND I WON'T GO EASY ON YOU!

CHAPTER 282: TEACHER'S FUTURE

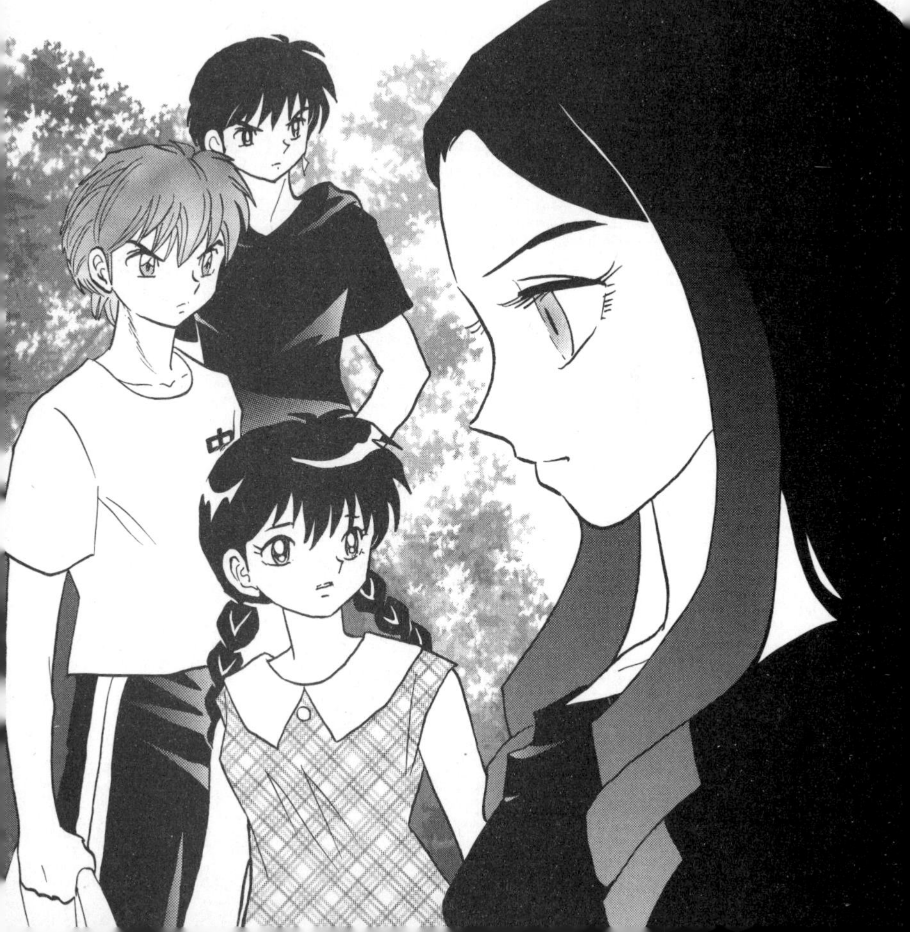
中

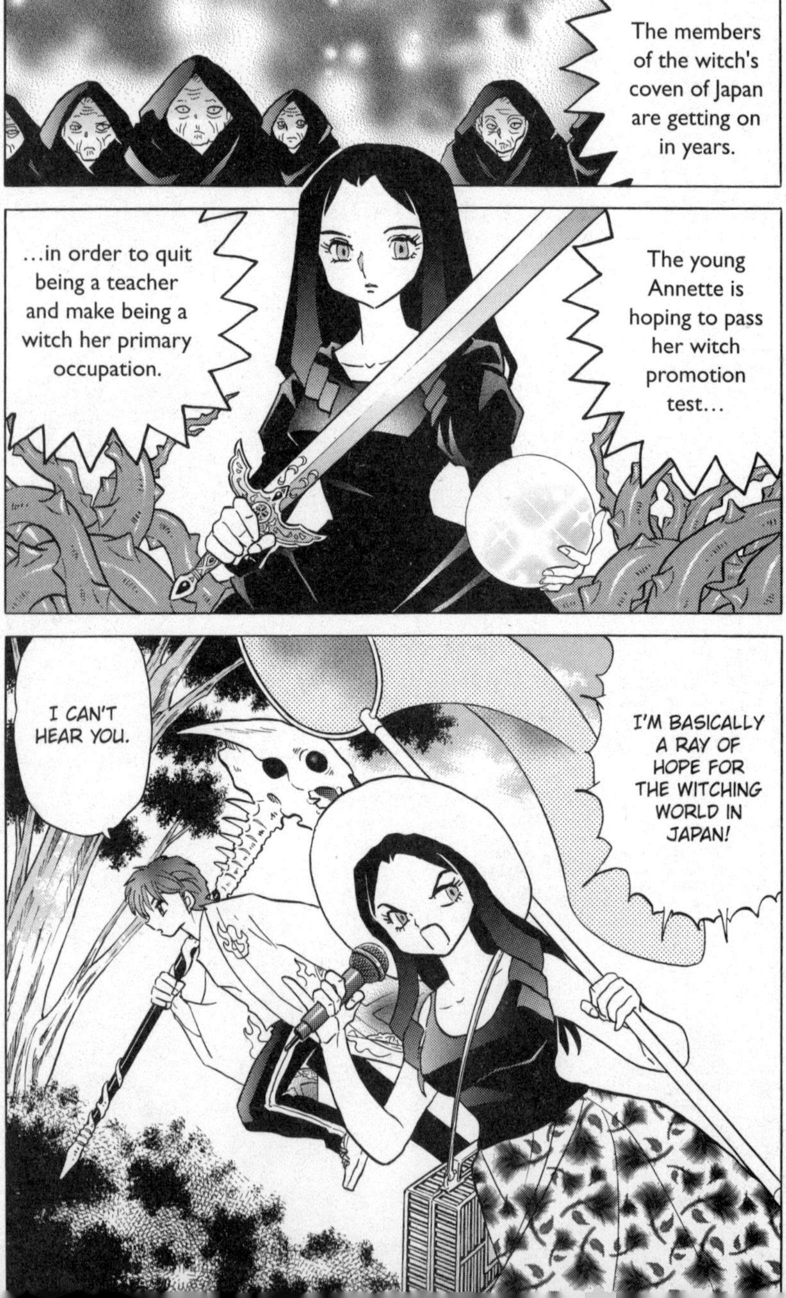
The members of the witch's coven of Japan are getting on in years.
The young Annette is hoping to pass her witch promotion test…
…in order to quit being a teacher and make being a witch her primary occupation.
I'M BASICALLY A RAY OF HOPE FOR THE WITCHING WORLD IN JAPAN!
I CAN'T HEAR YOU.

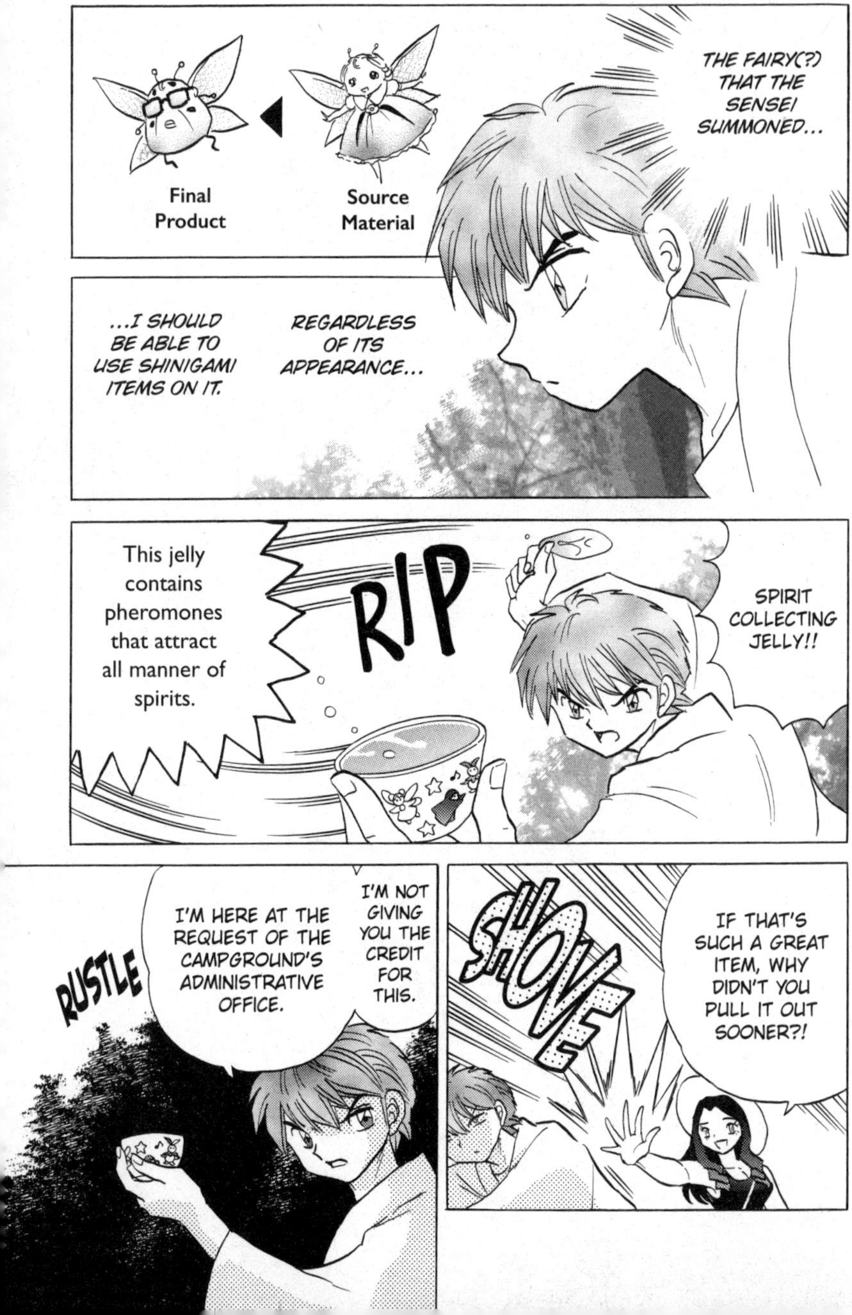
THE FAIRY(?) THAT THE SENSEI SUMMONED...
Source Material
Final Product
REGARDLESS OF ITS APPEARANCE...
...I SHOULD BE ABLE TO USE SHINIGAMI ITEMS ON IT.
SPIRIT COLLECTING JELLY!!
RIP
This jelly contains pheromones that attract all manner of spirits.
SHOVE
IF THAT'S SUCH A GREAT ITEM, WHY DIDN'T YOU PULL IT OUT SOONER?!
I'M NOT GIVING YOU THE CREDIT FOR THIS.
I'M HERE AT THE REQUEST OF THE CAMPGROUND'S ADMINISTRATIVE OFFICE.
RUSTLE

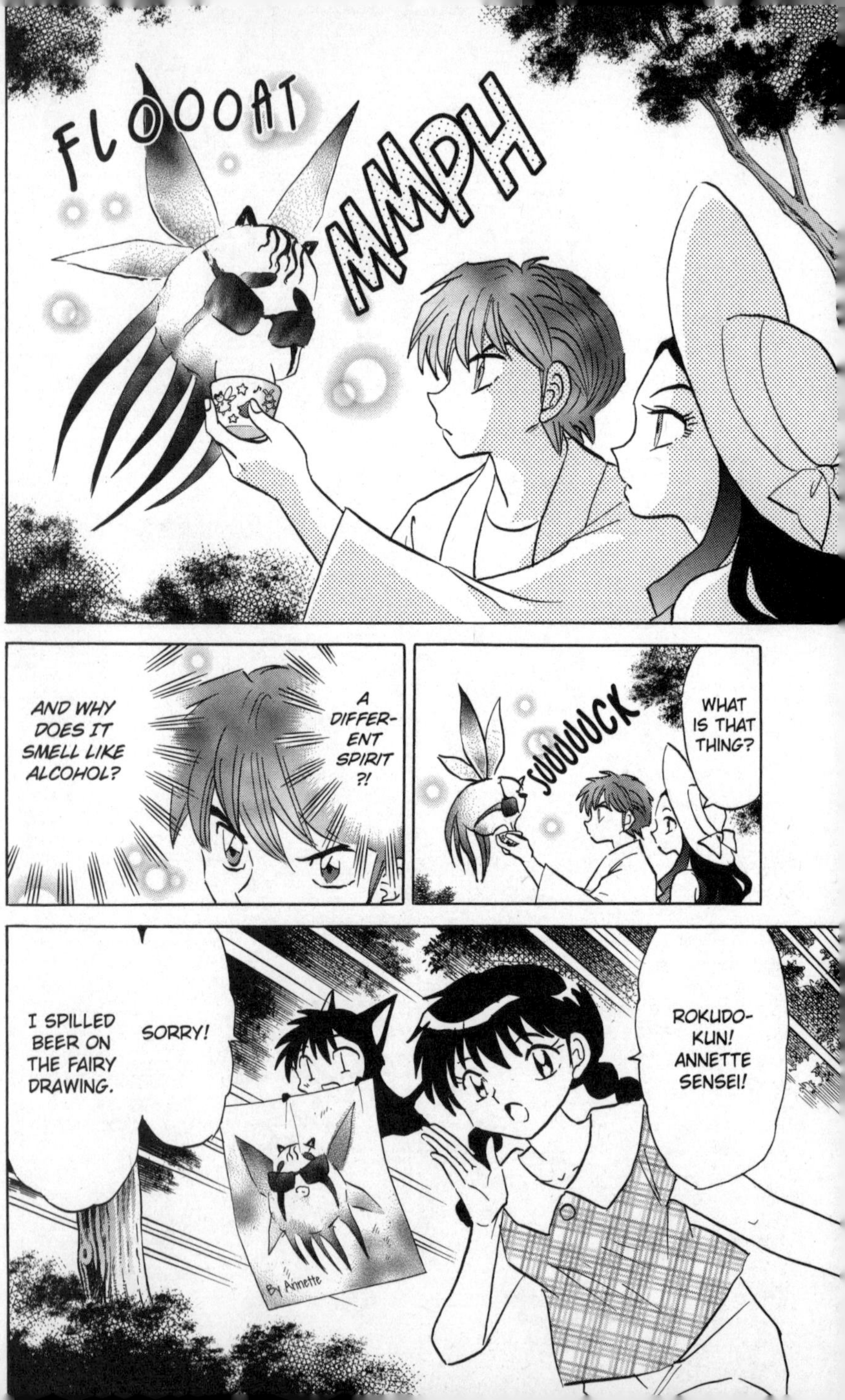
MMPH
FLOOOAT
WHAT IS THAT THING?
SUUUUUCK
A DIFFER-ENT SPIRIT ?!
AND WHY DOES IT SMELL LIKE ALCOHOL?
ROKUDO-KUN! ANNETTE SENSEI!
SORRY!
I SPILLED BEER ON THE FAIRY DRAWING.
By Annette

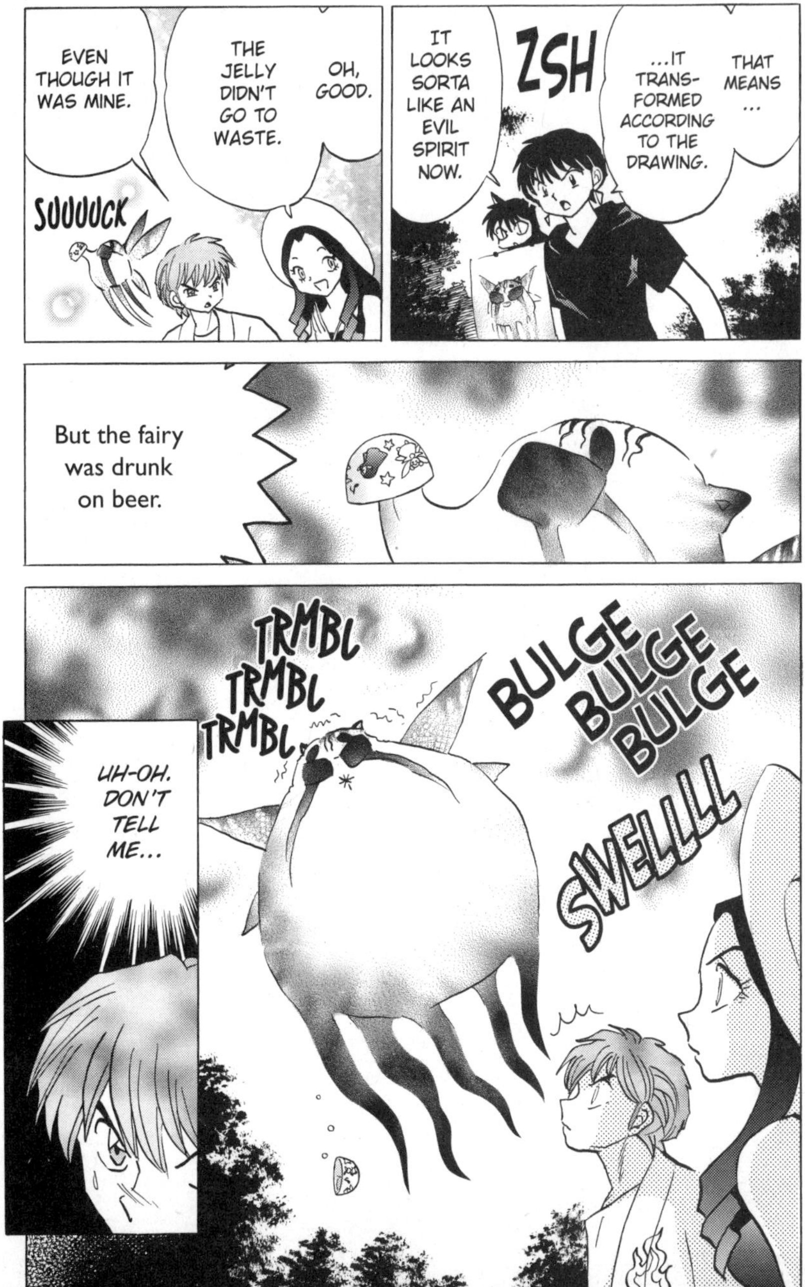
THAT MEANS ...
...IT TRANS-FORMED ACCORDING TO THE DRAWING.
ZSH
IT LOOKS SORTA LIKE AN EVIL SPIRIT NOW.
OH, GOOD.
THE JELLY DIDN'T GO TO WASTE.
EVEN THOUGH IT WAS MINE.
SUUUUCK
But the fairy was drunk on beer.
BULGE BULGE BULGE
TRMBL TRMBL TRMBL
SWELLLL
UH-OH. DON'T TELL ME...

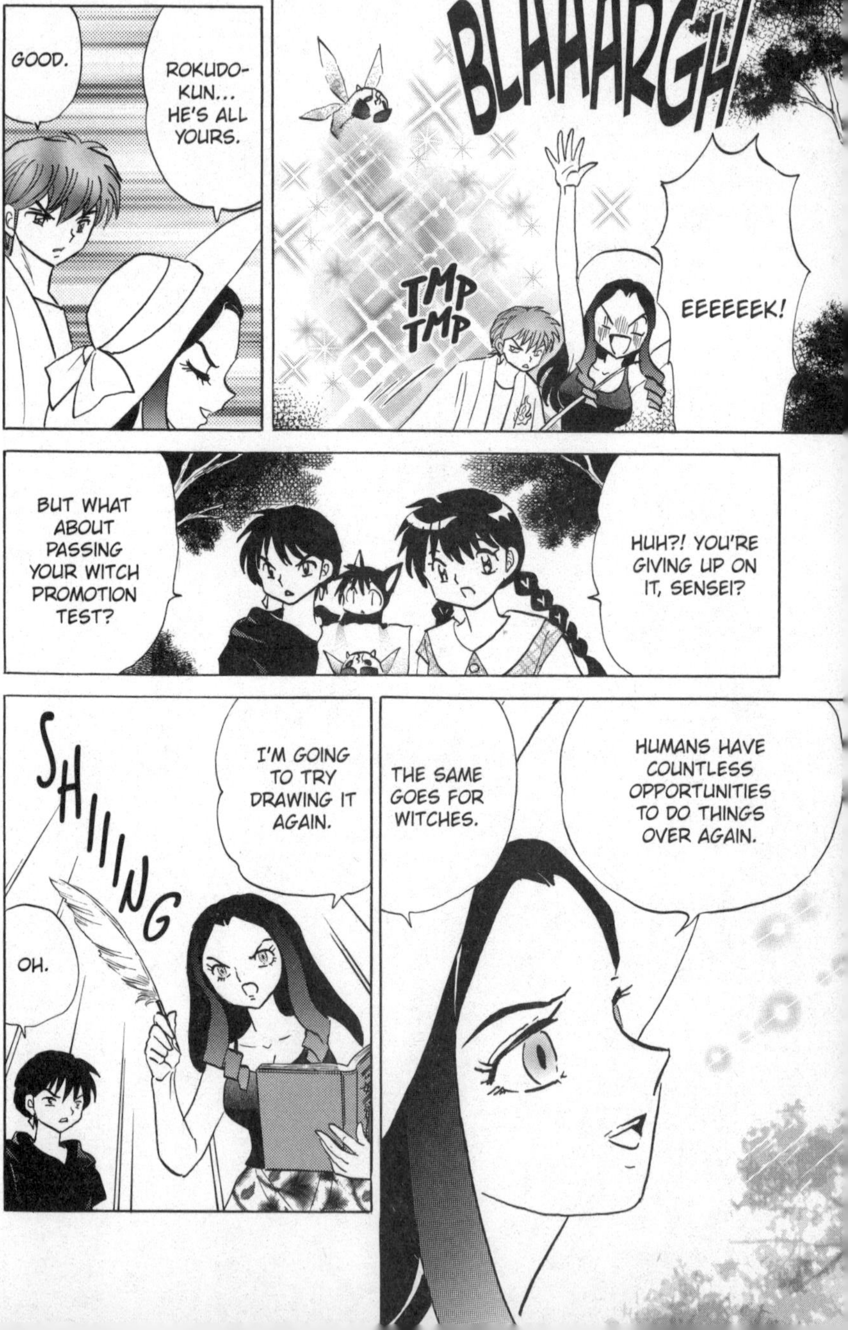
BLAAARGH
TMP TMP
EEEEEEK!
ROKUDO-KUN... HE'S ALL YOURS.
GOOD.
HUH?! YOU'RE GIVING UP ON IT, SENSEI?
BUT WHAT ABOUT PASSING YOUR WITCH PROMOTION TEST?
HUMANS HAVE COUNTLESS OPPORTUNITIES TO DO THINGS OVER AGAIN.
THE SAME GOES FOR WITCHES.
I'M GOING TO TRY DRAWING IT AGAIN.
SHIIING
OH.

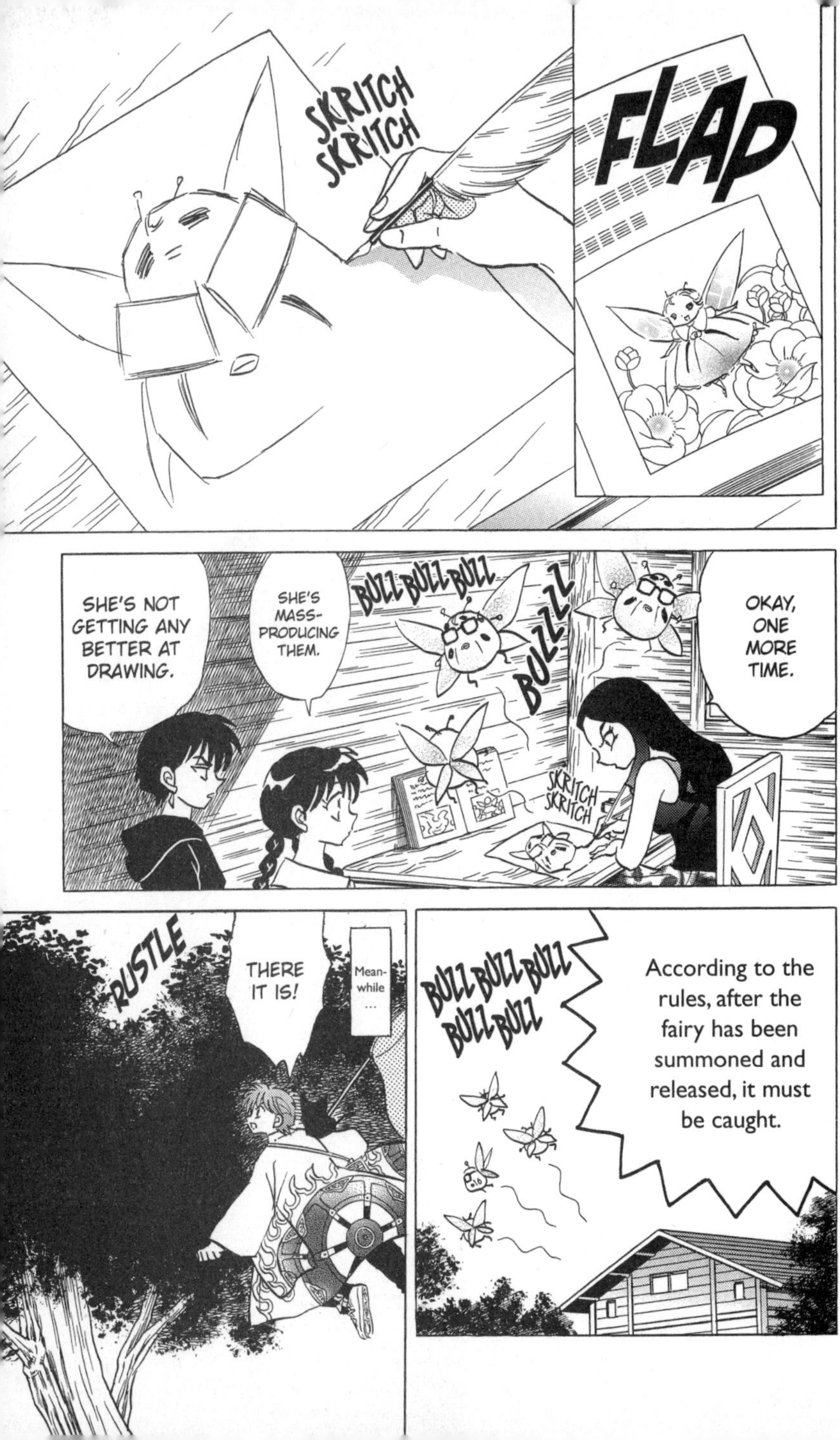
FLAP
SKRITCH SKRITCH
OKAY, ONE MORE TIME.
BUZZZZ
BUZZ BUZZ BUZZ
SHE'S MASS-PRODUCING THEM.
SHE'S NOT GETTING ANY BETTER AT DRAWING.
SKRITCH SKRITCH
According to the rules, after the fairy has been summoned and released, it must be caught.
BUZZ BUZZ BUZZ BUZZ BUZZ
Meanwhile …
THERE IT IS!
RUSTLE

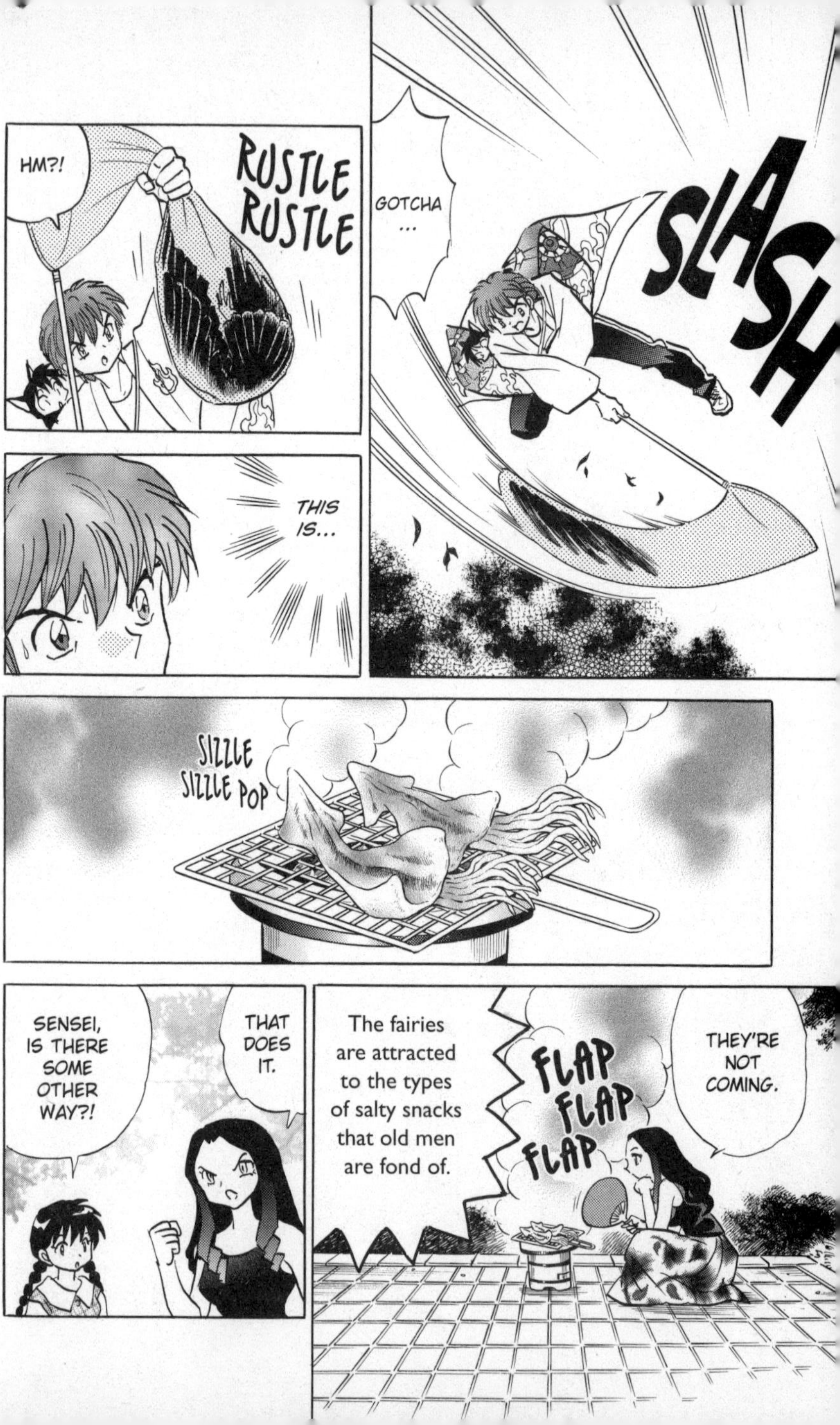
GOTCHA...
SLASH
HM?!
RUSTLE RUSTLE
THIS IS...
SIZZLE SIZZLE POP
THEY'RE NOT COMING.
FLAP FLAP FLAP
The fairies are attracted to the types of salty snacks that old men are fond of.
THAT DOES IT.
SENSEI, IS THERE SOME OTHER WAY?!

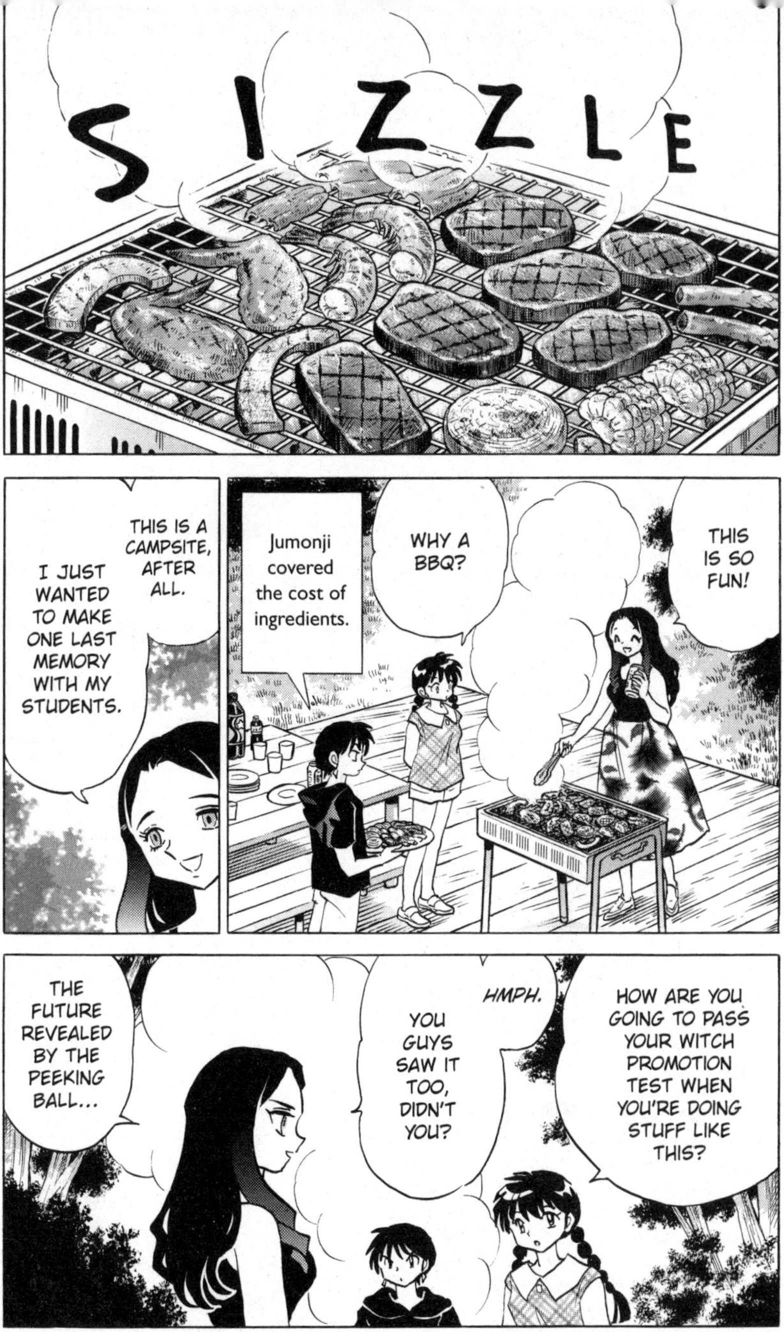
SIZZLE
THIS IS SO FUN!
WHY A BBQ?
Jumonji covered the cost of ingredients.
THIS IS A CAMPSITE, AFTER ALL.
I JUST WANTED TO MAKE ONE LAST MEMORY WITH MY STUDENTS.
HOW ARE YOU GOING TO PASS YOUR WITCH PROMOTION TEST WHEN YOU'RE DOING STUFF LIKE THIS?
HMPH.
YOU GUYS SAW IT TOO, DIDN'T YOU?
THE FUTURE REVEALED BY THE PEEKING BALL...

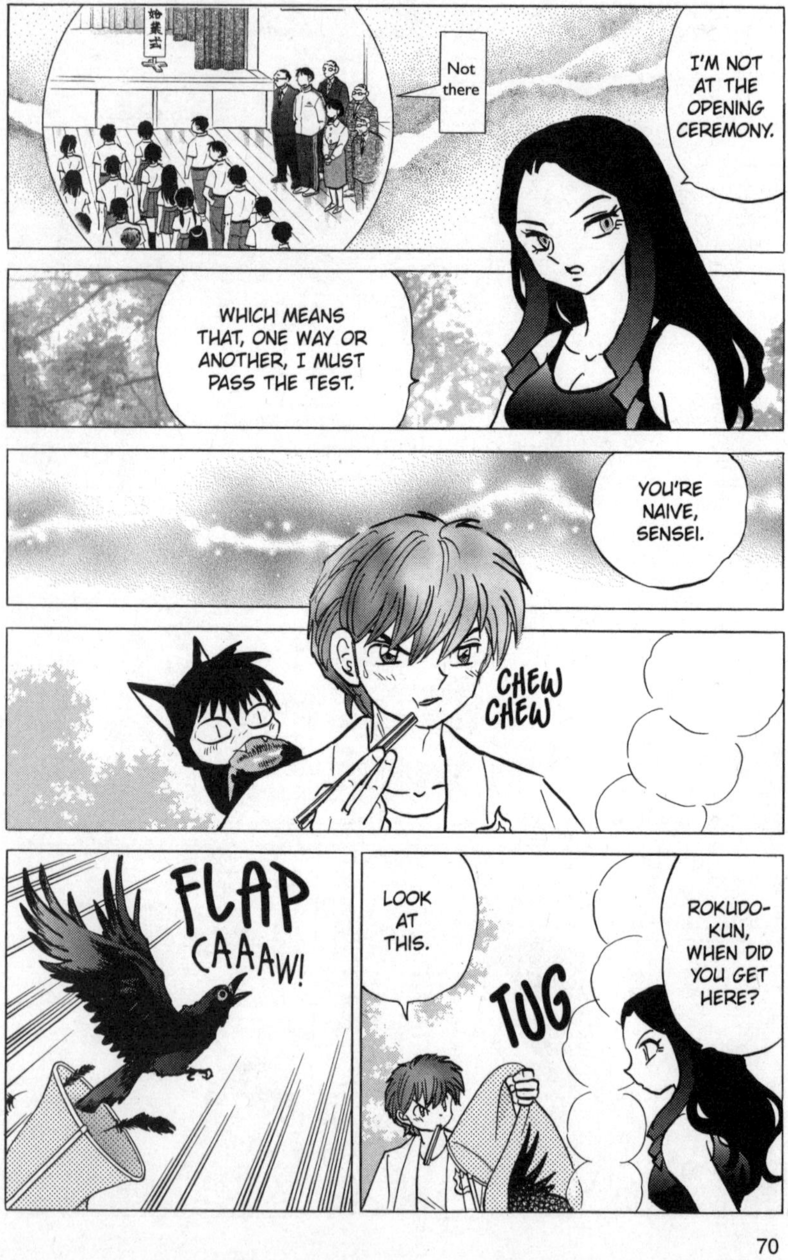
I'M NOT AT THE OPENING CEREMONY.
Not there
始業式
WHICH MEANS THAT, ONE WAY OR ANOTHER, I MUST PASS THE TEST.
YOU'RE NAIVE, SENSEI.
CHEW CHEW
ROKUDO-KUN, WHEN DID YOU GET HERE?
LOOK AT THIS.
TUG
FLAP
CAAAW!

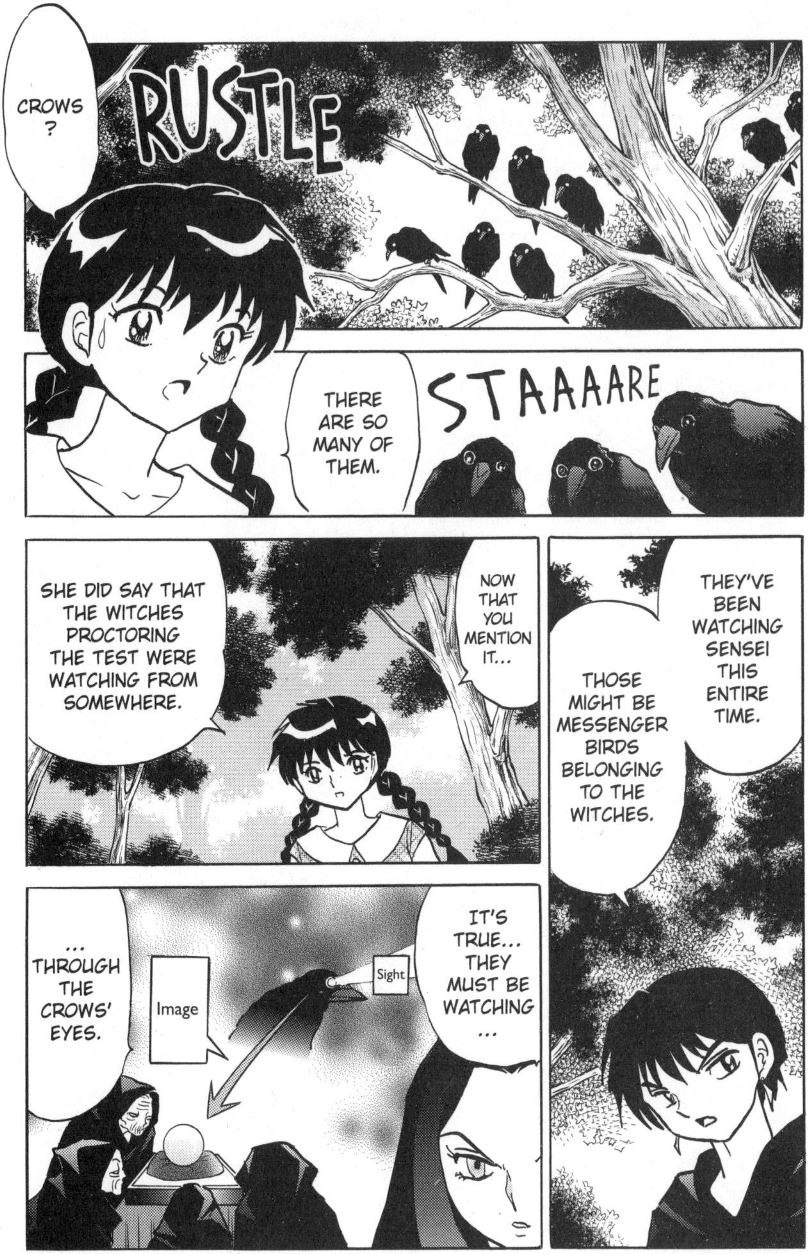
RUSTLE
CROWS ?
STAAAARE
THERE ARE SO MANY OF THEM.
THEY'VE BEEN WATCHING SENSEI THIS ENTIRE TIME.
THOSE MIGHT BE MESSENGER BIRDS BELONGING TO THE WITCHES.
NOW THAT YOU MENTION IT...
SHE DID SAY THAT THE WITCHES PROCTORING THE TEST WERE WATCHING FROM SOMEWHERE.
IT'S TRUE... THEY MUST BE WATCHING ...
Sight
Image
... THROUGH THE CROWS' EYES.

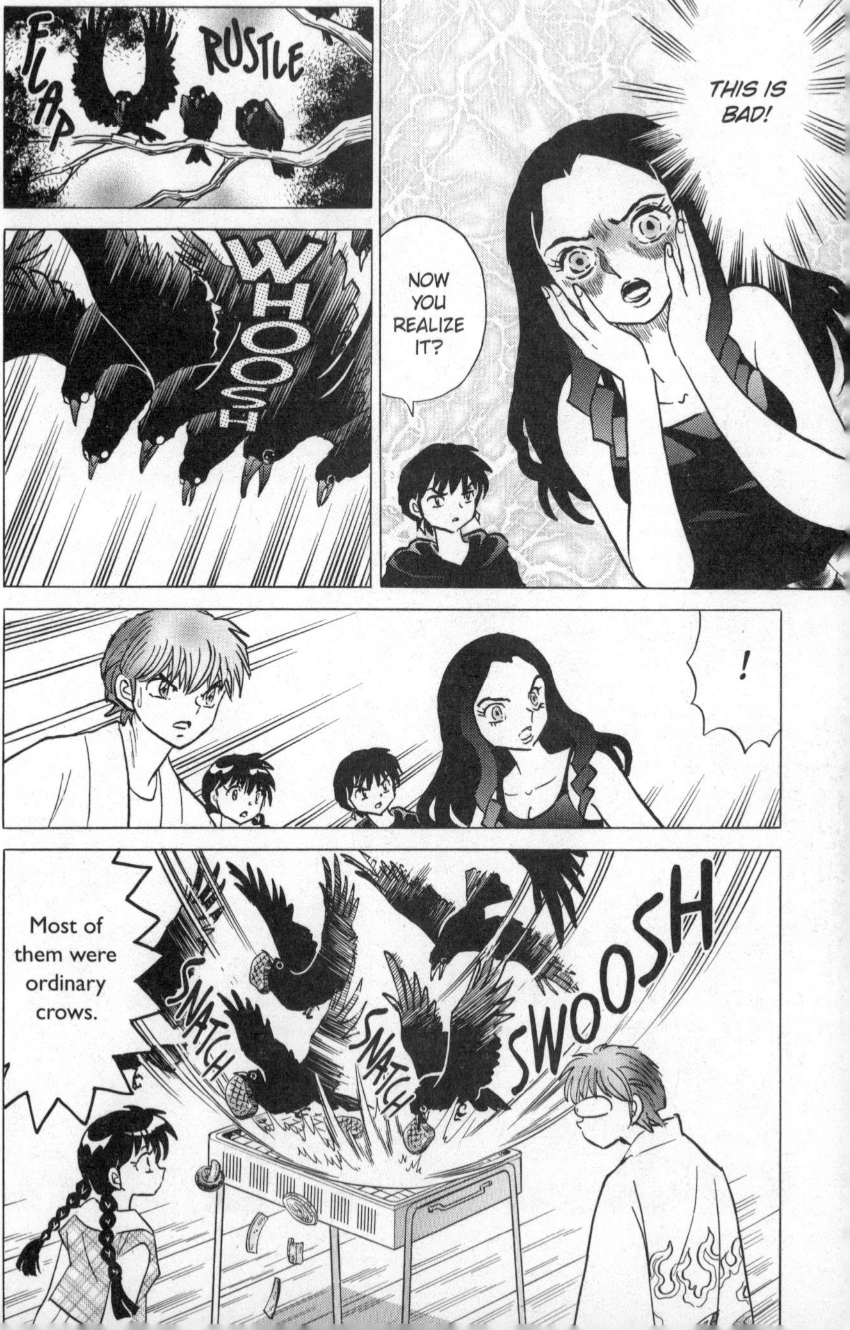
THIS IS BAD!
NOW YOU REALIZE IT?
FLAP
RUSTLE
WHOOSH
!
SWOOSH
Most of them were ordinary crows.
SNATCH
SNATCH

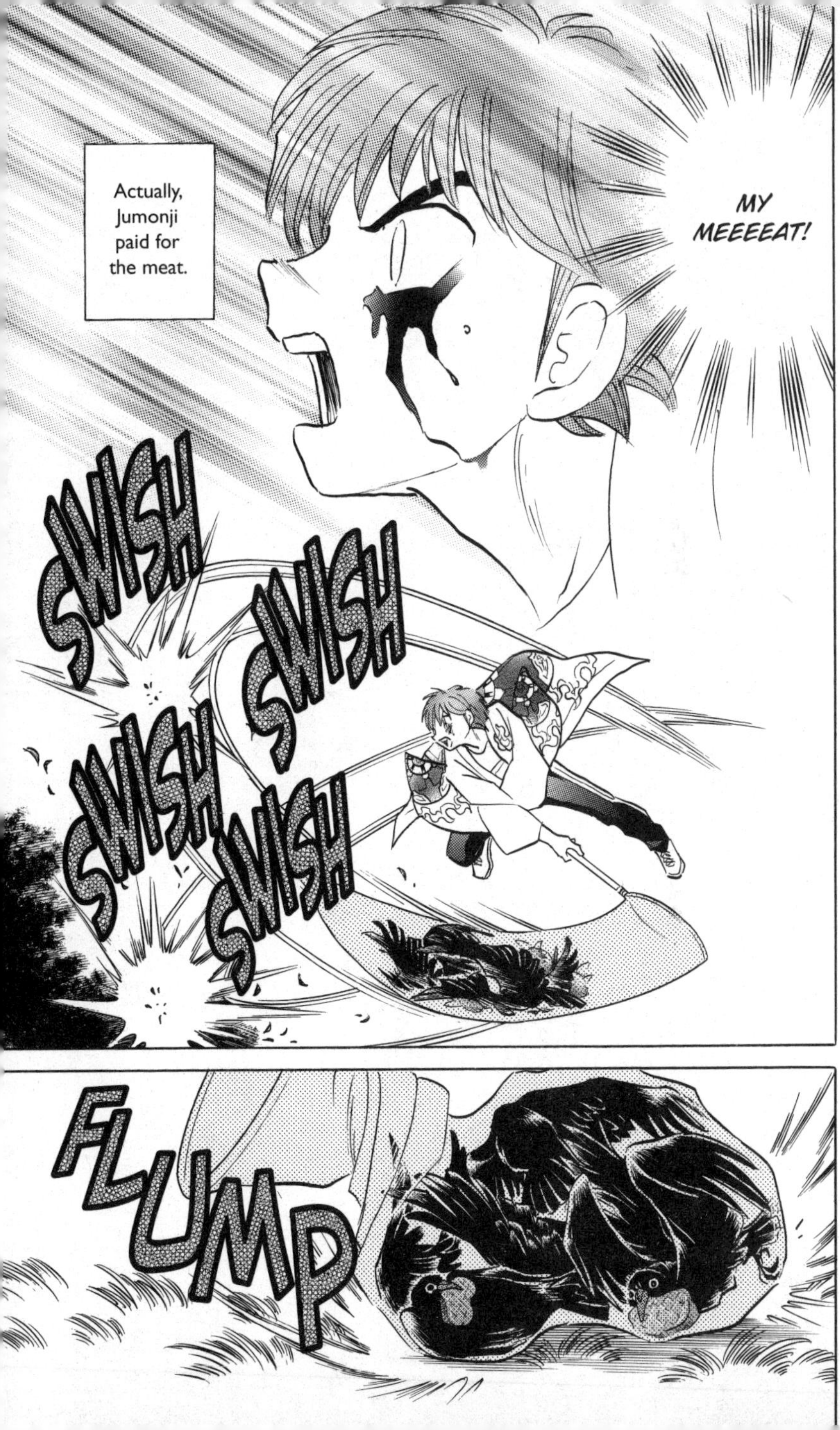
MY MEEEEAT!
Actually, Jumonji paid for the meat.
SWISH
SWISH
SWISH
SWISH
FLUMP

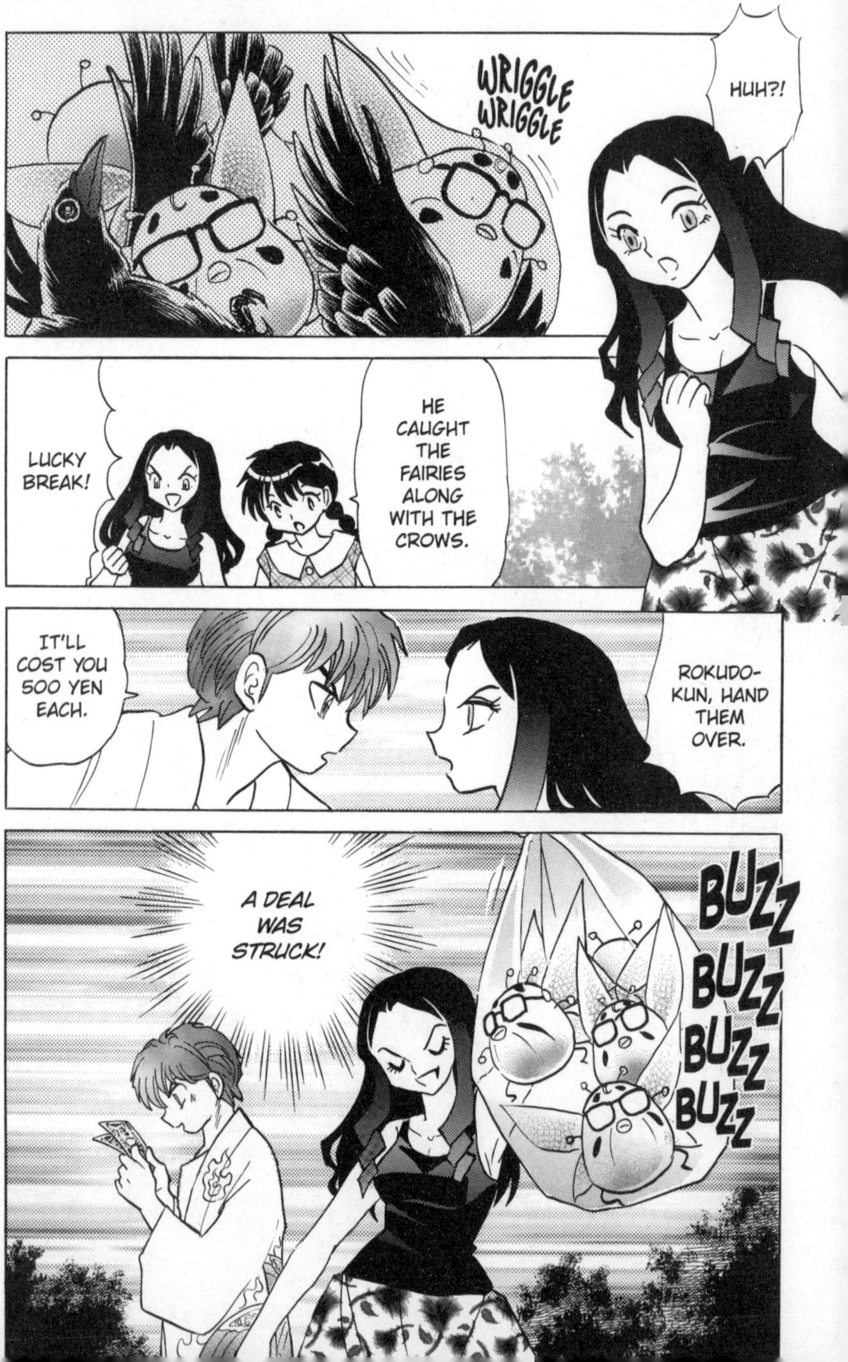
HUH?!
WRIGGLE WRIGGLE
HE CAUGHT THE FAIRIES ALONG WITH THE CROWS.
LUCKY BREAK!
ROKUDO-KUN, HAND THEM OVER.
IT'LL COST YOU 500 YEN EACH.
BUZZ BUZZ BUZZ BUZZ
A DEAL WAS STRUCK!

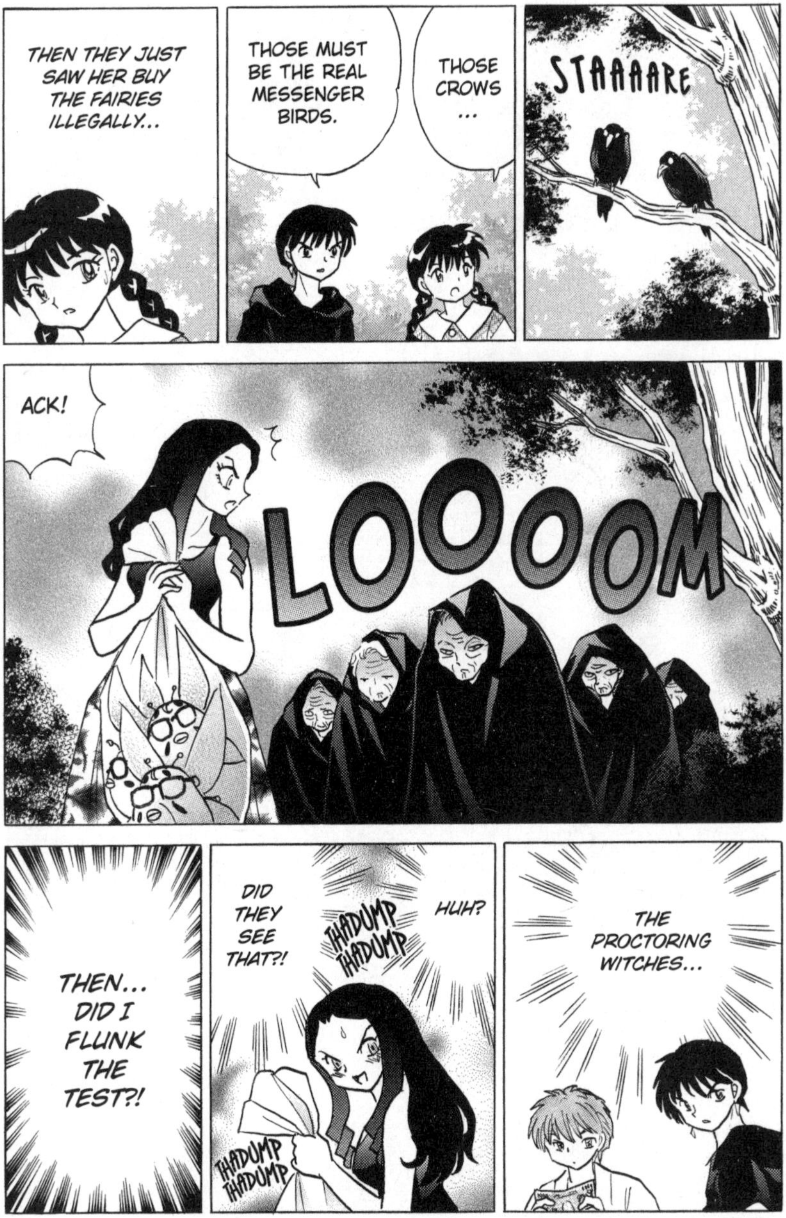
STAAAARE
THOSE CROWS ...
THOSE MUST BE THE REAL MESSENGER BIRDS.
THEN THEY JUST SAW HER BUY THE FAIRIES ILLEGALLY...
ACK!
LOOOOM
THE PROCTORING WITCHES...
HUH?
DID THEY SEE THAT?!
THADUMP THADUMP
THADUMP THADUMP
THEN... DID I FLUNK THE TEST?!

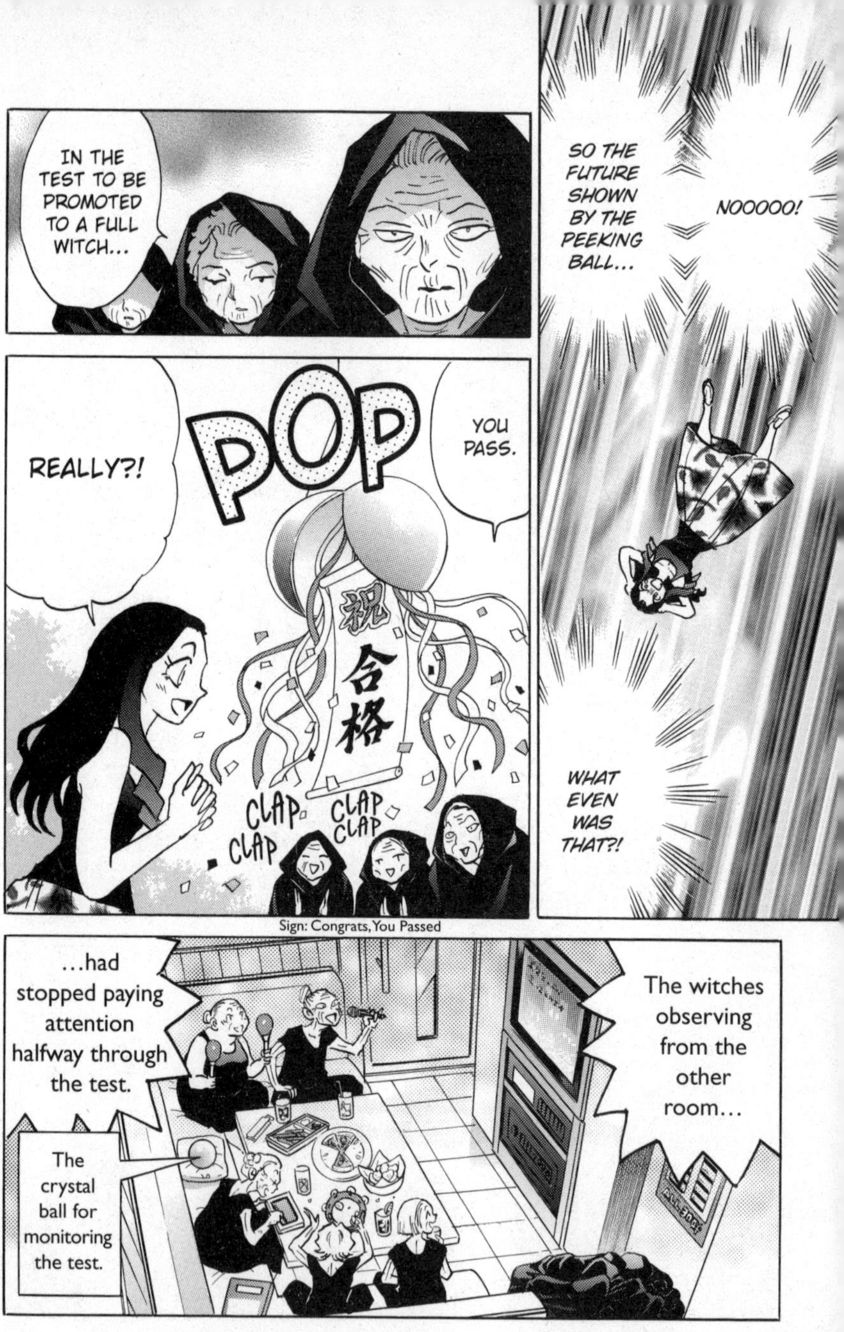
SO THE FUTURE SHOWN BY THE PEEKING BALL...
NOOOOO!
WHAT EVEN WAS THAT?!
IN THE TEST TO BE PROMOTED TO A FULL WITCH...
YOU PASS.
POP
REALLY?!
祝
合格
CLAP CLAP
CLAP CLAP
Sign: Congrats, You Passed
The witches observing from the other room…
…had stopped paying attention halfway through the test.
The crystal ball for monitoring the test.

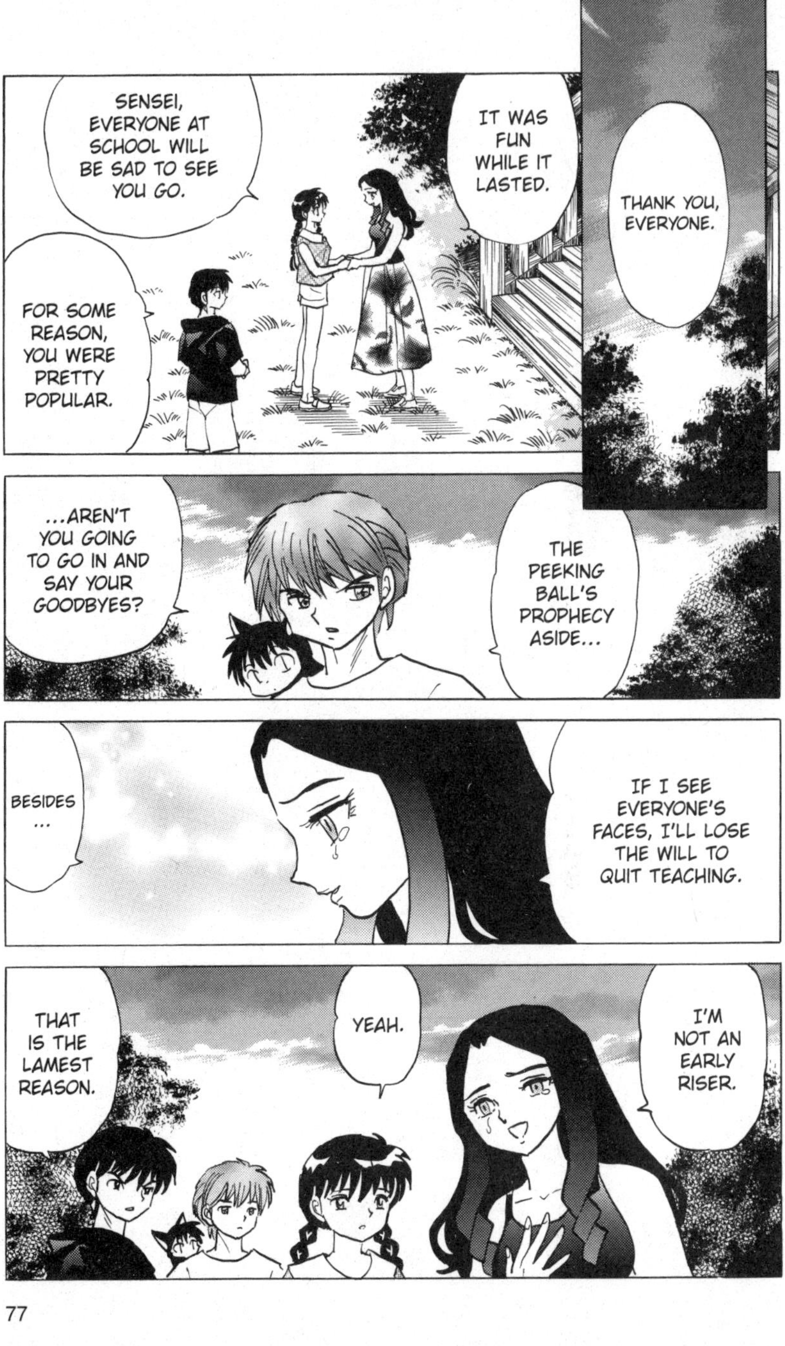
THANK YOU, EVERYONE.
IT WAS FUN WHILE IT LASTED.
SENSEI, EVERYONE AT SCHOOL WILL BE SAD TO SEE YOU GO.
FOR SOME REASON, YOU WERE PRETTY POPULAR.
THE PEEKING BALL'S PROPHECY ASIDE...
...AREN'T YOU GOING TO GO IN AND SAY YOUR GOODBYES?
IF I SEE EVERYONE'S FACES, I'LL LOSE THE WILL TO QUIT TEACHING.
BESIDES ...
I'M NOT AN EARLY RISER.
YEAH.
THAT IS THE LAMEST REASON.

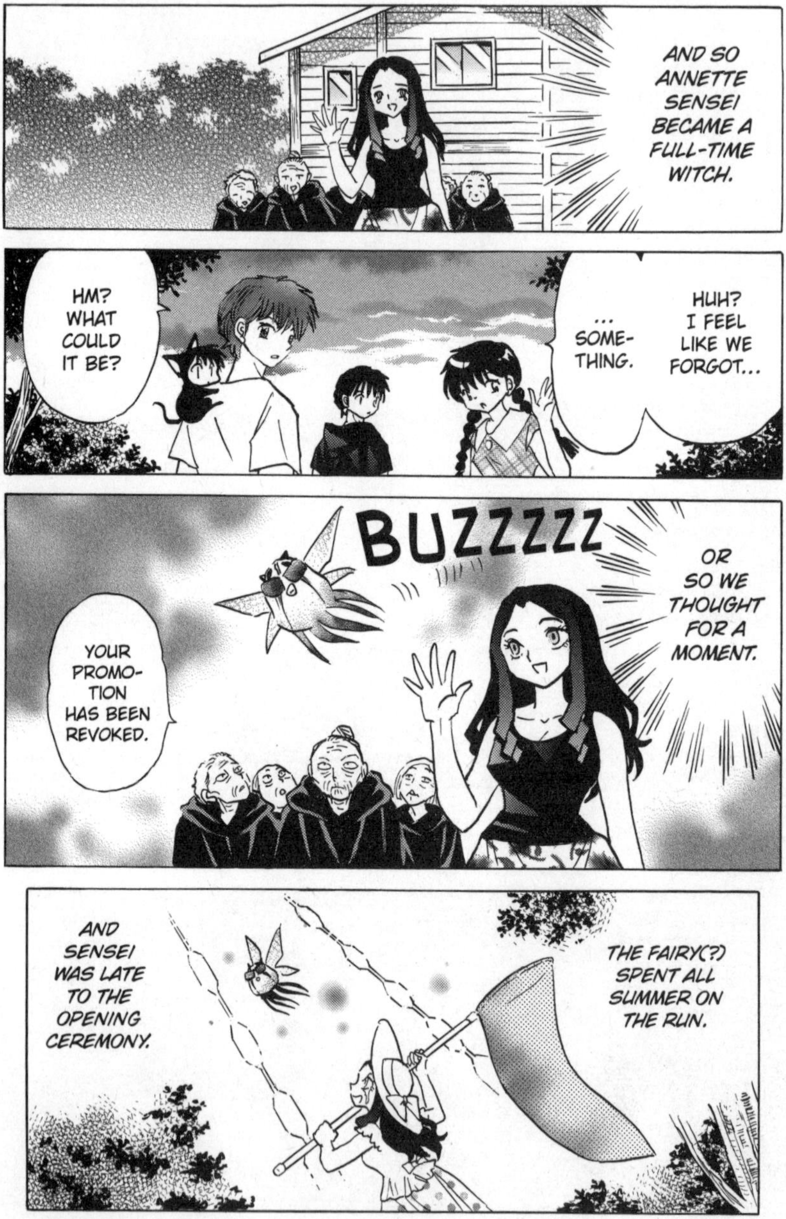
AND SO ANNETTE SENSEI BECAME A FULL-TIME WITCH.
HUH? I FEEL LIKE WE FORGOT...
... SOMETHING.
HM? WHAT COULD IT BE?
OR SO WE THOUGHT FOR A MOMENT.
BUZZZZZ
YOUR PROMOTION HAS BEEN REVOKED.
THE FAIRY(?) SPENT ALL SUMMER ON THE RUN.
AND SENSEI WAS LATE TO THE OPENING CEREMONY.

CHAPTER 383: THE CURSE OF MAMMON

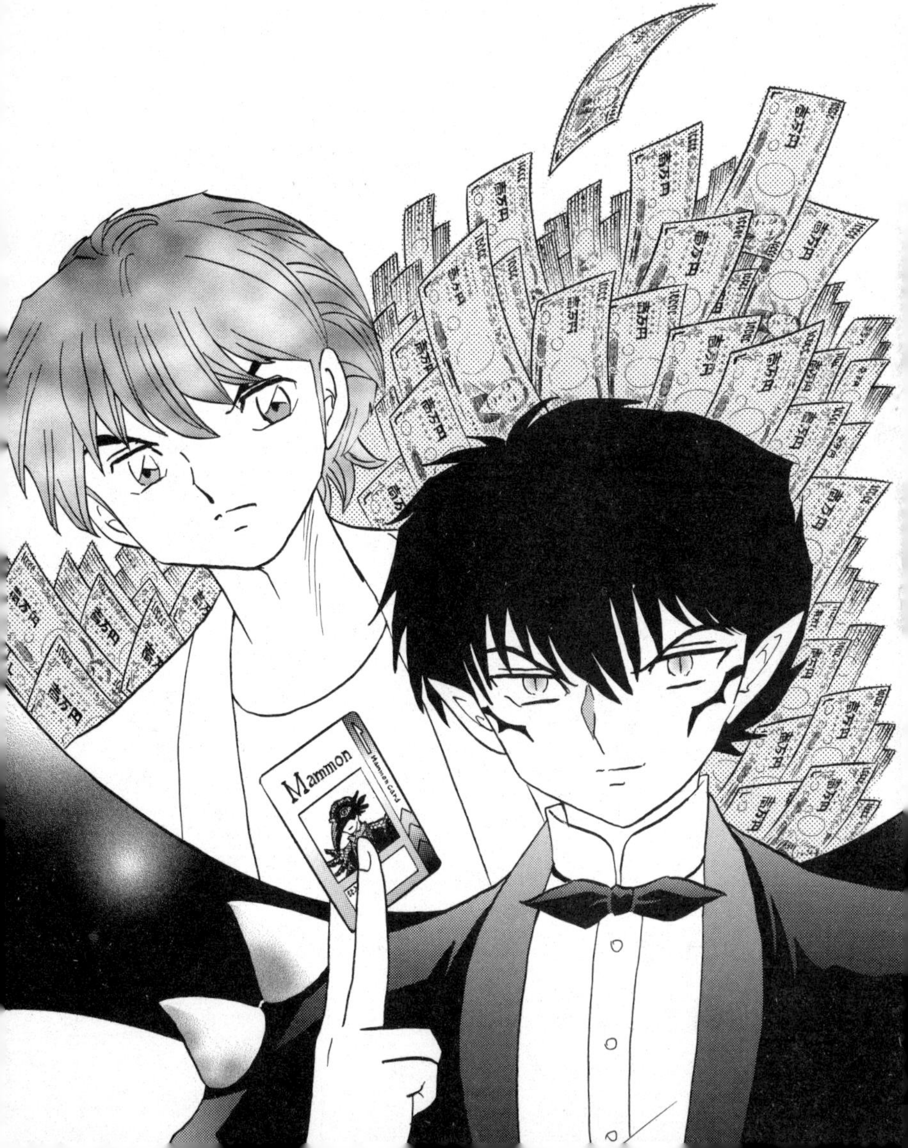
Mammon

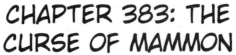

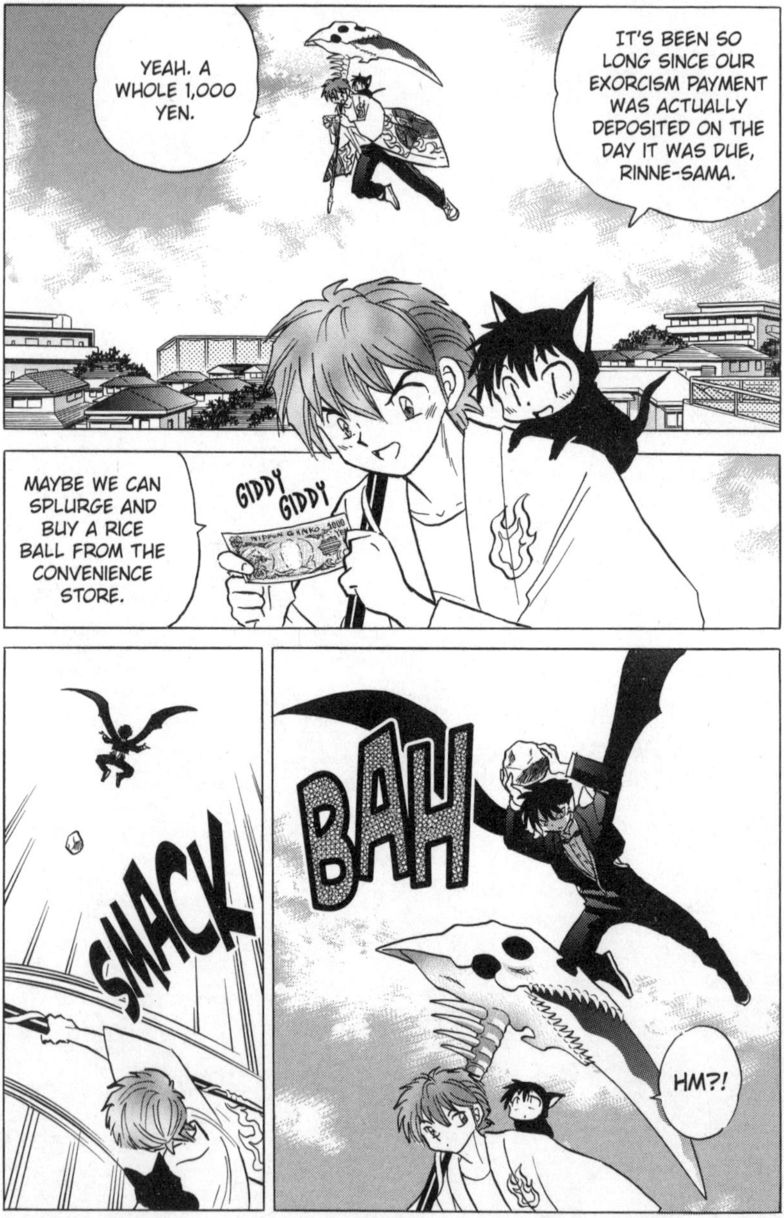
IT'S BEEN SO LONG SINCE OUR EXORCISM PAYMENT WAS ACTUALLY DEPOSITED ON THE DAY IT WAS DUE, RINNE-SAMA.
YEAH. A WHOLE 1,000 YEN.
GIDDY GIDDY
MAYBE WE CAN SPLURGE AND BUY A RICE BALL FROM THE CONVENIENCE STORE.
BAH
HM?!
SMACK

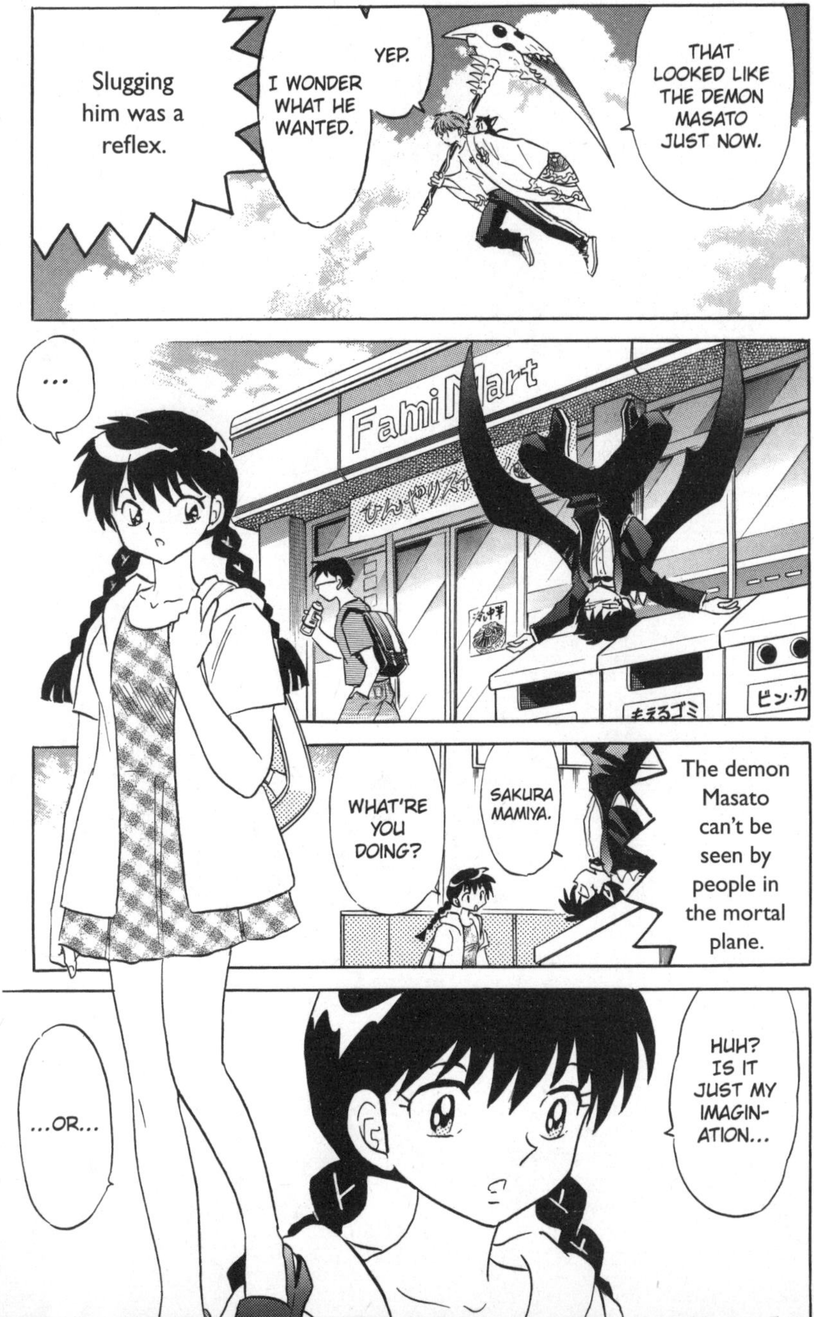
THAT LOOKED LIKE THE DEMON MASATO JUST NOW.
YEP.
I WONDER WHAT HE WANTED.
Slugging him was a reflex.
もえるゴミ
...
The demon Masato can't be seen by people in the mortal plane.
SAKURA MAMIYA.
WHAT'RE YOU DOING?
HUH? IS IT JUST MY IMAGINATION...
...OR...

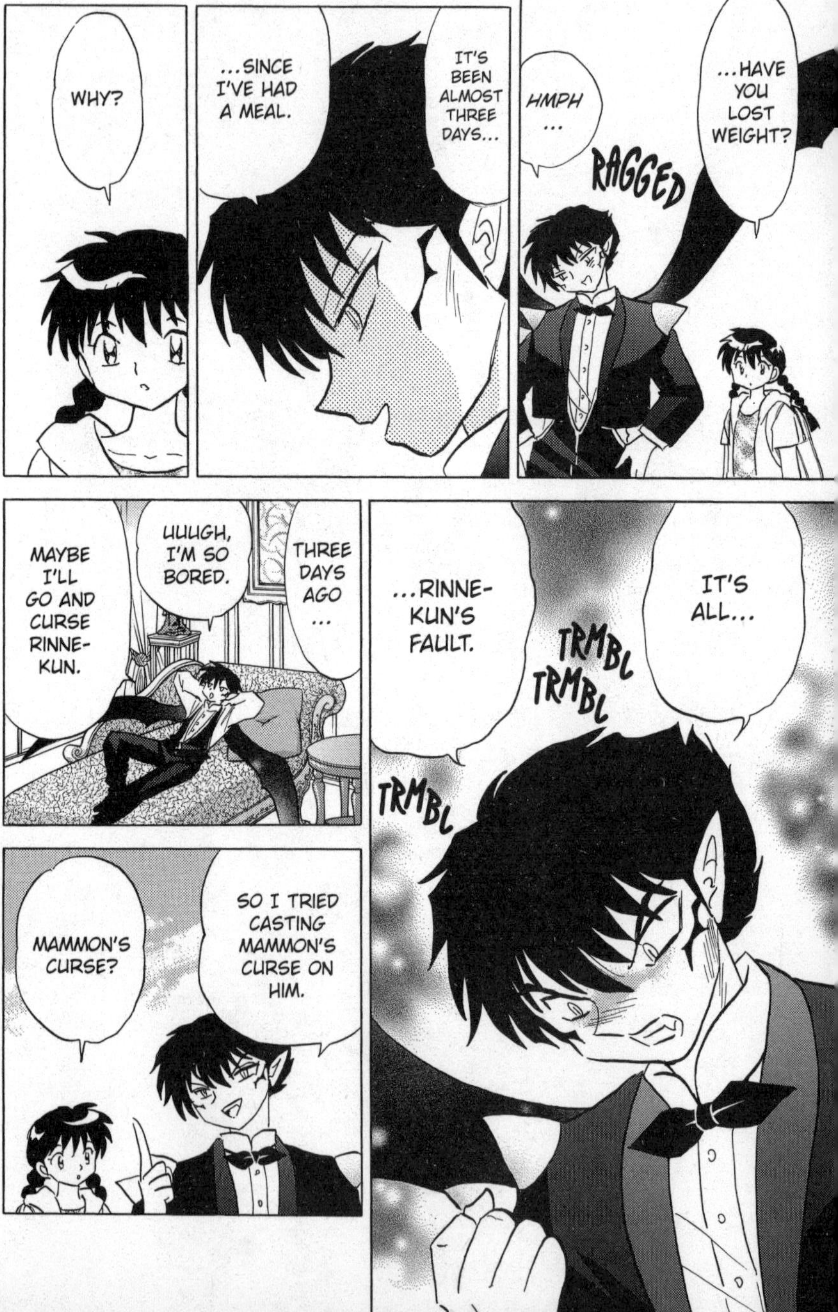
...HAVE YOU LOST WEIGHT?
HMPH ...
RAGGED
IT'S BEEN ALMOST THREE DAYS...
...SINCE I'VE HAD A MEAL.
WHY?
IT'S ALL...
...RINNE-KUN'S FAULT.
TRMBL TRMBL
TRMBL
THREE DAYS AGO ...
UUUGH, I'M SO BORED.
MAYBE I'LL GO AND CURSE RINNE-KUN.
SO I TRIED CASTING MAMMON'S CURSE ON HIM.
MAMMON'S CURSE?

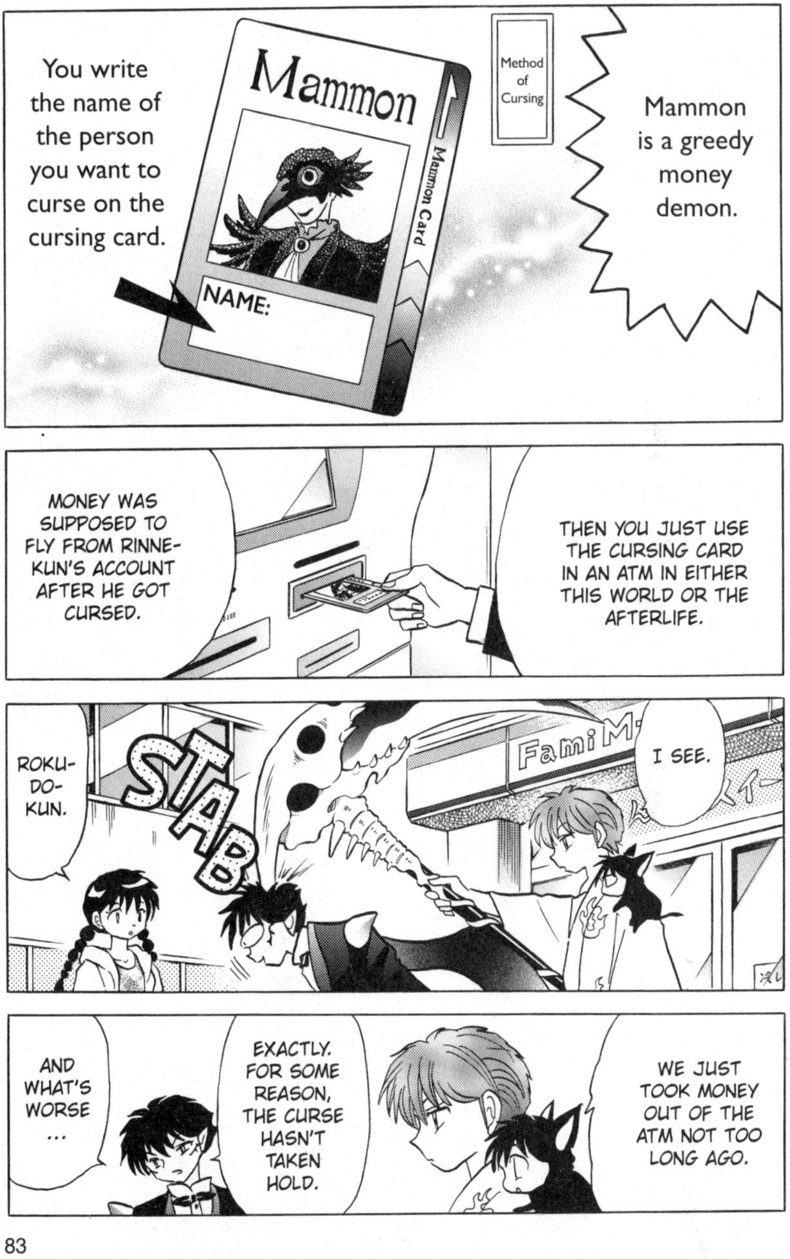
Method of Cursing
Mammon is a greedy money demon.
Mammon
Mammon Card
NAME:
You write the name of the person you want to curse on the cursing card.
THEN YOU JUST USE THE CURSING CARD IN AN ATM IN EITHER THIS WORLD OR THE AFTERLIFE.
MONEY WAS SUPPOSED TO FLY FROM RINNE-KUN'S ACCOUNT AFTER HE GOT CURSED.
I SEE.
FamiM
STAB
ROKU-DO-KUN.
WE JUST TOOK MONEY OUT OF THE ATM NOT TOO LONG AGO.
EXACTLY. FOR SOME REASON, THE CURSE HASN'T TAKEN HOLD.
AND WHAT'S WORSE ...

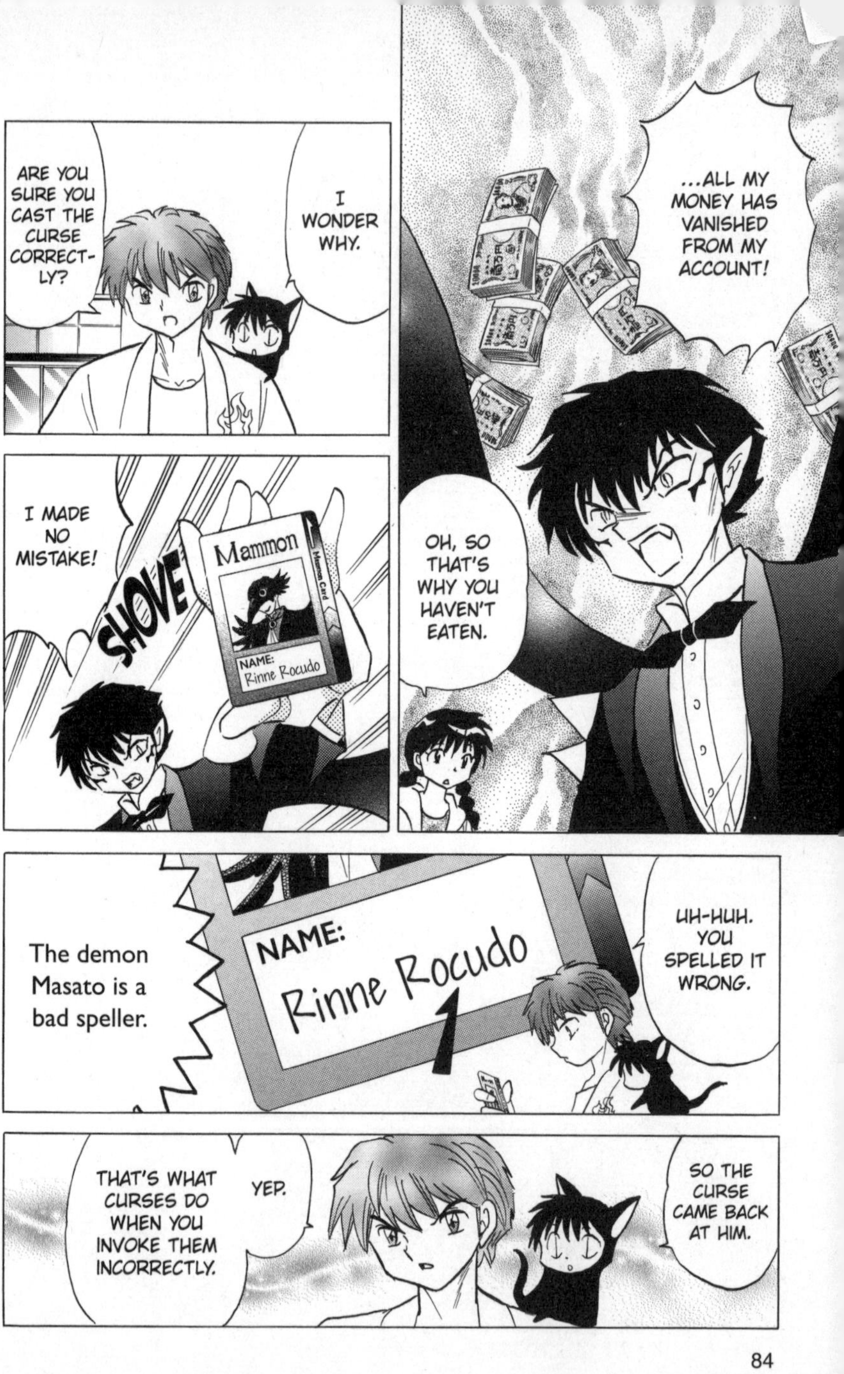
...ALL MY MONEY HAS VANISHED FROM MY ACCOUNT!
OH, SO THAT'S WHY YOU HAVEN'T EATEN.
I WONDER WHY.
ARE YOU SURE YOU CAST THE CURSE CORRECT-LY?
Mammon
Mammon Card
NAME: Rinne Rocudo
SHOVE
I MADE NO MISTAKE!
UH-HUH. YOU SPELLED IT WRONG.
NAME: Rinne Rocudo
The demon Masato is a bad speller.
SO THE CURSE CAME BACK AT HIM.
YEP.
THAT'S WHAT CURSES DO WHEN YOU INVOKE THEM INCORRECTLY.

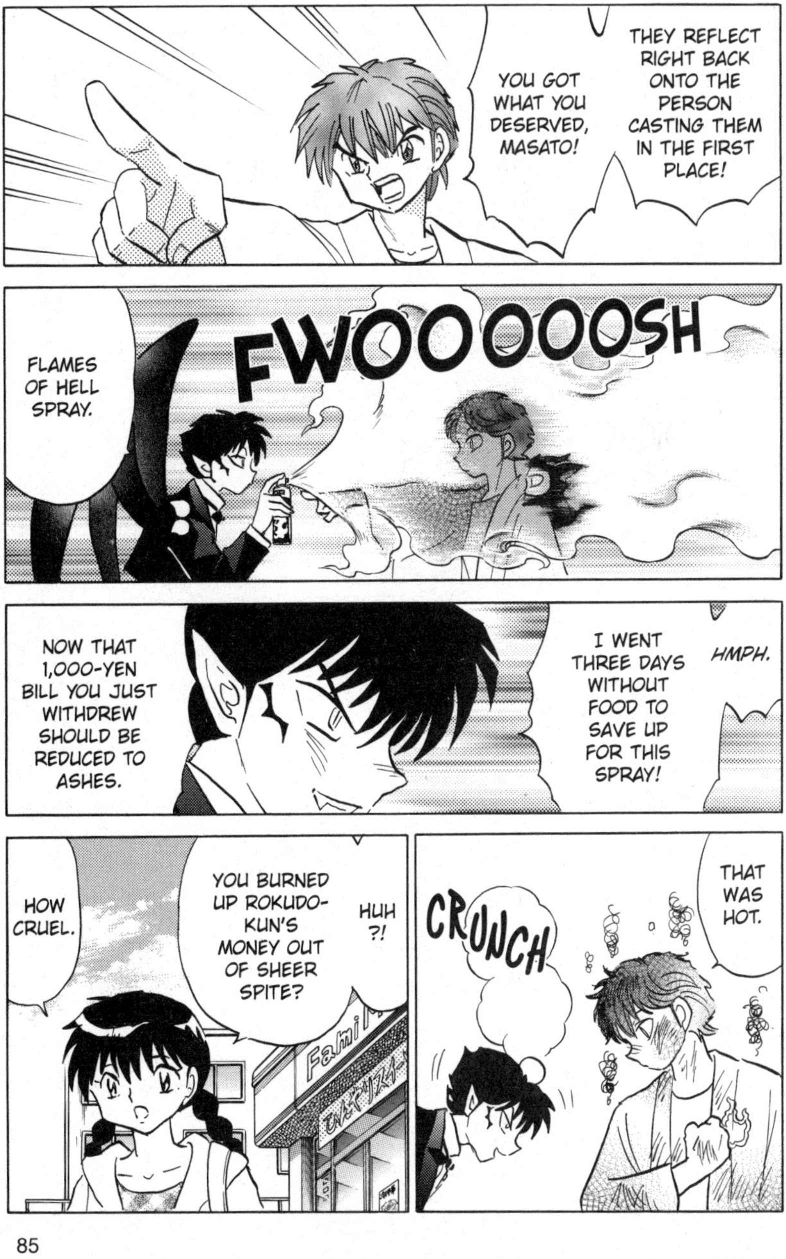
THEY REFLECT RIGHT BACK ONTO THE PERSON CASTING THEM IN THE FIRST PLACE!
YOU GOT WHAT YOU DESERVED, MASATO!
FWOOOOOSH
FLAMES OF HELL SPRAY.
HMPH.
I WENT THREE DAYS WITHOUT FOOD TO SAVE UP FOR THIS SPRAY!
NOW THAT 1,000-YEN BILL YOU JUST WITHDREW SHOULD BE REDUCED TO ASHES.
THAT WAS HOT.
CRUNCH
HUH ?!
YOU BURNED UP ROKUDO-KUN'S MONEY OUT OF SHEER SPITE?
HOW CRUEL.

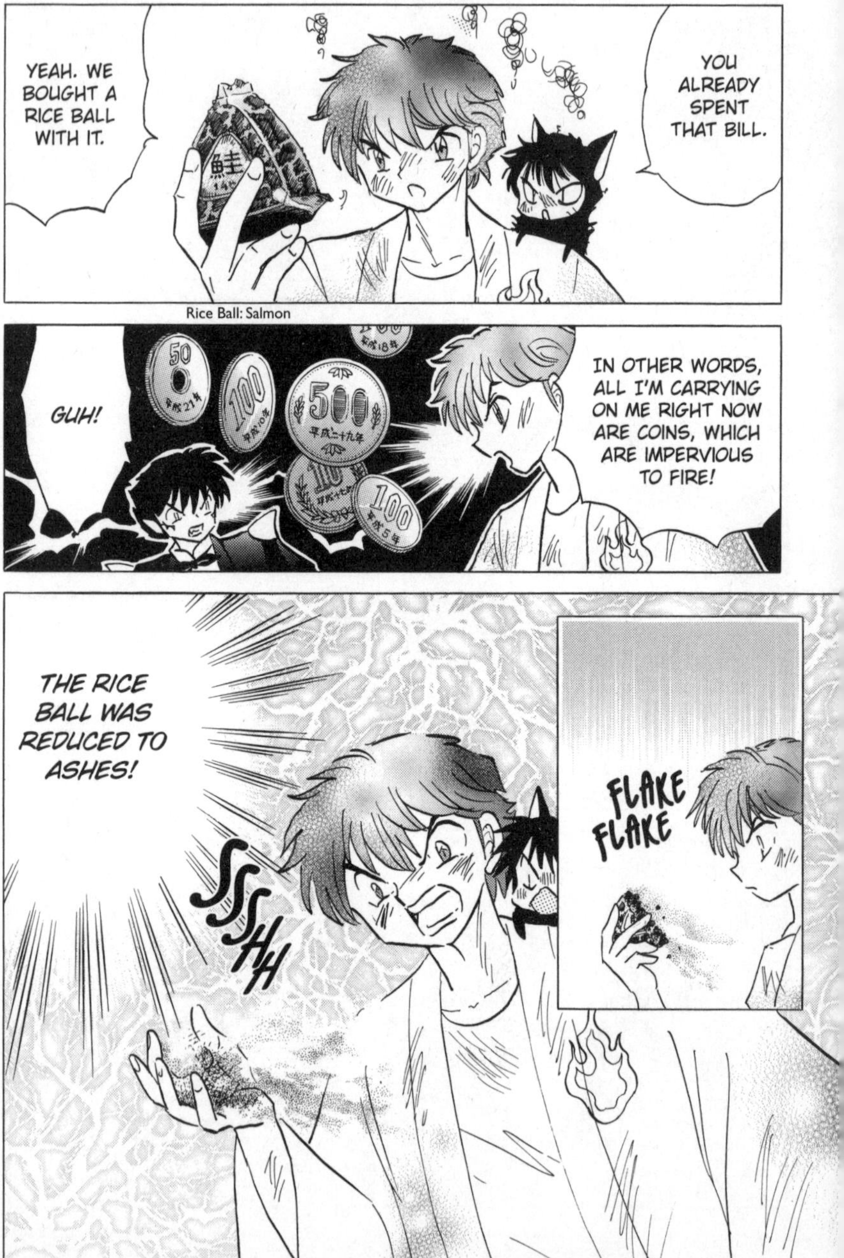
YOU ALREADY SPENT THAT BILL.
YEAH. WE BOUGHT A RICE BALL WITH IT.
Rice Ball: Salmon
IN OTHER WORDS, ALL I'M CARRYING ON ME RIGHT NOW ARE COINS, WHICH ARE IMPERVIOUS TO FIRE!
GUH!
FLAKE FLAKE
THE RICE BALL WAS REDUCED TO ASHES!
SSSHH

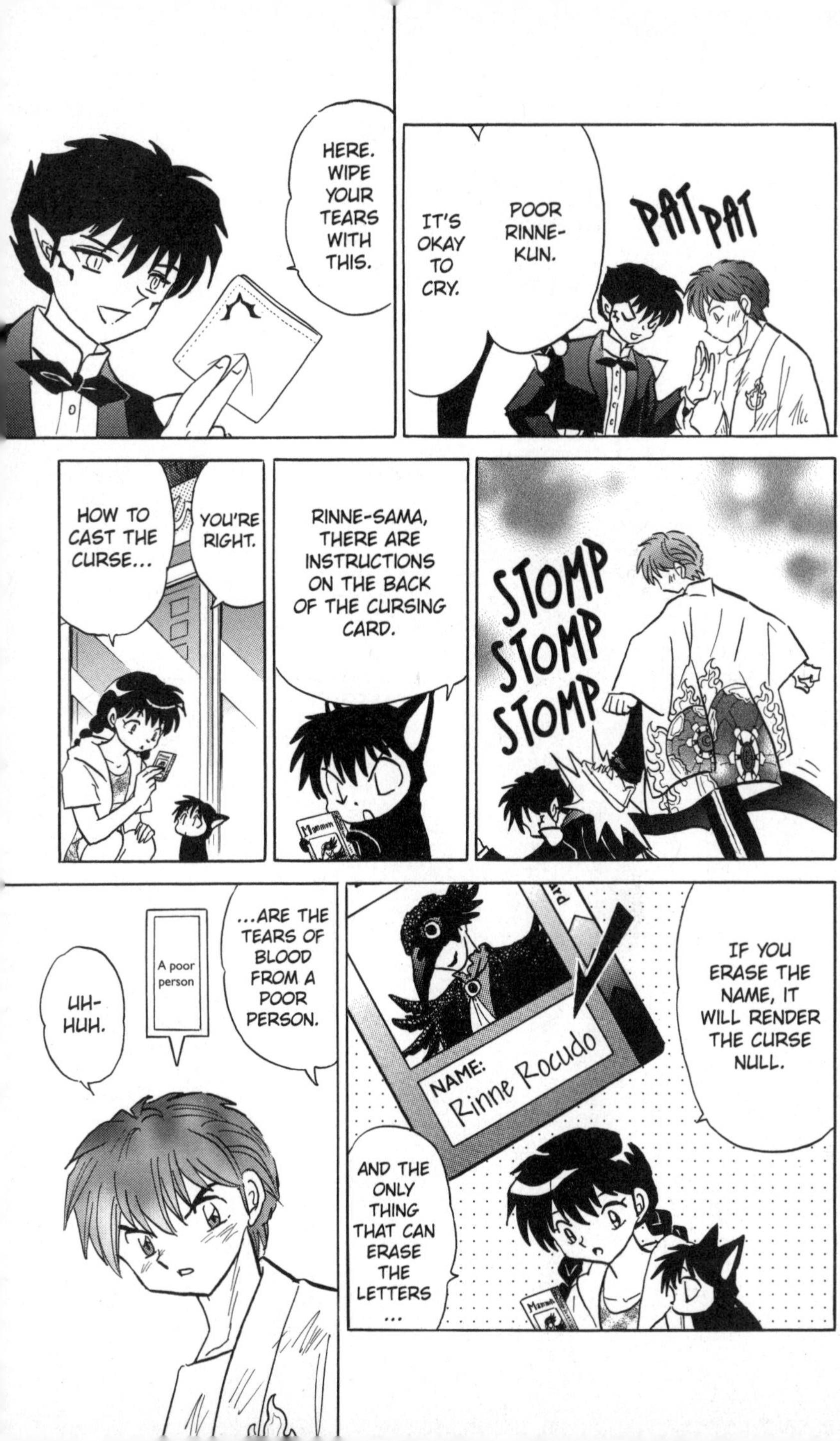
PAT PAT
POOR RINNE-KUN.
IT'S OKAY TO CRY.
HERE. WIPE YOUR TEARS WITH THIS.
STOMP STOMP STOMP
RINNE-SAMA, THERE ARE INSTRUCTIONS ON THE BACK OF THE CURSING CARD.
YOU'RE RIGHT.
HOW TO CAST THE CURSE...
IF YOU ERASE THE NAME, IT WILL RENDER THE CURSE NULL.
NAME: Rinne Rocudo
AND THE ONLY THING THAT CAN ERASE THE LETTERS...
...ARE THE TEARS OF BLOOD FROM A POOR PERSON.
A poor person
UH-HUH.

WHAT'LL HAPPEN IF YOU CAN'T LIFT THE CURSE?
EVERY-BODY KNOWS THAT.
EVEN IF I DEPOSIT MORE MONEY...
...IT'LL JUST VANISH AGAIN.
AN ETERNALLY ZEROED-OUT ACCOUNT.
GAAH!
THAT'S SO CRUEL, EVEN IF IT'S NOT HAPPENING TO ME...
TRMBL TRMBL SHAKE SHAKE
YOU CAN SYMPATHIZE WITH ME SO STRONGLY THAT YOU VOMIT BLOOD...?
SHAKE SHAKE SHAKE
RINNE-KUN!
YOU'RE A GOOD GUY!
JINGLE JANGLE
I'LL BE TAKING THAT!
LUNGE

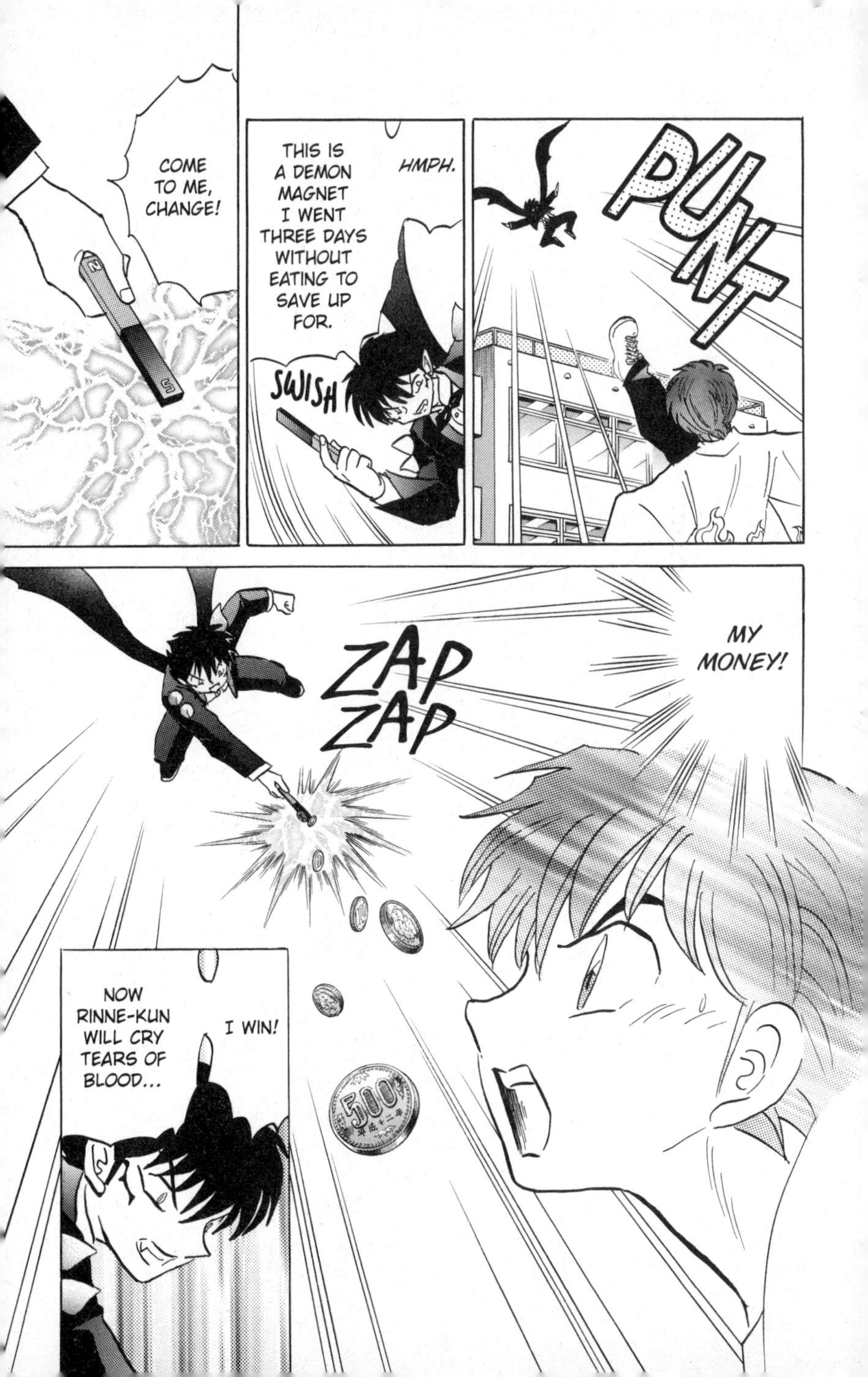
PUNT
HMPH.
THIS IS A DEMON MAGNET I WENT THREE DAYS WITHOUT EATING TO SAVE UP FOR.
SWISH
COME TO ME, CHANGE!
MY MONEY!
ZAP ZAP
I WIN!
NOW RINNE-KUN WILL CRY TEARS OF BLOOD...

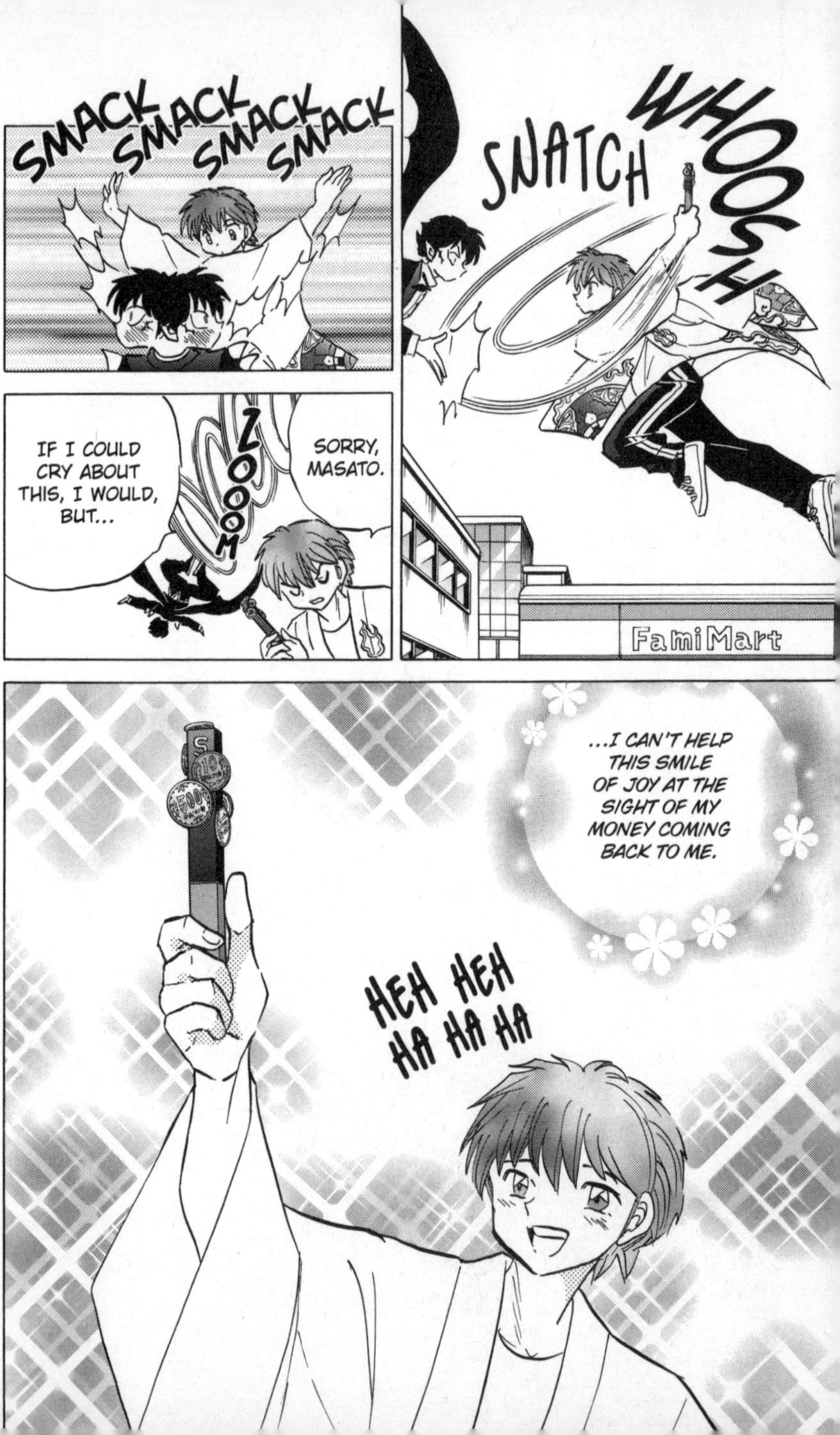
WHOOSH
SNATCH
FamiMart
SMACK SMACK SMACK SMACK
SORRY, MASATO.
ZOOOOM
IF I COULD CRY ABOUT THIS, I WOULD, BUT...
...I CAN'T HELP THIS SMILE OF JOY AT THE SIGHT OF MY MONEY COMING BACK TO ME.
HEH HEH HA HA HA

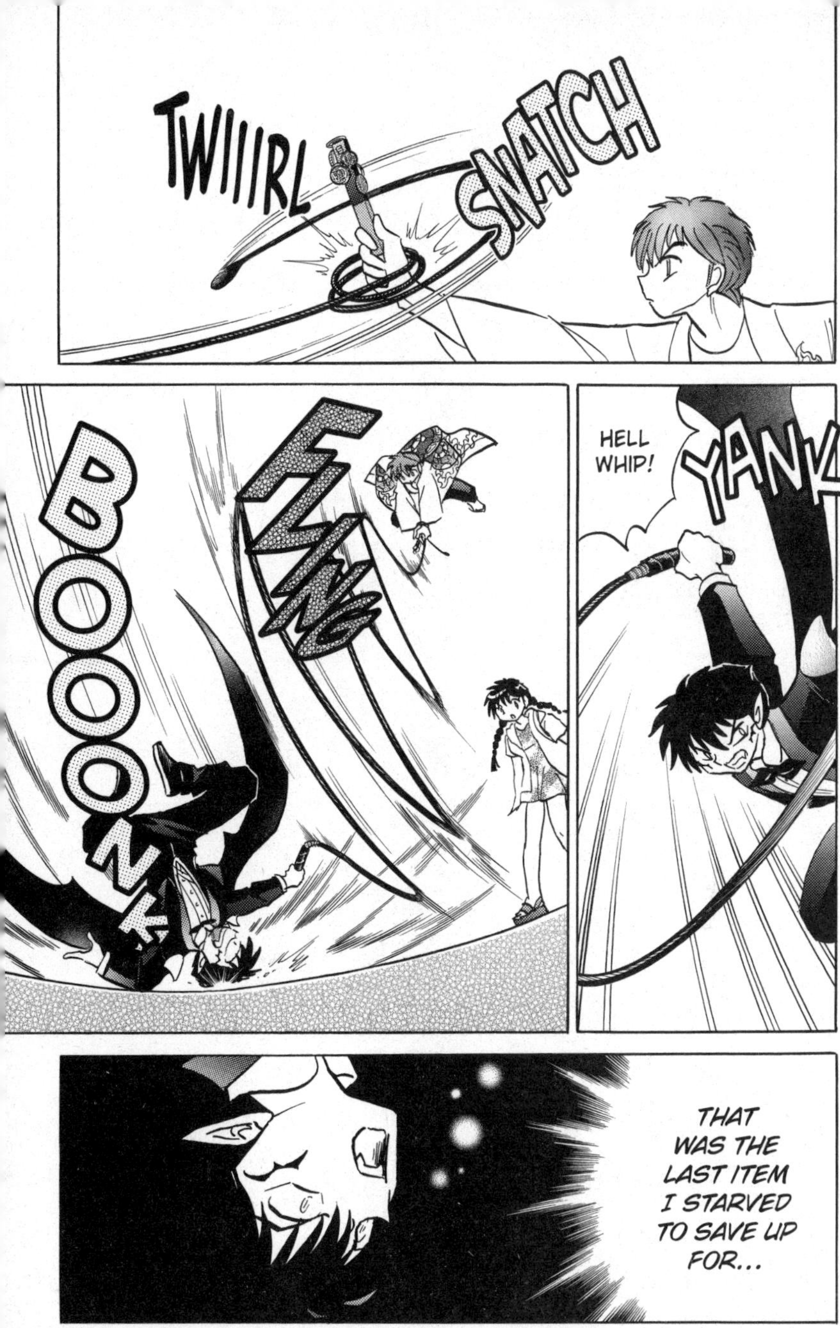
SNATCH
TWIIIRL
YANK
HELL WHIP!
FLING
BOOOOONK
THAT WAS THE LAST ITEM I STARVED TO SAVE UP FOR...

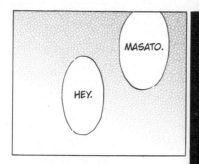

MASATO.

HEY.

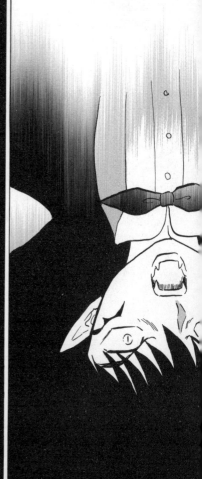

I'M ALL OUT
OF MONEY...

BLINK

HE'S
AWAKE.

YOU
OKAY?

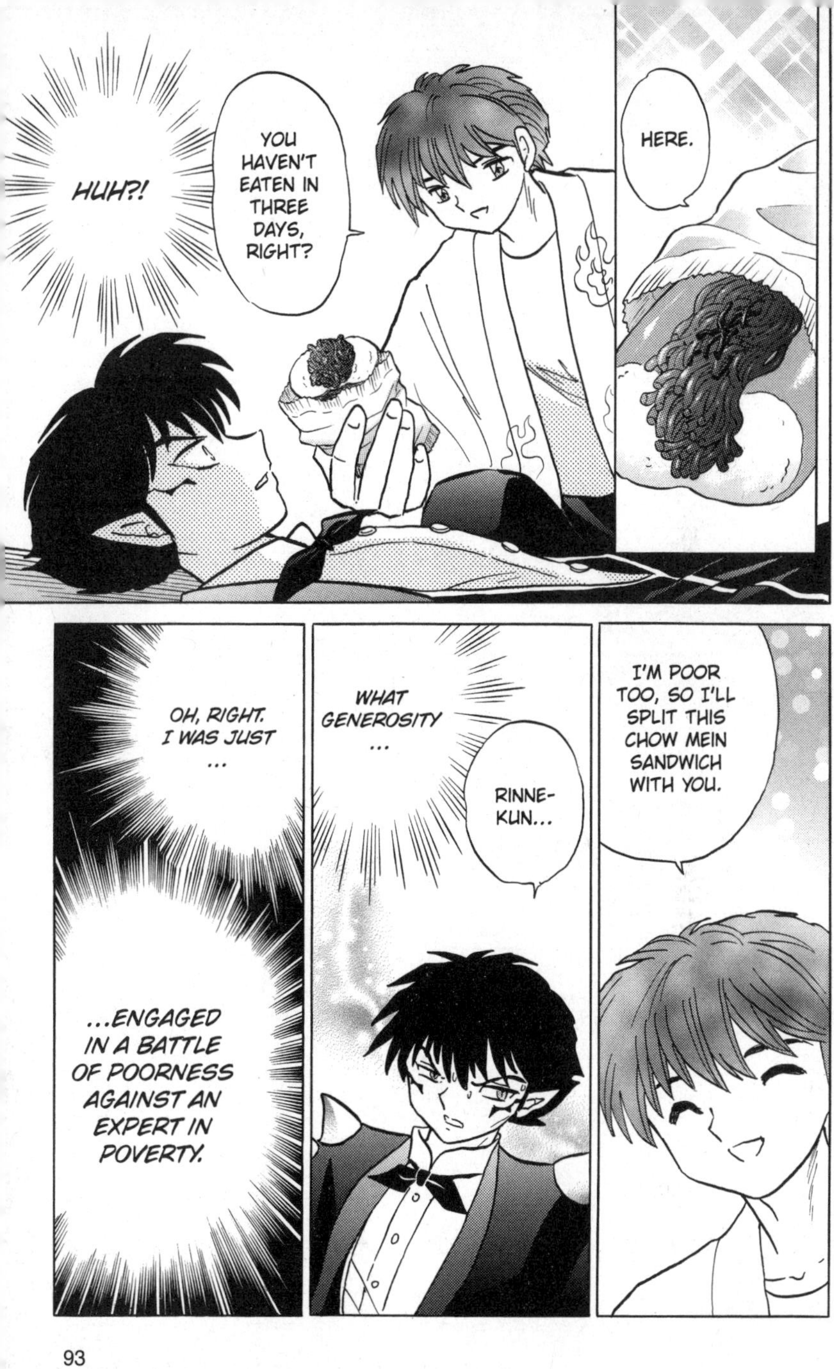
HERE.
YOU HAVEN'T EATEN IN THREE DAYS, RIGHT?
HUH?!
I'M POOR TOO, SO I'LL SPLIT THIS CHOW MEIN SANDWICH WITH YOU.
RINNE-KUN...
WHAT GENEROSITY ...
OH, RIGHT. I WAS JUST ...
...ENGAGED IN A BATTLE OF POORNESS AGAINST AN EXPERT IN POVERTY.

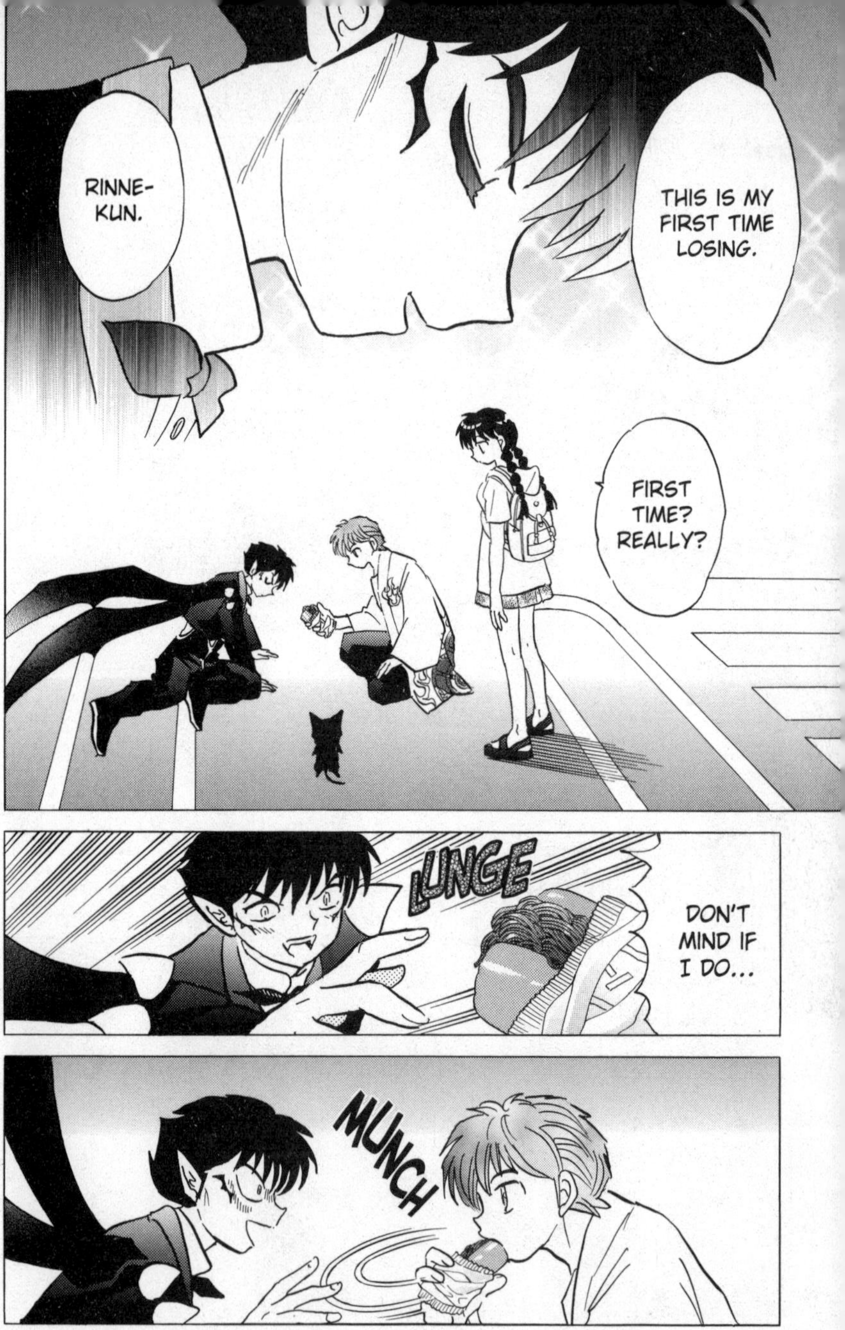
THIS IS MY FIRST TIME LOSING.
RINNE-KUN.
FIRST TIME? REALLY?
DON'T MIND IF I DO...
LUNGE
MUNCH

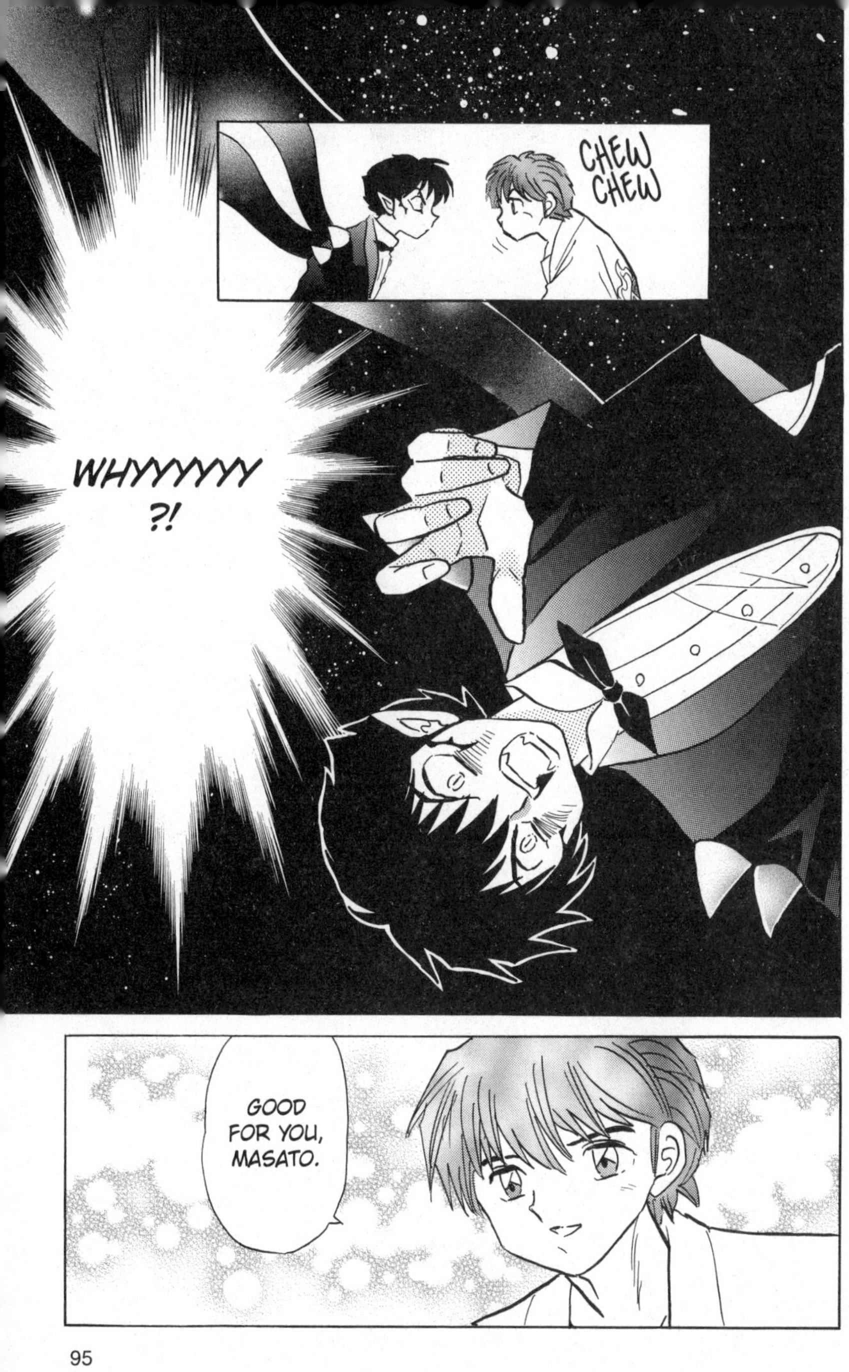
CHEW CHEW
WHYYYYYY ?!
GOOD FOR YOU, MASATO.

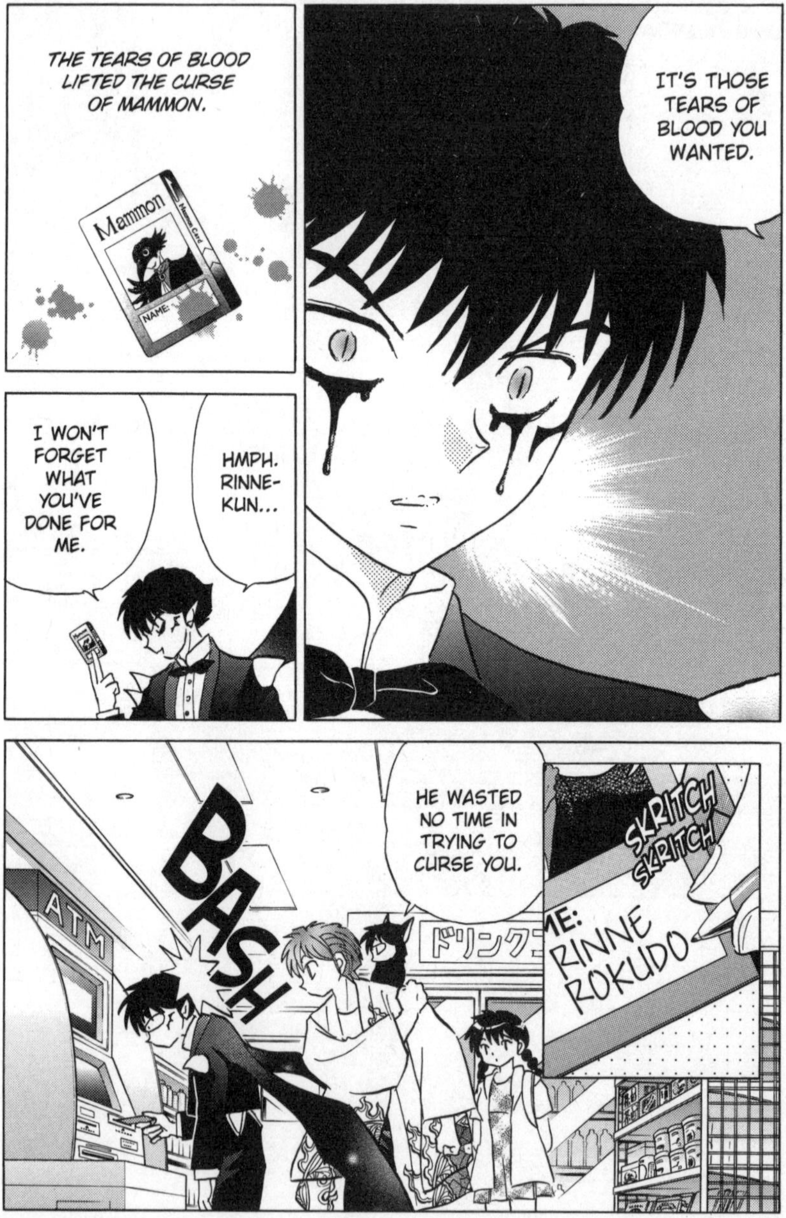
IT'S THOSE TEARS OF BLOOD YOU WANTED.
THE TEARS OF BLOOD LIFTED THE CURSE OF MAMMON.
Mammon
NAME:
HMPH. RINNE-KUN...
I WON'T FORGET WHAT YOU'VE DONE FOR ME.
SKRITCH SKRITCH
ME: RINNE ROKUDO
HE WASTED NO TIME IN TRYING TO CURSE YOU.
BASH
ATM
ドリンクコ

CHAPTER 384: BEAUTIFUL HOME

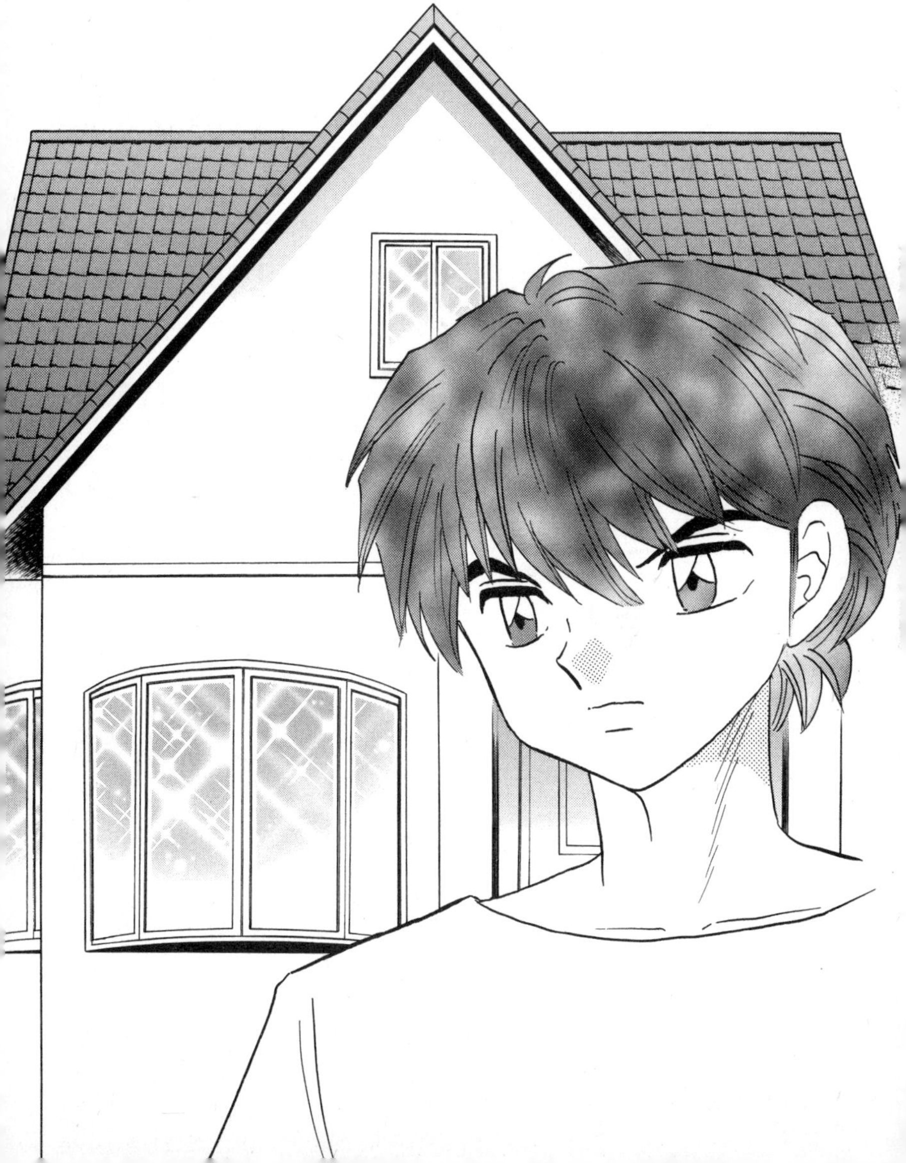

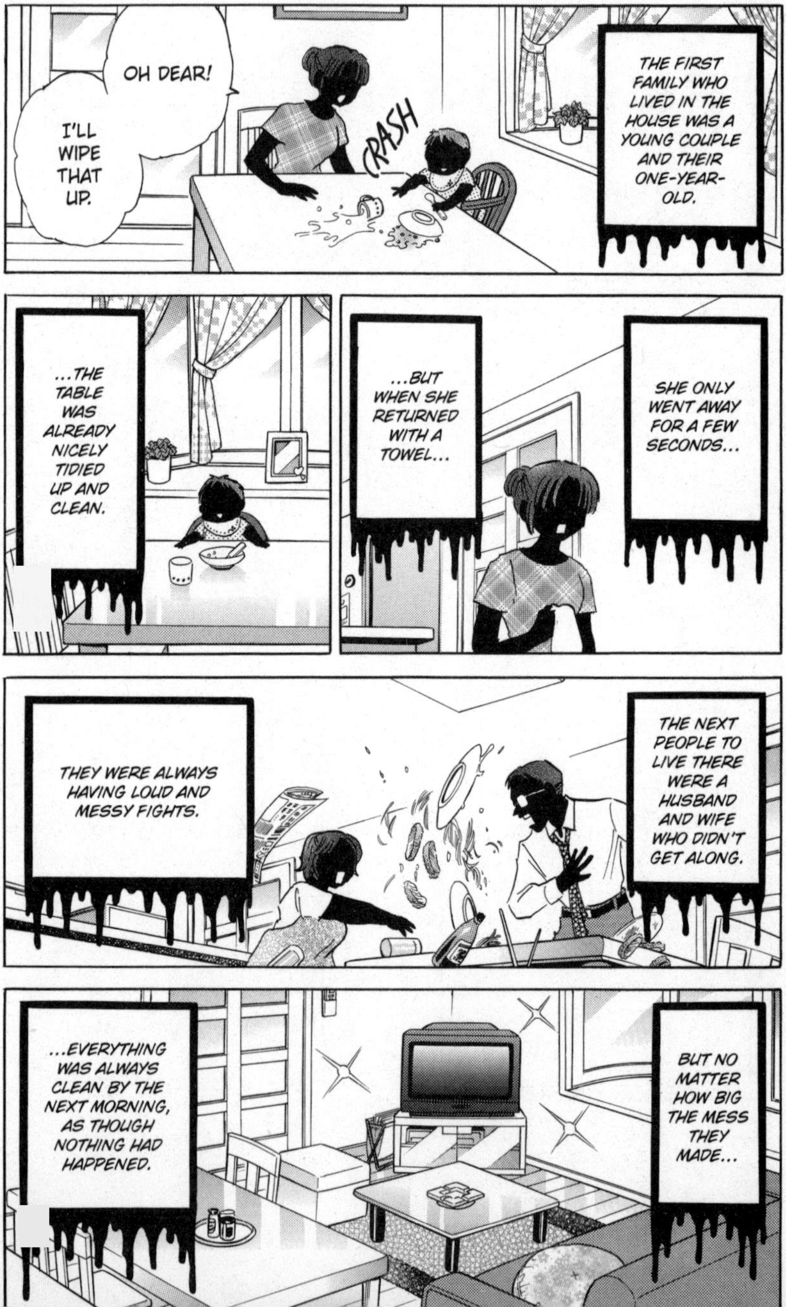
THE FIRST FAMILY WHO LIVED IN THE HOUSE WAS A YOUNG COUPLE AND THEIR ONE-YEAR-OLD.
CRASH
OH DEAR!
I'LL WIPE THAT UP.
SHE ONLY WENT AWAY FOR A FEW SECONDS...
...BUT WHEN SHE RETURNED WITH A TOWEL...
...THE TABLE WAS ALREADY NICELY TIDIED UP AND CLEAN.
THE NEXT PEOPLE TO LIVE THERE WERE A HUSBAND AND WIFE WHO DIDN'T GET ALONG.
CRASH
THEY WERE ALWAYS HAVING LOUD AND MESSY FIGHTS.
BUT NO MATTER HOW BIG THE MESS THEY MADE...
...EVERYTHING WAS ALWAYS CLEAN BY THE NEXT MORNING, AS THOUGH NOTHING HAD HAPPENED.

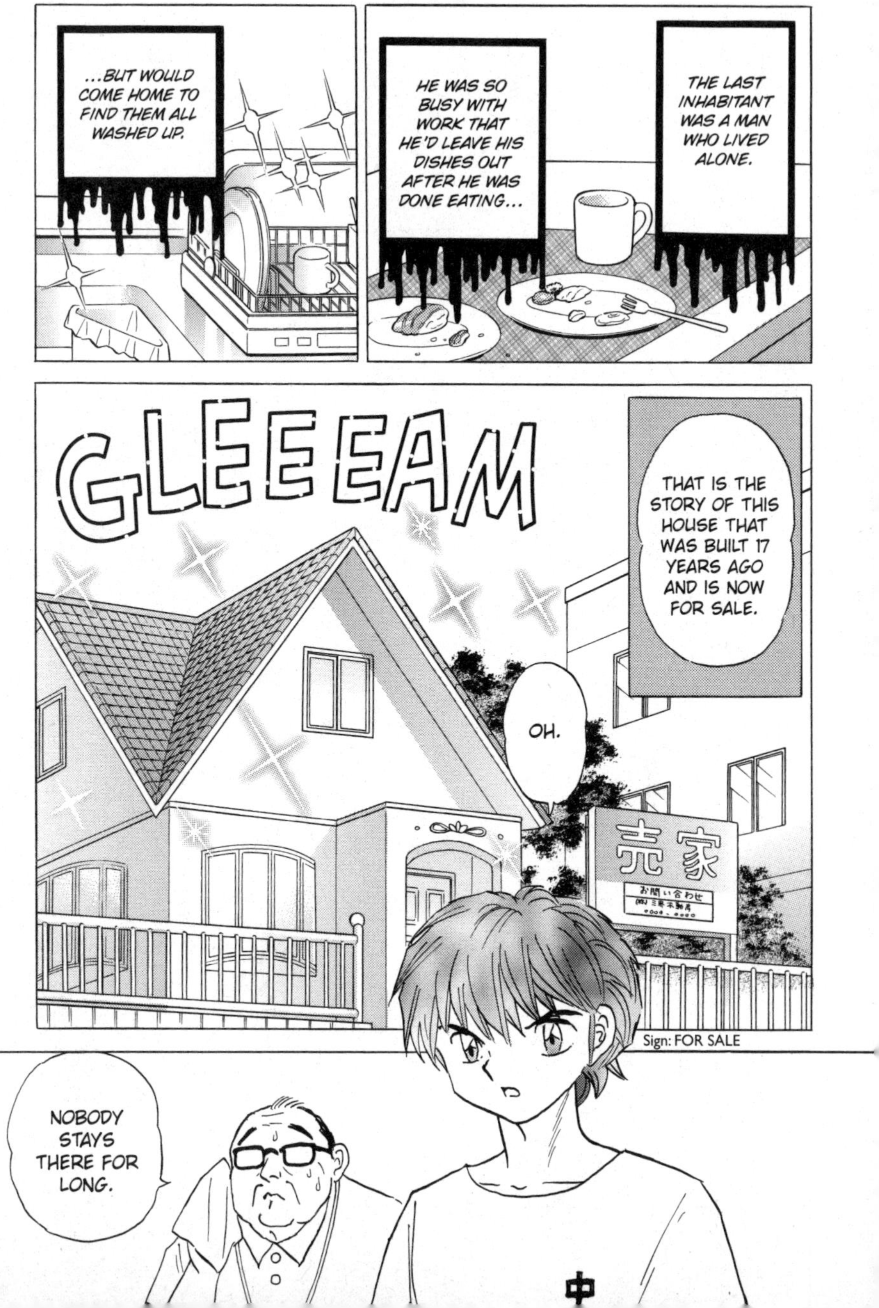
THE LAST INHABITANT WAS A MAN WHO LIVED ALONE.
HE WAS SO BUSY WITH WORK THAT HE'D LEAVE HIS DISHES OUT AFTER HE WAS DONE EATING...
...BUT WOULD COME HOME TO FIND THEM ALL WASHED UP.
THAT IS THE STORY OF THIS HOUSE THAT WAS BUILT 17 YEARS AGO AND IS NOW FOR SALE.
GLEEEAM
OH.
売家
Sign: FOR SALE
NOBODY STAYS THERE FOR LONG.

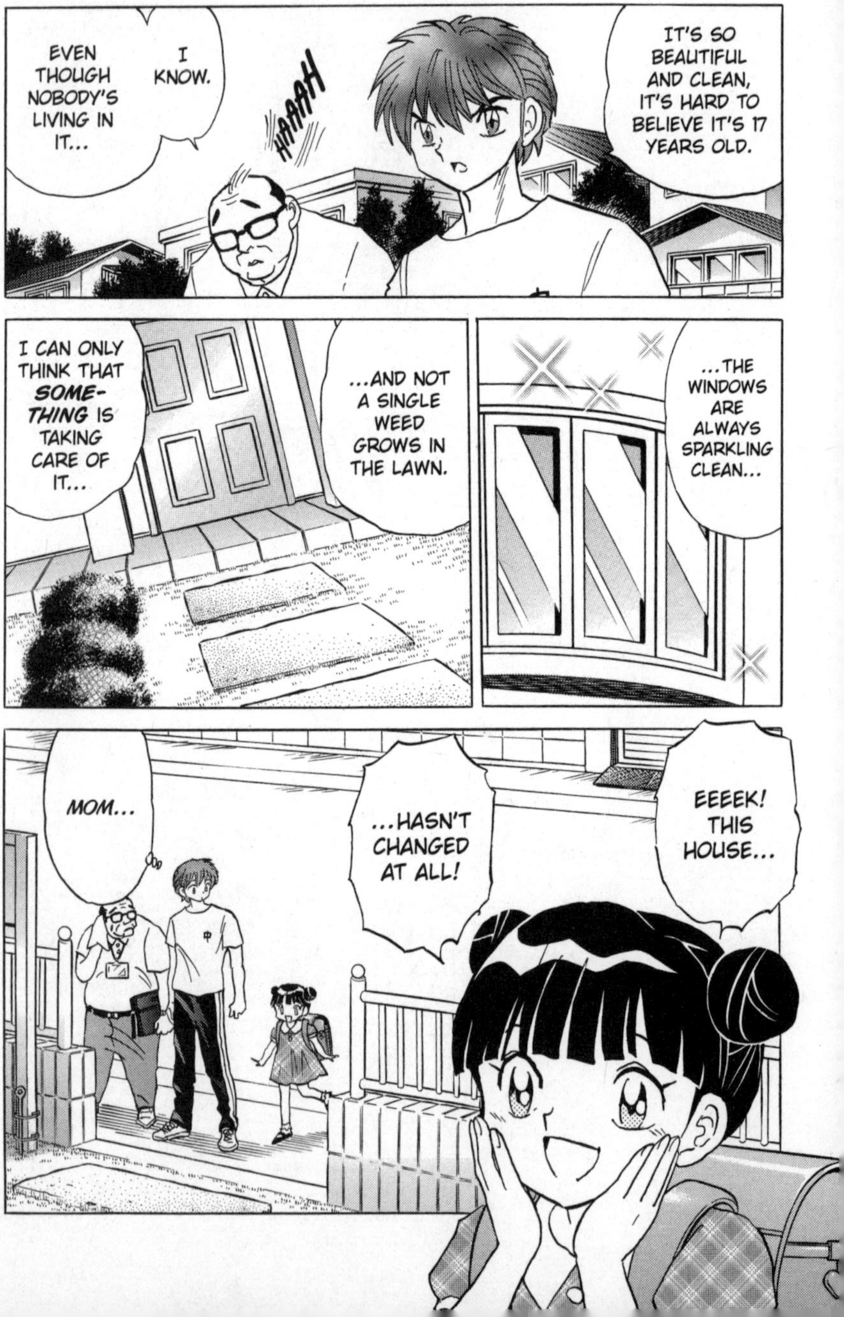
IT'S SO BEAUTIFUL AND CLEAN, IT'S HARD TO BELIEVE IT'S 17 YEARS OLD.
HAAAH
I KNOW.
EVEN THOUGH NOBODY'S LIVING IN IT...
...THE WINDOWS ARE ALWAYS SPARKLING CLEAN...
...AND NOT A SINGLE WEED GROWS IN THE LAWN.
I CAN ONLY THINK THAT *SOMETHING* IS TAKING CARE OF IT...
EEEEK! THIS HOUSE...
...HASN'T CHANGED AT ALL!
MOM...

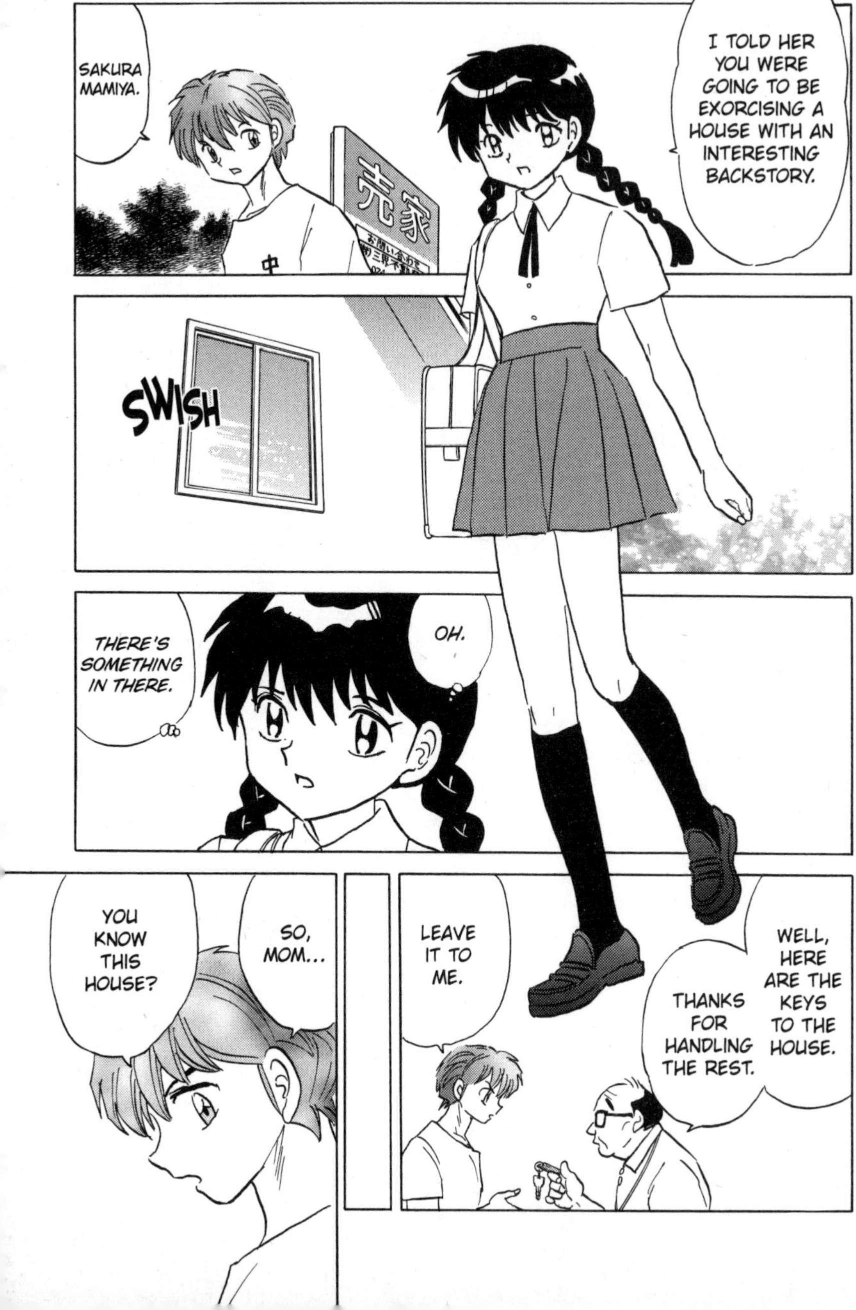
I TOLD HER YOU WERE GOING TO BE EXORCISING A HOUSE WITH AN INTERESTING BACKSTORY.
SAKURA MAMIYA.
売家
SWISH
OH.
THERE'S SOMETHING IN THERE.
WELL, HERE ARE THE KEYS TO THE HOUSE.
THANKS FOR HANDLING THE REST.
LEAVE IT TO ME.
SO, MOM...
YOU KNOW THIS HOUSE?

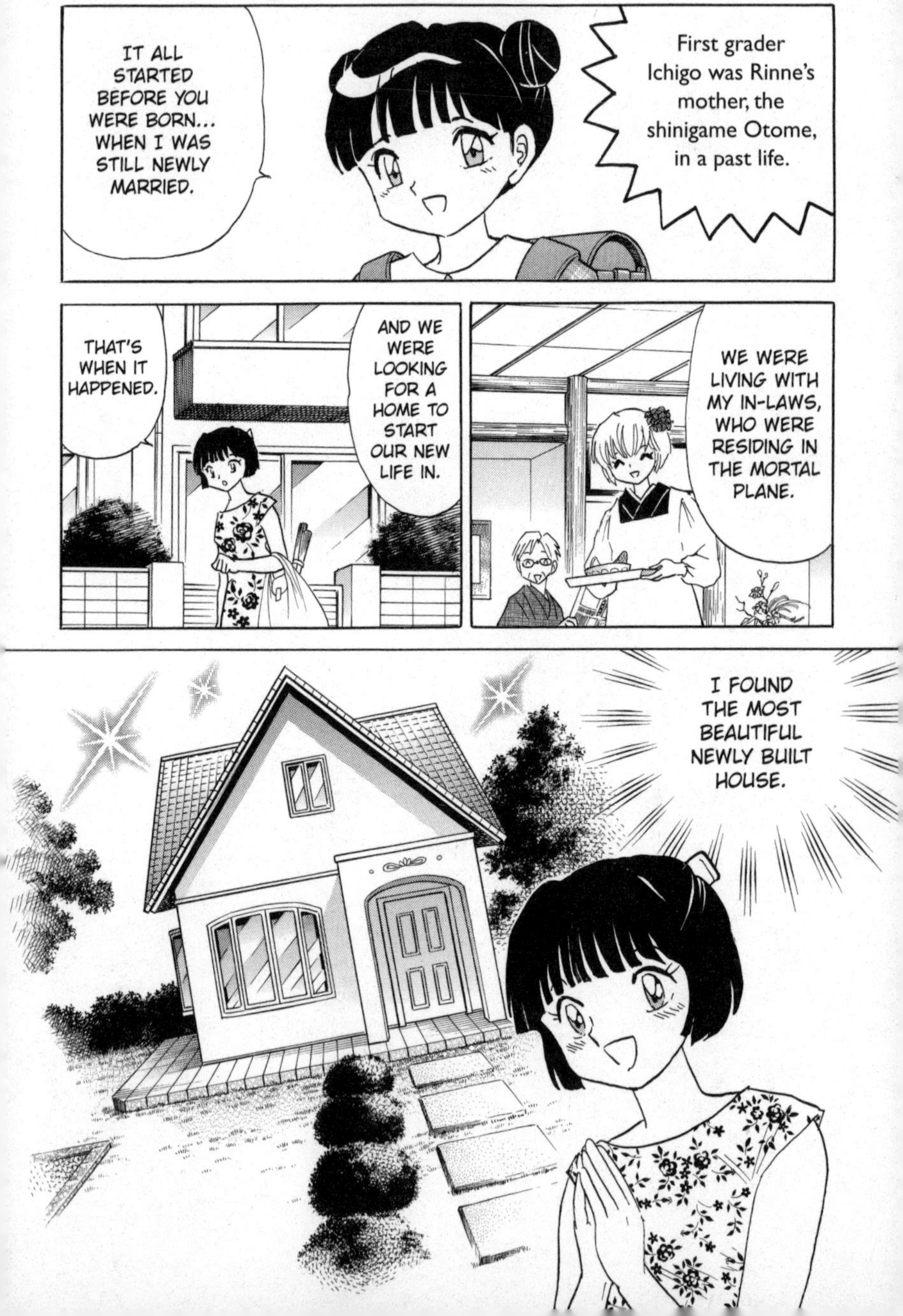
First grader Ichigo was Rinne's mother, the shinigame Otome, in a past life.
IT ALL STARTED BEFORE YOU WERE BORN... WHEN I WAS STILL NEWLY MARRIED.
WE WERE LIVING WITH MY IN-LAWS, WHO WERE RESIDING IN THE MORTAL PLANE.
AND WE WERE LOOKING FOR A HOME TO START OUR NEW LIFE IN.
THAT'S WHEN IT HAPPENED.
I FOUND THE MOST BEAUTIFUL NEWLY BUILT HOUSE.

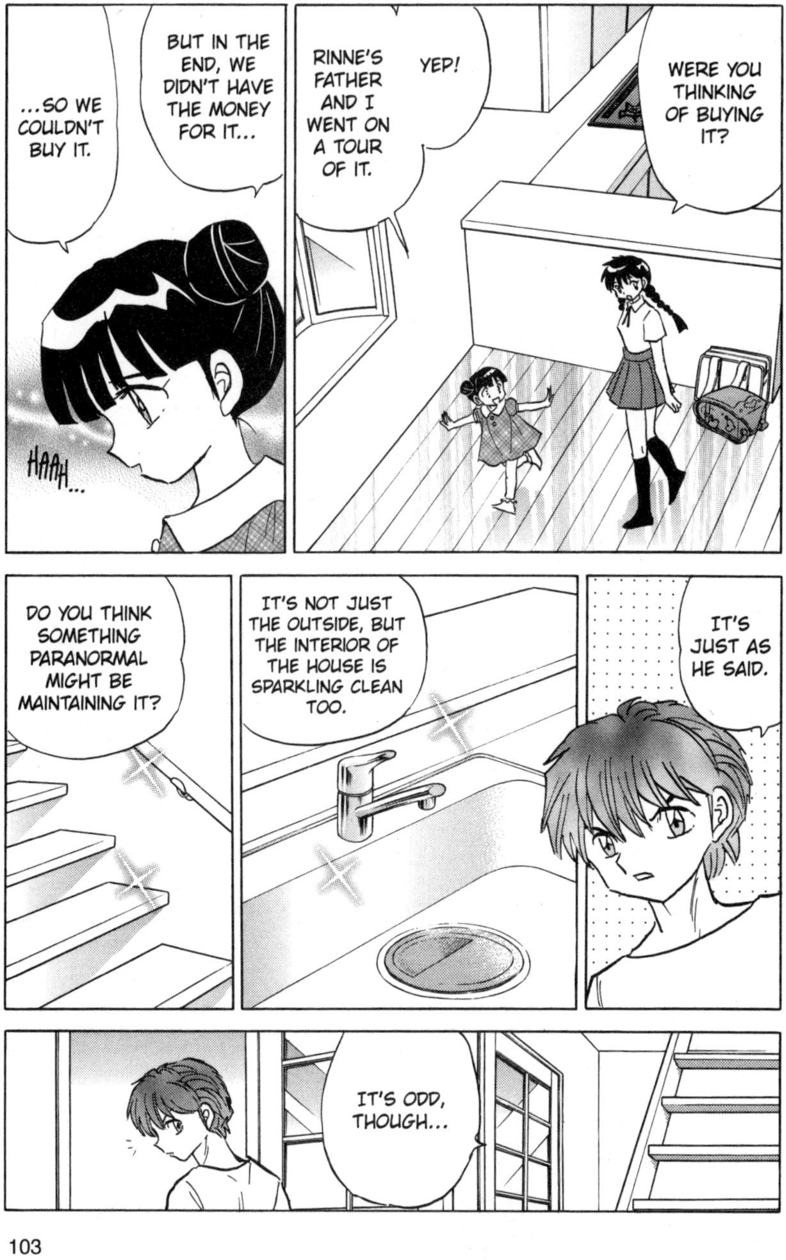
WERE YOU THINKING OF BUYING IT?
YEP!
RINNE'S FATHER AND I WENT ON A TOUR OF IT.
BUT IN THE END, WE DIDN'T HAVE THE MONEY FOR IT...
...SO WE COULDN'T BUY IT.
HAAH...
IT'S JUST AS HE SAID.
IT'S NOT JUST THE OUTSIDE, BUT THE INTERIOR OF THE HOUSE IS SPARKLING CLEAN TOO.
DO YOU THINK SOMETHING PARANORMAL MIGHT BE MAINTAINING IT?
IT'S ODD, THOUGH...

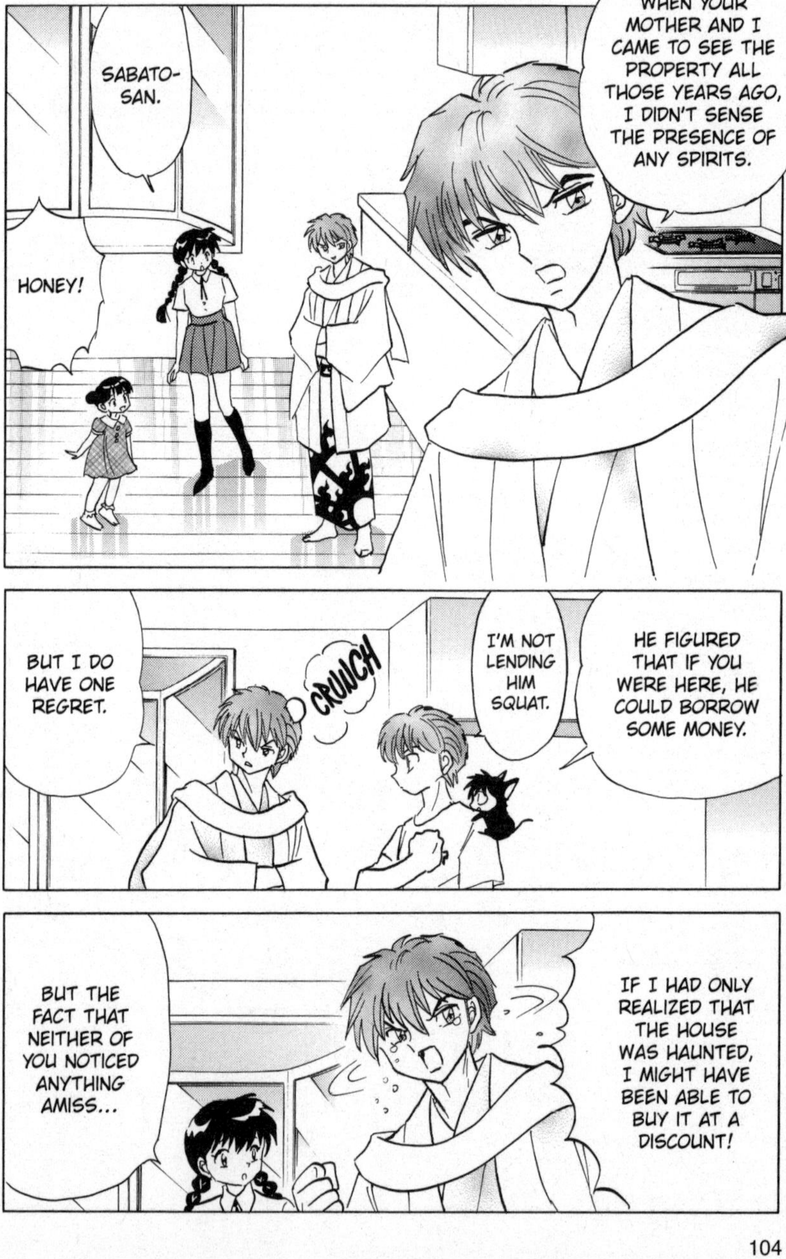
WHEN YOUR MOTHER AND I CAME TO SEE THE PROPERTY ALL THOSE YEARS AGO, I DIDN'T SENSE THE PRESENCE OF ANY SPIRITS.
SABATO-SAN.
HONEY!
HE FIGURED THAT IF YOU WERE HERE, HE COULD BORROW SOME MONEY.
I'M NOT LENDING HIM SQUAT.
CRUNCH
BUT I DO HAVE ONE REGRET.
IF I HAD ONLY REALIZED THAT THE HOUSE WAS HAUNTED, I MIGHT HAVE BEEN ABLE TO BUY IT AT A DISCOUNT!
BUT THE FACT THAT NEITHER OF YOU NOTICED ANYTHING AMISS...

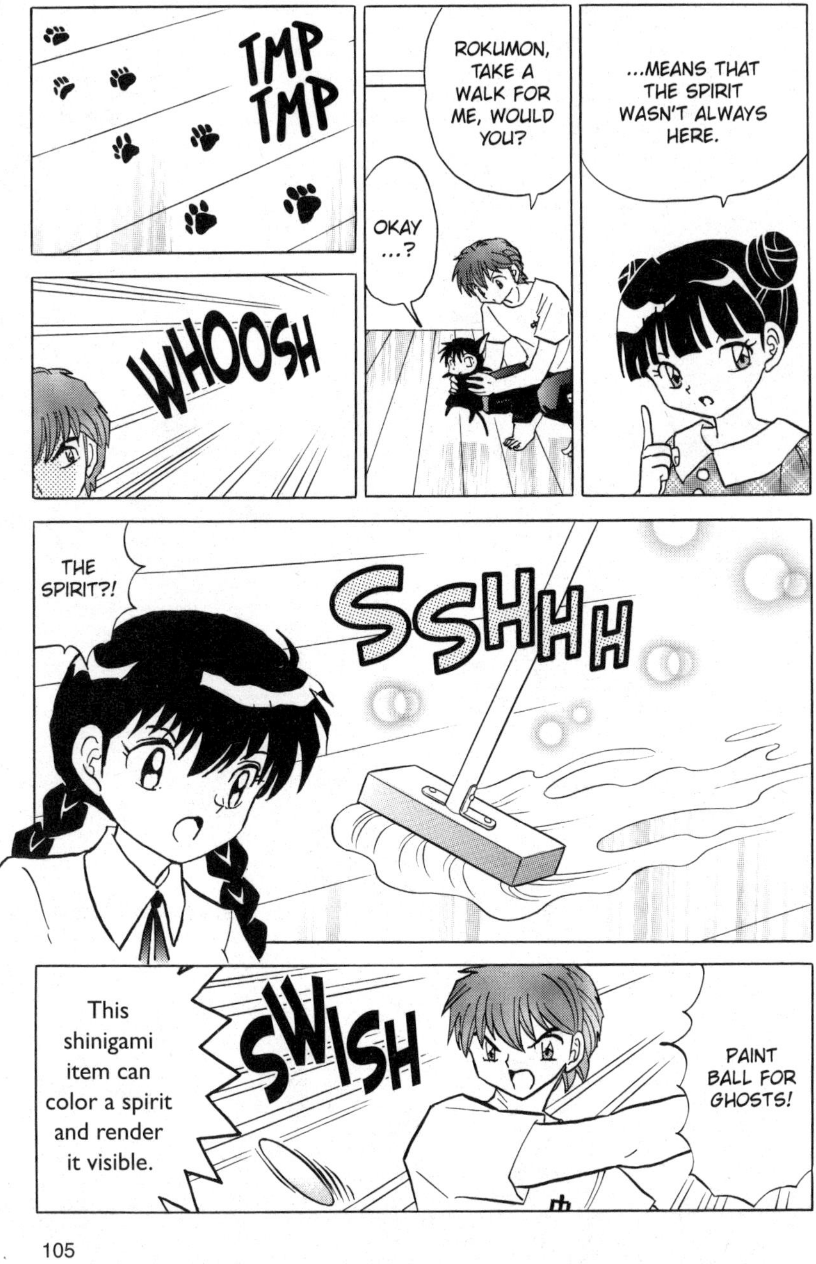
...MEANS THAT THE SPIRIT WASN'T ALWAYS HERE.
ROKUMON, TAKE A WALK FOR ME, WOULD YOU?
OKAY ...?
TMP TMP
WHOOSH
THE SPIRIT?!
SSHHH
PAINT BALL FOR GHOSTS!
SWISH
This shinigami item can color a spirit and render it visible.

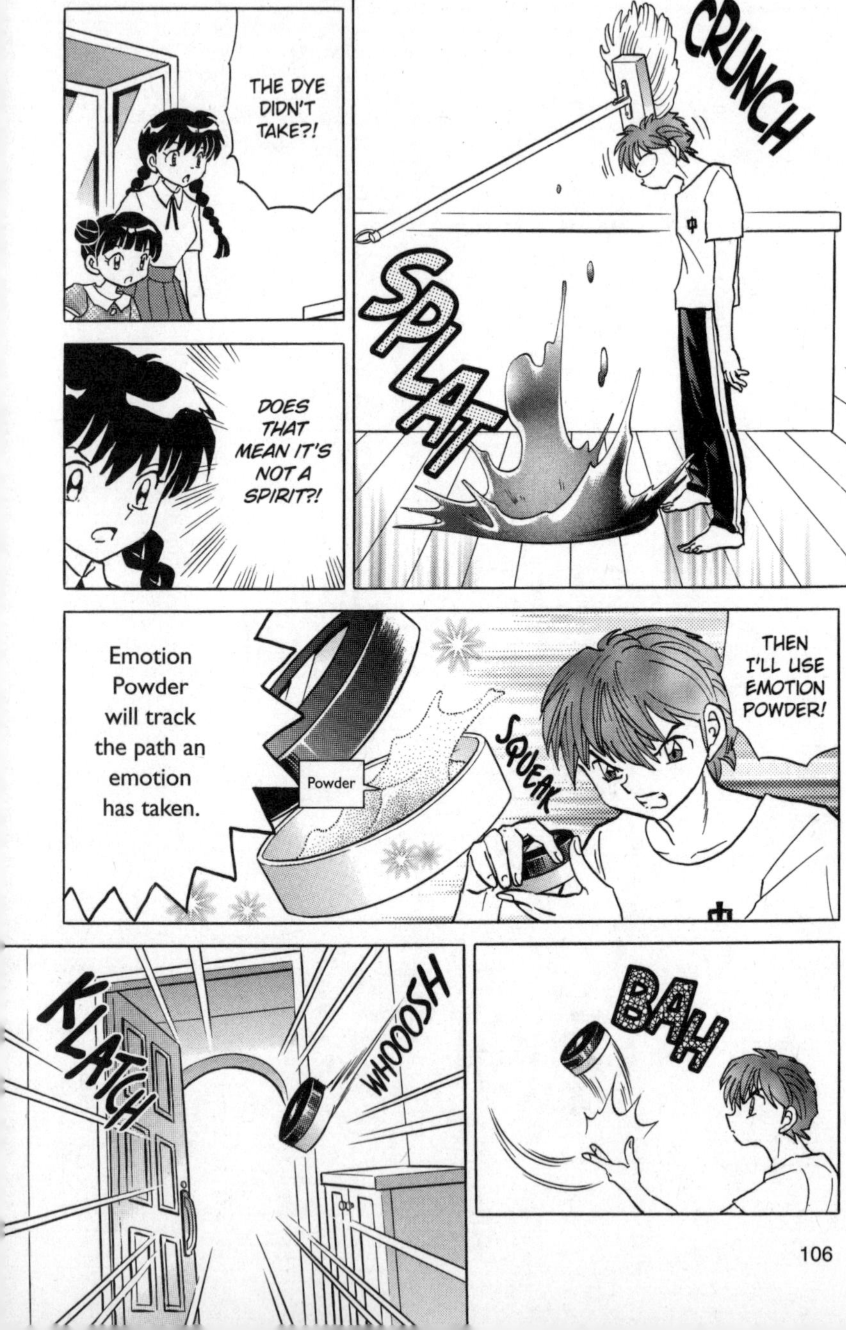
CRUNCH
SPLAT
THE DYE DIDN'T TAKE?!
DOES THAT MEAN IT'S NOT A SPIRIT?!
THEN I'LL USE EMOTION POWDER!
SQUEAK
Powder
Emotion Powder will track the path an emotion has taken.
BAH
WHOOOSH
KLATCH

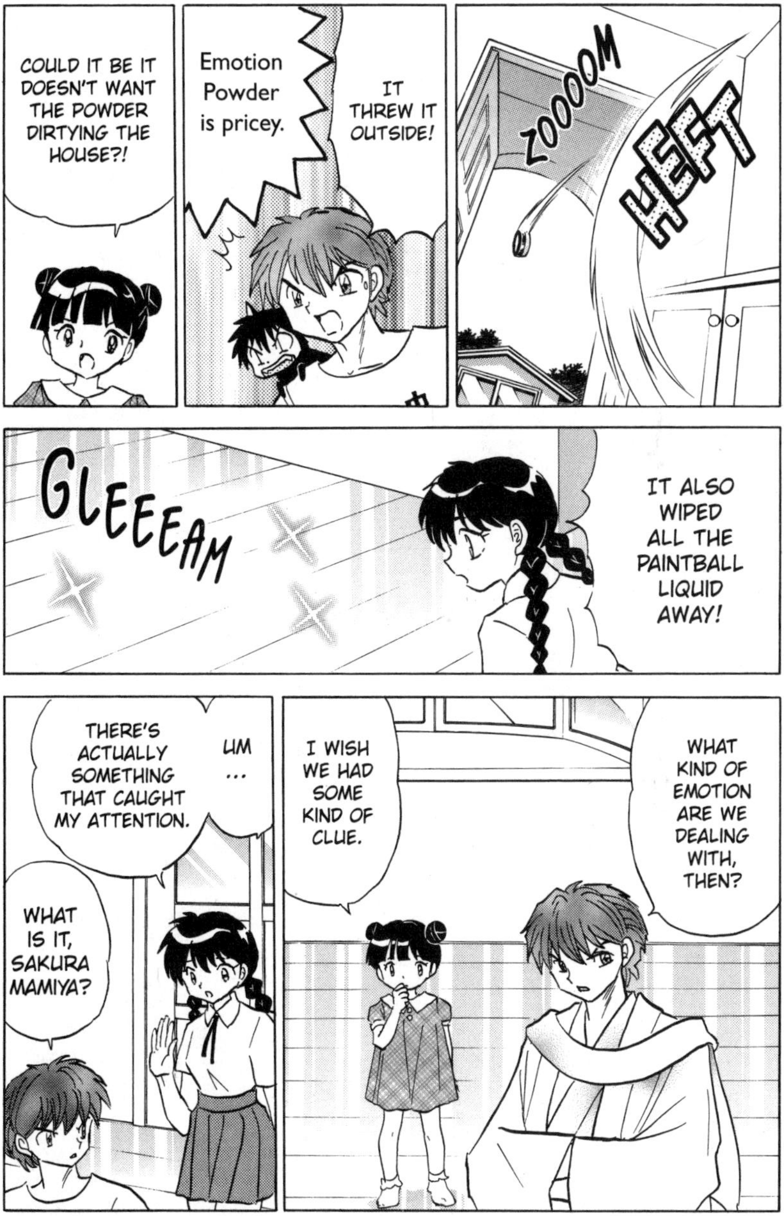
ZOOOOM
HEFT
IT THREW IT OUTSIDE!
Emotion Powder is pricey.
COULD IT BE IT DOESN'T WANT THE POWDER DIRTYING THE HOUSE?!
IT ALSO WIPED ALL THE PAINTBALL LIQUID AWAY!
GLEEEAM
WHAT KIND OF EMOTION ARE WE DEALING WITH, THEN?
I WISH WE HAD SOME KIND OF CLUE.
UM ...
THERE'S ACTUALLY SOMETHING THAT CAUGHT MY ATTENTION.
WHAT IS IT, SAKURA MAMIYA?

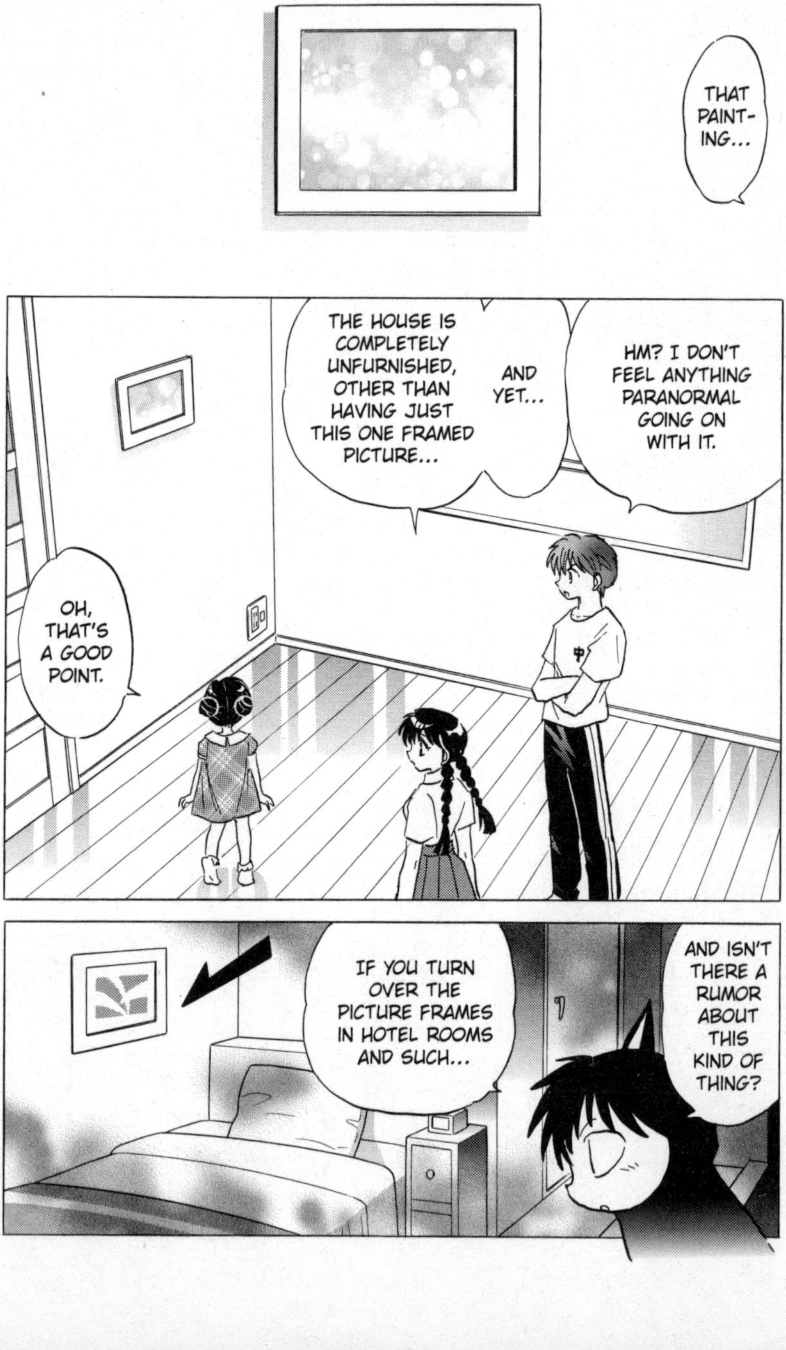
THAT PAINT-ING...
HM? I DON'T FEEL ANYTHING PARANORMAL GOING ON WITH IT.
THE HOUSE IS COMPLETELY UNFURNISHED, OTHER THAN HAVING JUST THIS ONE FRAMED PICTURE...
AND YET...
OH, THAT'S A GOOD POINT.
AND ISN'T THERE A RUMOR ABOUT THIS KIND OF THING?
IF YOU TURN OVER THE PICTURE FRAMES IN HOTEL ROOMS AND SUCH...

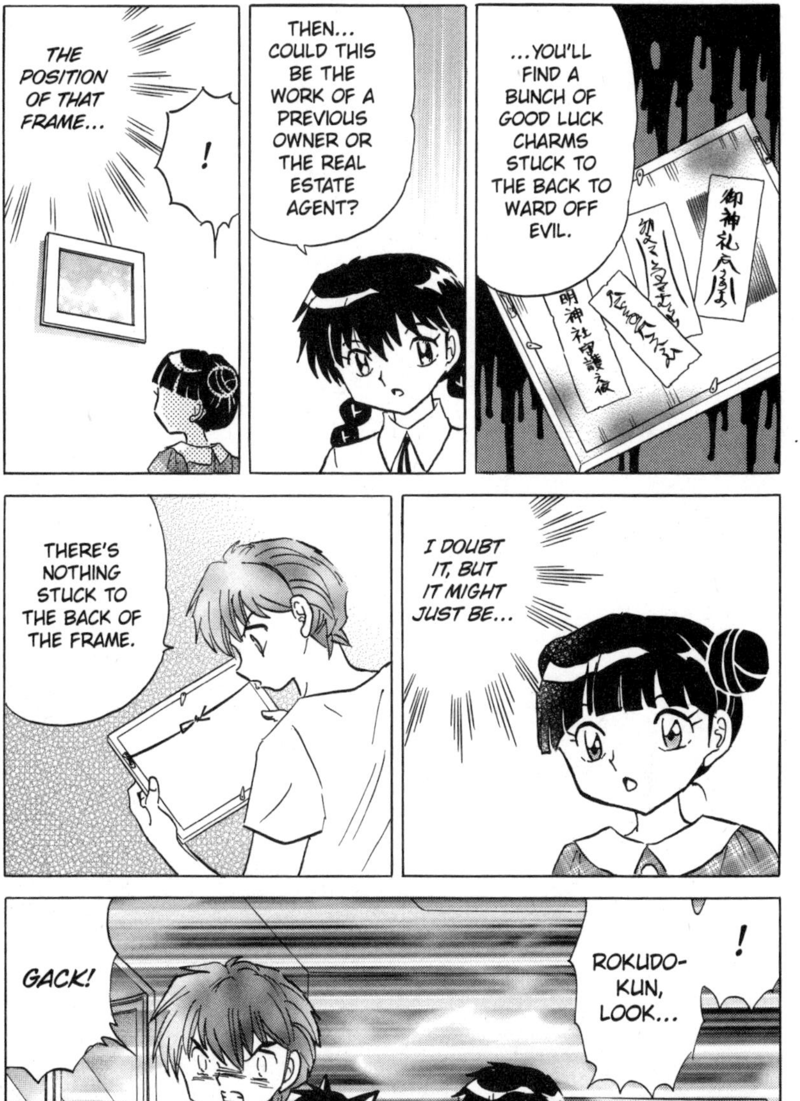
...YOU'LL FIND A BUNCH OF GOOD LUCK CHARMS STUCK TO THE BACK TO WARD OFF EVIL.
THEN... COULD THIS BE THE WORK OF A PREVIOUS OWNER OR THE REAL ESTATE AGENT?
THE POSITION OF THAT FRAME...
!
I DOUBT IT, BUT IT MIGHT JUST BE...
THERE'S NOTHING STUCK TO THE BACK OF THE FRAME.
!
ROKUDO-KUN, LOOK...
GACK!

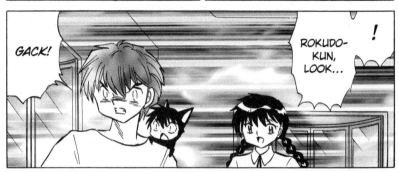

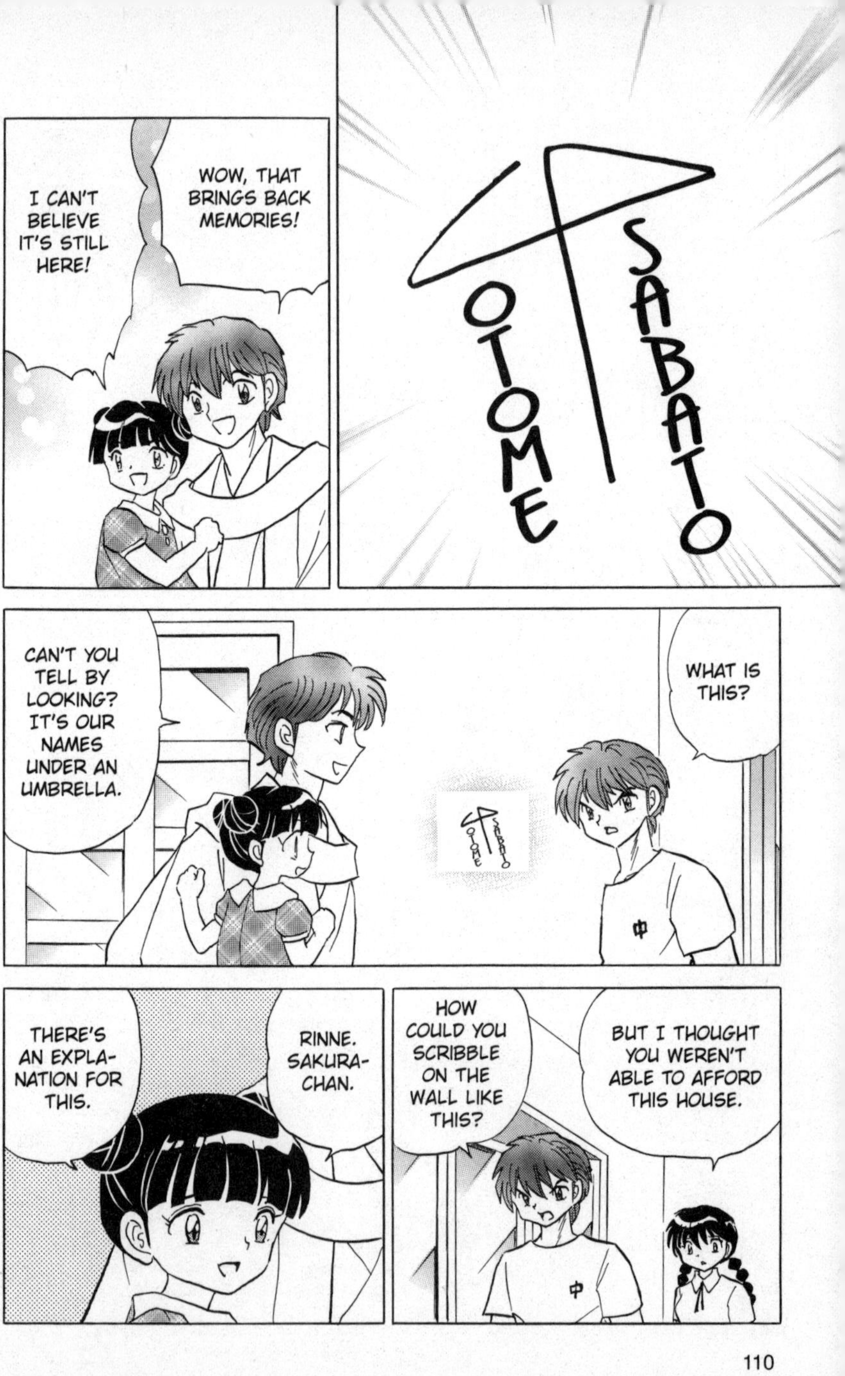
SABATO
OTOME
WOW, THAT BRINGS BACK MEMORIES!
I CAN'T BELIEVE IT'S STILL HERE!
WHAT IS THIS?
CAN'T YOU TELL BY LOOKING? IT'S OUR NAMES UNDER AN UMBRELLA.
BUT I THOUGHT YOU WEREN'T ABLE TO AFFORD THIS HOUSE.
HOW COULD YOU SCRIBBLE ON THE WALL LIKE THIS?
RINNE. SAKURA-CHAN.
THERE'S AN EXPLA-NATION FOR THIS.

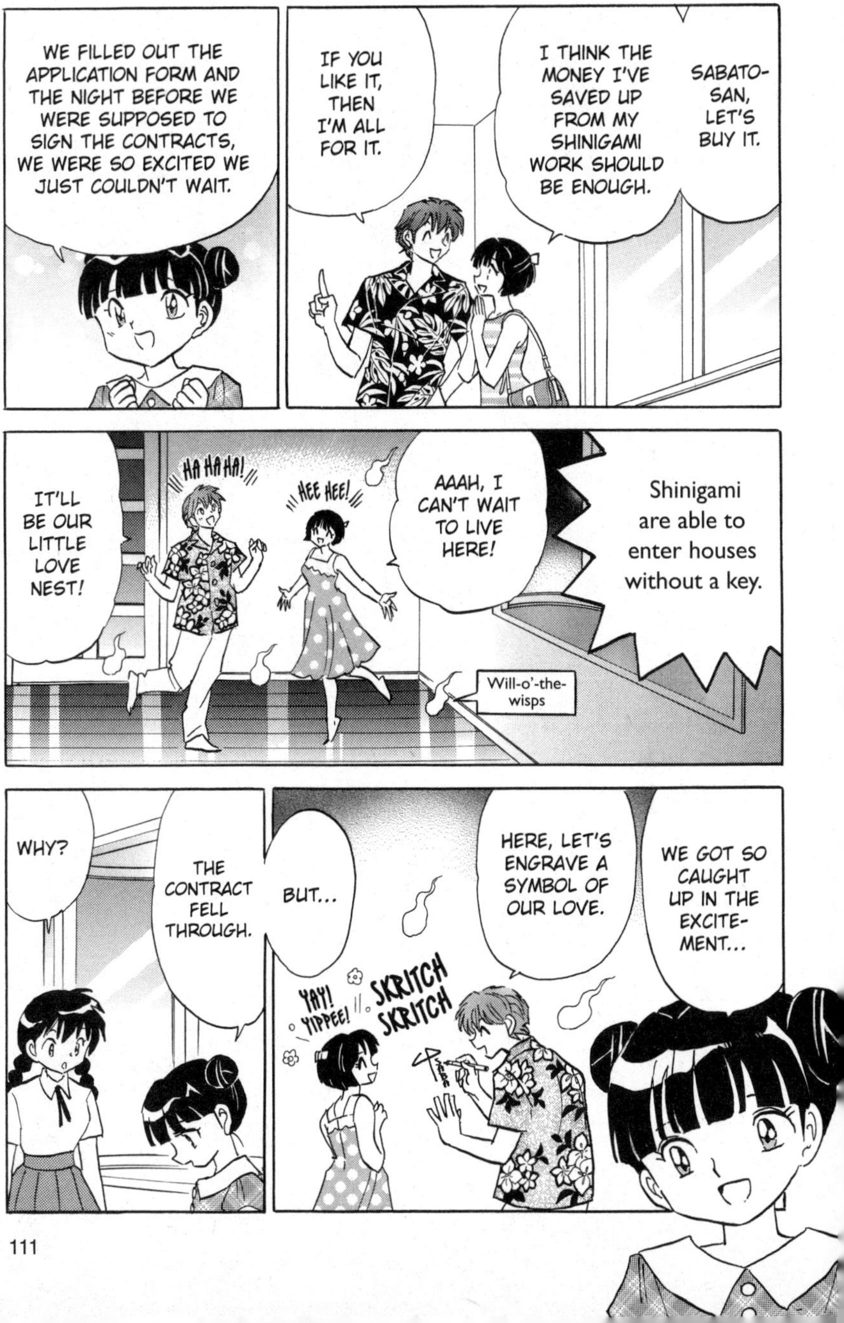
SABATO-SAN, LET'S BUY IT.
I THINK THE MONEY I'VE SAVED UP FROM MY SHINIGAMI WORK SHOULD BE ENOUGH.
IF YOU LIKE IT, THEN I'M ALL FOR IT.
WE FILLED OUT THE APPLICATION FORM AND THE NIGHT BEFORE WE WERE SUPPOSED TO SIGN THE CONTRACTS, WE WERE SO EXCITED WE JUST COULDN'T WAIT.
Shinigami are able to enter houses without a key.
AAAH, I CAN'T WAIT TO LIVE HERE!
HEE HEE!
HA HA HA!
IT'LL BE OUR LITTLE LOVE NEST!
Will-o'-the-wisps
WE GOT SO CAUGHT UP IN THE EXCITE-MENT...
HERE, LET'S ENGRAVE A SYMBOL OF OUR LOVE.
SKRITCH SKRITCH
YAY! YIPPEE!
BUT...
THE CONTRACT FELL THROUGH.
WHY?

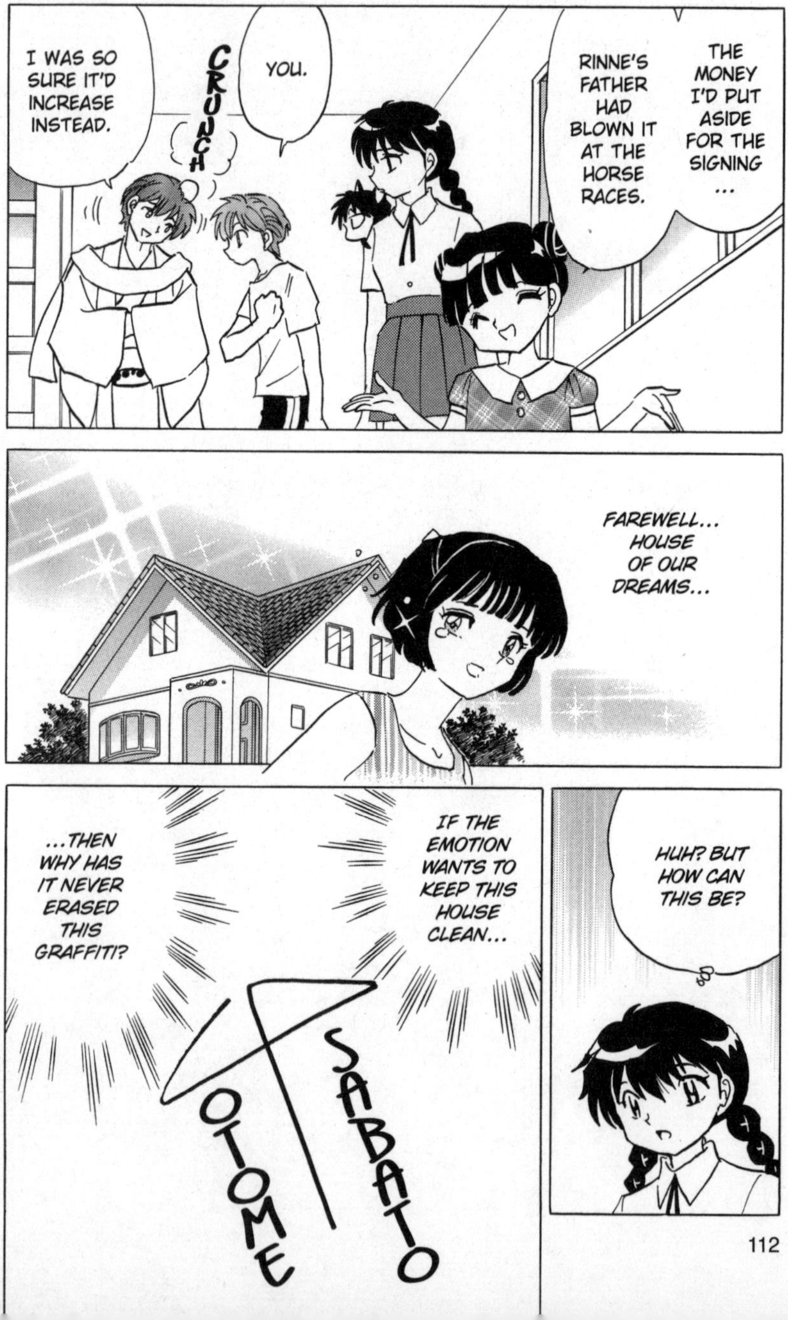
THE MONEY I'D PUT ASIDE FOR THE SIGNING...
RINNE'S FATHER HAD BLOWN IT AT THE HORSE RACES.
YOU.
CRUNCH
I WAS SO SURE IT'D INCREASE INSTEAD.
FAREWELL... HOUSE OF OUR DREAMS...
HUH? BUT HOW CAN THIS BE?
IF THE EMOTION WANTS TO KEEP THIS HOUSE CLEAN...
...THEN WHY HAS IT NEVER ERASED THIS GRAFFITI?
SABATO
OTOME

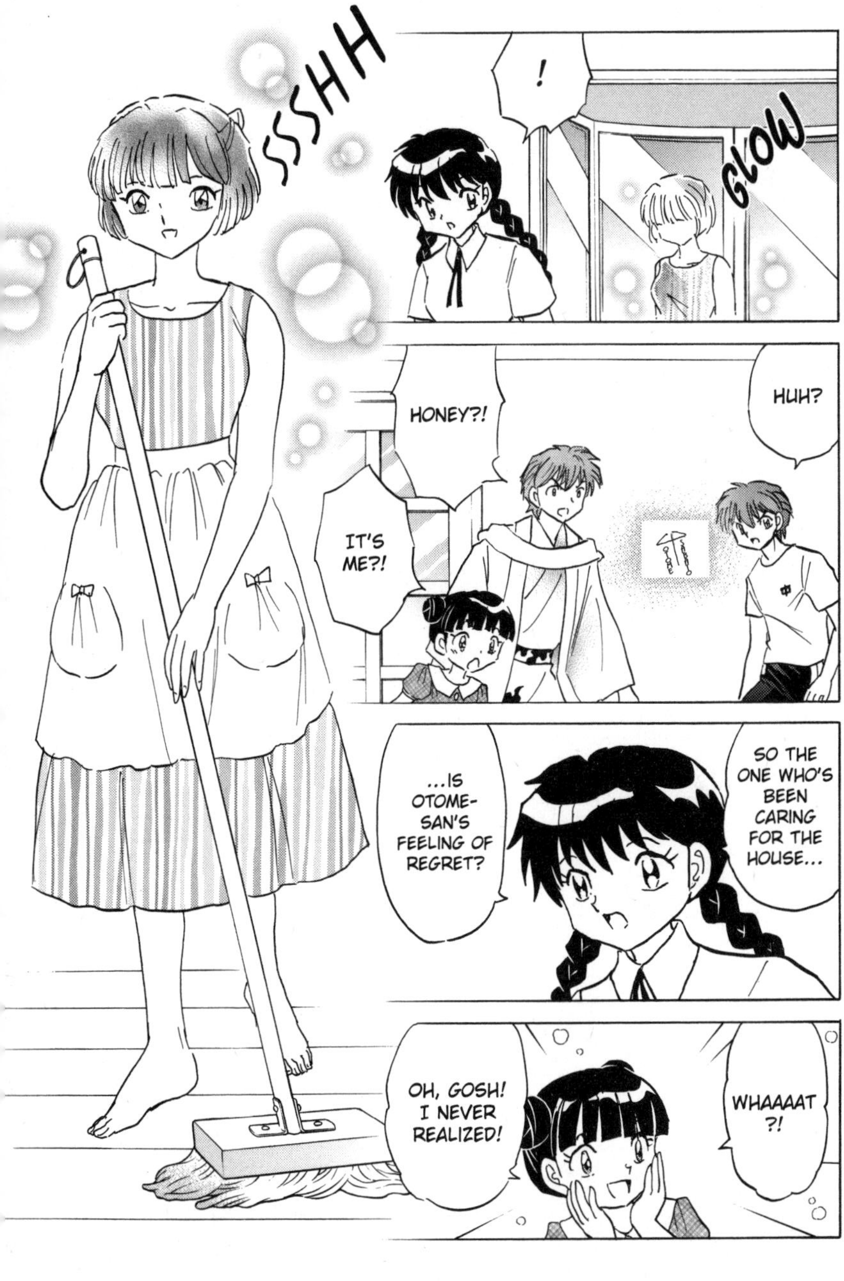
!
GLOW
HUH?
HONEY?!
IT'S ME?!
SO THE ONE WHO'S BEEN CARING FOR THE HOUSE...
...IS OTOME-SAN'S FEELING OF REGRET?
WHAAAAT?!
OH, GOSH! I NEVER REALIZED!
SSSHH

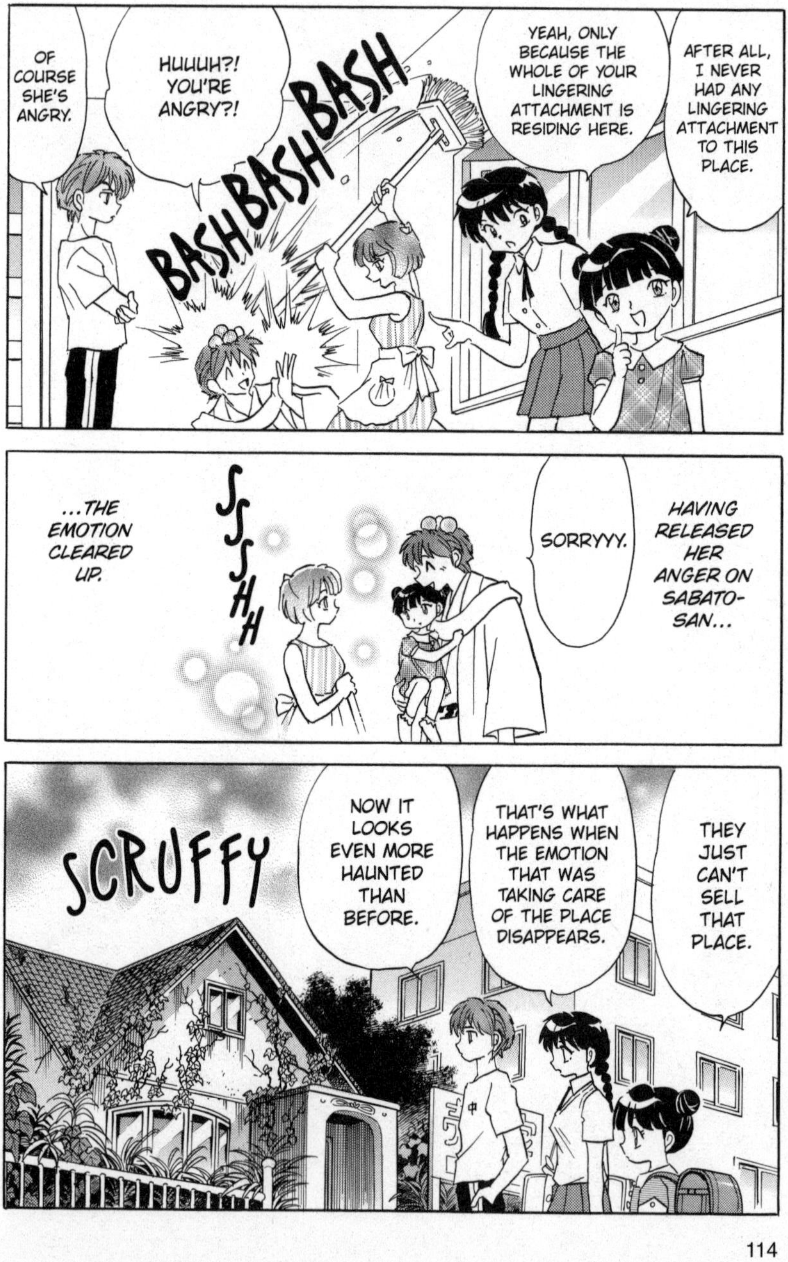
AFTER ALL, I NEVER HAD ANY LINGERING ATTACHMENT TO THIS PLACE.
YEAH, ONLY BECAUSE THE WHOLE OF YOUR LINGERING ATTACHMENT IS RESIDING HERE.
BASH BASH BASH
HUUUH?! YOU'RE ANGRY?!
OF COURSE SHE'S ANGRY.
HAVING RELEASED HER ANGER ON SABATO-SAN...
SORRYYY.
SSSHH
...THE EMOTION CLEARED UP.
THEY JUST CAN'T SELL THAT PLACE.
THAT'S WHAT HAPPENS WHEN THE EMOTION THAT WAS TAKING CARE OF THE PLACE DISAPPEARS.
NOW IT LOOKS EVEN MORE HAUNTED THAN BEFORE.
SCRUFFY

CHAPTER 385: THE BELOVED

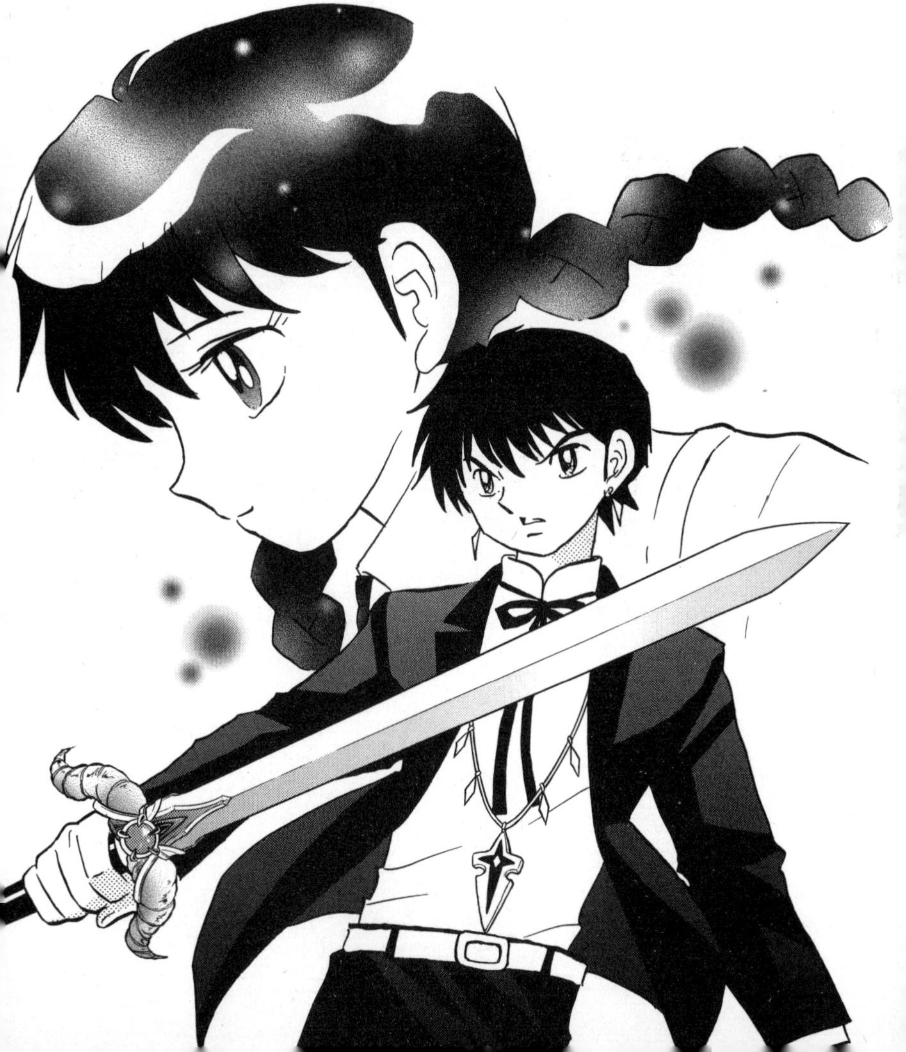

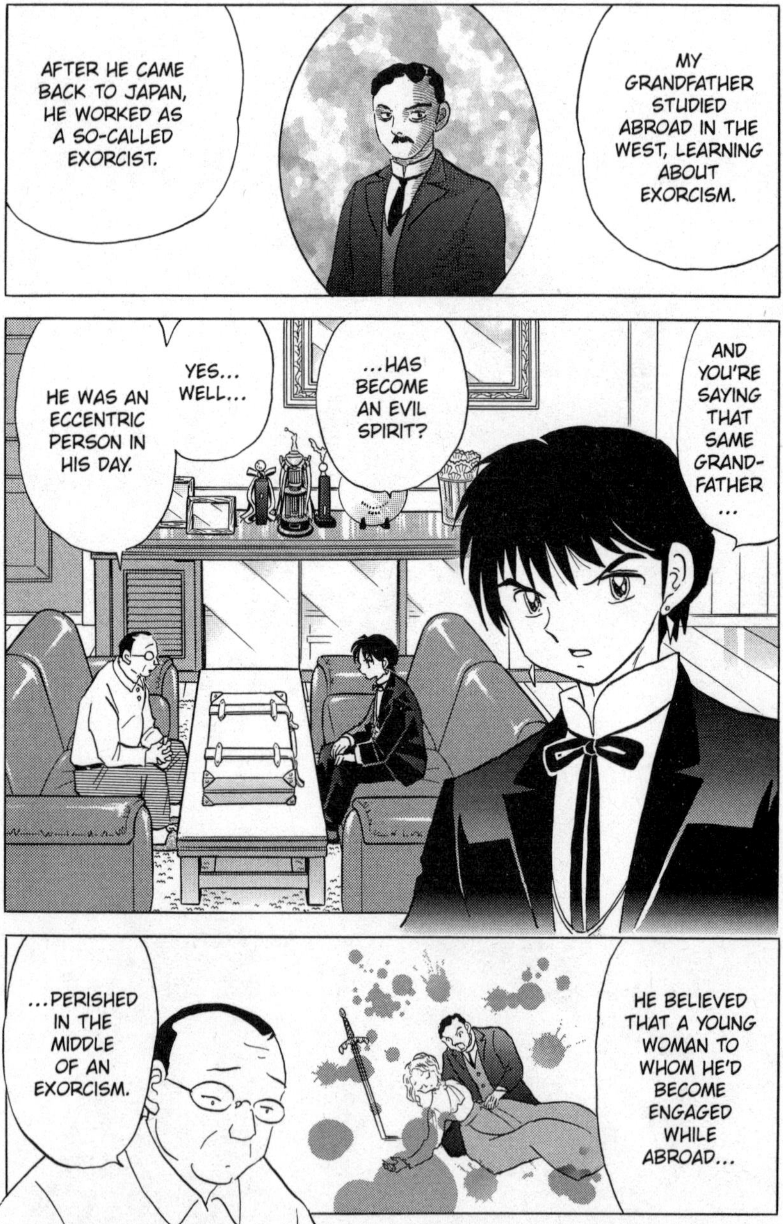
MY GRANDFATHER STUDIED ABROAD IN THE WEST, LEARNING ABOUT EXORCISM.
AFTER HE CAME BACK TO JAPAN, HE WORKED AS A SO-CALLED EXORCIST.
AND YOU'RE SAYING THAT SAME GRANDFATHER...
...HAS BECOME AN EVIL SPIRIT?
YES... WELL...
HE WAS AN ECCENTRIC PERSON IN HIS DAY.
HE BELIEVED THAT A YOUNG WOMAN TO WHOM HE'D BECOME ENGAGED WHILE ABROAD...
...PERISHED IN THE MIDDLE OF AN EXORCISM.

WHILE STILL GRIEVING, HE RETURNED HOME TO JAPAN AND MARRIED MY GRANDMOTHER.

BUT IT SEEMS HE NEVER ONCE STOPPED THINKING ABOUT HIS LOST FIANCÉE.

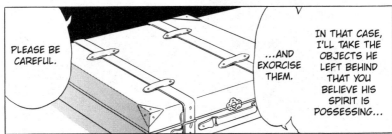

IN THAT CASE, I'LL TAKE THE OBJECTS HE LEFT BEHIND THAT YOU BELIEVE HIS SPIRIT IS POSSESSING...

...AND EXORCISE THEM.

PLEASE BE CAREFUL.

IF YOU SPEAK TO SOMEONE OF THE OPPOSITE SEX WHILE NEAR THESE ARTICLES LEFT BY MY DECEASED GRAND-FATHER...

...AND GET A TWINKLE IN YOUR EYE AND DO A MERRY LITTLE SKIP, YOU'LL BE CURSED INSTANTLY.

HAVING A CONVERSATION WITH SOMEONE OF THE OPPOSITE SEX IS ONE THING...

HAH ...

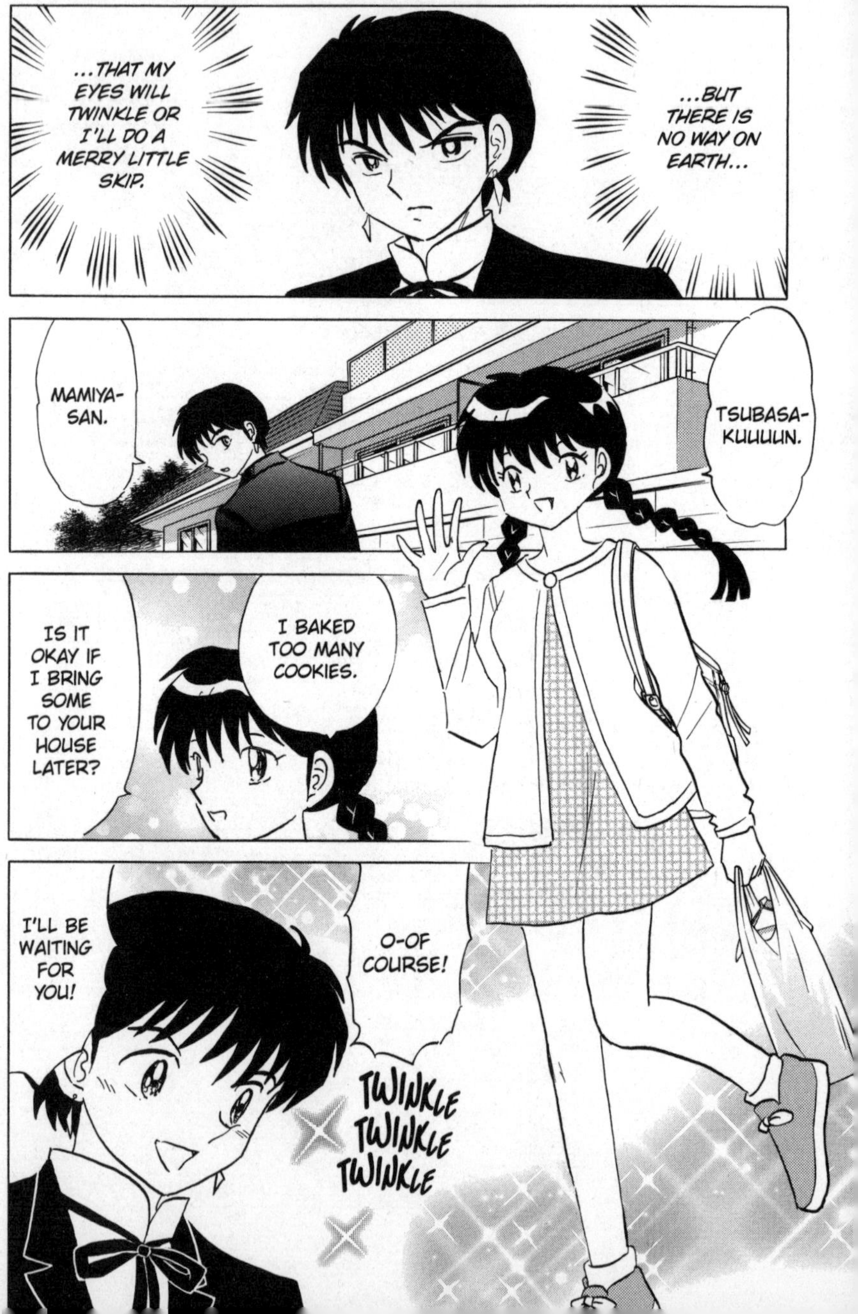
...BUT THERE IS NO WAY ON EARTH...
...THAT MY EYES WILL TWINKLE OR I'LL DO A MERRY LITTLE SKIP.
TSUBASA-KUUUUN.
MAMIYA-SAN.
I BAKED TOO MANY COOKIES.
IS IT OKAY IF I BRING SOME TO YOUR HOUSE LATER?
O-OF COURSE!
I'LL BE WAITING FOR YOU!
TWINKLE TWINKLE TWINKLE

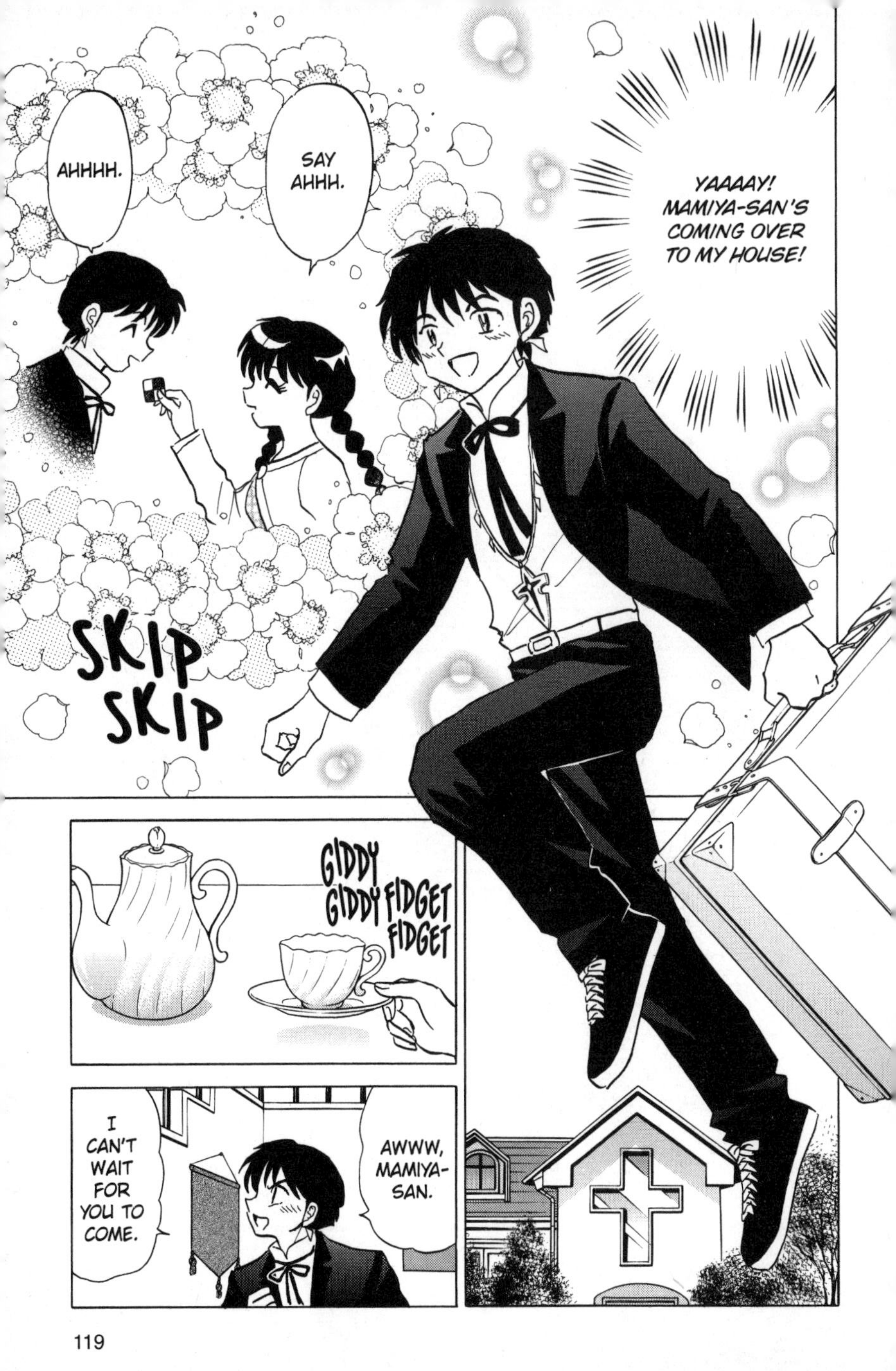
YAAAAY! MAMIYA-SAN'S COMING OVER TO MY HOUSE!
SAY AHHH.
AHHHH.
SKIP SKIP
GIDDY GIDDY FIDGET FIDGET
AWWW, MAMIYA-SAN.
I CAN'T WAIT FOR YOU TO COME.

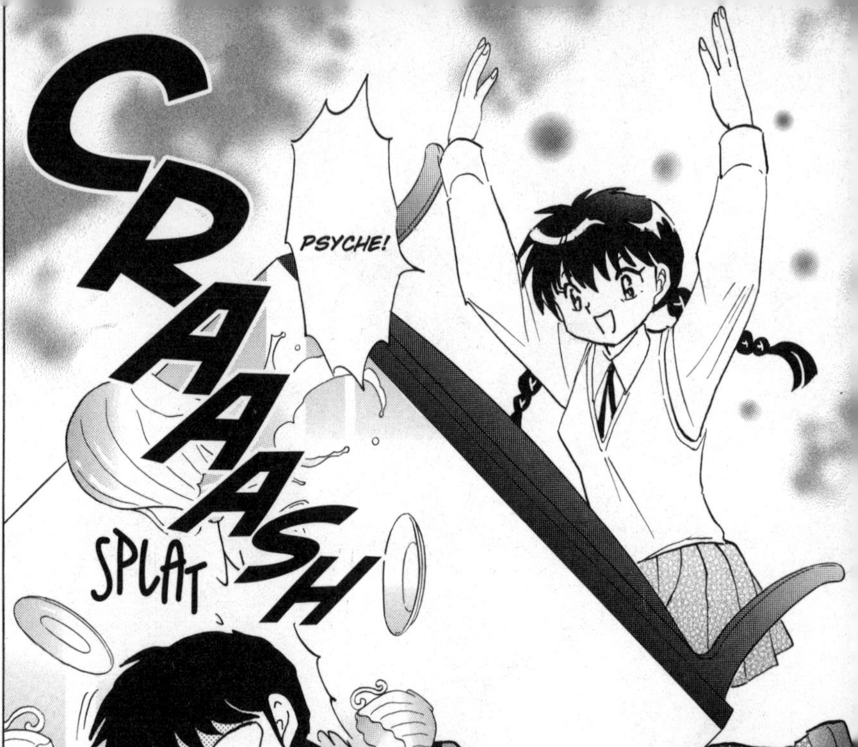
PSYCHE!
CRAAASH
SPLAT
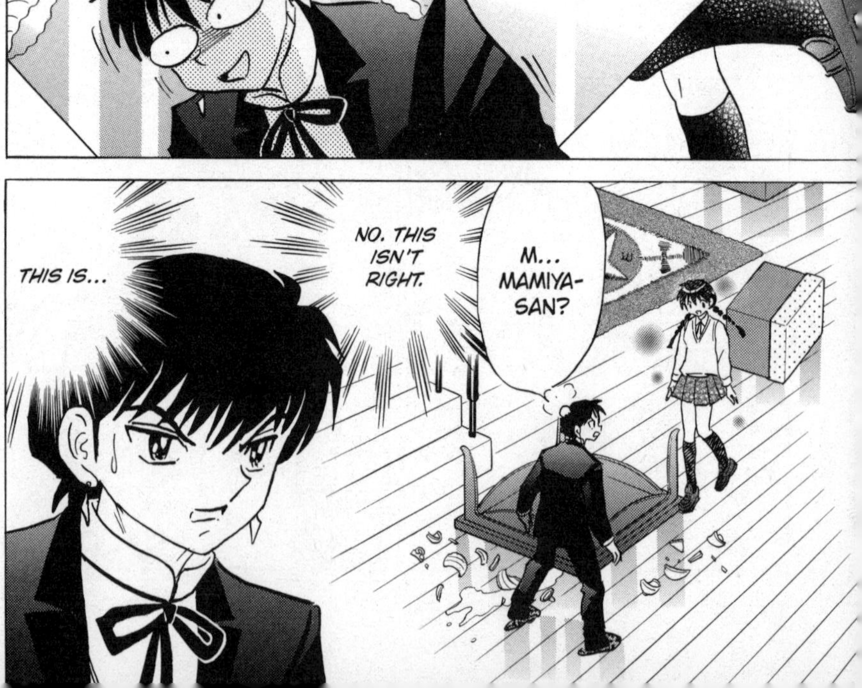
M... MAMIYA-SAN?
NO. THIS ISN'T RIGHT.
THIS IS...

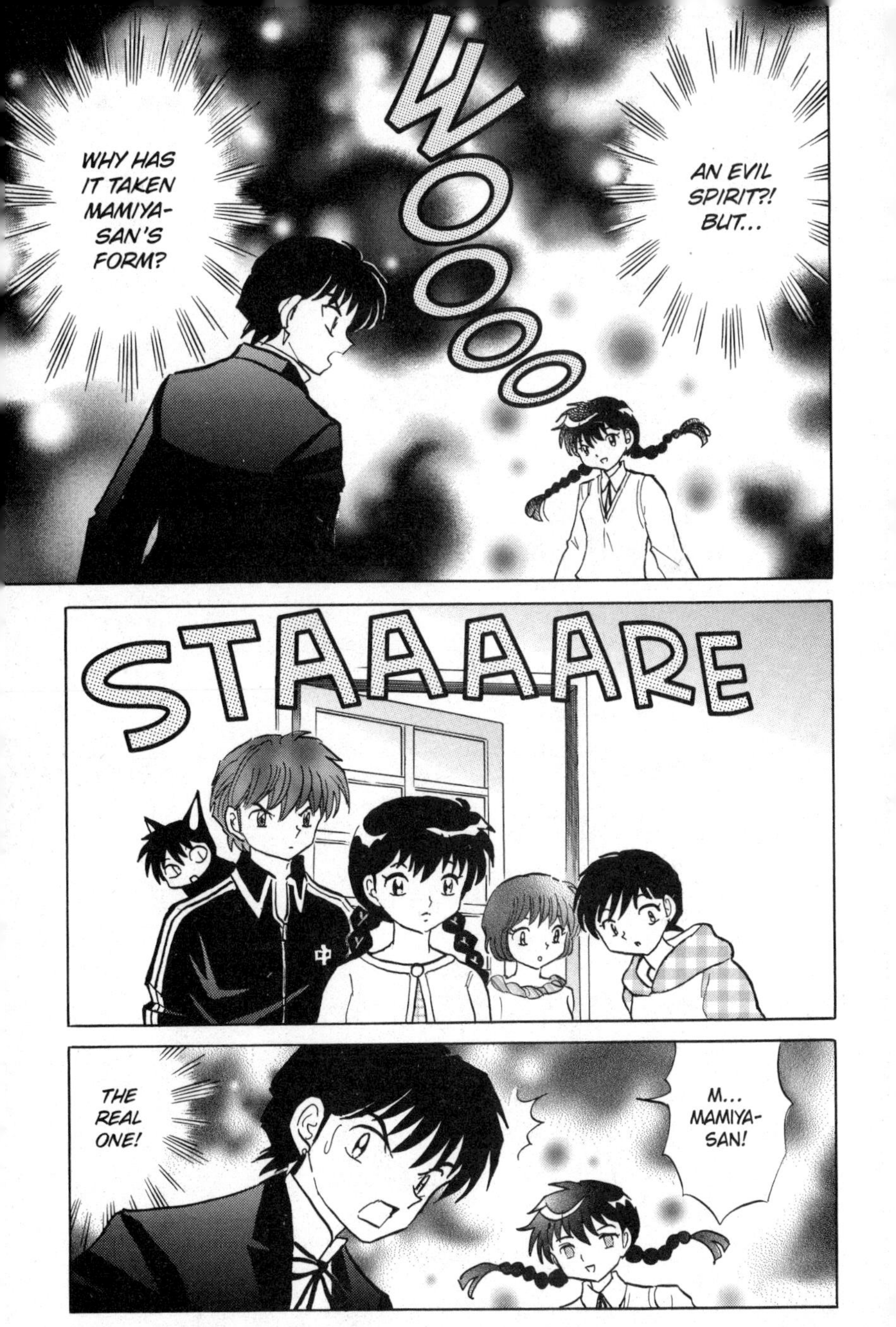
AN EVIL SPIRIT?! BUT...
WOOOOO
WHY HAS IT TAKEN MAMIYA-SAN'S FORM?
STAAAARE
M... MAMIYA-SAN!
THE REAL ONE!

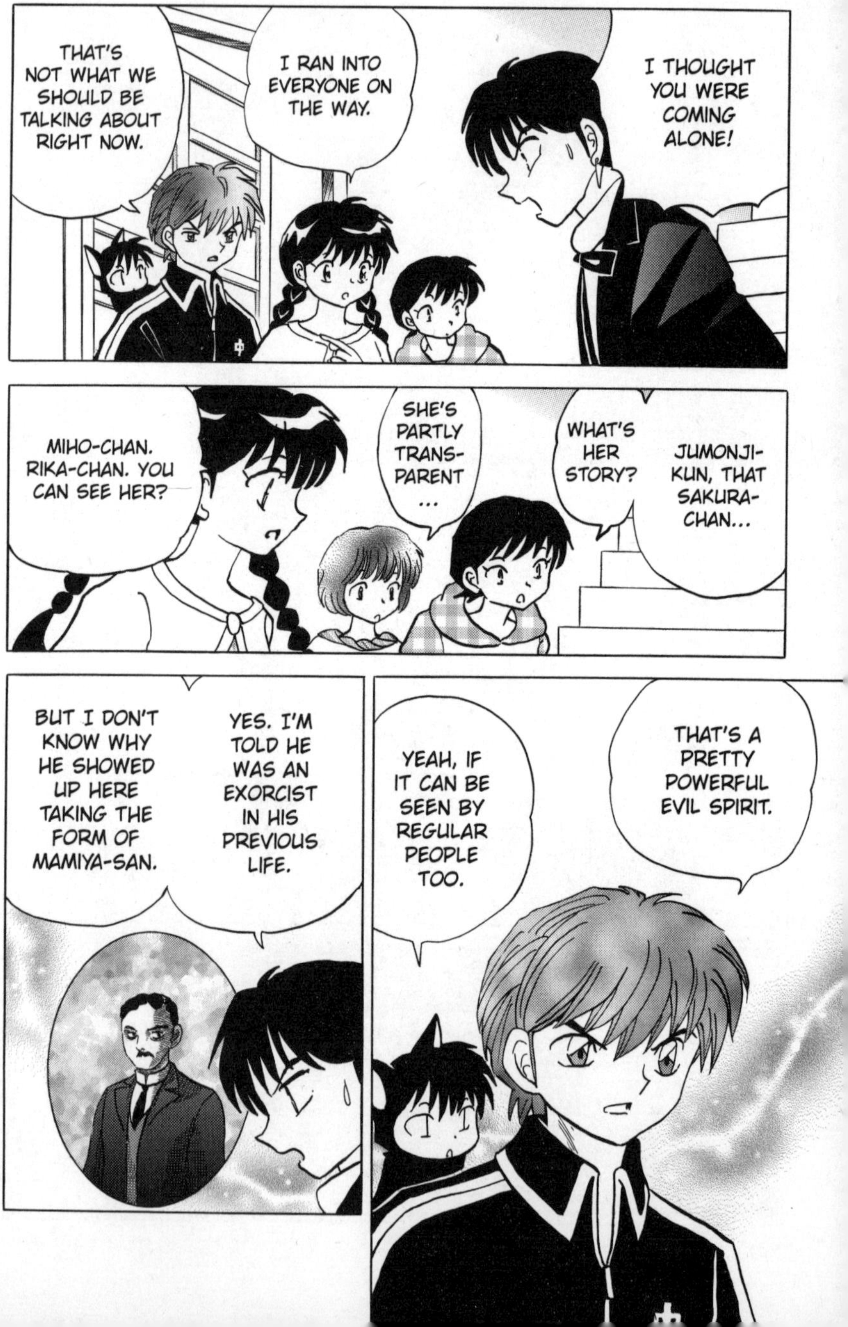
I THOUGHT YOU WERE COMING ALONE!
I RAN INTO EVERYONE ON THE WAY.
THAT'S NOT WHAT WE SHOULD BE TALKING ABOUT RIGHT NOW.
JUMONJI-KUN, THAT SAKURA-CHAN...
WHAT'S HER STORY?
SHE'S PARTLY TRANS-PARENT ...
MIHO-CHAN. RIKA-CHAN. YOU CAN SEE HER?
THAT'S A PRETTY POWERFUL EVIL SPIRIT.
YEAH, IF IT CAN BE SEEN BY REGULAR PEOPLE TOO.
YES. I'M TOLD HE WAS AN EXORCIST IN HIS PREVIOUS LIFE.
BUT I DON'T KNOW WHY HE SHOWED UP HERE TAKING THE FORM OF MAMIYA-SAN.

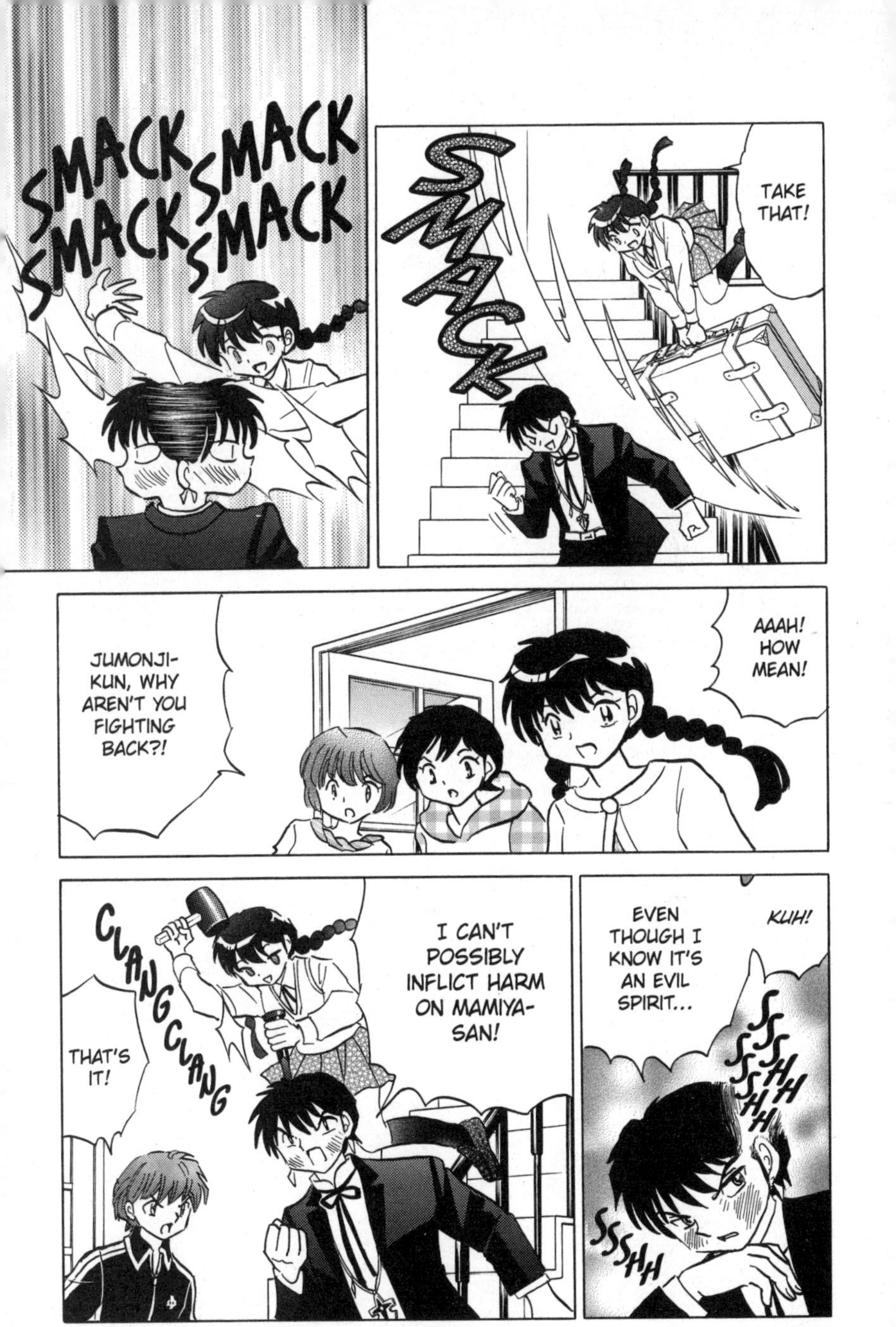
SMACK
TAKE THAT!
SMACK SMACK
SMACK SMACK
AAAH! HOW MEAN!
JUMONJI-KUN, WHY AREN'T YOU FIGHTING BACK?!
KUH!
EVEN THOUGH I KNOW IT'S AN EVIL SPIRIT...
SSSHH SSSHH
SSSHH
I CAN'T POSSIBLY INFLICT HARM ON MAMIYA-SAN!
CLANG CLANG
THAT'S IT!

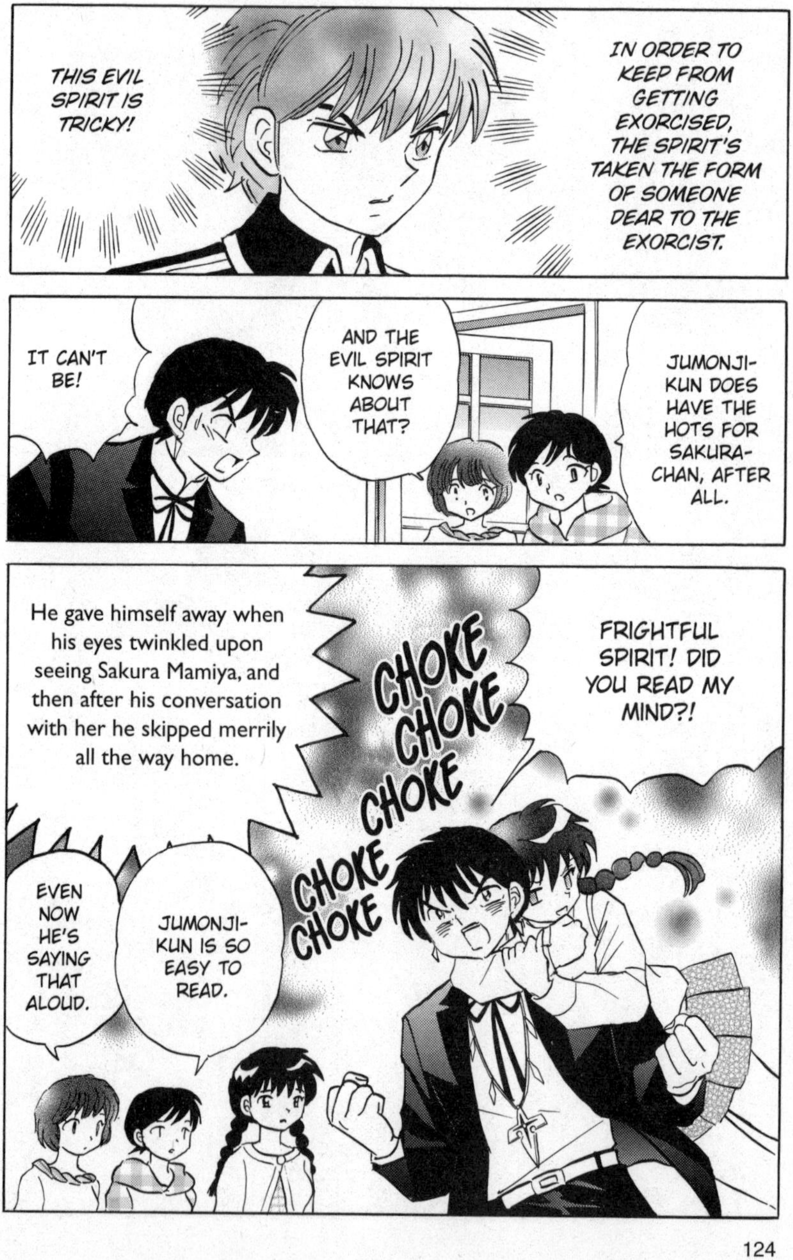
IN ORDER TO KEEP FROM GETTING EXORCISED, THE SPIRIT'S TAKEN THE FORM OF SOMEONE DEAR TO THE EXORCIST.
THIS EVIL SPIRIT IS TRICKY!
JUMONJI-KUN DOES HAVE THE HOTS FOR SAKURA-CHAN, AFTER ALL.
AND THE EVIL SPIRIT KNOWS ABOUT THAT?
IT CAN'T BE!
FRIGHTFUL SPIRIT! DID YOU READ MY MIND?!
He gave himself away when his eyes twinkled upon seeing Sakura Mamiya, and then after his conversation with her he skipped merrily all the way home.
CHOKE CHOKE CHOKE CHOKE CHOKE
JUMONJI-KUN IS SO EASY TO READ.
EVEN NOW HE'S SAYING THAT ALOUD.

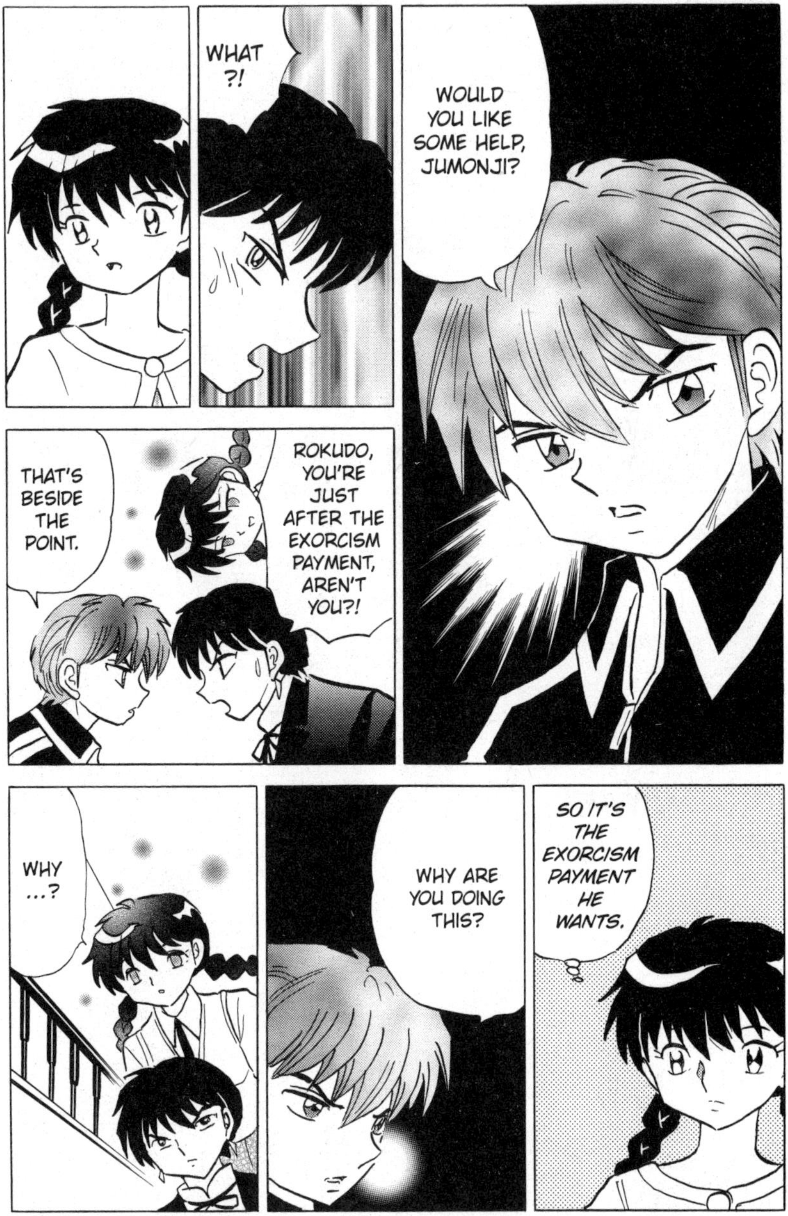
WOULD YOU LIKE SOME HELP, JUMONJI?
WHAT ?!
ROKUDO, YOU'RE JUST AFTER THE EXORCISM PAYMENT, AREN'T YOU?!
THAT'S BESIDE THE POINT.
SO IT'S THE EXORCISM PAYMENT HE WANTS.
WHY ARE YOU DOING THIS?
WHY ...?

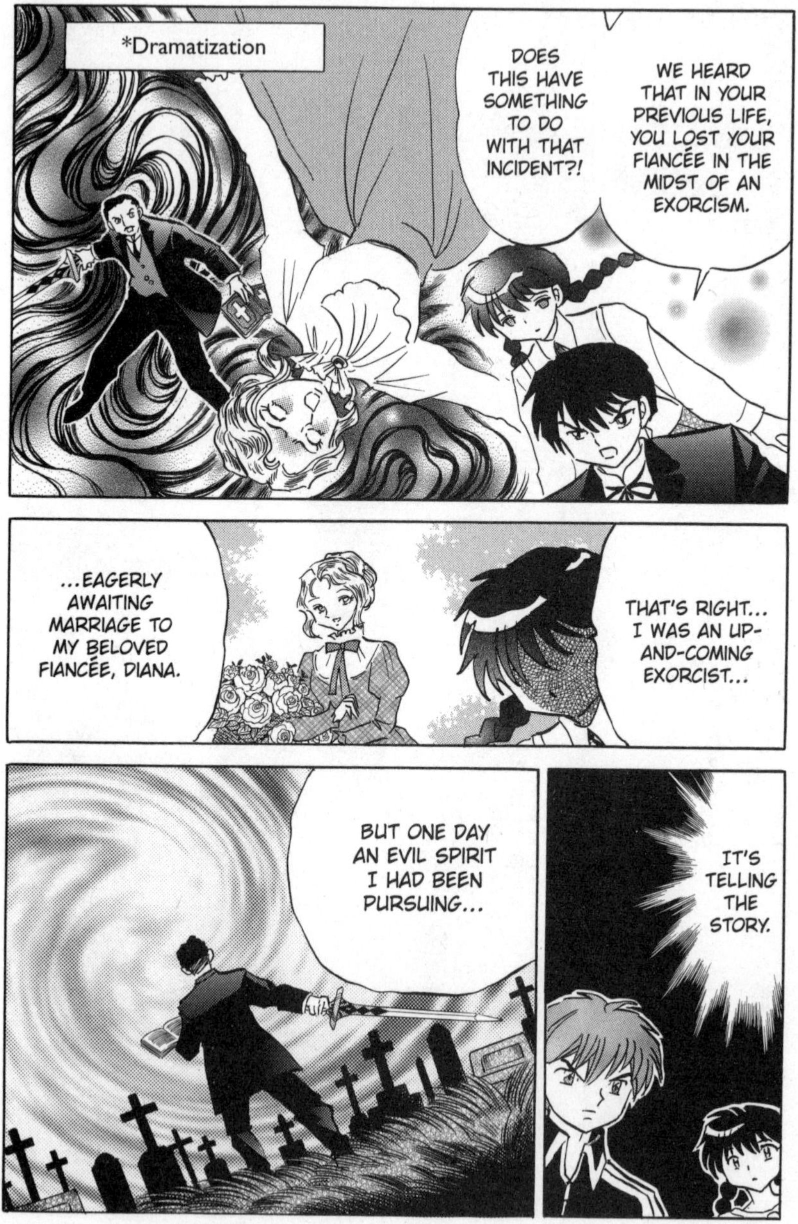
WE HEARD THAT IN YOUR PREVIOUS LIFE, YOU LOST YOUR FIANCÉE IN THE MIDST OF AN EXORCISM.
DOES THIS HAVE SOMETHING TO DO WITH THAT INCIDENT?!
*Dramatization
THAT'S RIGHT... I WAS AN UP-AND-COMING EXORCIST...
...EAGERLY AWAITING MARRIAGE TO MY BELOVED FIANCÉE, DIANA.
IT'S TELLING THE STORY.
BUT ONE DAY AN EVIL SPIRIT I HAD BEEN PURSUING...

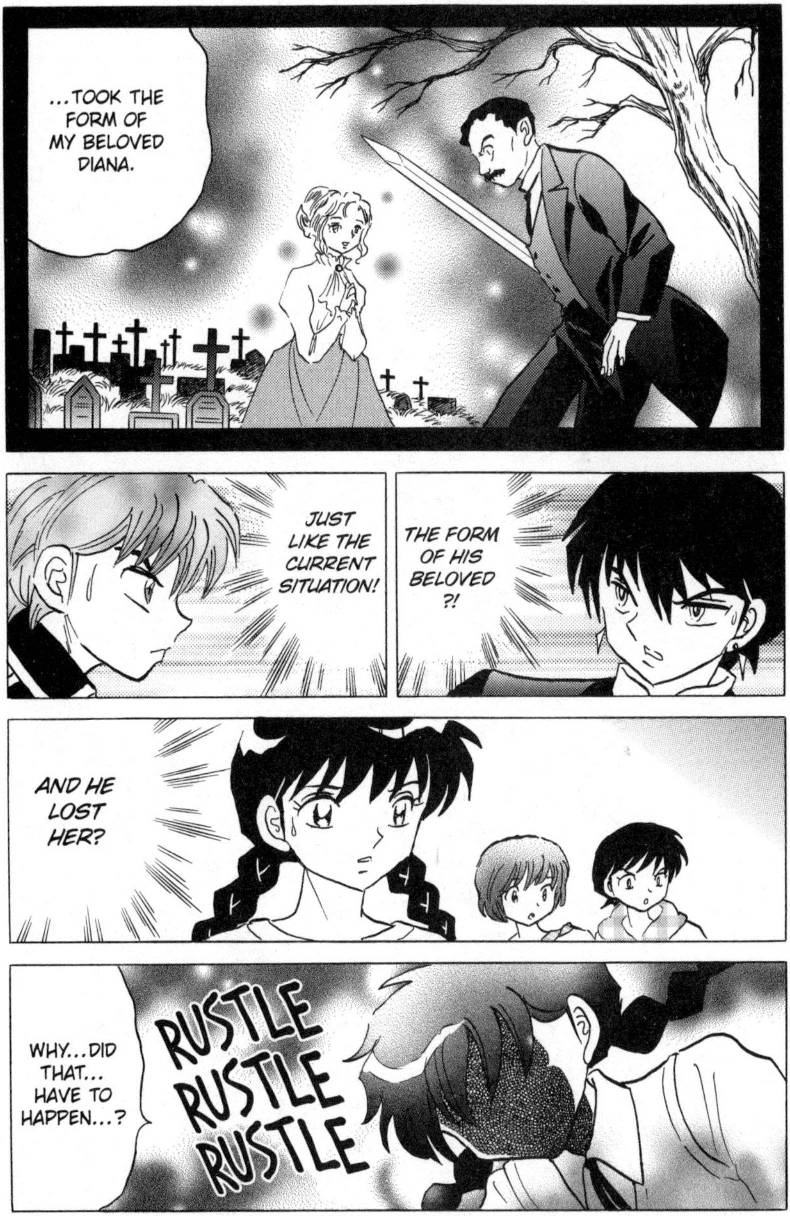
...TOOK THE FORM OF MY BELOVED DIANA.
THE FORM OF HIS BELOVED ?!
JUST LIKE THE CURRENT SITUATION!
AND HE LOST HER?
RUSTLE RUSTLE RUSTLE
WHY...DID THAT... HAVE TO HAPPEN...?

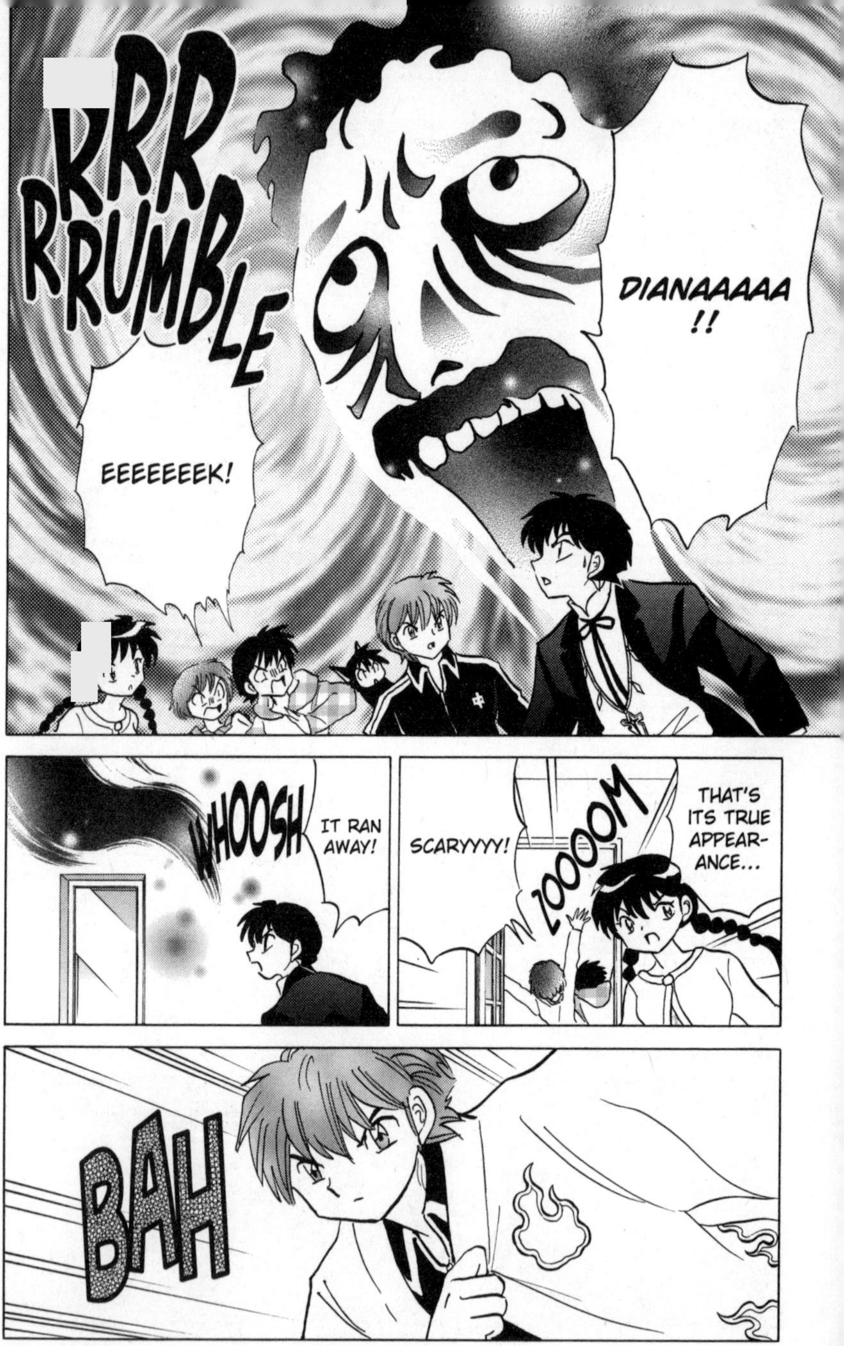
DIANAAAAA !!
RRR RRUMBLE
EEEEEEEK!
THAT'S ITS TRUE APPEAR-ANCE...
ZOOOOM
SCARYYYY!
IT RAN AWAY!
WHOOSH
BAH

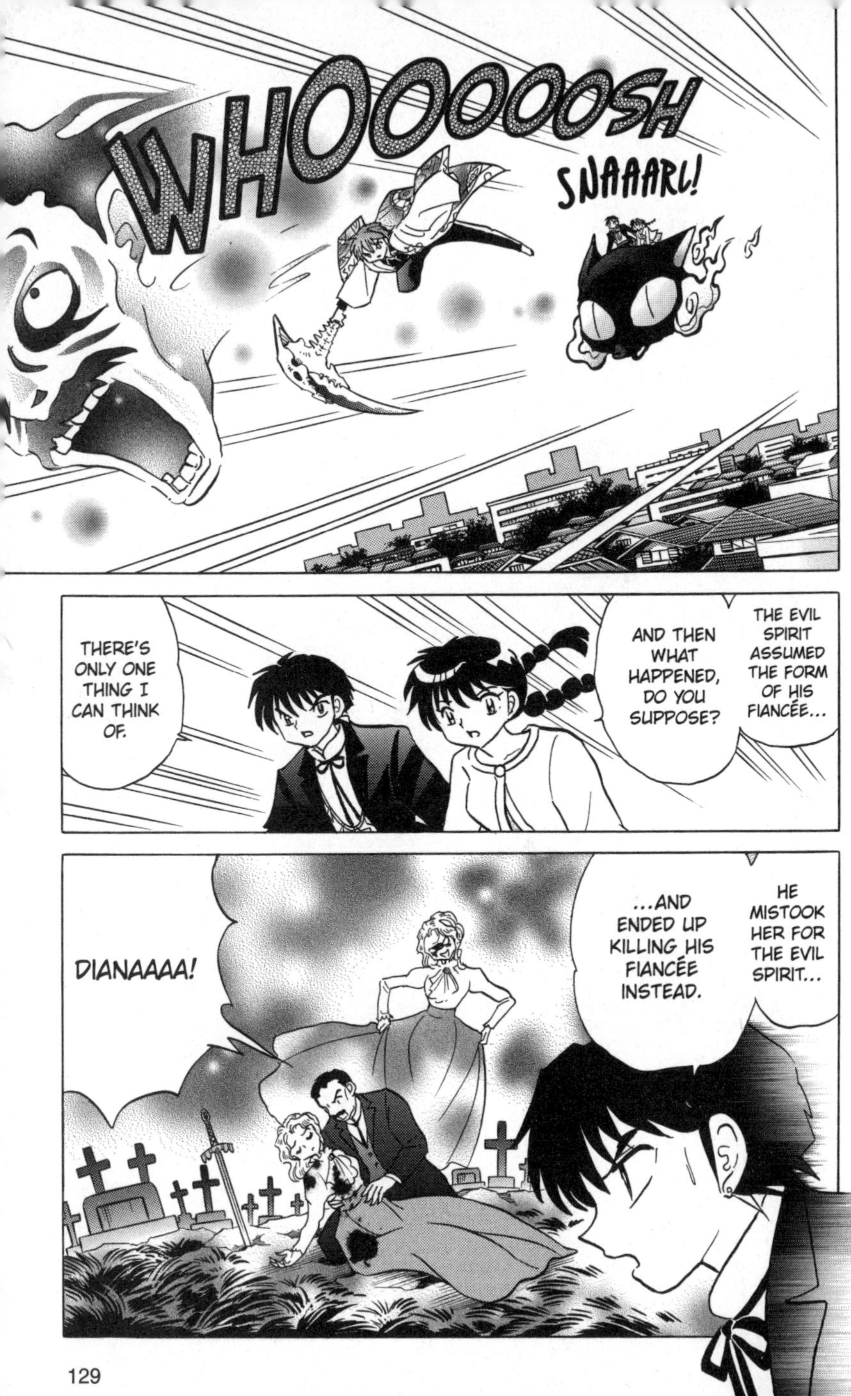
SNAAARL!
WHOOOOOOSH
THE EVIL SPIRIT ASSUMED THE FORM OF HIS FIANCÉE...
AND THEN WHAT HAPPENED, DO YOU SUPPOSE?
THERE'S ONLY ONE THING I CAN THINK OF.
HE MISTOOK HER FOR THE EVIL SPIRIT...
...AND ENDED UP KILLING HIS FIANCÉE INSTEAD.
DIANAAAA!

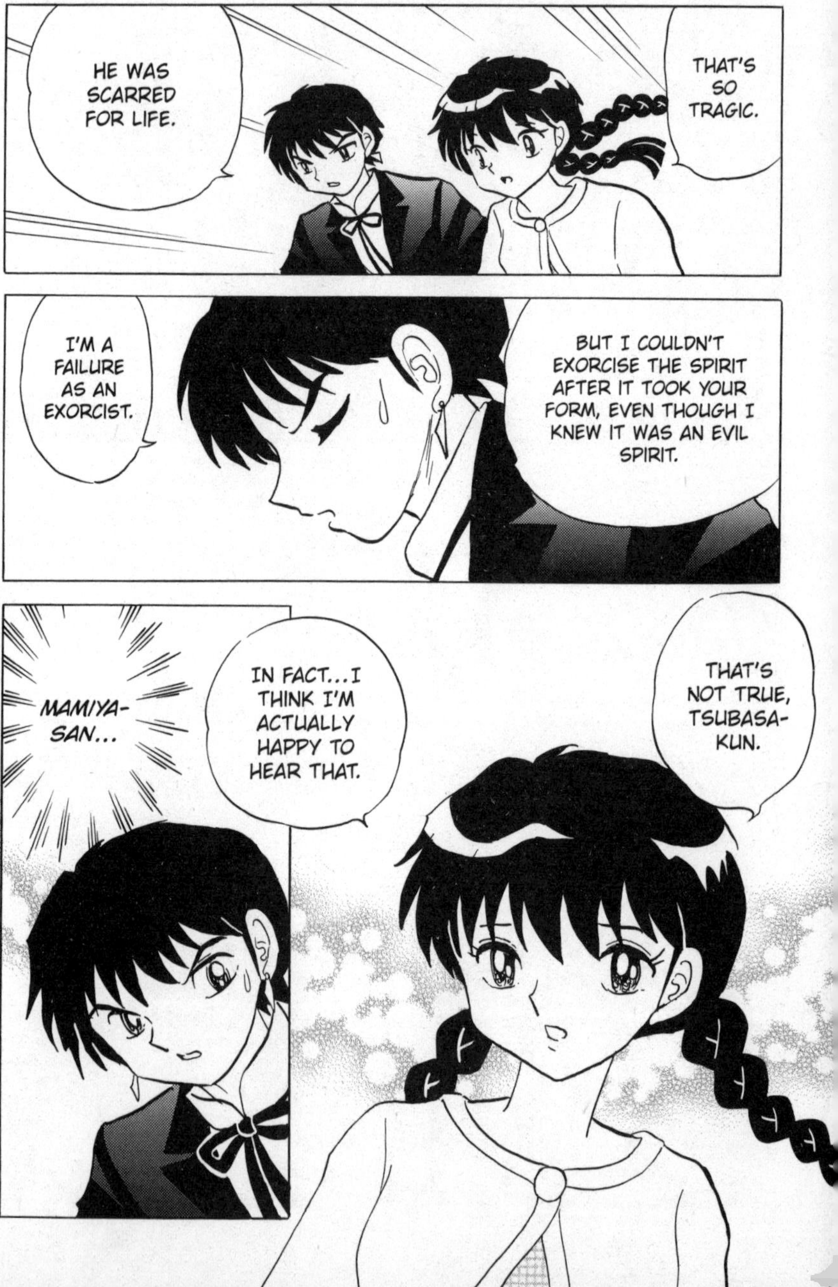
THAT'S SO TRAGIC.
HE WAS SCARRED FOR LIFE.
BUT I COULDN'T EXORCISE THE SPIRIT AFTER IT TOOK YOUR FORM, EVEN THOUGH I KNEW IT WAS AN EVIL SPIRIT.
I'M A FAILURE AS AN EXORCIST.
THAT'S NOT TRUE, TSUBASA-KUN.
IN FACT...I THINK I'M ACTUALLY HAPPY TO HEAR THAT.
MAMIYA-SAN...

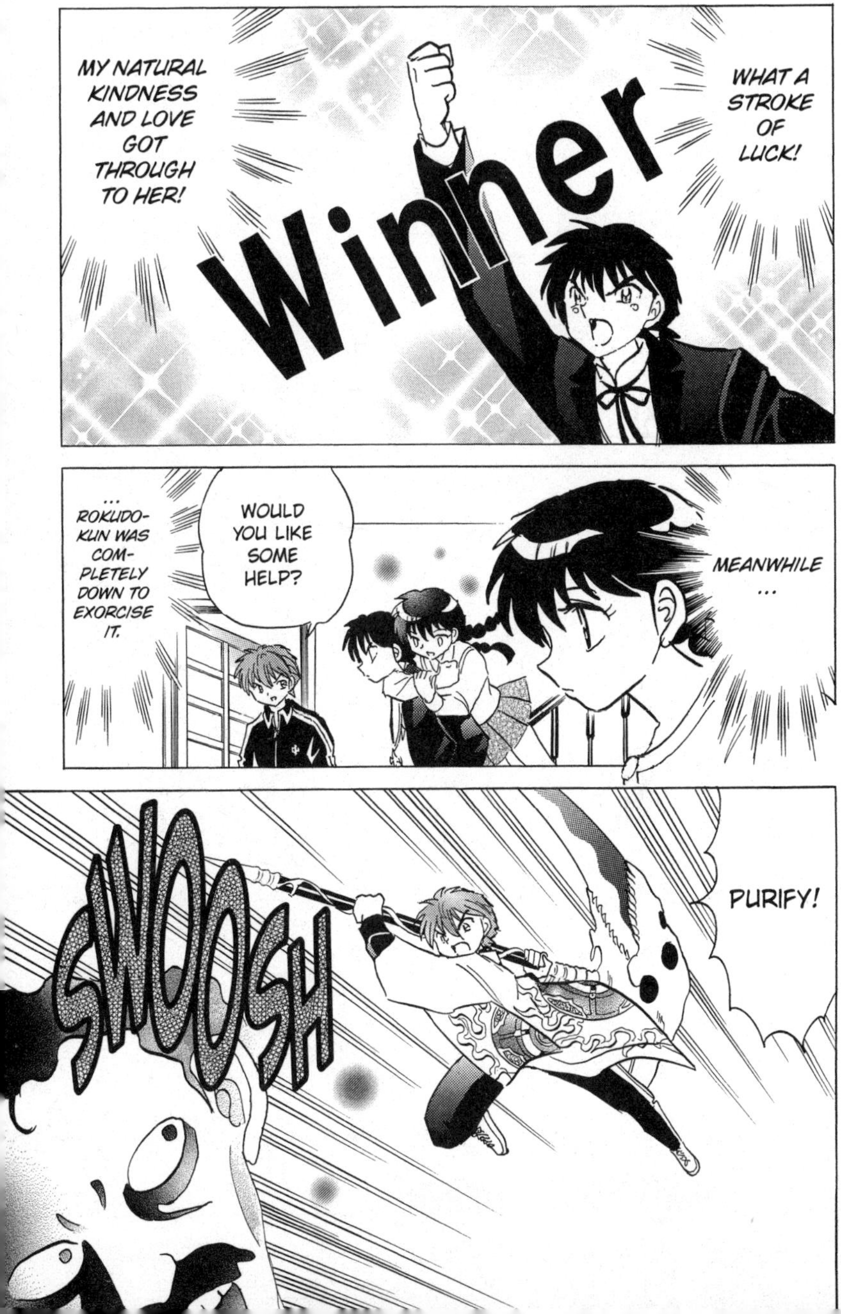
WHAT A STROKE OF LUCK!
MY NATURAL KINDNESS AND LOVE GOT THROUGH TO HER!
Winner
MEANWHILE ...
WOULD YOU LIKE SOME HELP?
... ROKUDO-KUN WAS COMPLETELY DOWN TO EXORCISE IT.
PURIFY!
SWOOSH

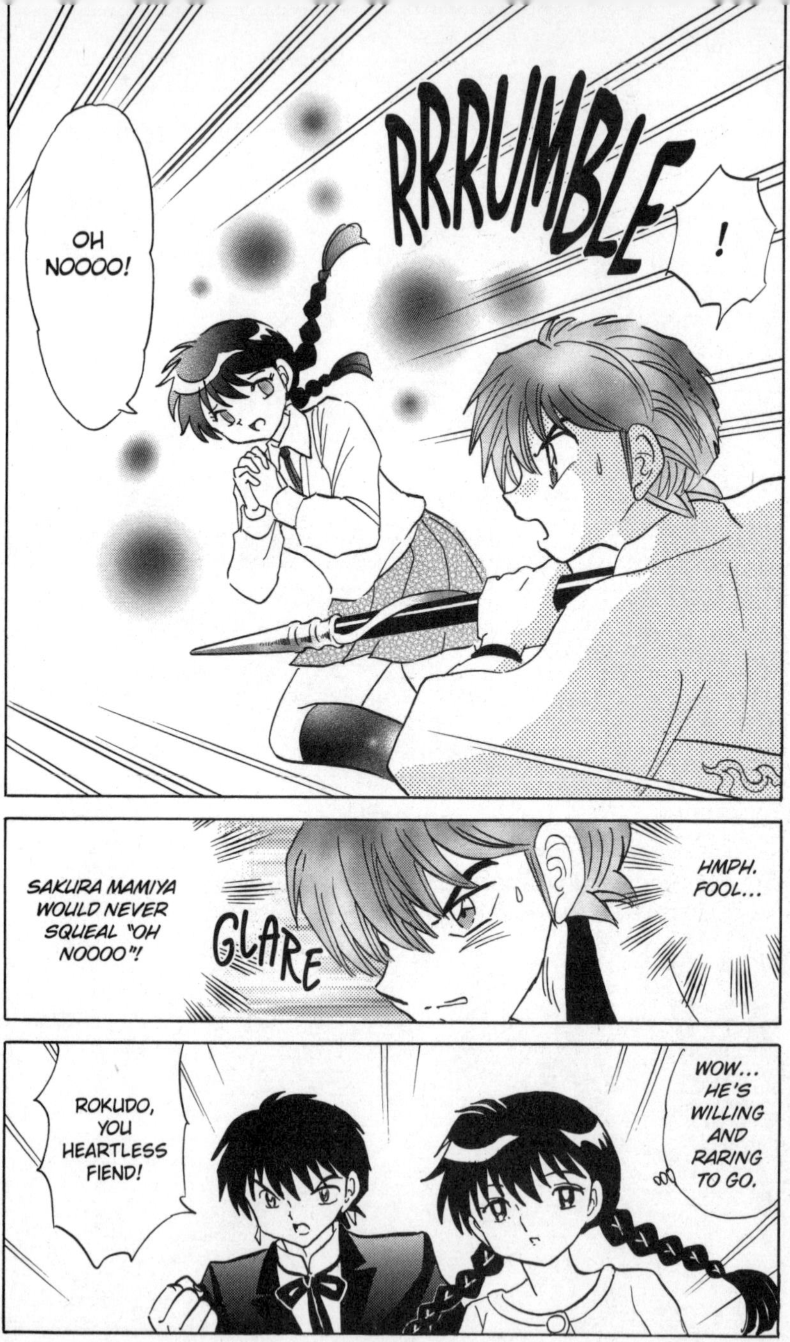
!
RRRUMBLE
OH NOOOO!
HMPH. FOOL...
GLARE
SAKURA MAMIYA WOULD NEVER SQUEAL "OH NOOOO"!
WOW... HE'S WILLING AND RARING TO GO.
ROKUDO, YOU HEARTLESS FIEND!

CHAPTER 386: I DON'T KNOW WHY

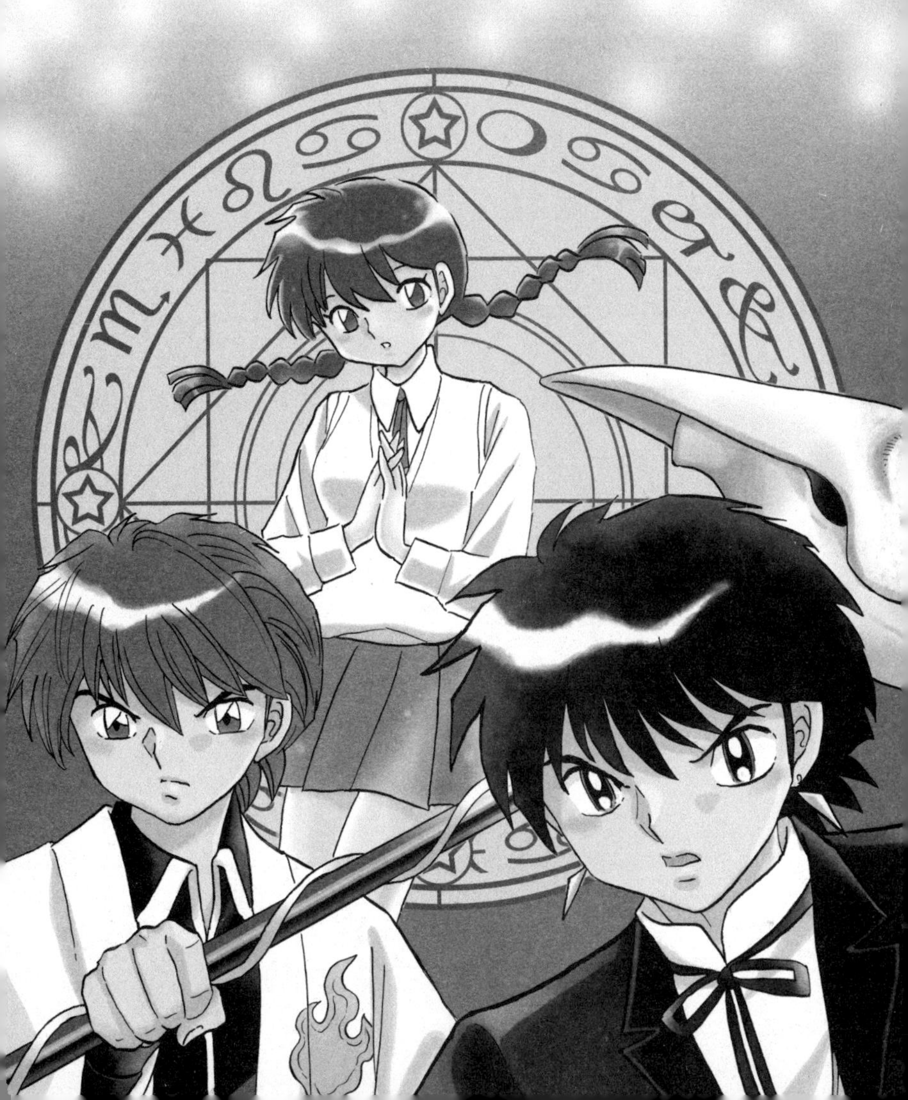

りんね

RIN-NE

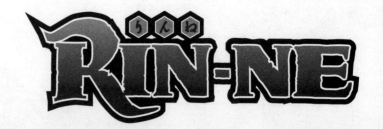

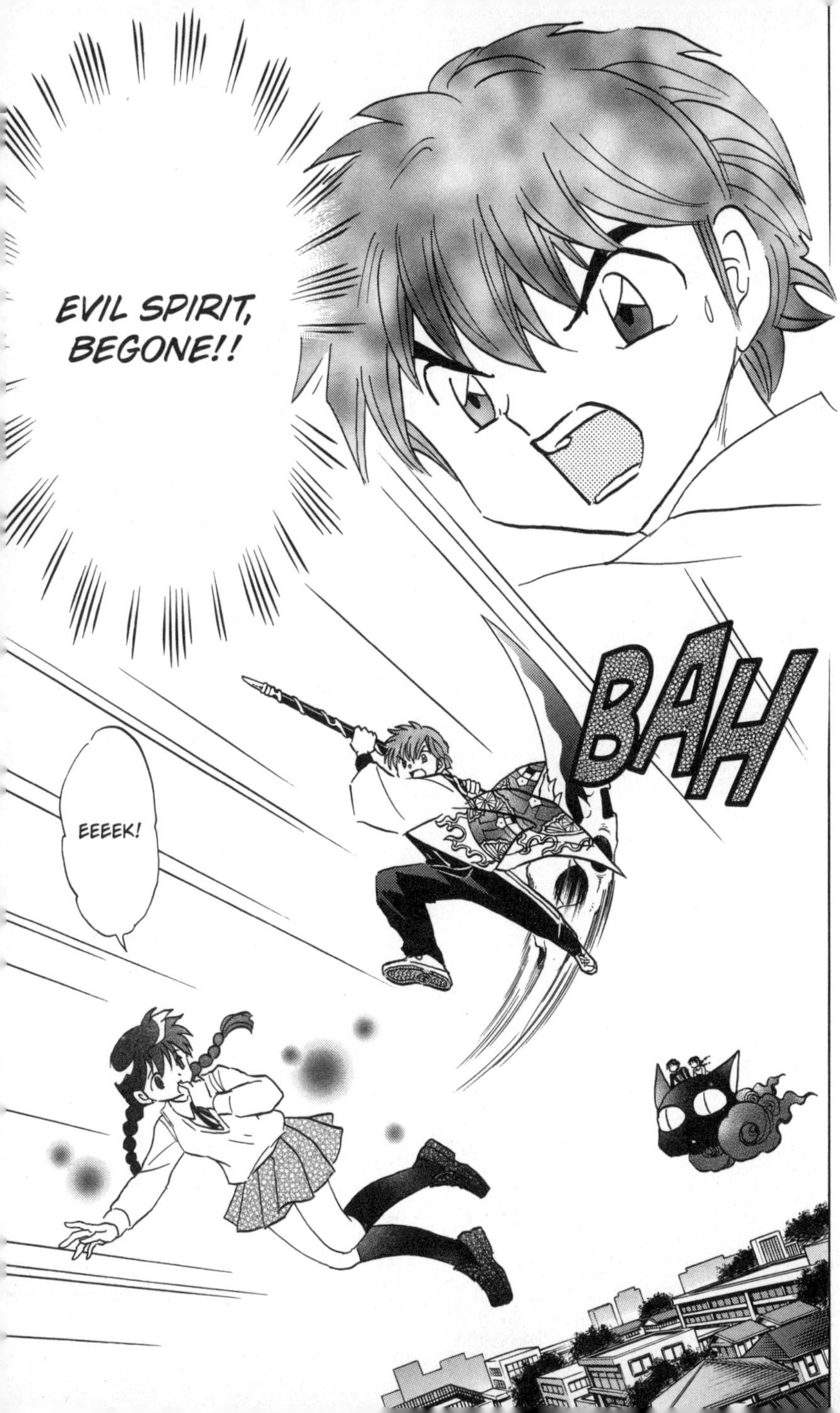
EVIL SPIRIT, BEGONE!!
BAH
EEEEK!

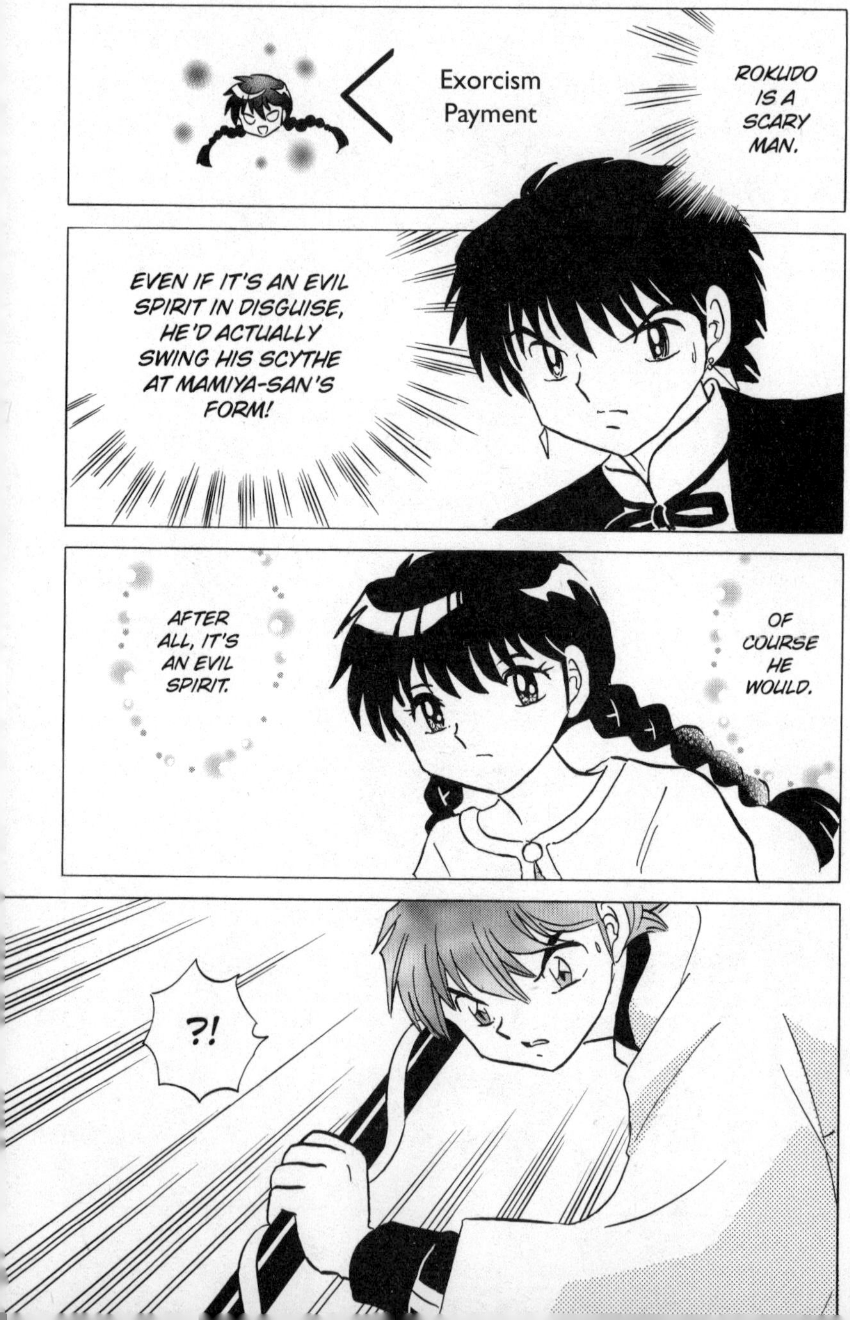
ROKUDO IS A SCARY MAN.
Exorcism Payment
EVEN IF IT'S AN EVIL SPIRIT IN DISGUISE, HE'D ACTUALLY SWING HIS SCYTHE AT MAMIYA-SAN'S FORM!
OF COURSE HE WOULD.
AFTER ALL, IT'S AN EVIL SPIRIT.
?!

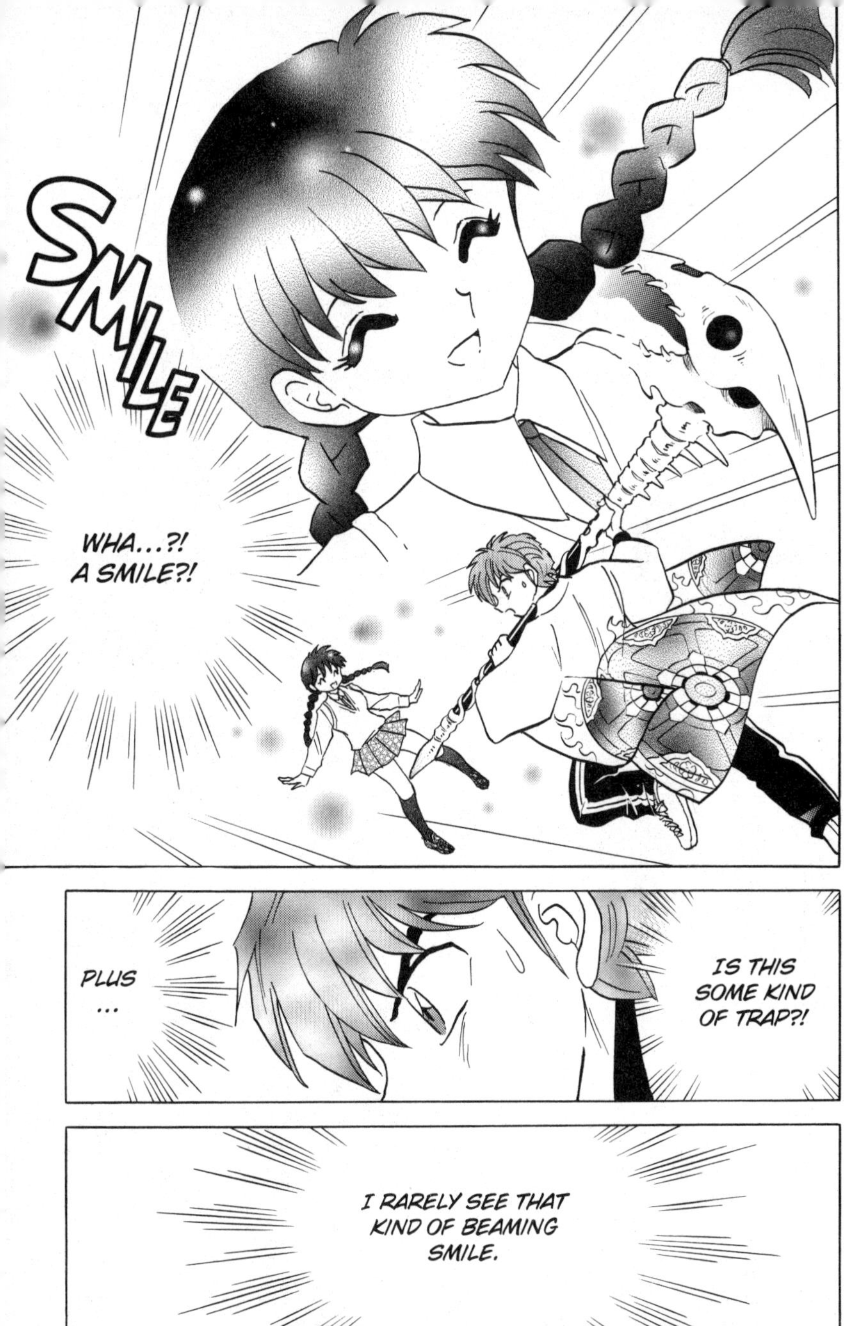
SMILE
WHA...?! A SMILE?!
IS THIS SOME KIND OF TRAP?!
PLUS ...
I RARELY SEE THAT KIND OF BEAMING SMILE.

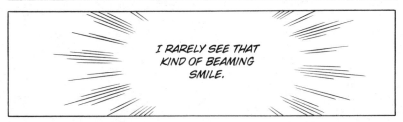

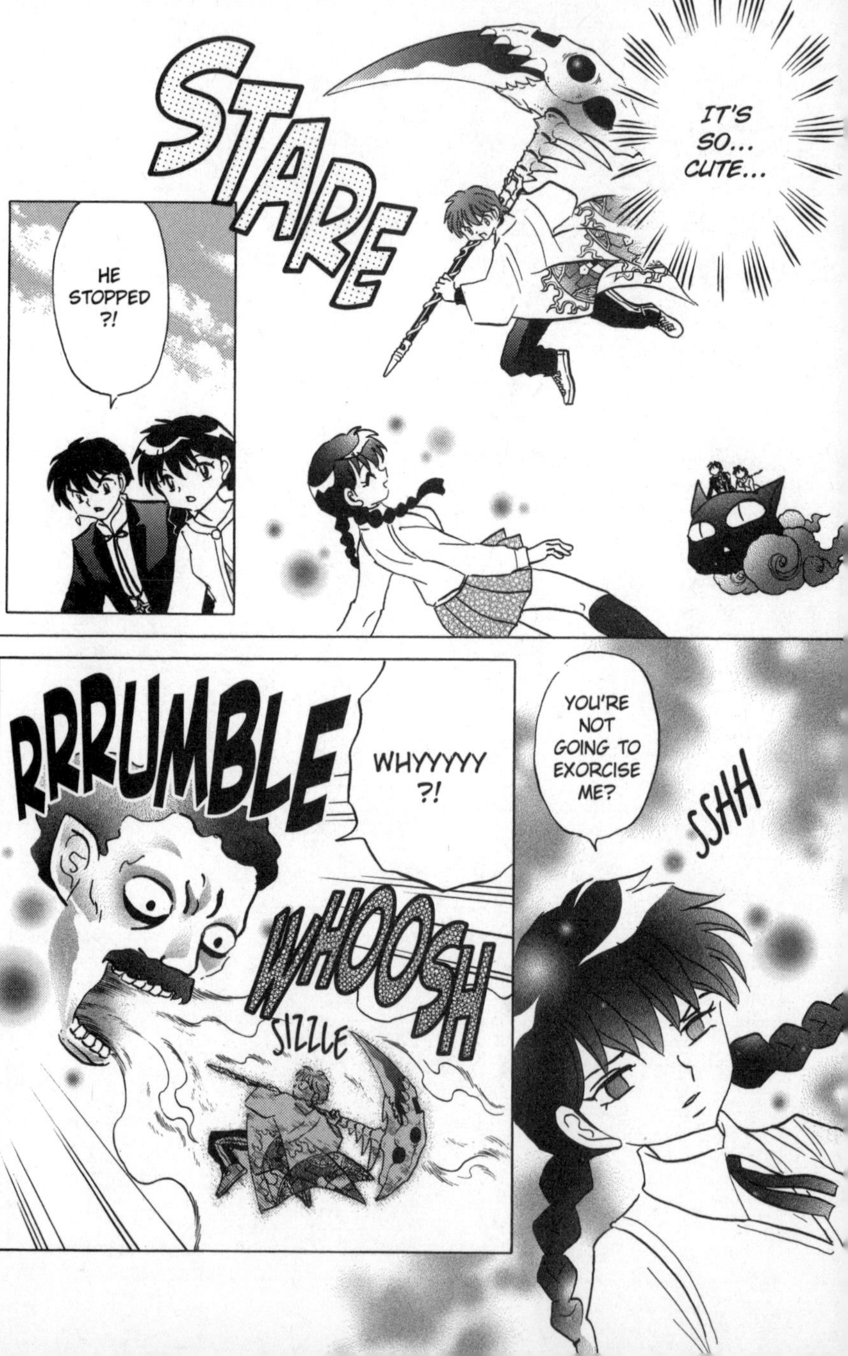
IT'S SO... CUTE...
STARE
HE STOPPED ?!
YOU'RE NOT GOING TO EXORCISE ME?
SSHH
WHYYYYY ?!
RRRUMBLE
WHOOSH
SIZZLE

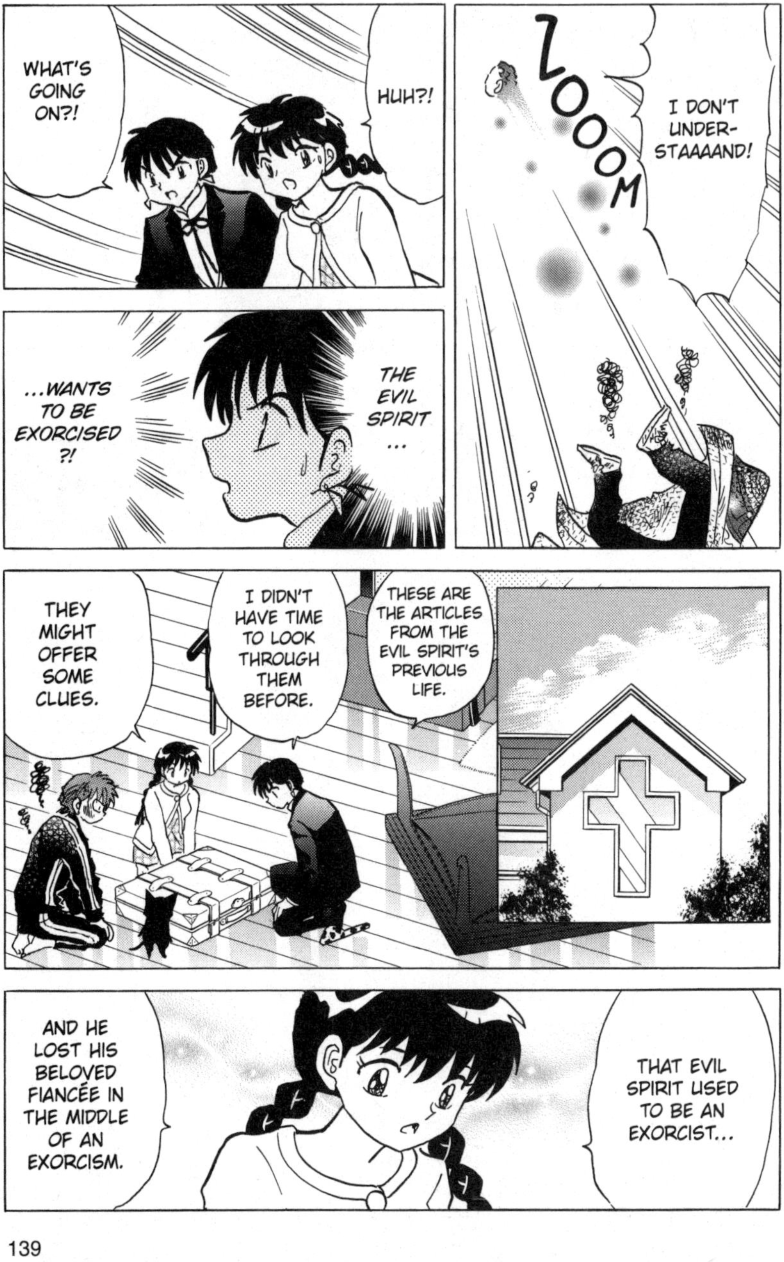
I DON'T UNDER-STAAAAND!
ZOOOM
HUH?!
WHAT'S GOING ON?!
THE EVIL SPIRIT...
...WANTS TO BE EXORCISED?!
THESE ARE THE ARTICLES FROM THE EVIL SPIRIT'S PREVIOUS LIFE.
I DIDN'T HAVE TIME TO LOOK THROUGH THEM BEFORE.
THEY MIGHT OFFER SOME CLUES.
THAT EVIL SPIRIT USED TO BE AN EXORCIST...
AND HE LOST HIS BELOVED FIANCÉE IN THE MIDDLE OF AN EXORCISM.

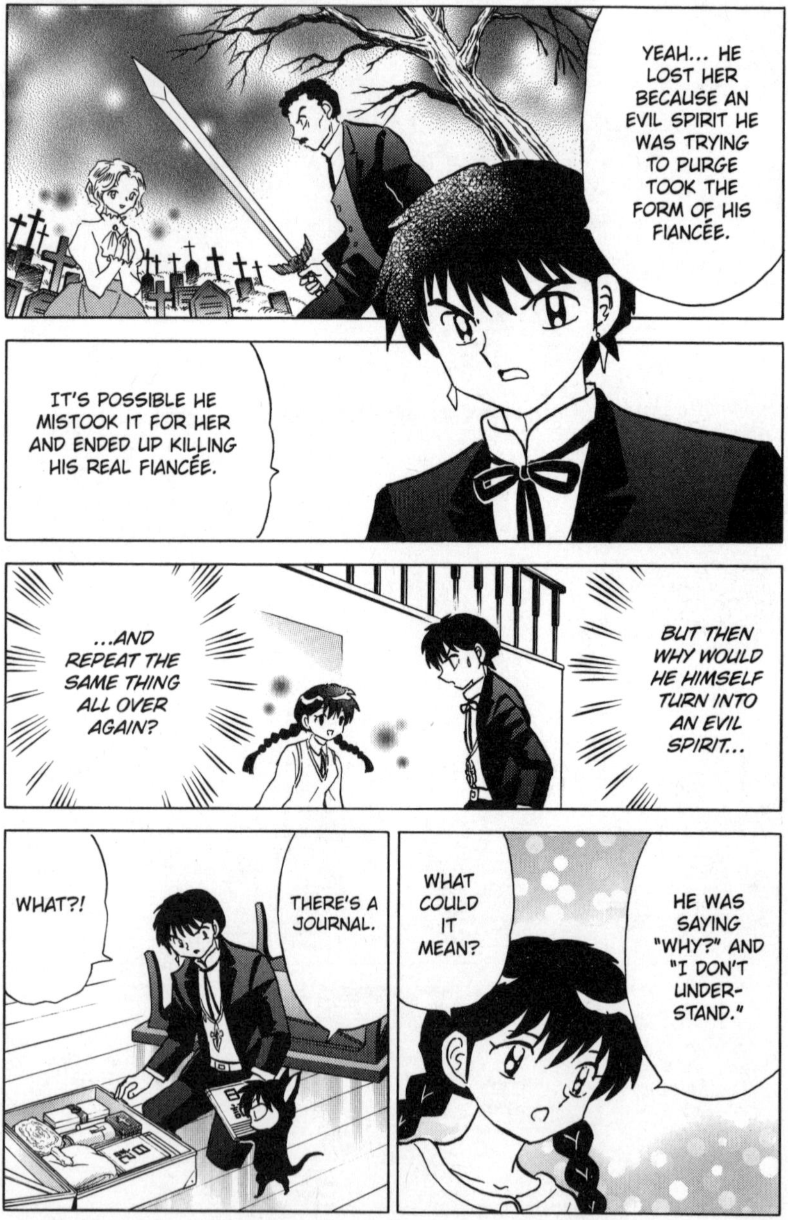
YEAH... HE LOST HER BECAUSE AN EVIL SPIRIT HE WAS TRYING TO PURGE TOOK THE FORM OF HIS FIANCÉE.
IT'S POSSIBLE HE MISTOOK IT FOR HER AND ENDED UP KILLING HIS REAL FIANCÉE.
BUT THEN WHY WOULD HE HIMSELF TURN INTO AN EVIL SPIRIT...
...AND REPEAT THE SAME THING ALL OVER AGAIN?
HE WAS SAYING "WHY?" AND "I DON'T UNDER-STAND."
WHAT COULD IT MEAN?
THERE'S A JOURNAL.
WHAT?!

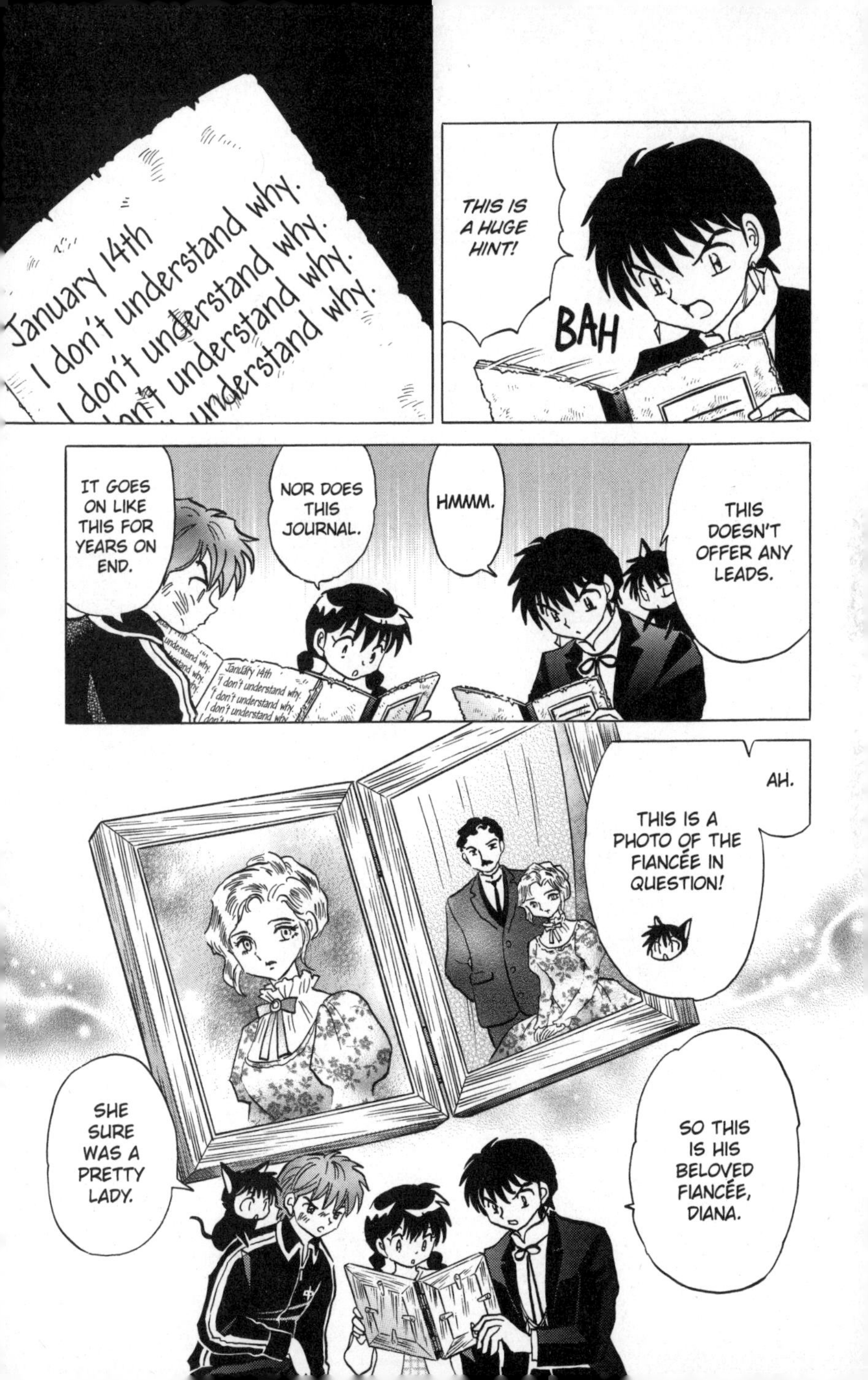
THIS IS A HUGE HINT!
BAH
January 14th
I don't understand why.
I don't understand why.
I don't understand why.
understand why.
THIS DOESN'T OFFER ANY LEADS.
HMMM.
NOR DOES THIS JOURNAL.
IT GOES ON LIKE THIS FOR YEARS ON END.
AH.
THIS IS A PHOTO OF THE FIANCÉE IN QUESTION!
SO THIS IS HIS BELOVED FIANCÉE, DIANA.
SHE SURE WAS A PRETTY LADY.

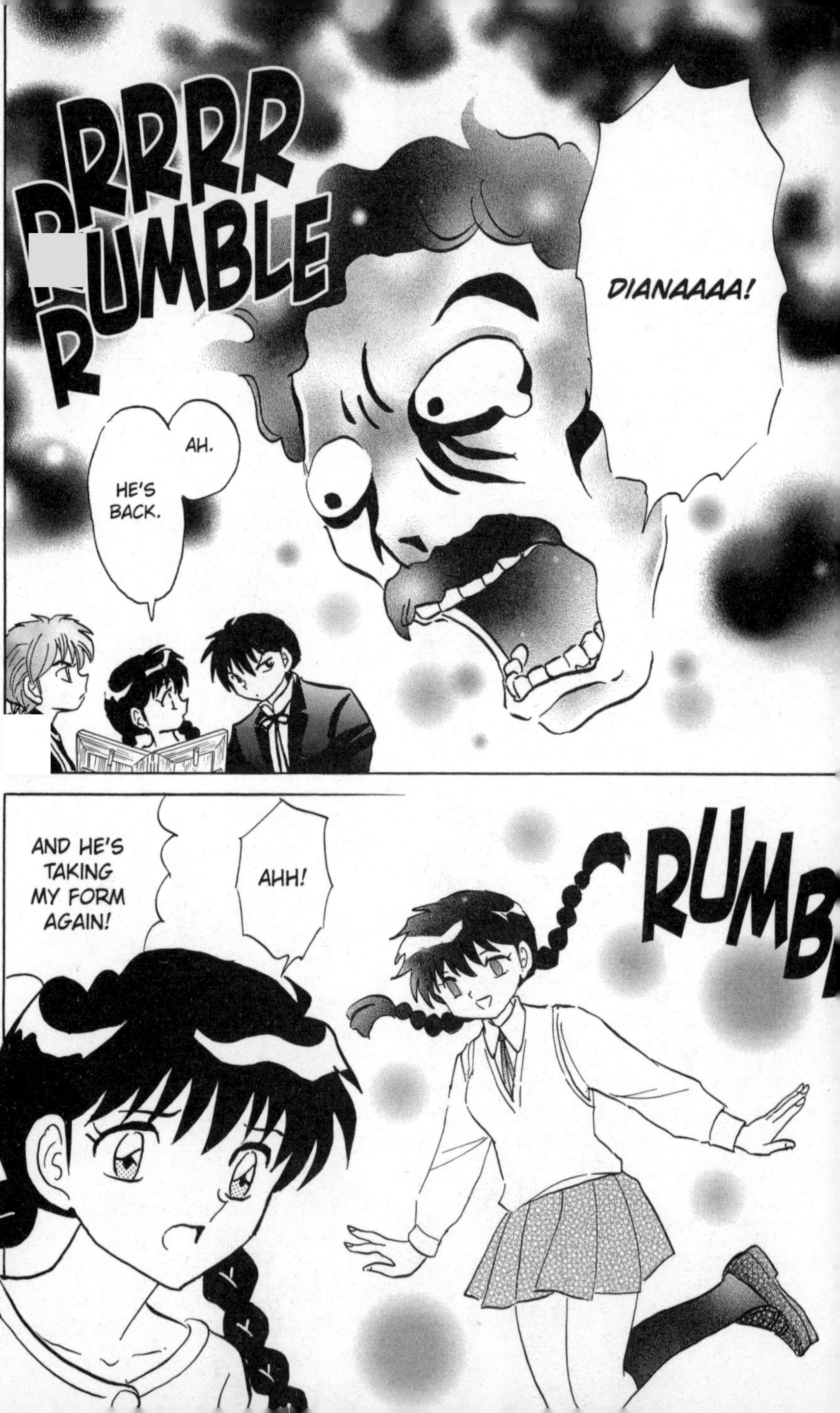
DIANAAAA!
RRRRR RUMBLE
AH.
HE'S BACK.
RUMB
AHH!
AND HE'S TAKING MY FORM AGAIN!

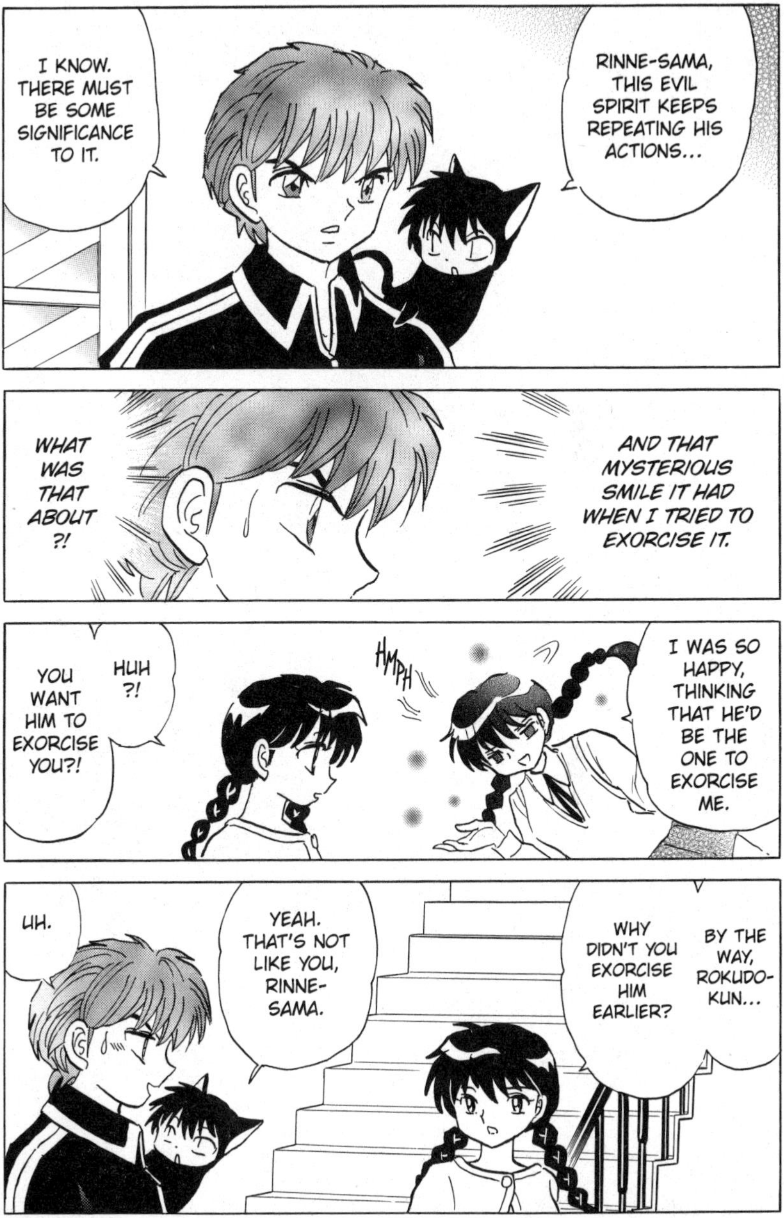
RINNE-SAMA, THIS EVIL SPIRIT KEEPS REPEATING HIS ACTIONS...
I KNOW. THERE MUST BE SOME SIGNIFICANCE TO IT.
AND THAT MYSTERIOUS SMILE IT HAD WHEN I TRIED TO EXORCISE IT.
WHAT WAS THAT ABOUT ?!
I WAS SO HAPPY, THINKING THAT HE'D BE THE ONE TO EXORCISE ME.
HMPH
HUH ?!
YOU WANT HIM TO EXORCISE YOU?!
BY THE WAY, ROKUDO-KUN...
WHY DIDN'T YOU EXORCISE HIM EARLIER?
YEAH. THAT'S NOT LIKE YOU, RINNE-SAMA.
UH.

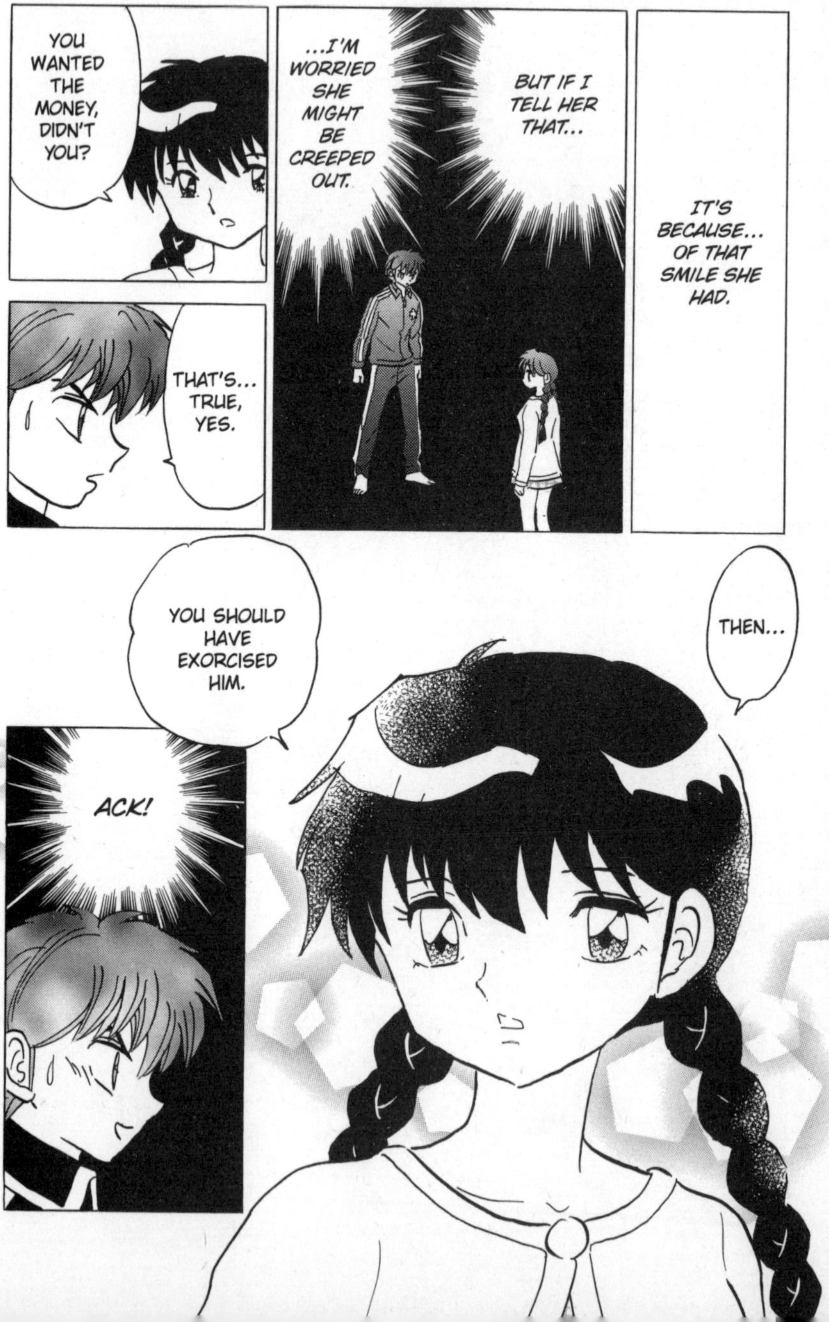
IT'S BECAUSE... OF THAT SMILE SHE HAD.
BUT IF I TELL HER THAT...
...I'M WORRIED SHE MIGHT BE CREEPED OUT.
YOU WANTED THE MONEY, DIDN'T YOU?
THAT'S... TRUE, YES.
THEN...
YOU SHOULD HAVE EXORCISED HIM.
ACK!

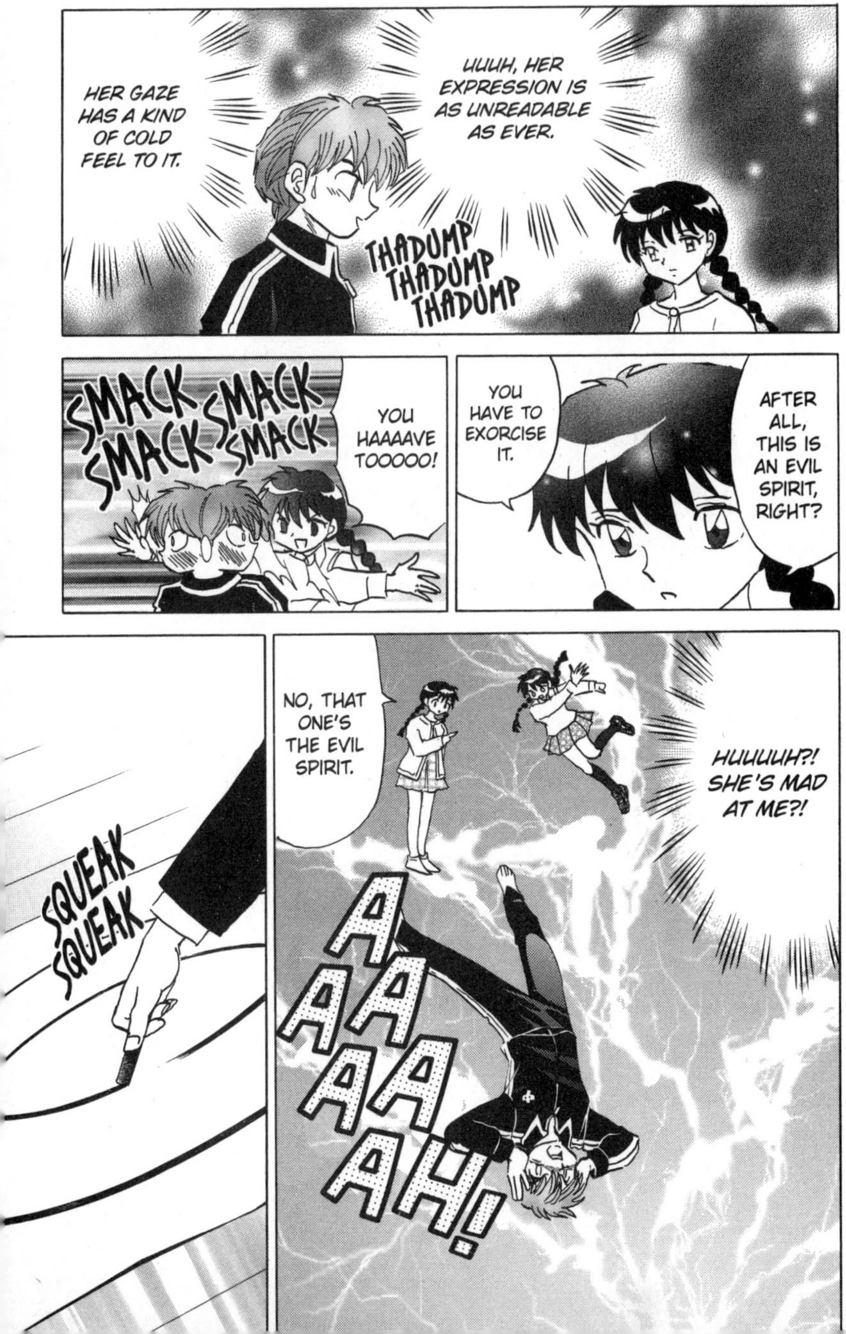
UUUH, HER EXPRESSION IS AS UNREADABLE AS EVER.
HER GAZE HAS A KIND OF COLD FEEL TO IT.
THADUMP THADUMP THADUMP
AFTER ALL, THIS IS AN EVIL SPIRIT, RIGHT?
YOU HAVE TO EXORCISE IT.
YOU HAAAAVE TOOOOO!
SMACK SMACK SMACK SMACK
HUUUUH?! SHE'S MAD AT ME?!
NO, THAT ONE'S THE EVIL SPIRIT.
AAAAAAAH!
SQUEAK SQUEAK

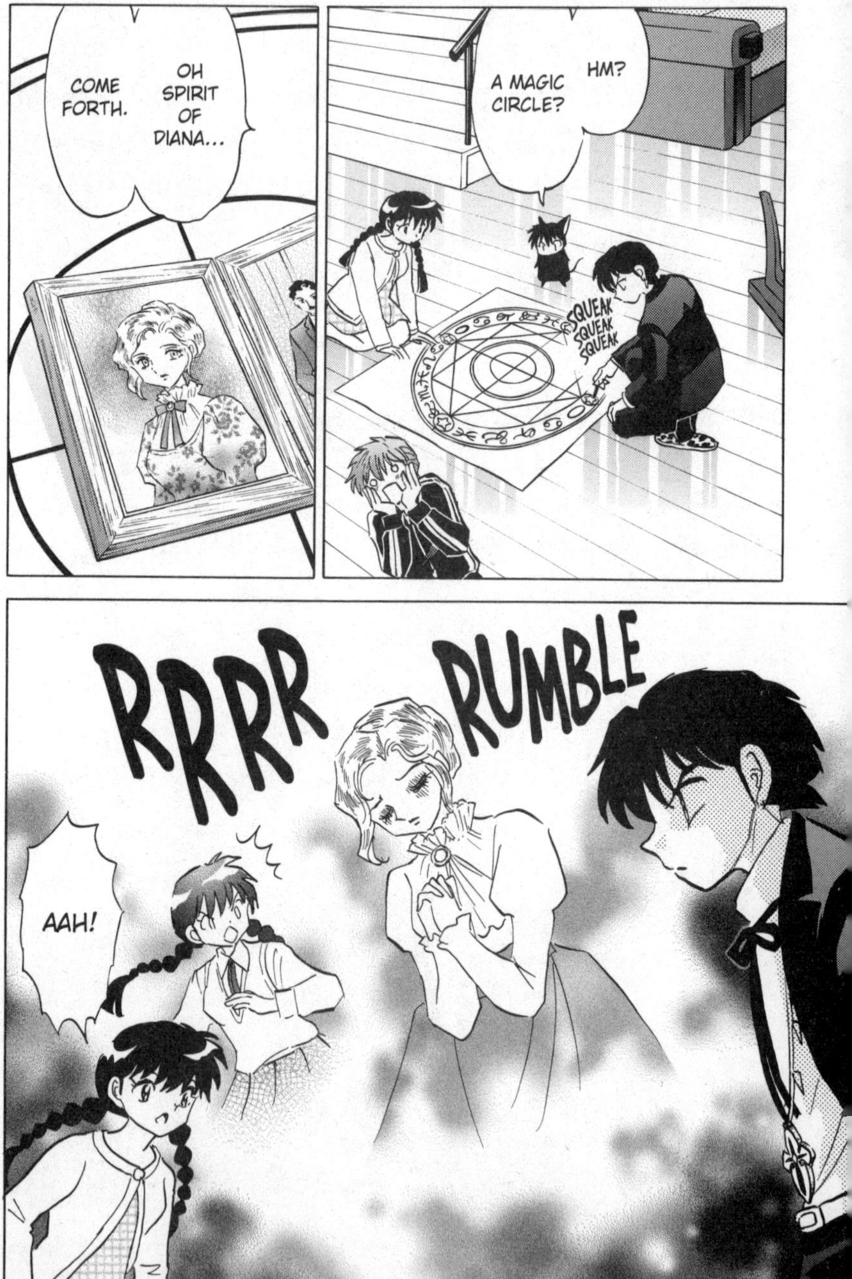
HM?
A MAGIC CIRCLE?
SQUEAK SQUEAK SQUEAK
OH SPIRIT OF DIANA...
COME FORTH.
RUMBLE
RRRR
AAH!

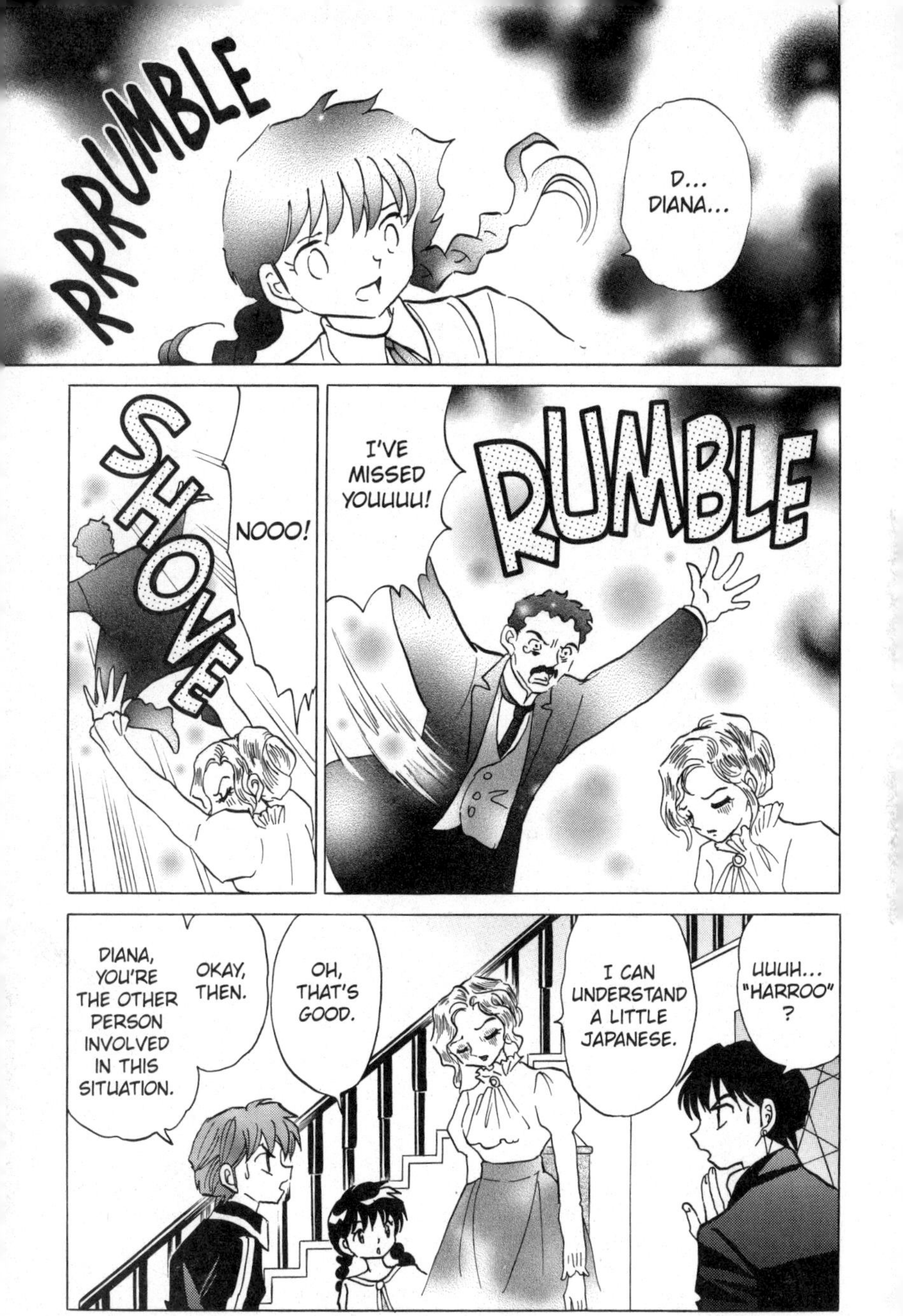
D... DIANA...
PRRUMBLE
RUMBLE
I'VE MISSED YOUUUU!
NOOO!
SHOVE
UUUH... "HARROO" ?
I CAN UNDERSTAND A LITTLE JAPANESE.
OH, THAT'S GOOD.
OKAY, THEN.
DIANA, YOU'RE THE OTHER PERSON INVOLVED IN THIS SITUATION.

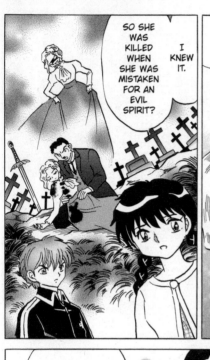

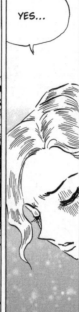

WERE YOU HURT BY THE MAN YOU WERE GOING TO MARRY AS HE WAS EXORCISING AN EVIL SPIRIT?!
YES...
SO SHE WAS KILLED WHEN SHE WAS MISTAKEN FOR AN EVIL SPIRIT? I KNEW IT.
WHAT ARE YOU TALKING ABOUT?
I EXORCISED THE EVIL SPIRIT, HAVE NO DOUBT ABOUT IT.
DONT LIE.
IT'S NOT A LIE.
YEAH.
IT'S NOT A LIE.
HOW CAN THAT BE?!

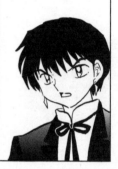

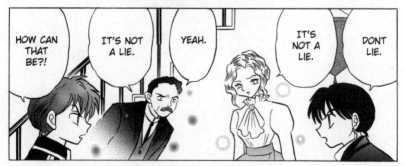

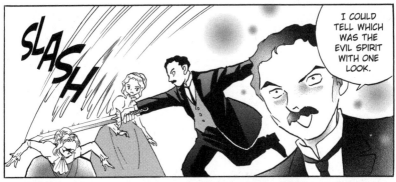

I COULD TELL WHICH WAS THE EVIL SPIRIT WITH ONE LOOK.
SLASH
SMACK SMACK SMACK
SMASH
UUUH...
AND YOU DID ALL THAT RIGHT IN FRONT OF DIANA-SAN?
HE BEAT "HER" TO A PULP BEFORE MY VERY EYES.
IT WAS A THOROUGH THRASHING.
AND THEN, IMMEDIATELY FOLLOWING THE SUCCESSFUL PURGING OF THE EVIL SPIRIT...

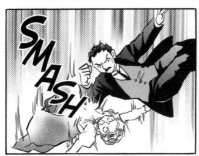

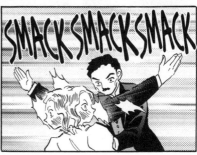

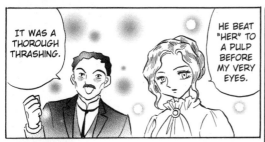

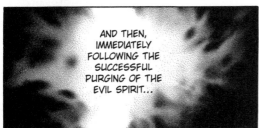

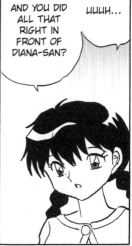

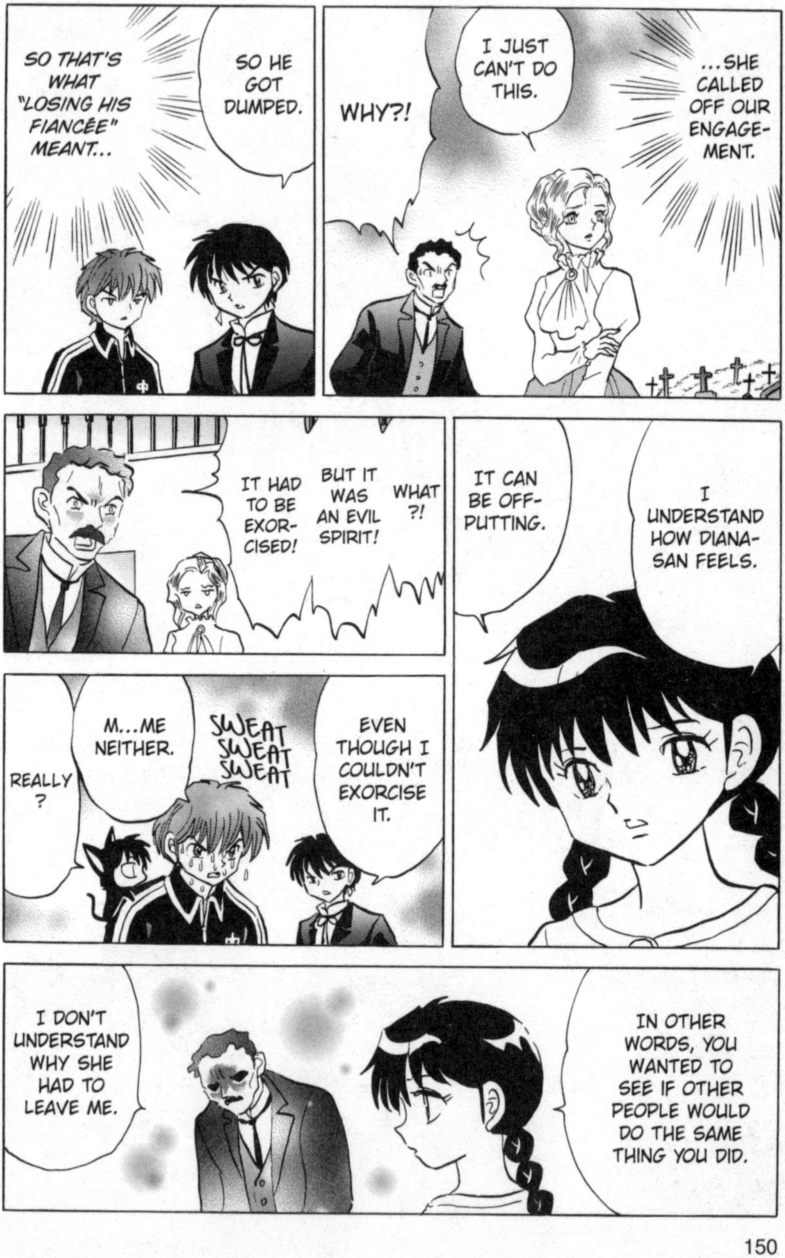
...SHE CALLED OFF OUR ENGAGEMENT.
I JUST CAN'T DO THIS.
WHY?!
SO HE GOT DUMPED.
SO THAT'S WHAT "LOSING HIS FIANCÉE" MEANT...
I UNDERSTAND HOW DIANA-SAN FEELS.
IT CAN BE OFF-PUTTING.
WHAT?!
BUT IT WAS AN EVIL SPIRIT!
IT HAD TO BE EXORCISED!
EVEN THOUGH I COULDN'T EXORCISE IT.
SWEAT SWEAT SWEAT
M...ME NEITHER.
REALLY?
IN OTHER WORDS, YOU WANTED TO SEE IF OTHER PEOPLE WOULD DO THE SAME THING YOU DID.
I DON'T UNDERSTAND WHY SHE HAD TO LEAVE ME.

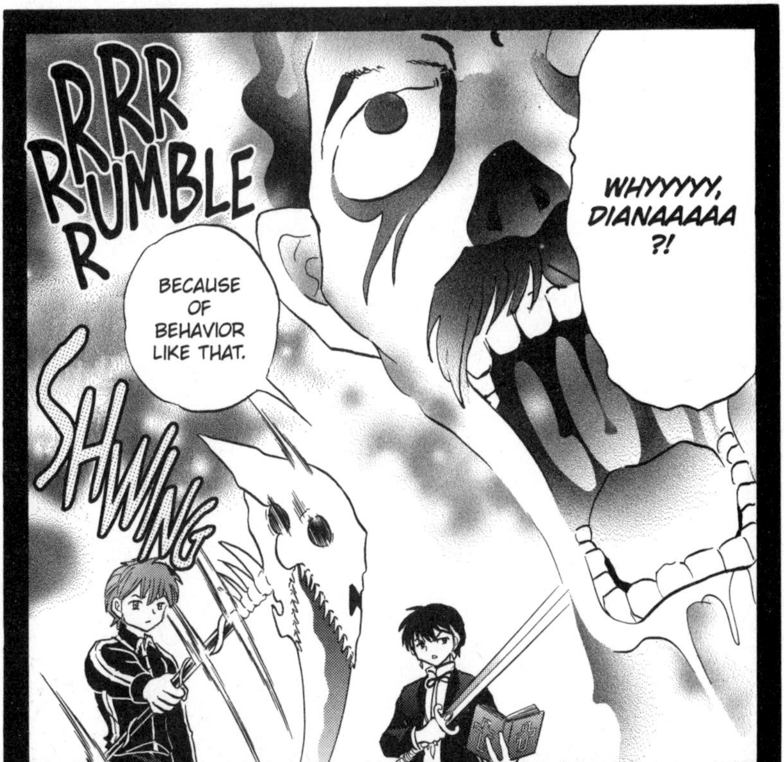
WHYYYYY, DIANAAAAA ?!
RRR RUMBLE
BECAUSE OF BEHAVIOR LIKE THAT.
SHWING

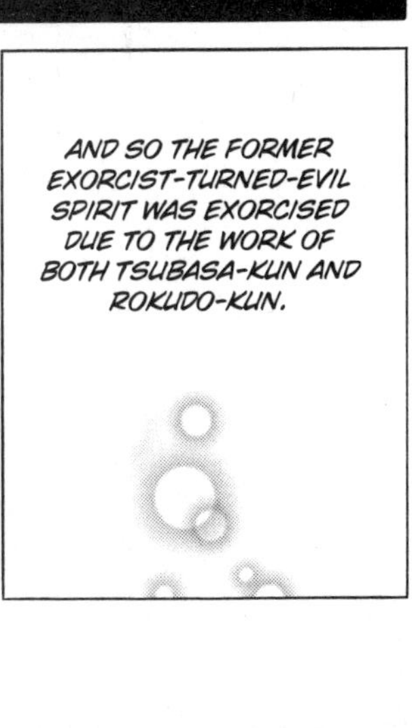
AND SO THE FORMER EXORCIST-TURNED-EVIL SPIRIT WAS EXORCISED DUE TO THE WORK OF BOTH TSUBASA-KUN AND ROKUDO-KUN.

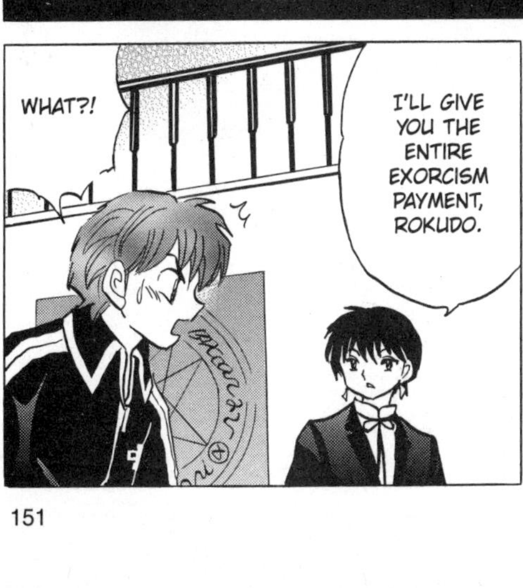
I'LL GIVE YOU THE ENTIRE EXORCISM PAYMENT, ROKUDO.
WHAT?!

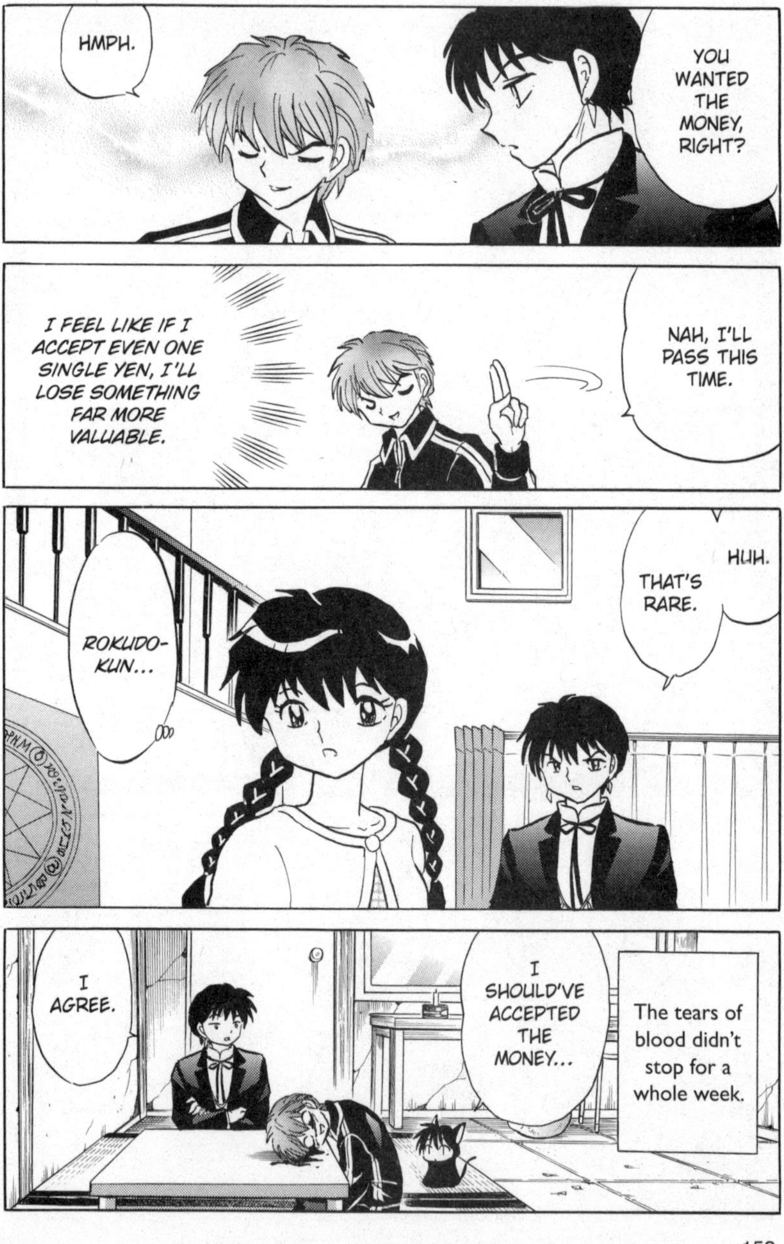
YOU WANTED THE MONEY, RIGHT?
HMPH.
NAH, I'LL PASS THIS TIME.
I FEEL LIKE IF I ACCEPT EVEN ONE SINGLE YEN, I'LL LOSE SOMETHING FAR MORE VALUABLE.
HUH.
THAT'S RARE.
ROKUDO-KUN...
The tears of blood didn't stop for a whole week.
I SHOULD'VE ACCEPTED THE MONEY...
I AGREE.

CHAPTER 387: RAPID JOB GROWTH

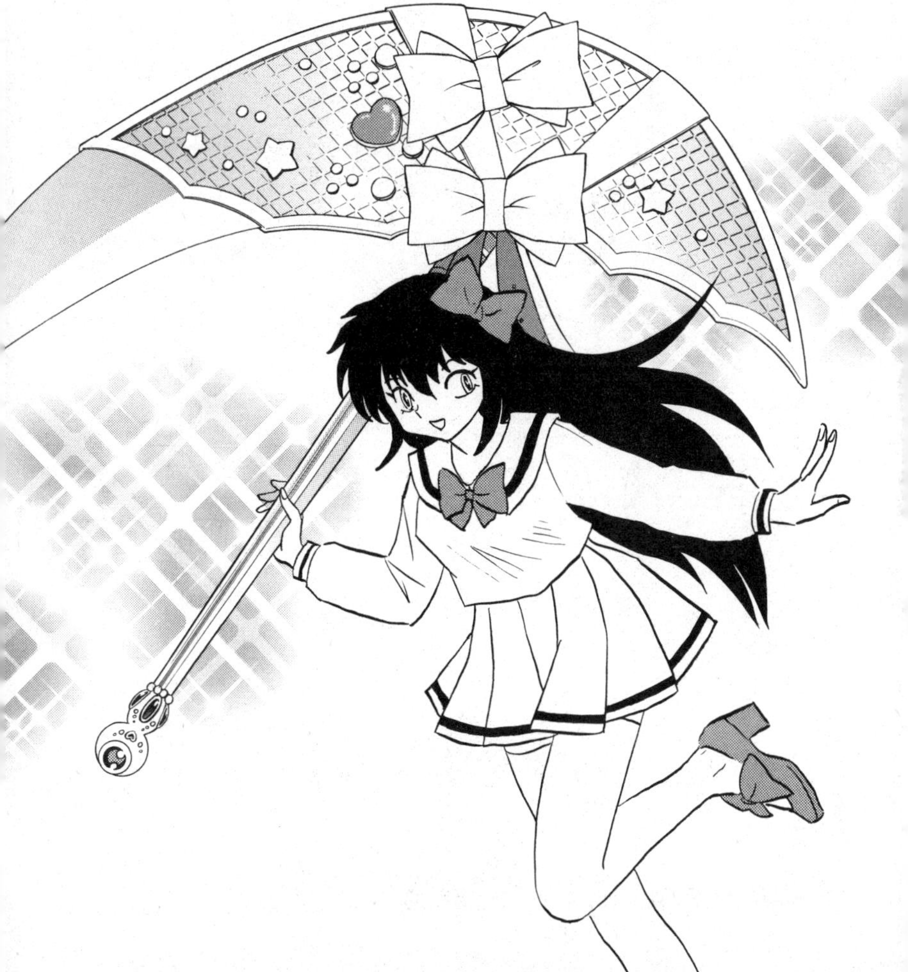

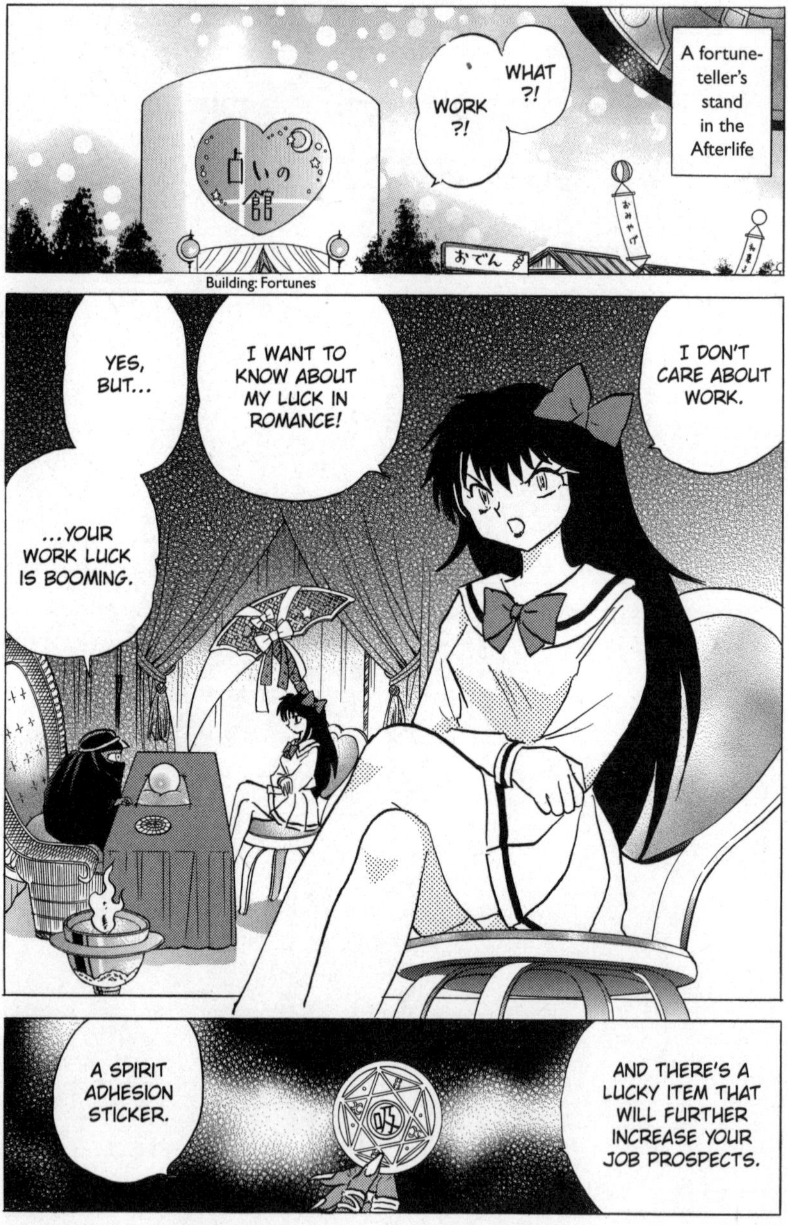
A fortune-teller's stand in the Afterlife
WHAT ?!
WORK ?!
占いの館
おでん
Building: Fortunes
I DON'T CARE ABOUT WORK.
I WANT TO KNOW ABOUT MY LUCK IN ROMANCE!
YES, BUT...
...YOUR WORK LUCK IS BOOMING.
AND THERE'S A LUCKY ITEM THAT WILL FURTHER INCREASE YOUR JOB PROSPECTS.
A SPIRIT ADHESION STICKER.

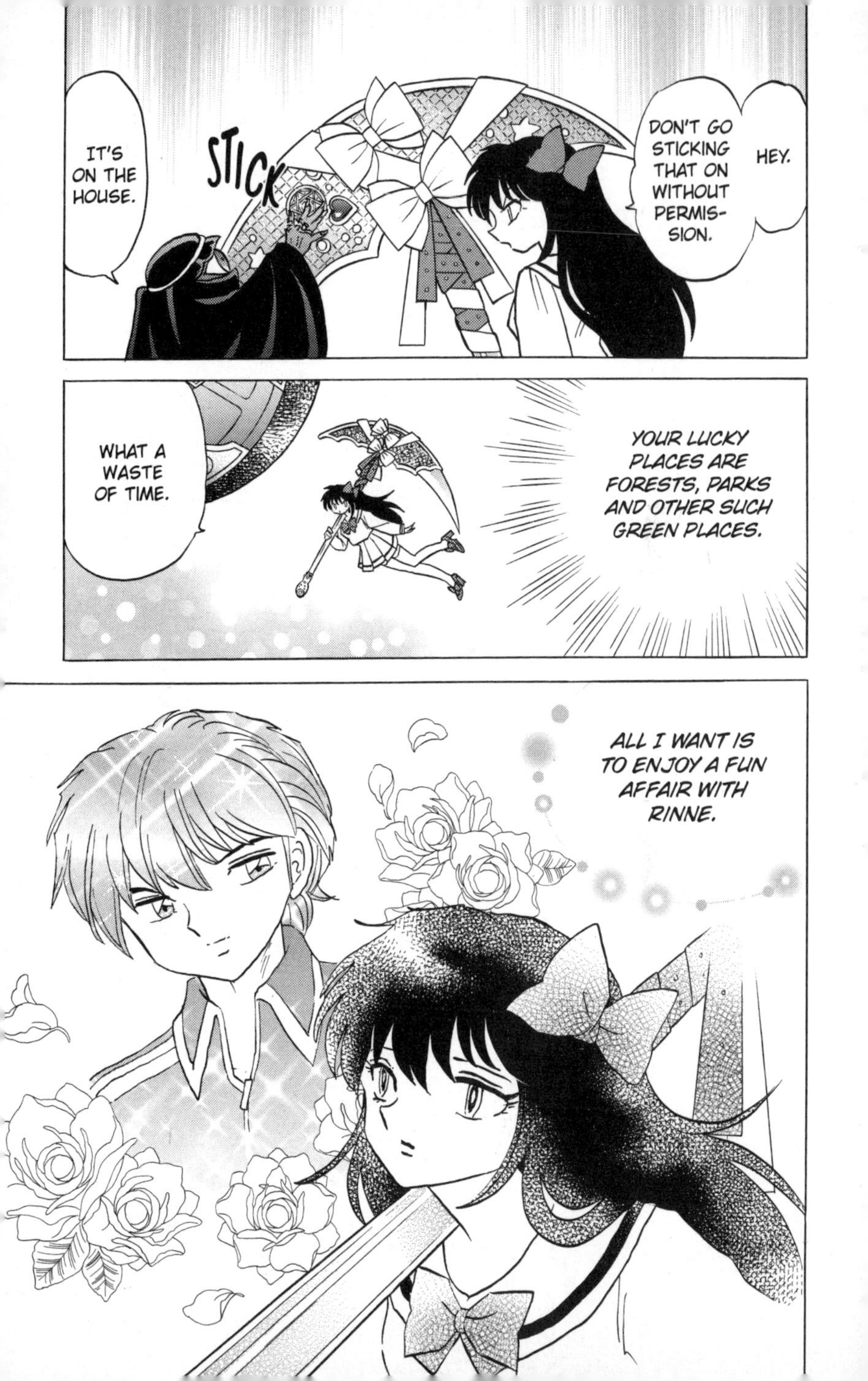
HEY.
DON'T GO STICKING THAT ON WITHOUT PERMIS-SION.
STICK
IT'S ON THE HOUSE.
YOUR LUCKY PLACES ARE FORESTS, PARKS AND OTHER SUCH GREEN PLACES.
WHAT A WASTE OF TIME.
ALL I WANT IS TO ENJOY A FUN AFFAIR WITH RINNE.

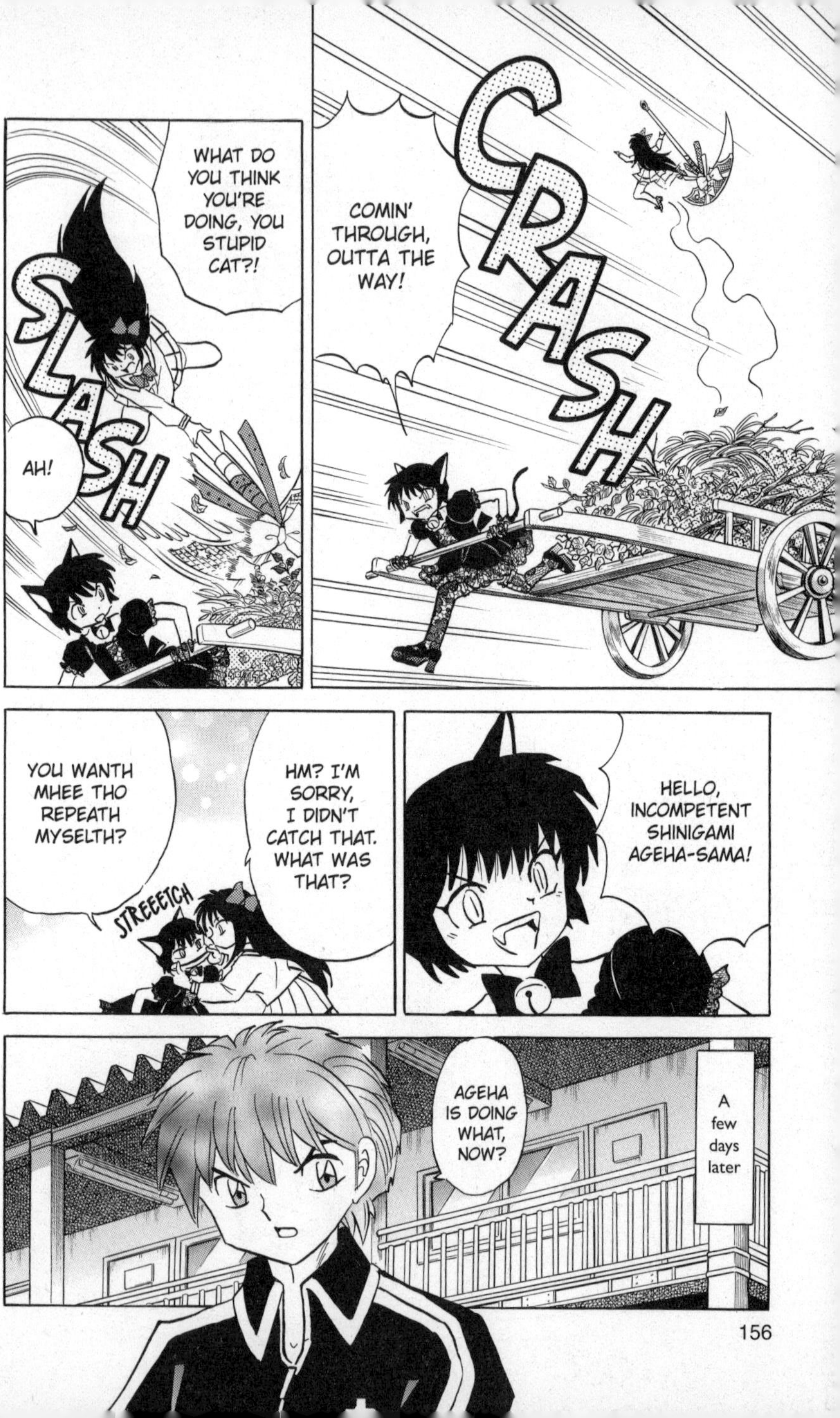
CRASH
COMIN' THROUGH, OUTTA THE WAY!
WHAT DO YOU THINK YOU'RE DOING, YOU STUPID CAT?!
SLASH
AH!
HELLO, INCOMPETENT SHINIGAMI AGEHA-SAMA!
HM? I'M SORRY, I DIDN'T CATCH THAT. WHAT WAS THAT?
YOU WANTH MHEE THO REPEATH MYSELTH?
STREEETCH
A few days later
AGEHA IS DOING WHAT, NOW?

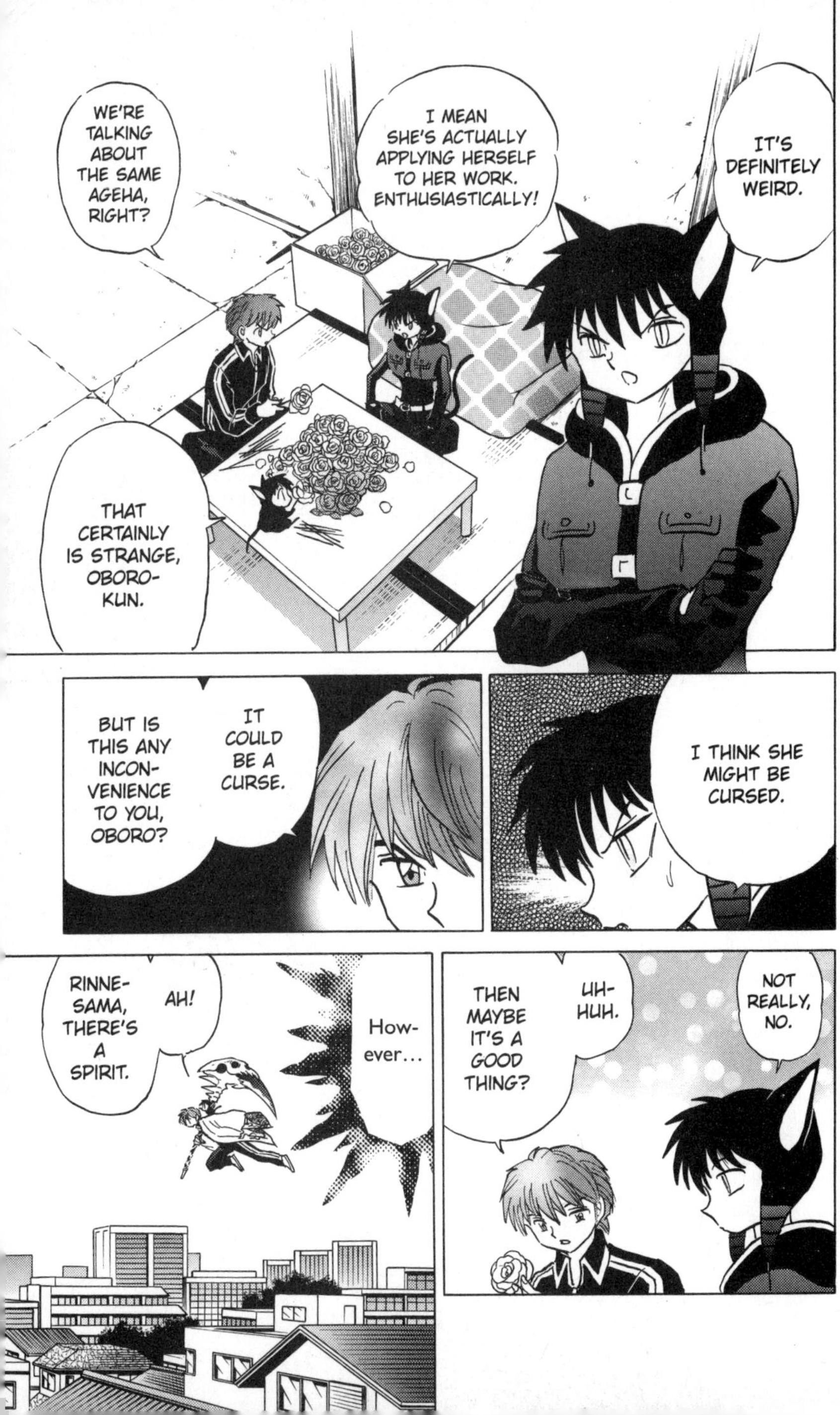
IT'S DEFINITELY WEIRD.
I MEAN SHE'S ACTUALLY APPLYING HERSELF TO HER WORK. ENTHUSIASTICALLY!
WE'RE TALKING ABOUT THE SAME AGEHA, RIGHT?
THAT CERTAINLY IS STRANGE, OBORO-KUN.
I THINK SHE MIGHT BE CURSED.
IT COULD BE A CURSE.
BUT IS THIS ANY INCONVENIENCE TO YOU, OBORO?
NOT REALLY, NO.
UH-HUH.
THEN MAYBE IT'S A GOOD THING?
However…
AH!
RINNE-SAMA, THERE'S A SPIRIT.

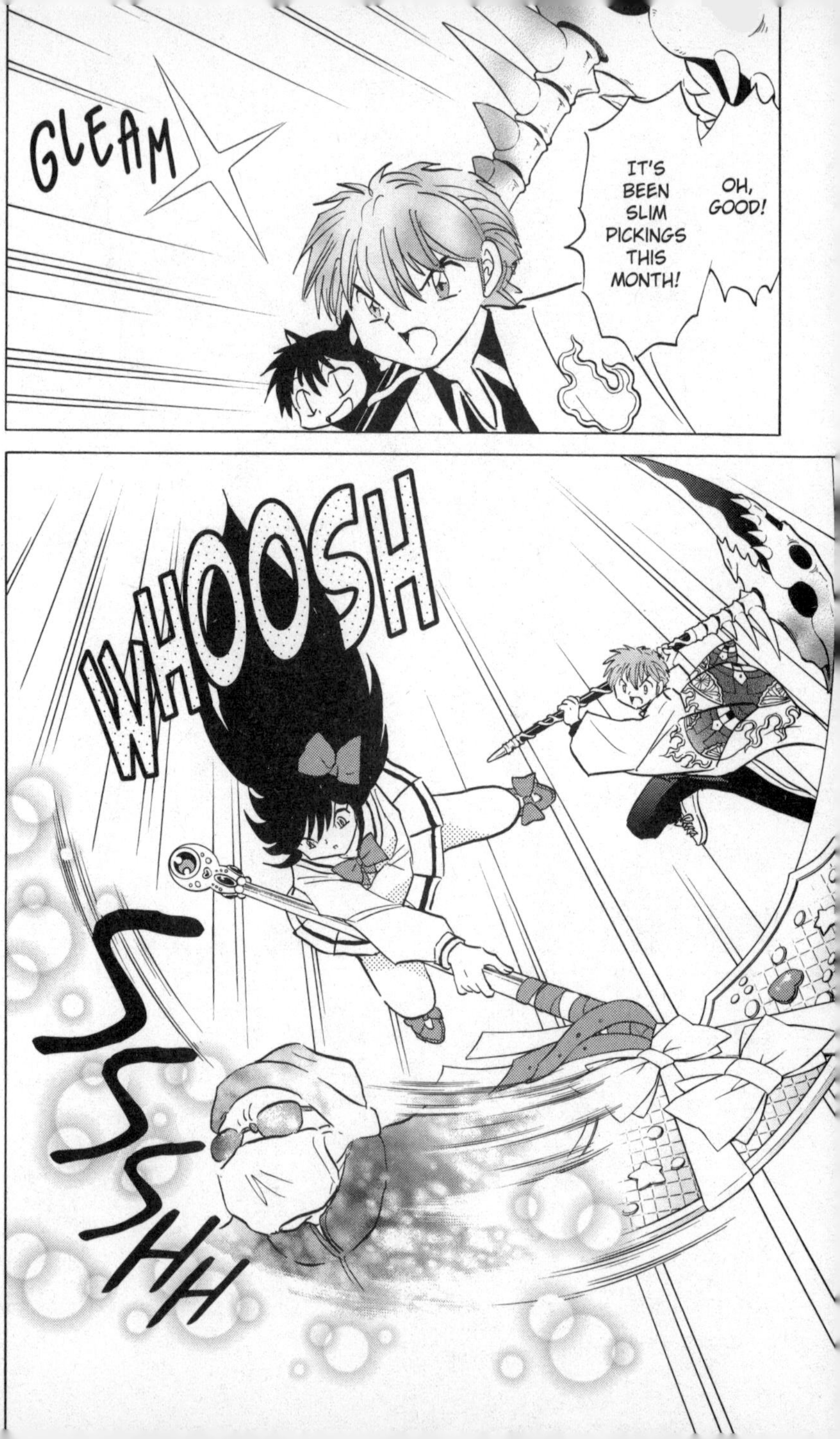
OH, GOOD!
IT'S BEEN SLIM PICKINGS THIS MONTH!
GLEAM
WHOOSH
SSSHH

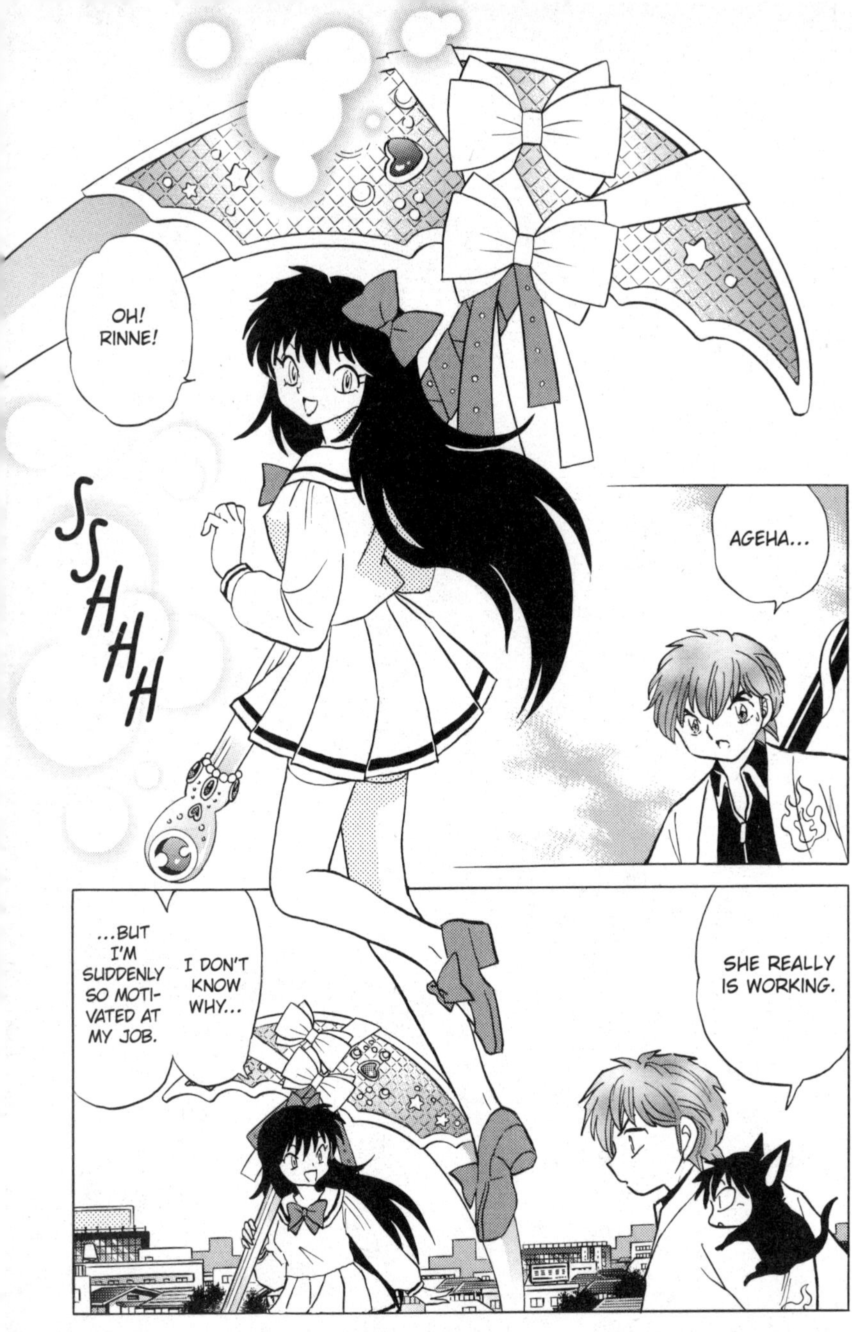
OH! RINNE!
SSHHH
AGEHA...
SHE REALLY IS WORKING.
I DON'T KNOW WHY...
...BUT I'M SUDDENLY SO MOTI-VATED AT MY JOB.

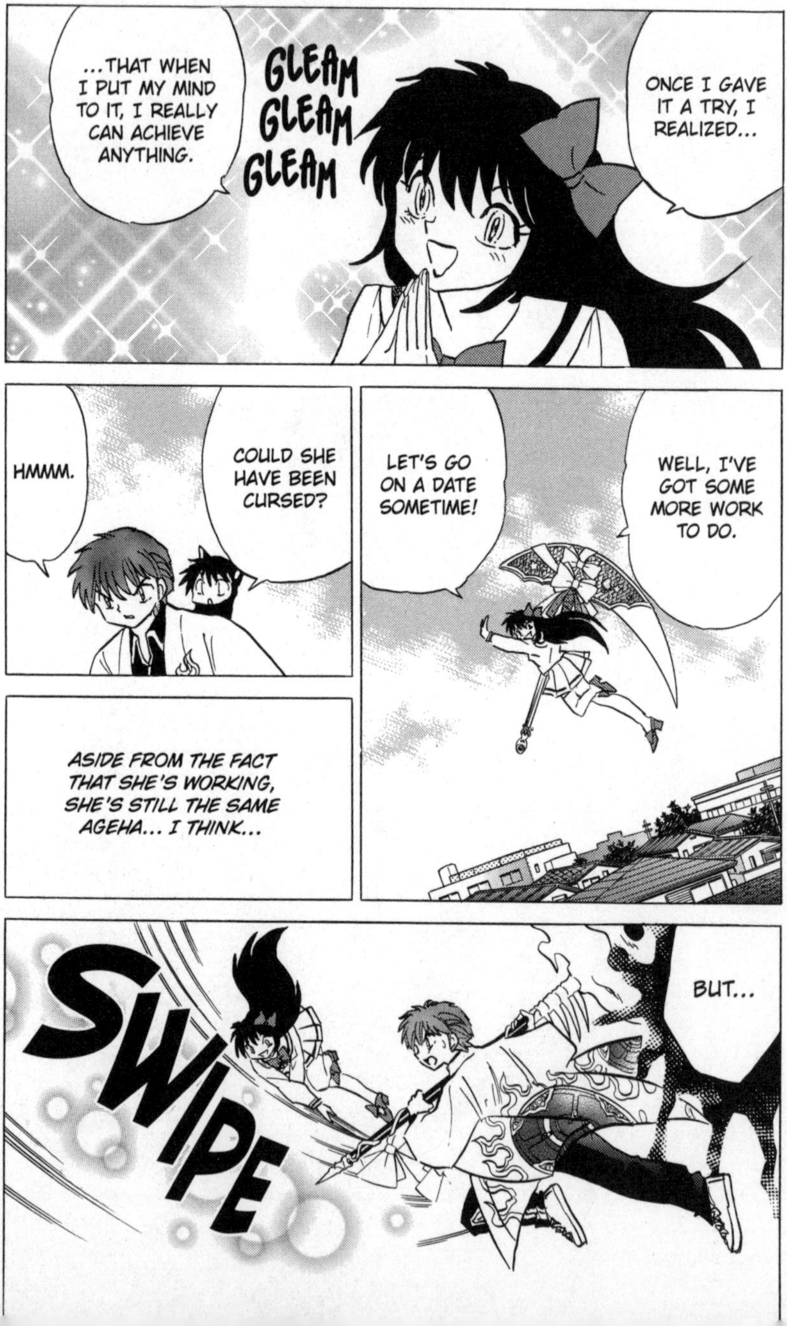
ONCE I GAVE IT A TRY, I REALIZED...
GLEAM GLEAM GLEAM
...THAT WHEN I PUT MY MIND TO IT, I REALLY CAN ACHIEVE ANYTHING.
WELL, I'VE GOT SOME MORE WORK TO DO.
LET'S GO ON A DATE SOMETIME!
COULD SHE HAVE BEEN CURSED?
HMMM.
ASIDE FROM THE FACT THAT SHE'S WORKING, SHE'S STILL THE SAME AGEHA... I THINK...
BUT...
SWIPE

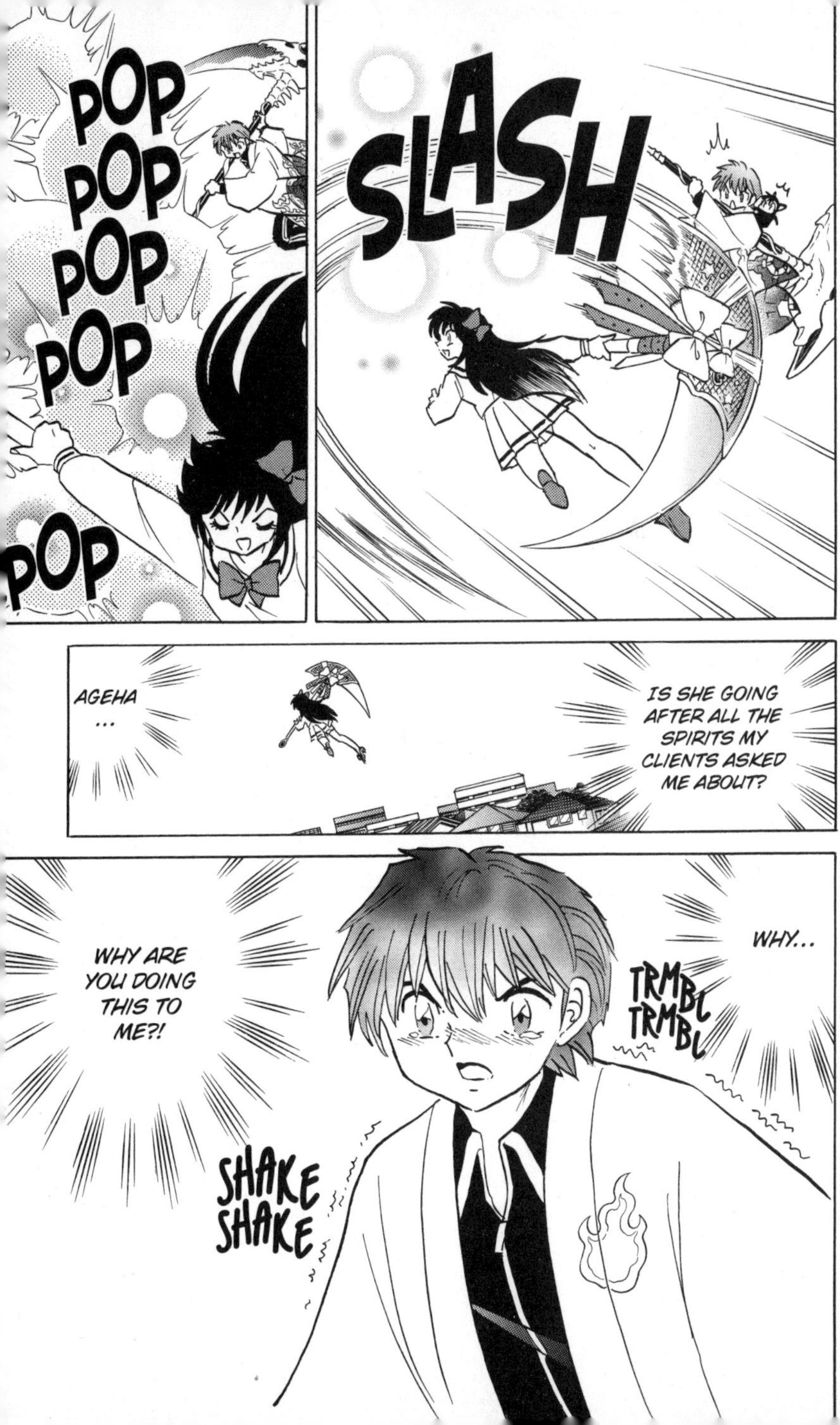
SLASH
POP POP POP POP
POP
IS SHE GOING AFTER ALL THE SPIRITS MY CLIENTS ASKED ME ABOUT?
AGEHA ...
WHY...
TRMBL TRMBL
WHY ARE YOU DOING THIS TO ME?!
SHAKE SHAKE

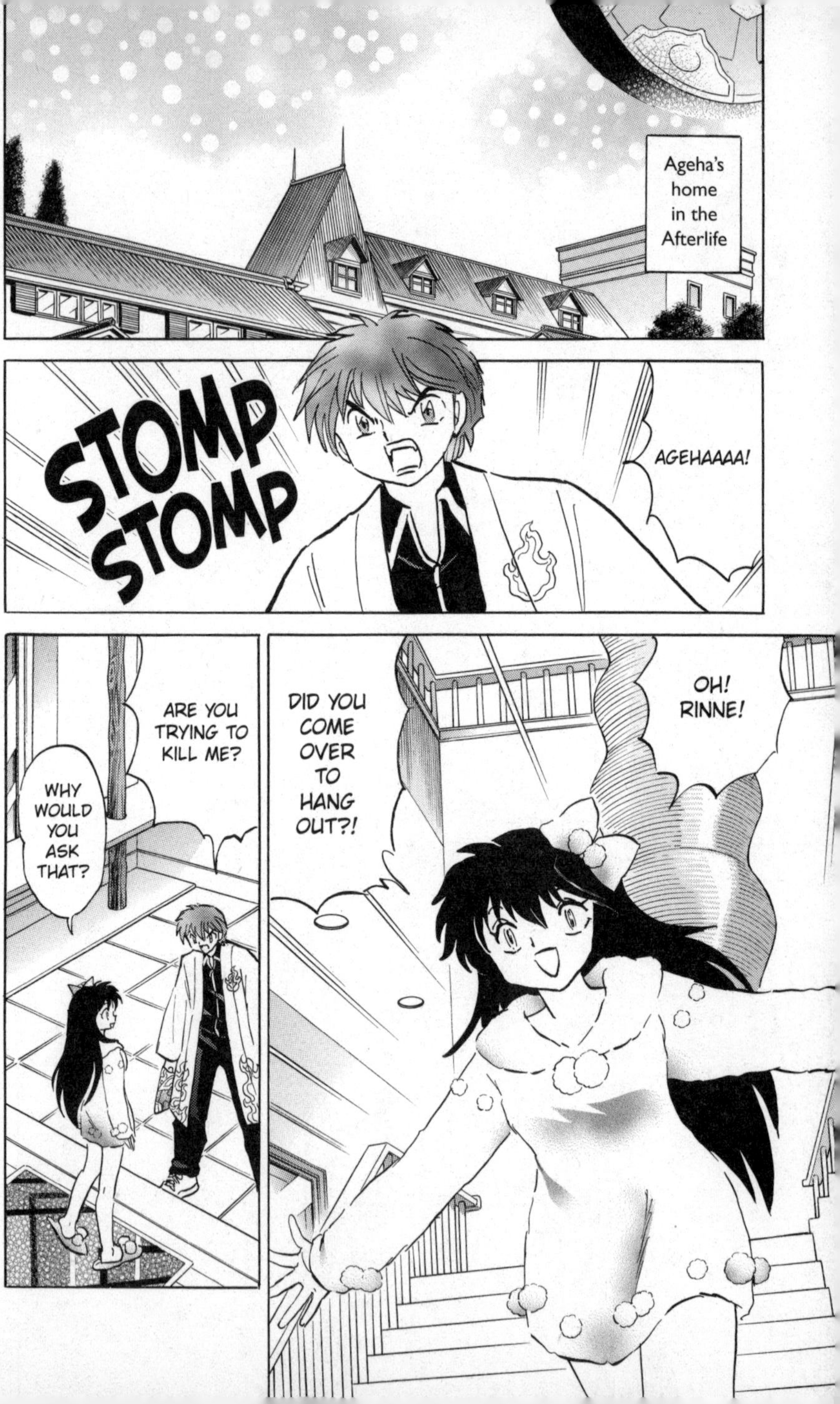
Ageha's home in the Afterlife
STOMP STOMP
AGEHAAAA!
OH! RINNE!
DID YOU COME OVER TO HANG OUT?!
ARE YOU TRYING TO KILL ME?
WHY WOULD YOU ASK THAT?

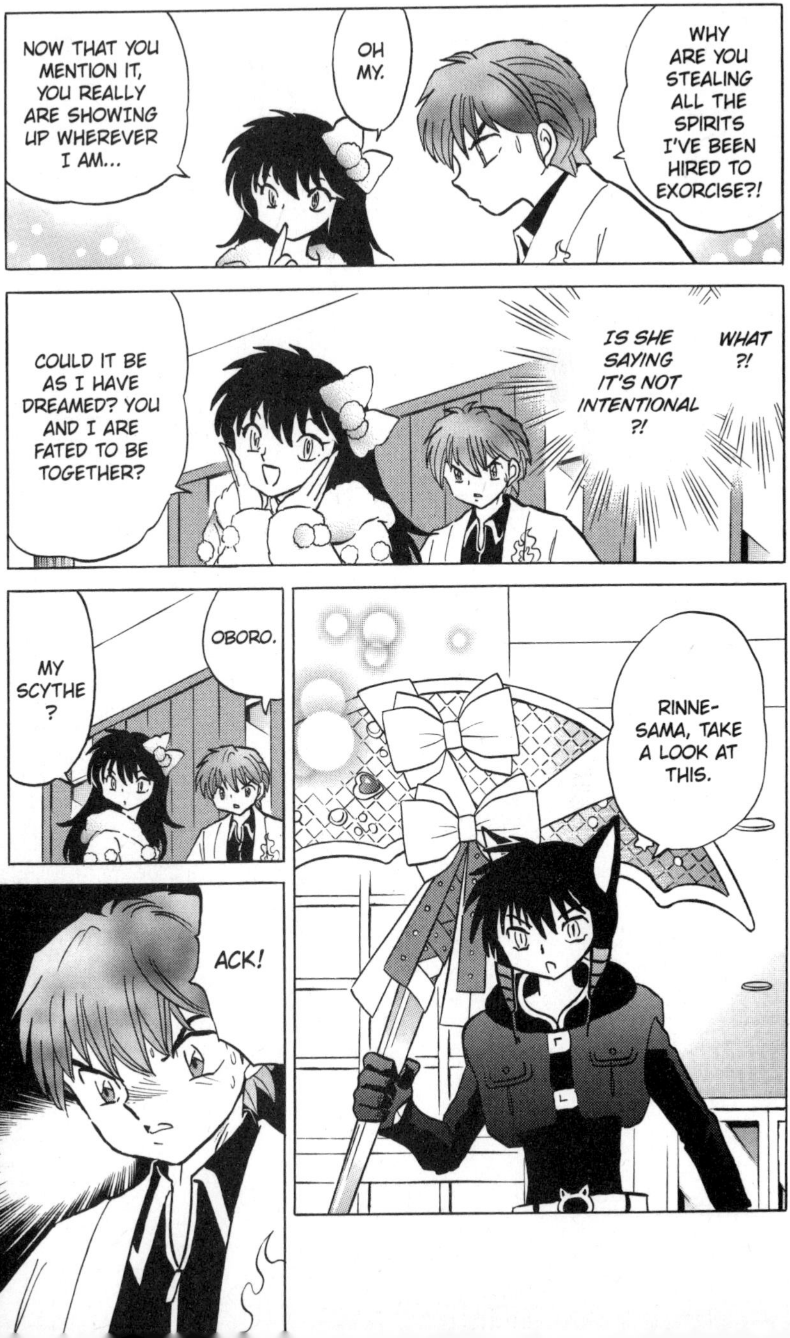
WHY ARE YOU STEALING ALL THE SPIRITS I'VE BEEN HIRED TO EXORCISE?!
OH MY.
NOW THAT YOU MENTION IT, YOU REALLY ARE SHOWING UP WHEREVER I AM...
WHAT ?!
IS SHE SAYING IT'S NOT INTENTIONAL ?!
COULD IT BE AS I HAVE DREAMED? YOU AND I ARE FATED TO BE TOGETHER?
RINNE-SAMA, TAKE A LOOK AT THIS.
OBORO.
MY SCYTHE ?
ACK!

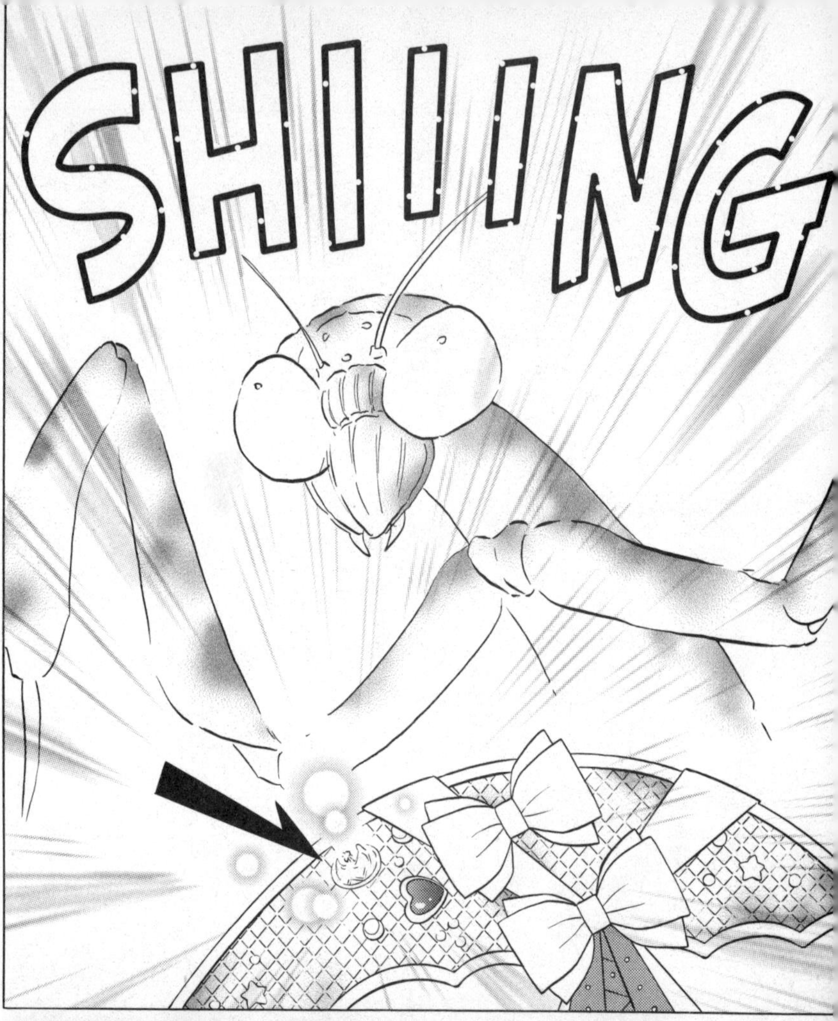
SHIIING

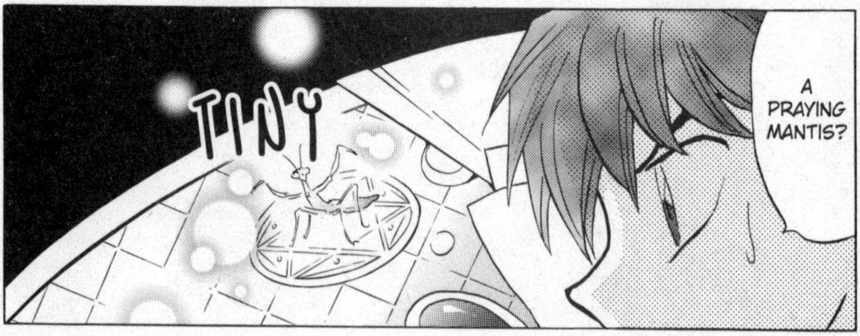
A PRAYING MANTIS?
TINY

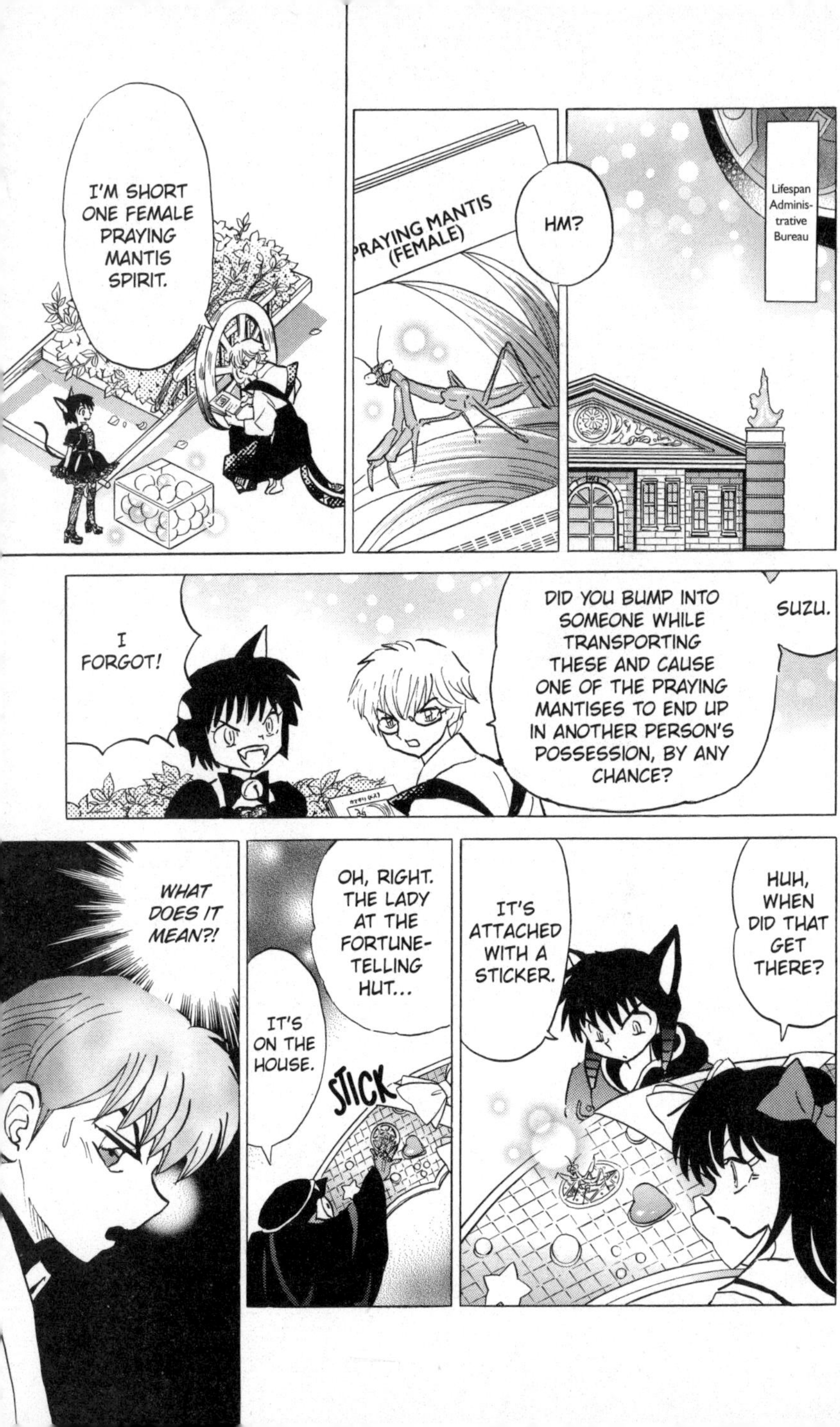
Lifespan Administrative Bureau
PRAYING MANTIS (FEMALE)
HM?
I'M SHORT ONE FEMALE PRAYING MANTIS SPIRIT.
SUZU.
DID YOU BUMP INTO SOMEONE WHILE TRANSPORTING THESE AND CAUSE ONE OF THE PRAYING MANTISES TO END UP IN ANOTHER PERSON'S POSSESSION, BY ANY CHANCE?
I FORGOT!
HUH, WHEN DID THAT GET THERE?
IT'S ATTACHED WITH A STICKER.
OH, RIGHT. THE LADY AT THE FORTUNE-TELLING HUT...
IT'S ON THE HOUSE.
STICK
WHAT DOES IT MEAN?!

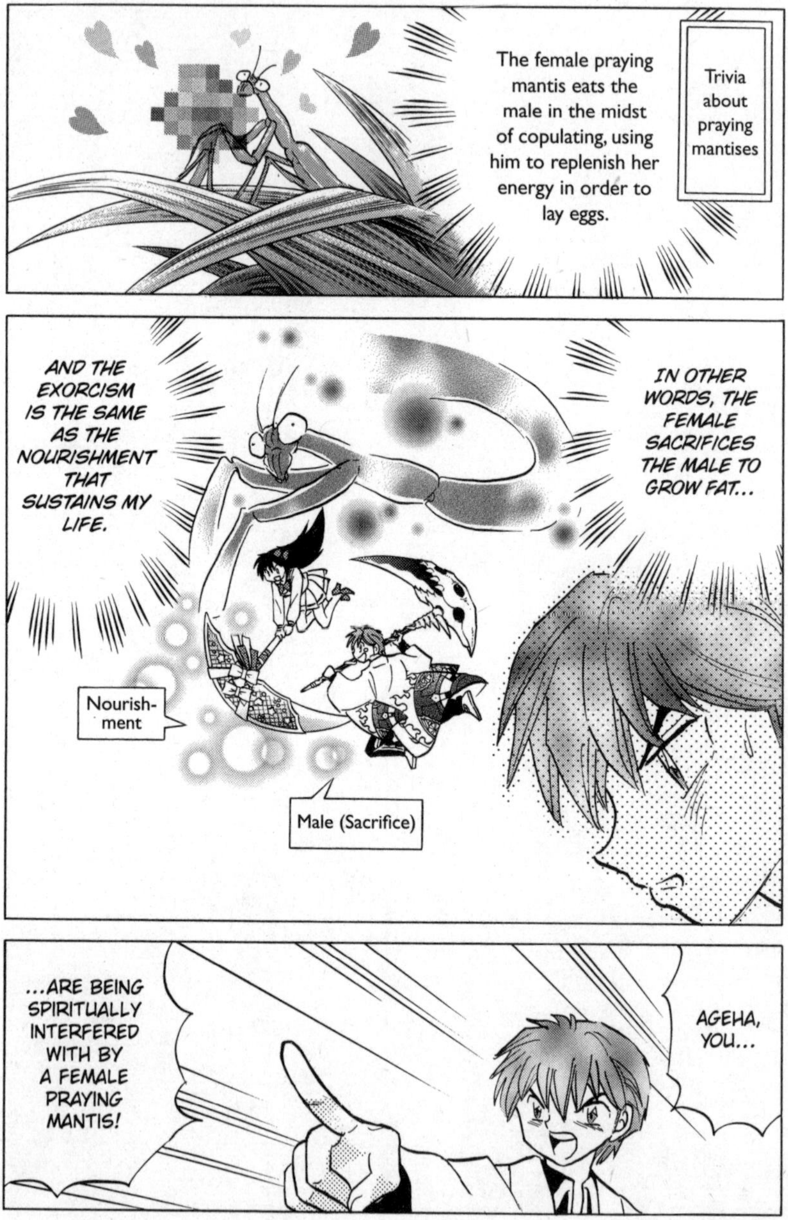
Trivia about praying mantises
The female praying mantis eats the male in the midst of copulating, using him to replenish her energy in order to lay eggs.
IN OTHER WORDS, THE FEMALE SACRIFICES THE MALE TO GROW FAT...
AND THE EXORCISM IS THE SAME AS THE NOURISHMENT THAT SUSTAINS MY LIFE.
Nourish-ment
Male (Sacrifice)
AGEHA, YOU...
...ARE BEING SPIRITUALLY INTERFERED WITH BY A FEMALE PRAYING MANTIS!

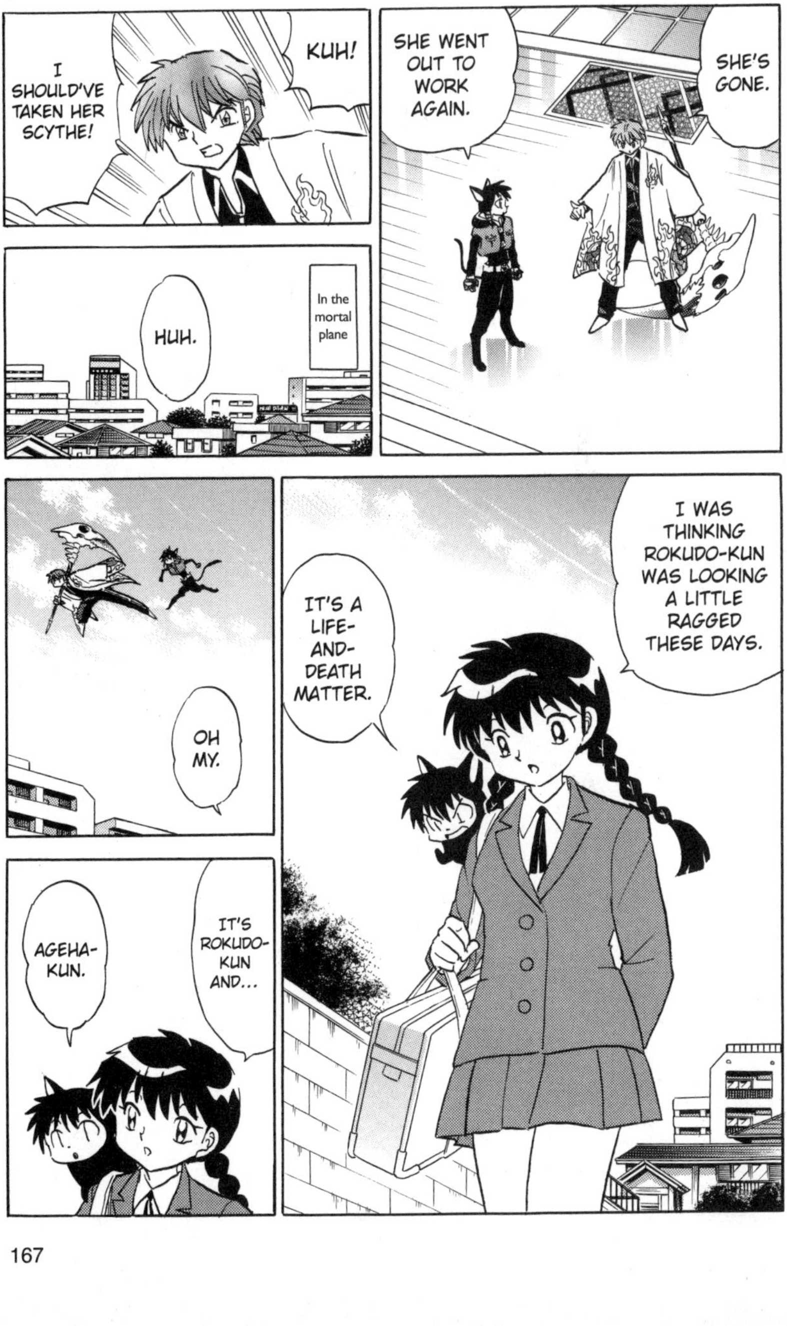
SHE'S GONE.
SHE WENT OUT TO WORK AGAIN.
KUH!
I SHOULD'VE TAKEN HER SCYTHE!
In the mortal plane
HUH.
I WAS THINKING ROKUDO-KUN WAS LOOKING A LITTLE RAGGED THESE DAYS.
IT'S A LIFE-AND-DEATH MATTER.
OH MY.
IT'S ROKUDO-KUN AND...
AGEHA-KUN.

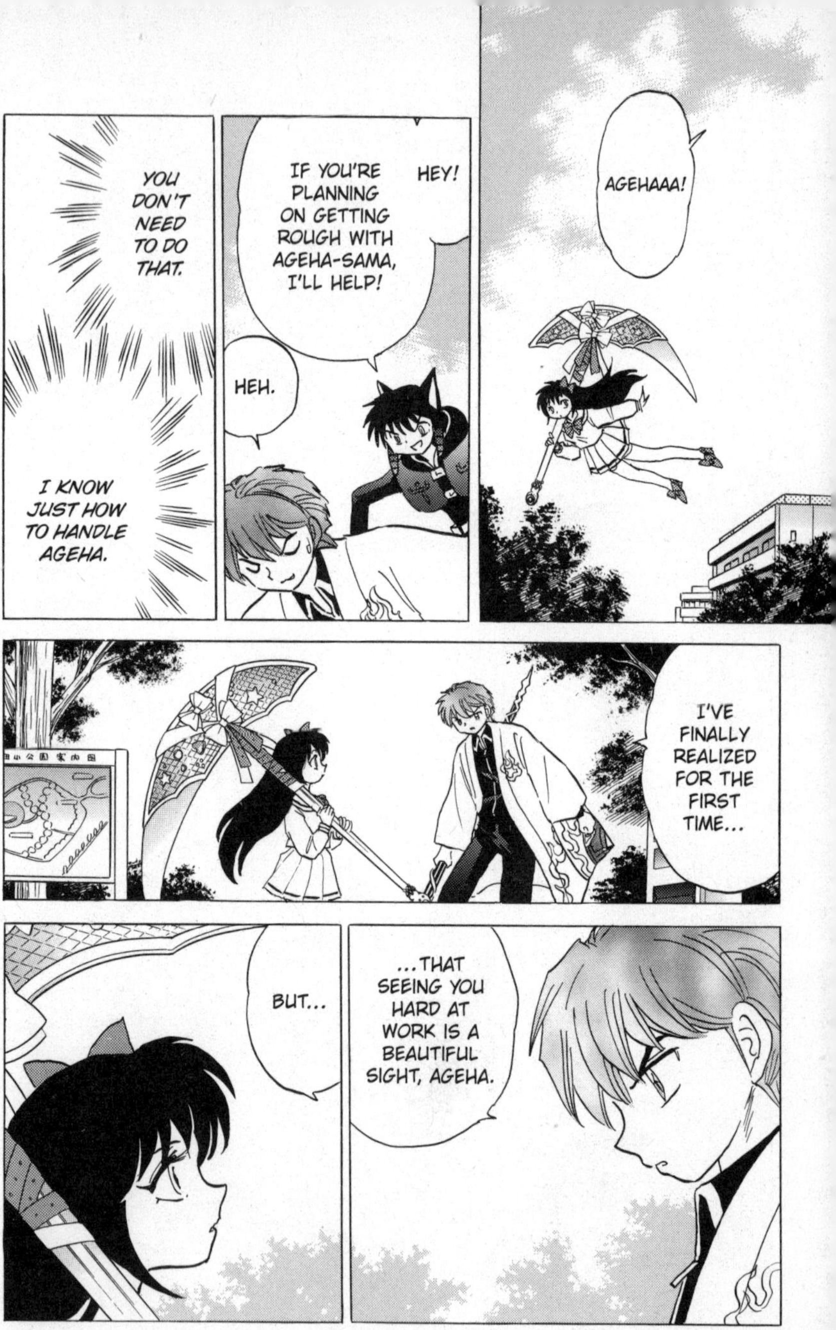
AGEHAAA!
HEY!
IF YOU'RE PLANNING ON GETTING ROUGH WITH AGEHA-SAMA, I'LL HELP!
HEH.
YOU DON'T NEED TO DO THAT.
I KNOW JUST HOW TO HANDLE AGEHA.
I'VE FINALLY REALIZED FOR THE FIRST TIME...
...THAT SEEING YOU HARD AT WORK IS A BEAUTIFUL SIGHT, AGEHA.
BUT...

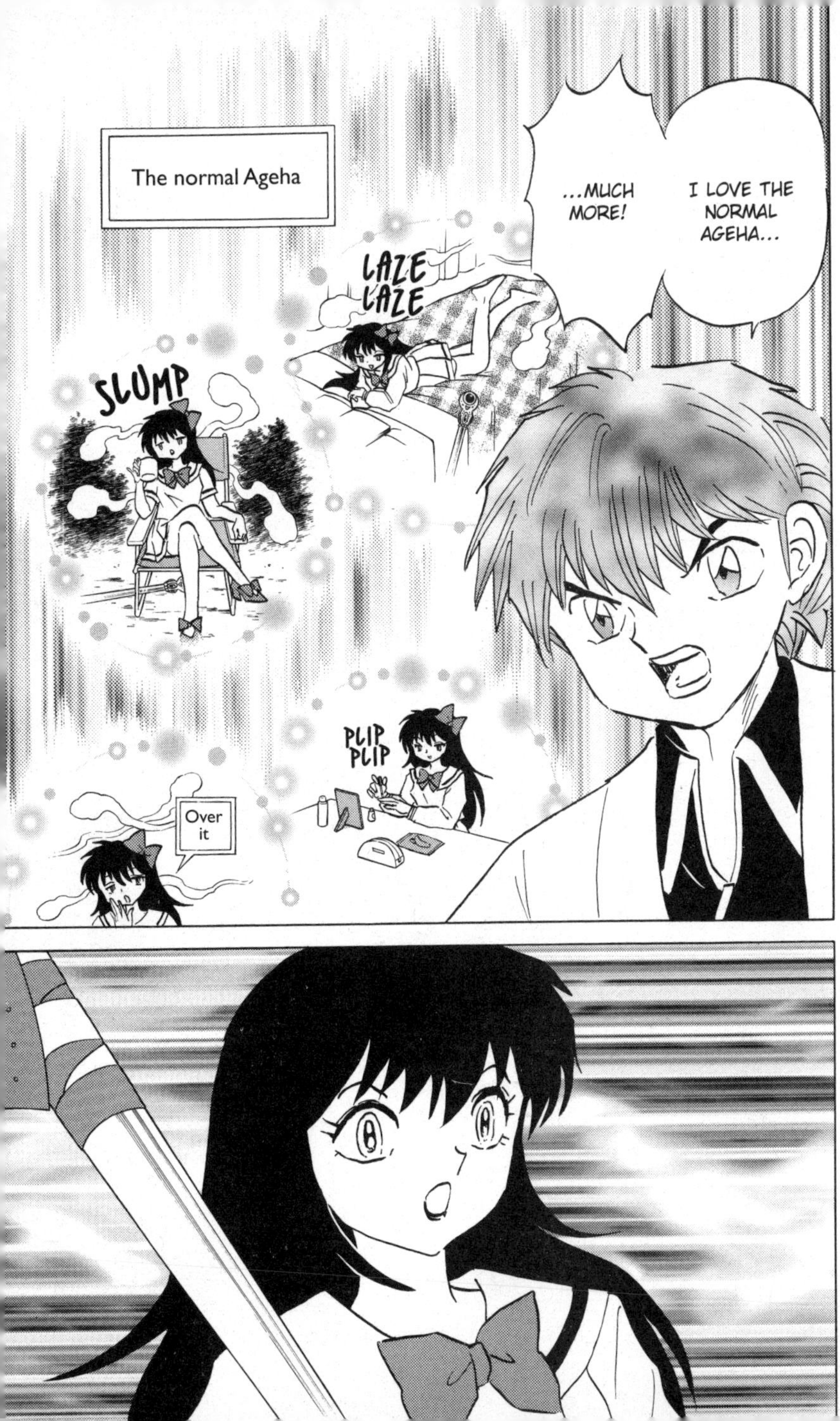
I LOVE THE NORMAL AGEHA...
...MUCH MORE!
The normal Ageha
LAZE LAZE
SLUMP
PLIP PLIP
Over it

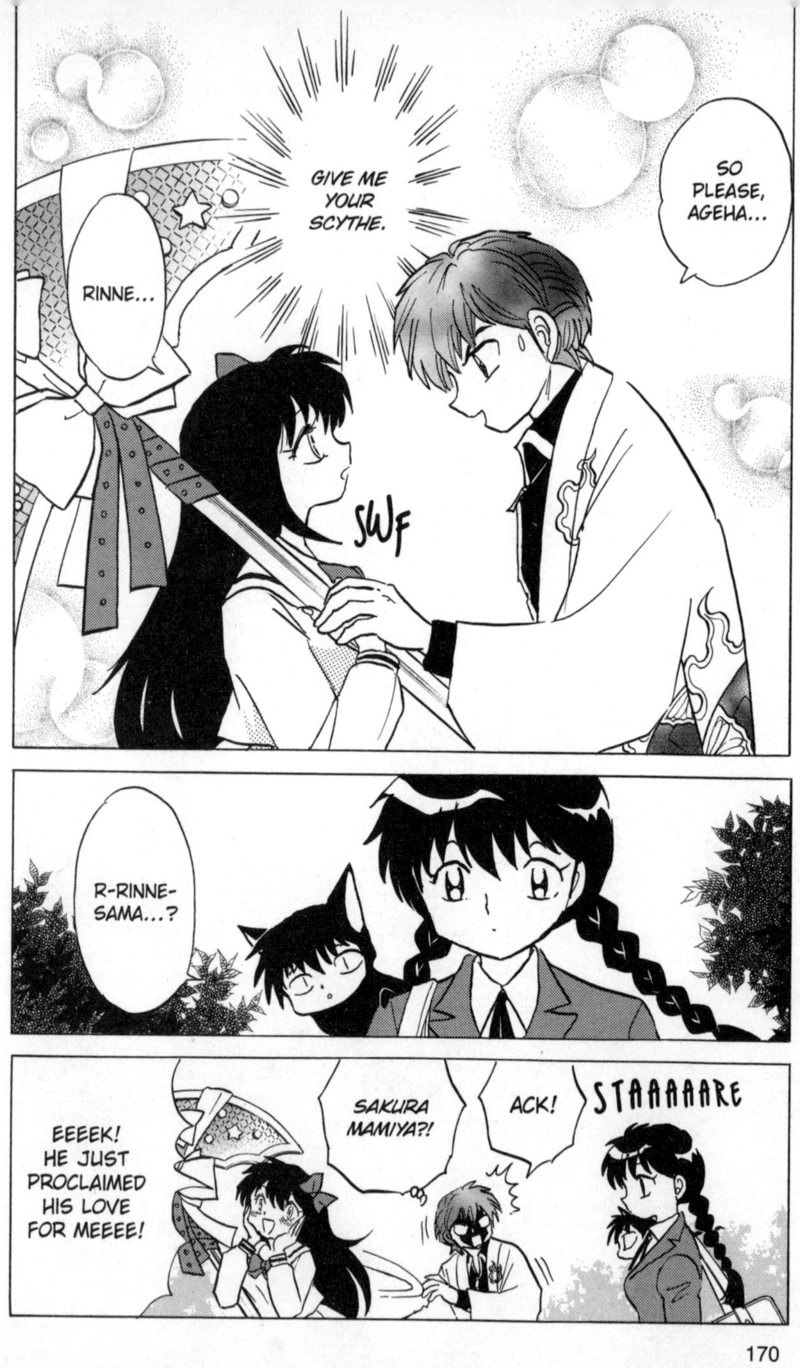
SO PLEASE, AGEHA...
GIVE ME YOUR SCYTHE.
RINNE...
SWF
R-RINNE-SAMA...?
STAAAAARE
ACK!
SAKURA MAMIYA?!
EEEEK! HE JUST PROCLAIMED HIS LOVE FOR MEEEE!

CHAPTER 388: THE SHINIGAMI CALLED AGEHA

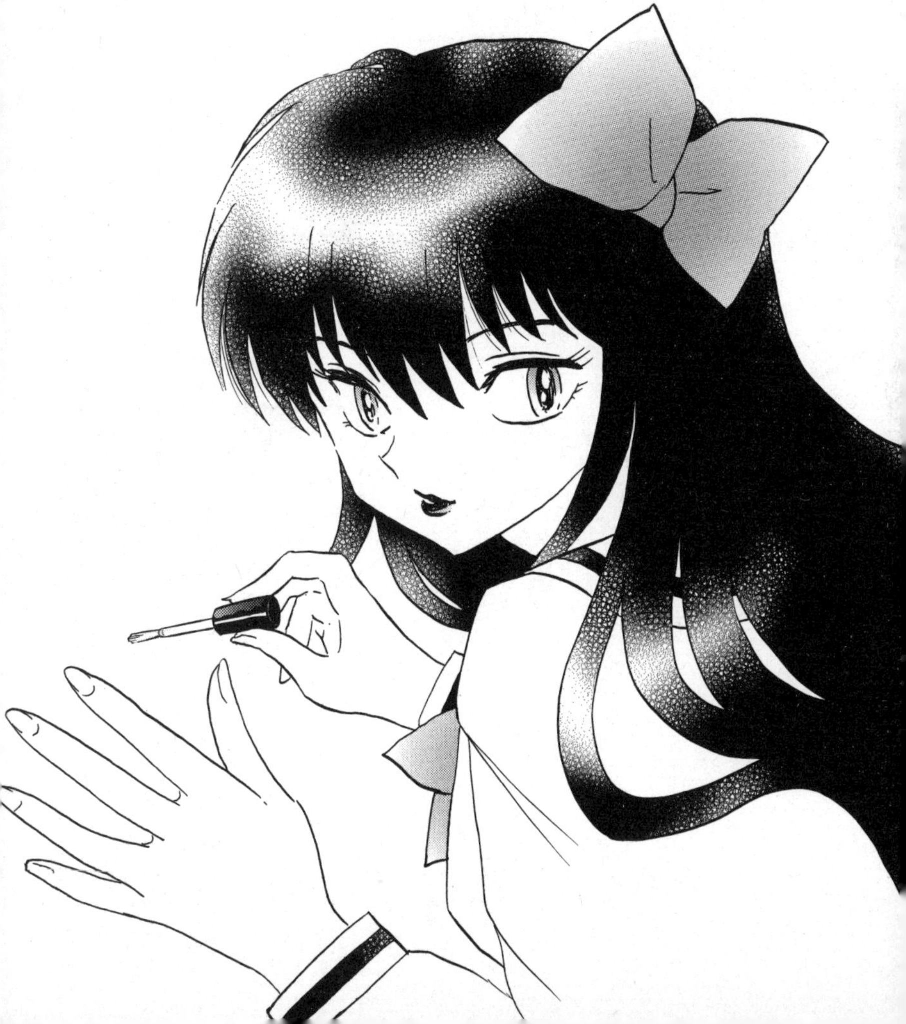

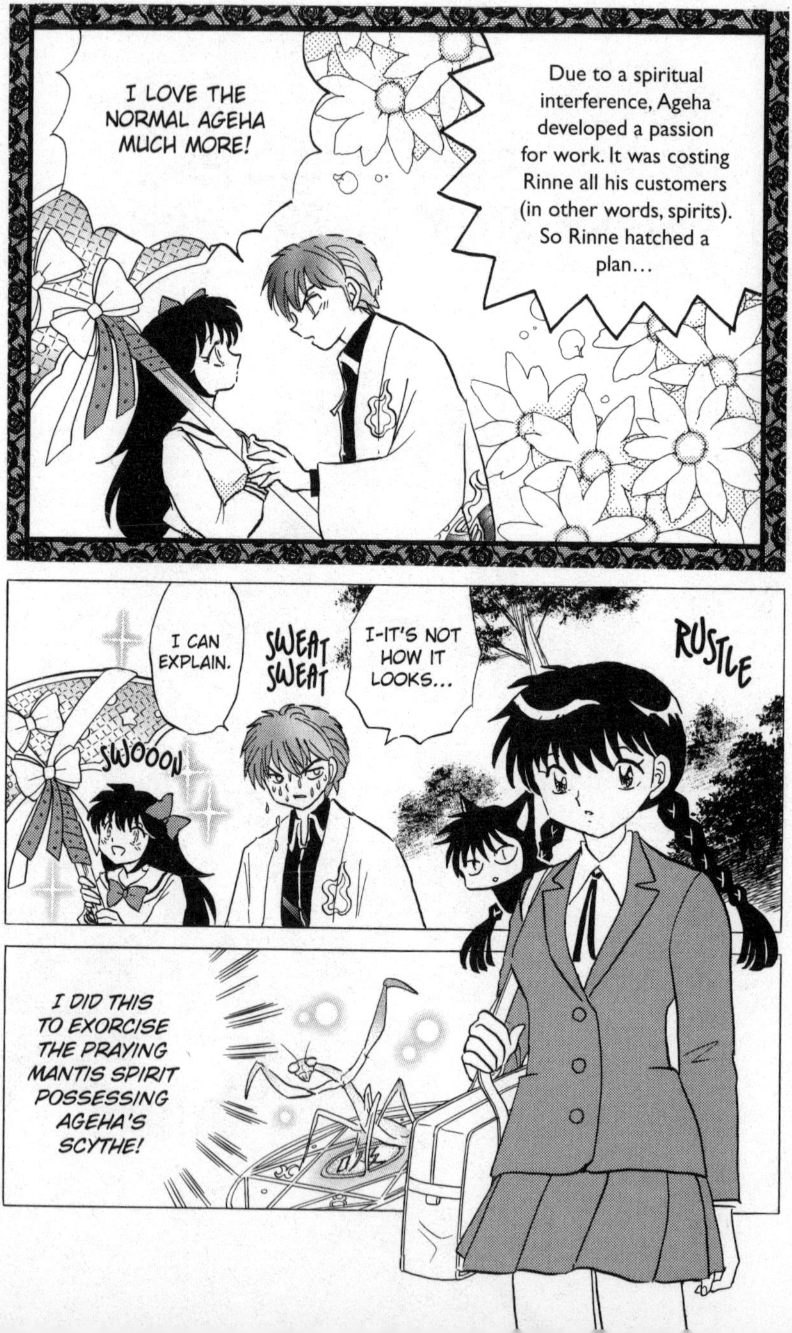
Due to a spiritual interference, Ageha developed a passion for work. It was costing Rinne all his customers (in other words, spirits). So Rinne hatched a plan…
I LOVE THE NORMAL AGEHA MUCH MORE!
RUSTLE
I-IT'S NOT HOW IT LOOKS…
SWEAT SWEAT
I CAN EXPLAIN.
SWOOON
I DID THIS TO EXORCISE THE PRAYING MANTIS SPIRIT POSSESSING AGEHA'S SCYTHE!

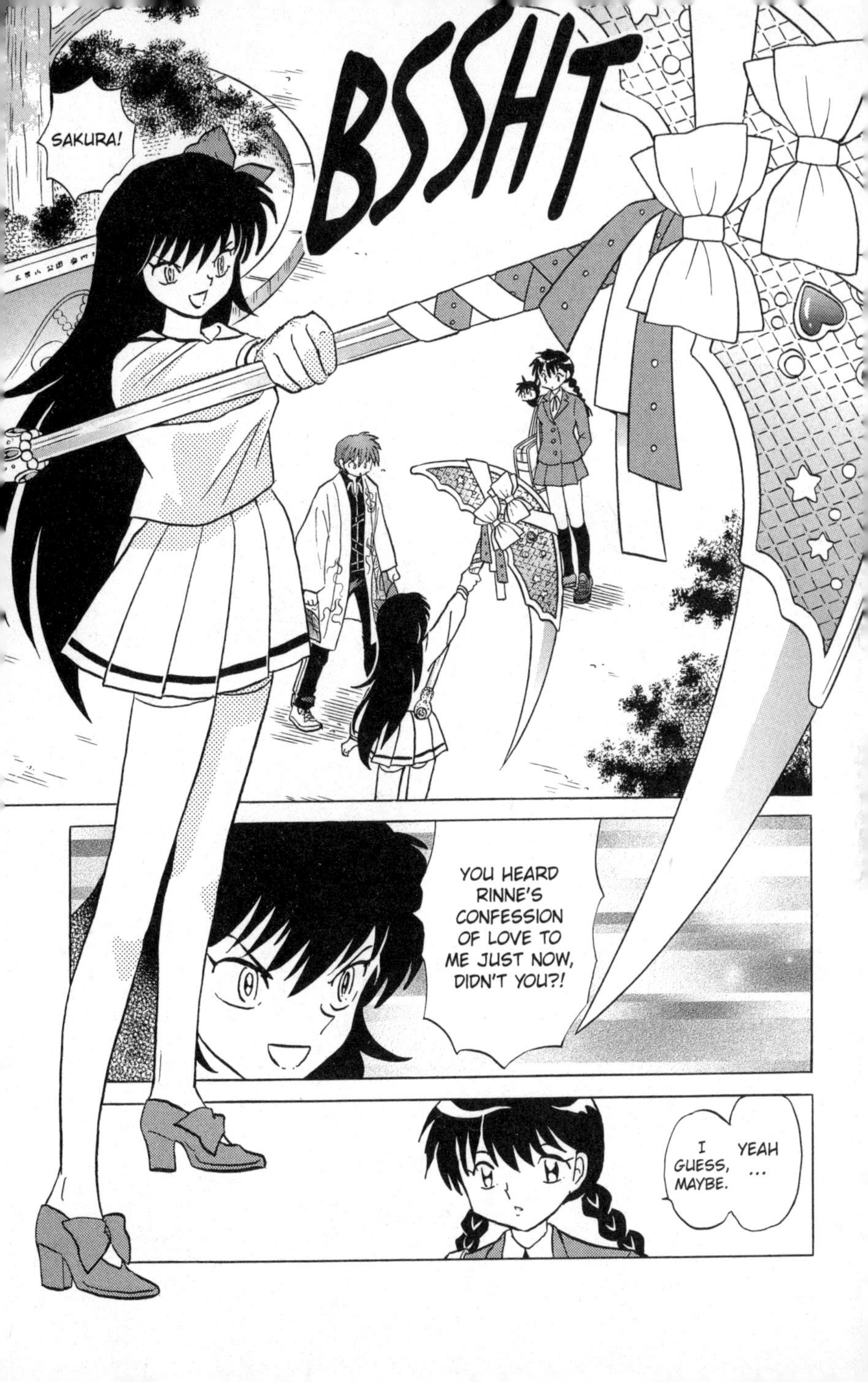
BSSHT
SAKURA!
YOU HEARD RINNE'S CONFESSION OF LOVE TO ME JUST NOW, DIDN'T YOU?!
YEAH... I GUESS, MAYBE.

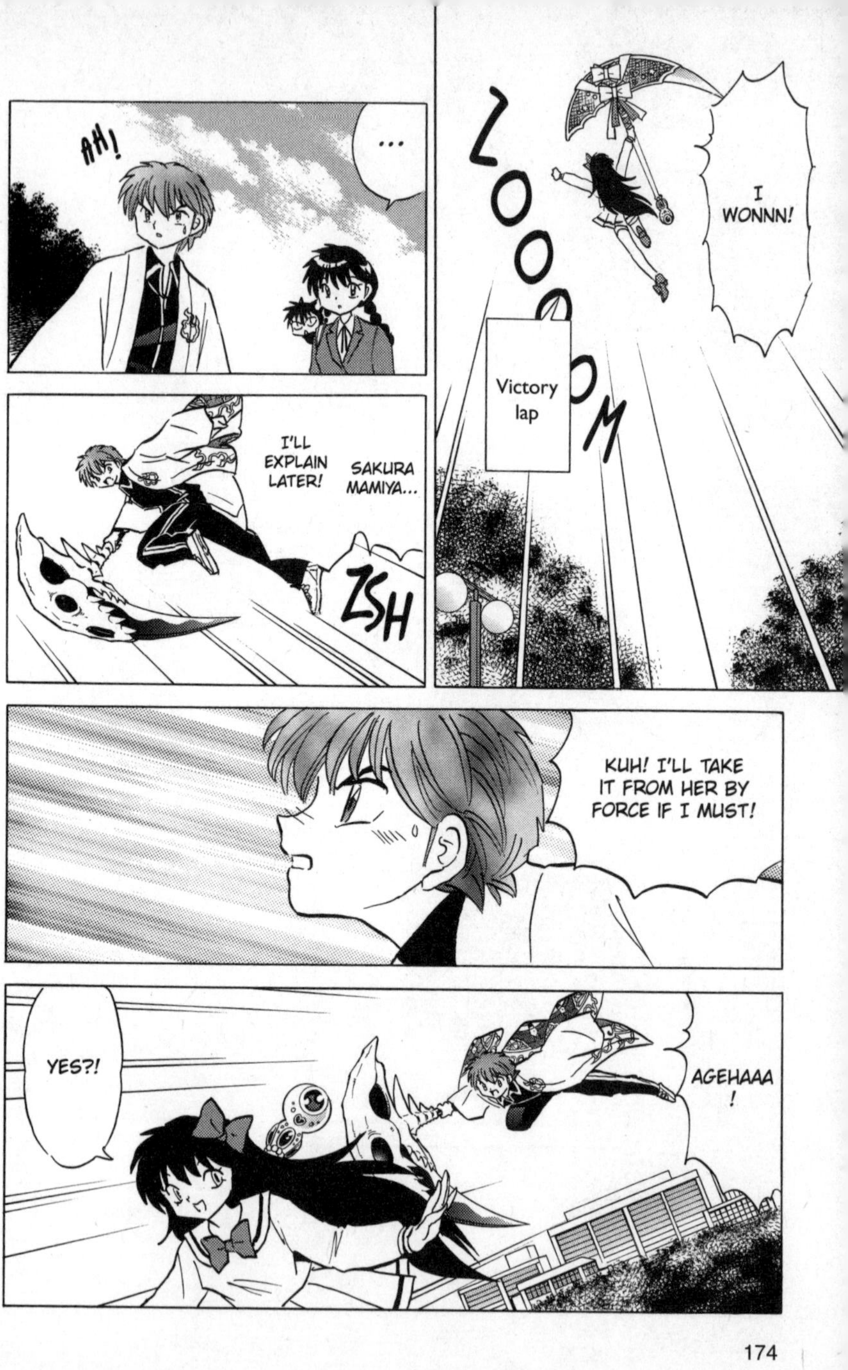
I WONNN!
ZOOOOOM
Victory lap
AH!
...
SAKURA MAMIYA...
I'LL EXPLAIN LATER!
ZSH
KUH! I'LL TAKE IT FROM HER BY FORCE IF I MUST!
AGEHAAA!
YES?!

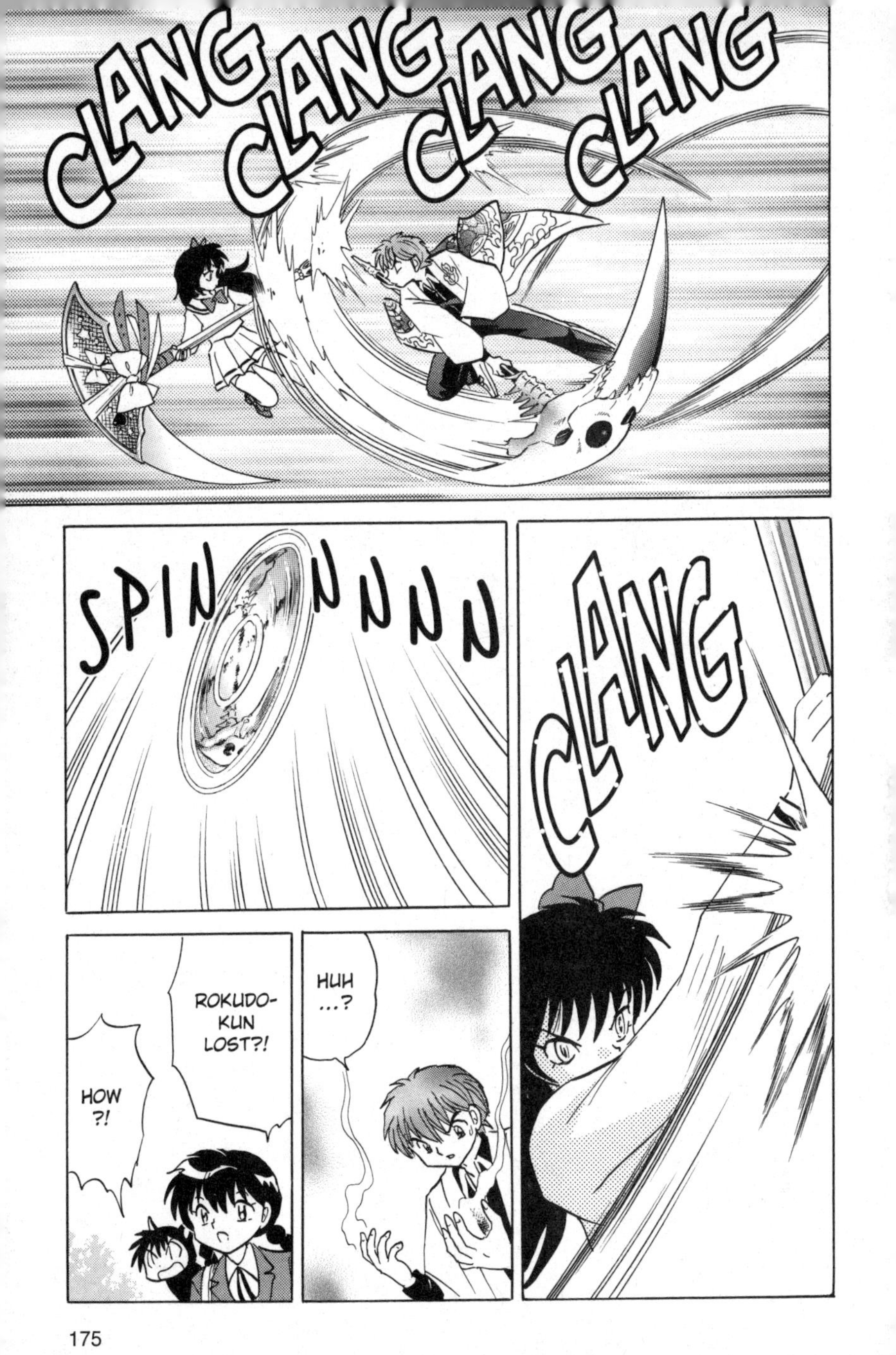
CLANG CLANG CLANG CLANG
CLANG
SPINNNNN
HUH ...?
ROKUDO-KUN LOST?!
HOW ?!

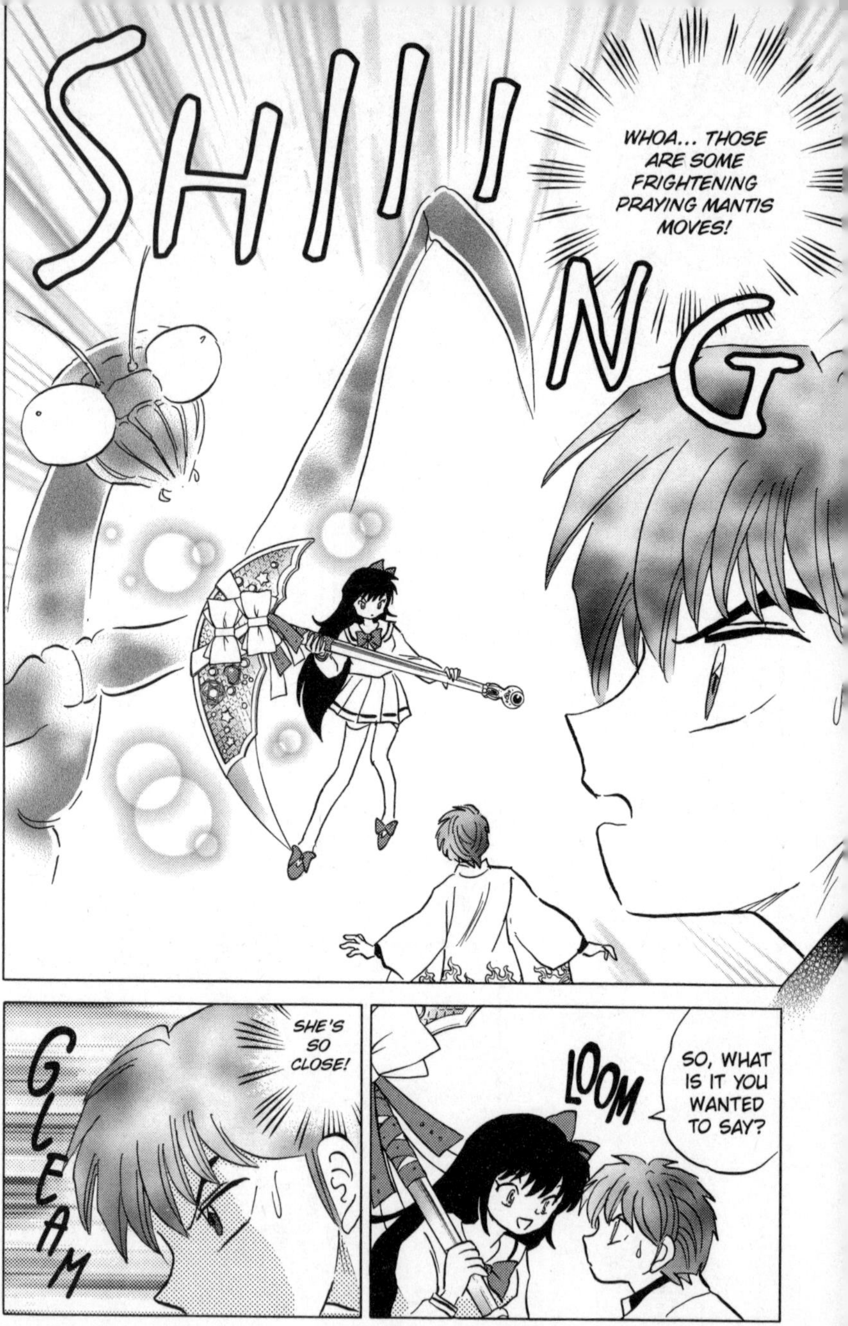
SHIIING
WHOA... THOSE ARE SOME FRIGHTENING PRAYING MANTIS MOVES!
LOOM
SO, WHAT IS IT YOU WANTED TO SAY?
SHE'S SO CLOSE!
GLEAM

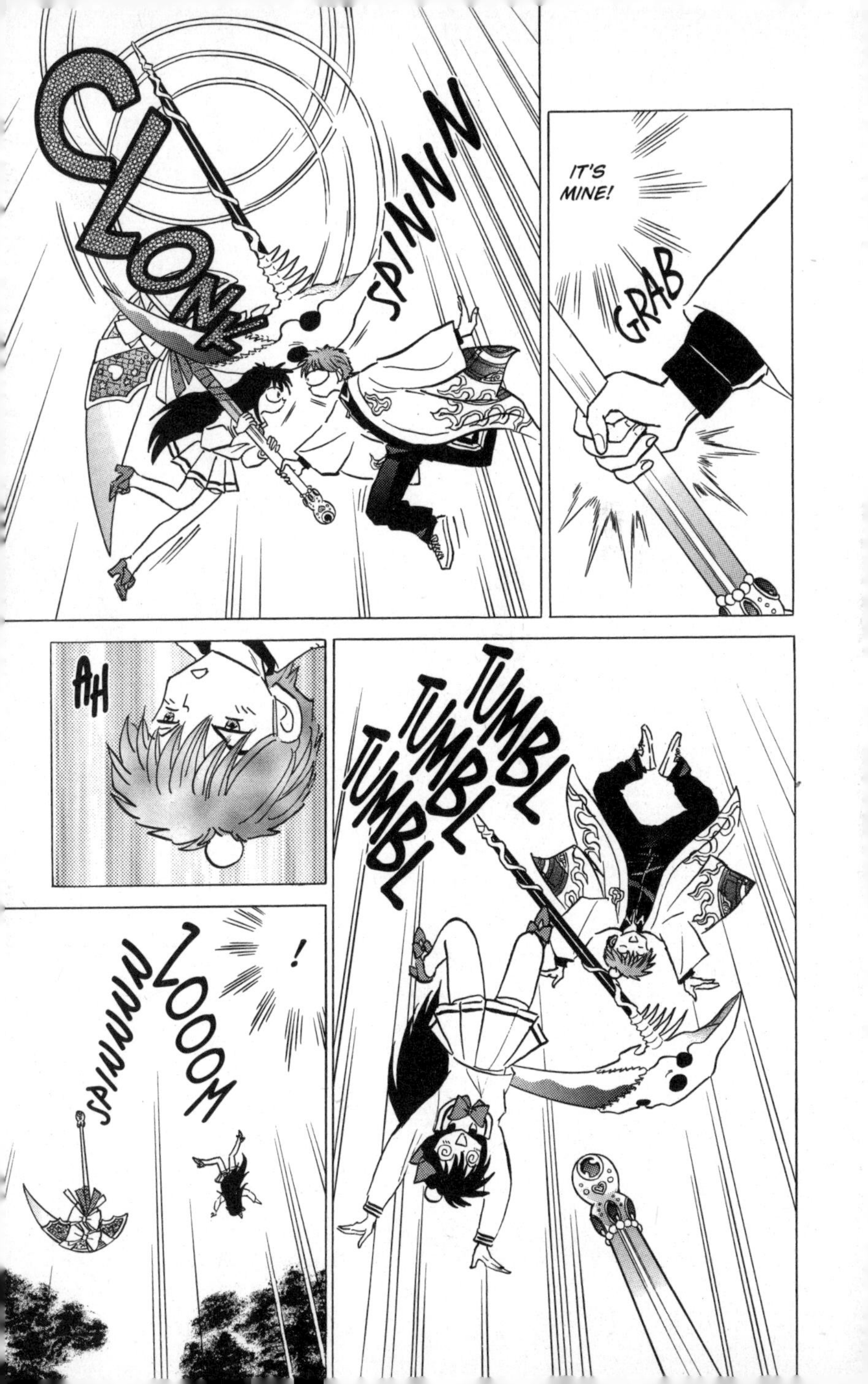
IT'S MINE!
GRAB
CLONK
SPINNN
TUMBL
TUMBL
TUMBL
AH
!
ZOOOM
SPINNNN

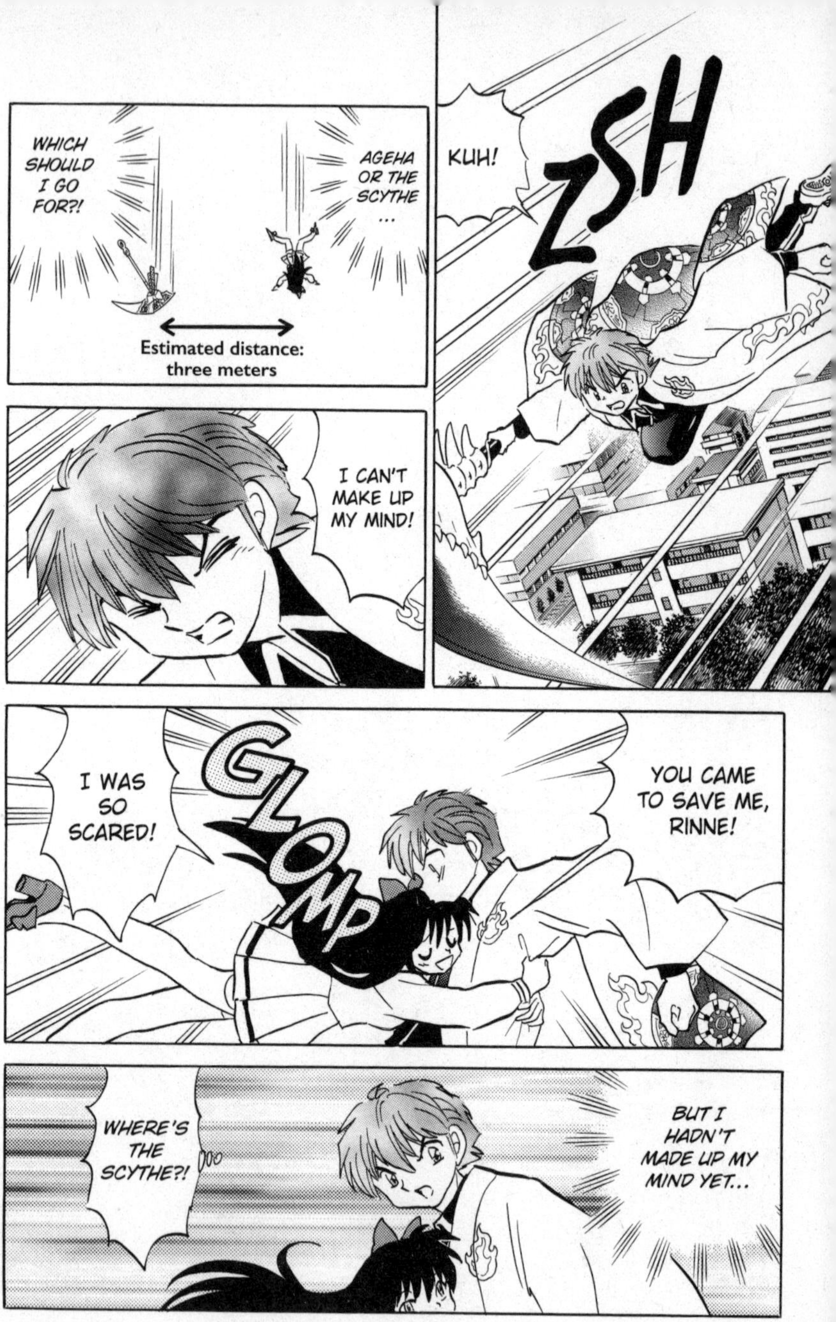
KUH!
ZSH
AGEHA OR THE SCYTHE ...
WHICH SHOULD I GO FOR?!
Estimated distance: three meters
I CAN'T MAKE UP MY MIND!
YOU CAME TO SAVE ME, RINNE!
GLOMP
I WAS SO SCARED!
BUT I HADN'T MADE UP MY MIND YET...
WHERE'S THE SCYTHE?!

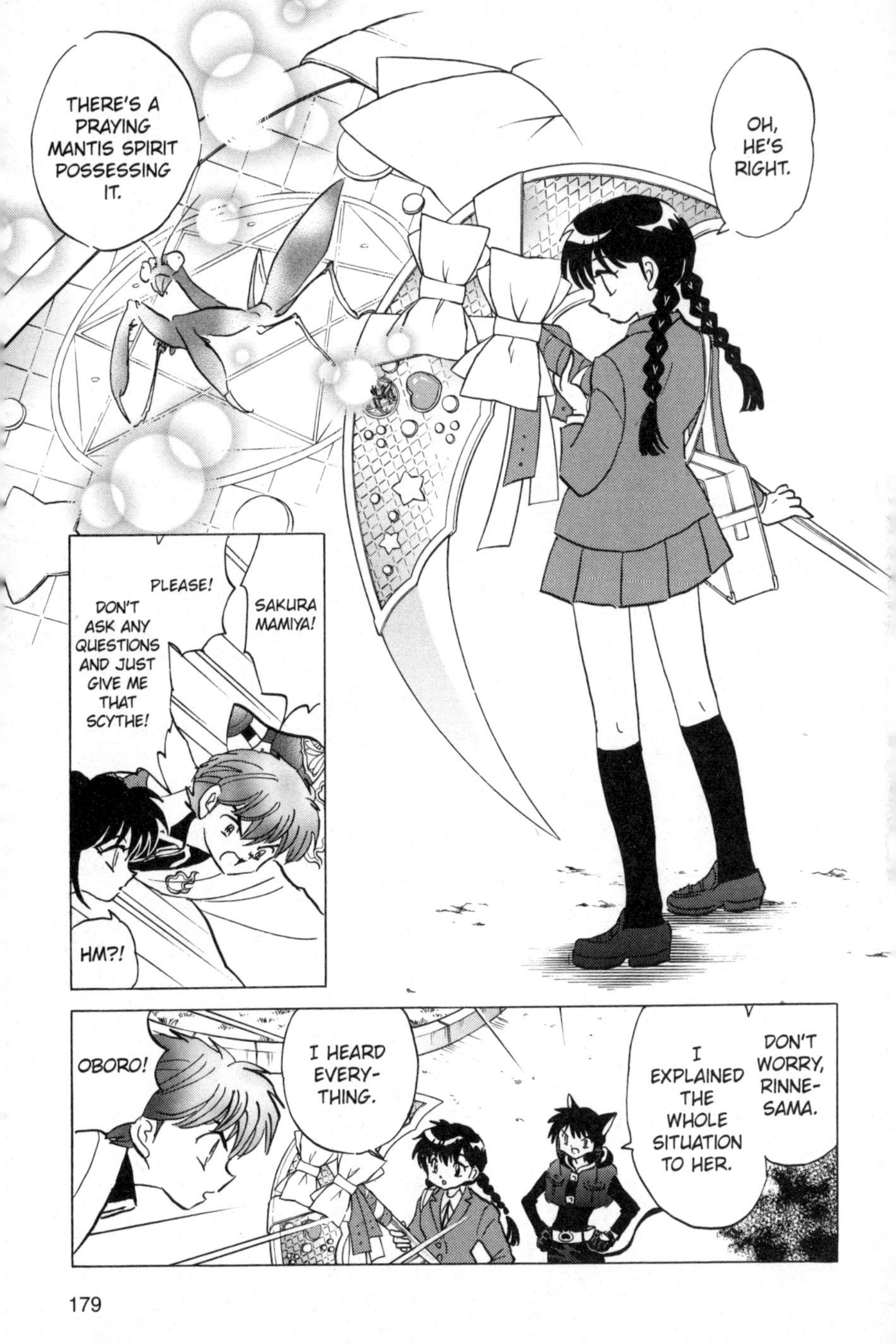
OH, HE'S RIGHT.
THERE'S A PRAYING MANTIS SPIRIT POSSESSING IT.
SAKURA MAMIYA!
PLEASE!
DON'T ASK ANY QUESTIONS AND JUST GIVE ME THAT SCYTHE!
HM?!
DON'T WORRY, RINNE-SAMA.
I EXPLAINED THE WHOLE SITUATION TO HER.
I HEARD EVERY-THING.
OBORO!

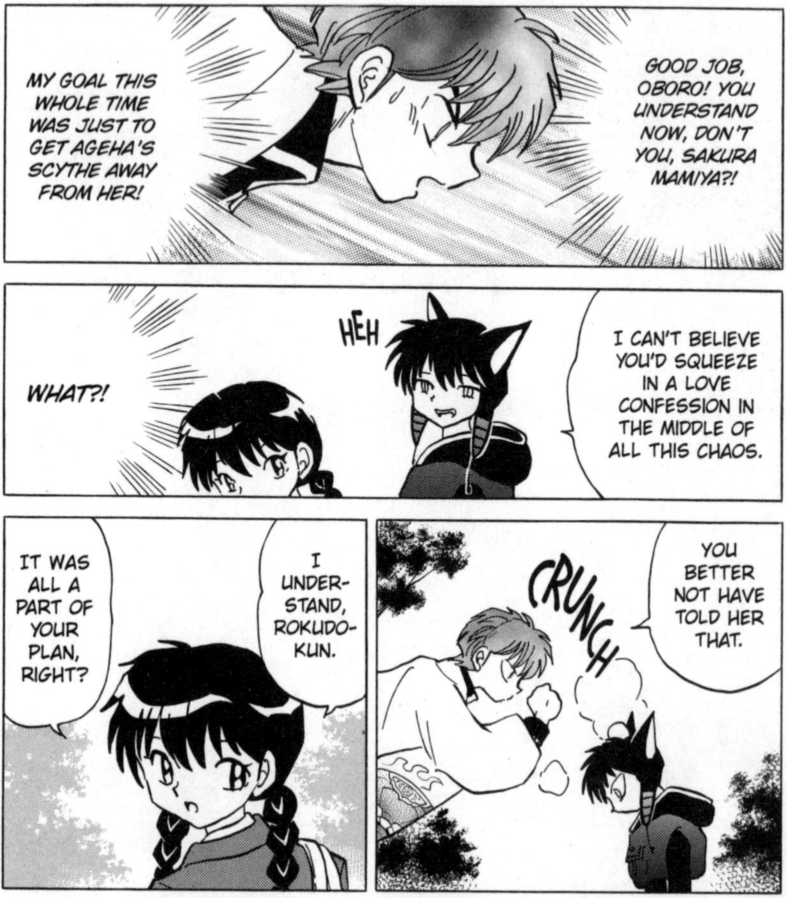
GOOD JOB, OBORO! YOU UNDERSTAND NOW, DON'T YOU, SAKURA MAMIYA?!
MY GOAL THIS WHOLE TIME WAS JUST TO GET AGEHA'S SCYTHE AWAY FROM HER!
I CAN'T BELIEVE YOU'D SQUEEZE IN A LOVE CONFESSION IN THE MIDDLE OF ALL THIS CHAOS.
HEH
WHAT?!
YOU BETTER NOT HAVE TOLD HER THAT.
CRUNCH
I UNDER-STAND, ROKUDO-KUN.
IT WAS ALL A PART OF YOUR PLAN, RIGHT?
SHE EVEN UNDER-STOOD THAT PART!
GLOW
YOINK
THAT'S OUR RINNE-SAMA.

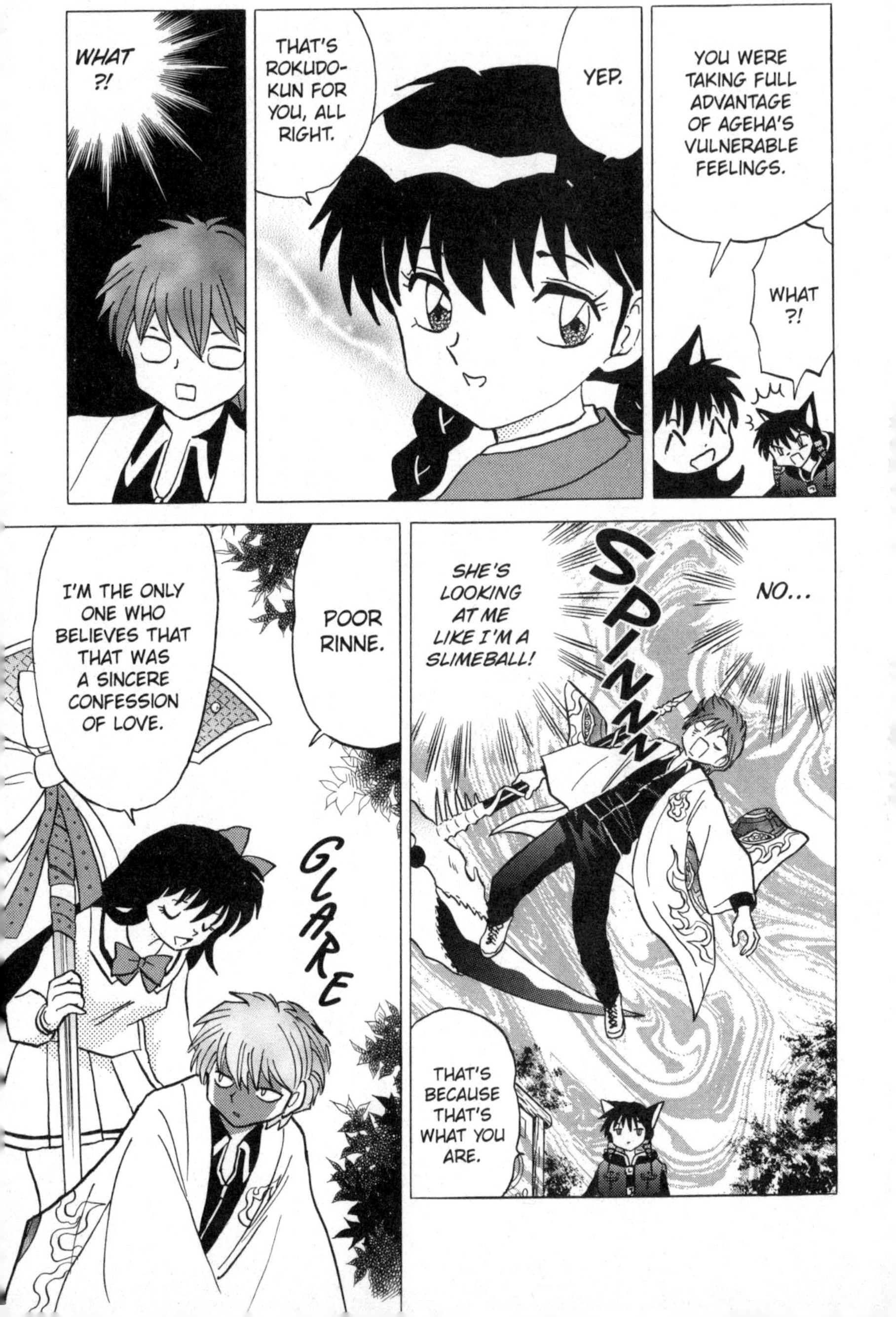
YOU WERE TAKING FULL ADVANTAGE OF AGEHA'S VULNERABLE FEELINGS.
WHAT ?!
YEP.
THAT'S ROKUDO-KUN FOR YOU, ALL RIGHT.
WHAT ?!
NO...
SHE'S LOOKING AT ME LIKE I'M A SLIMEBALL!
SPINNN
THAT'S BECAUSE THAT'S WHAT YOU ARE.
POOR RINNE.
I'M THE ONLY ONE WHO BELIEVES THAT THAT WAS A SINCERE CONFESSION OF LOVE.
GLARE

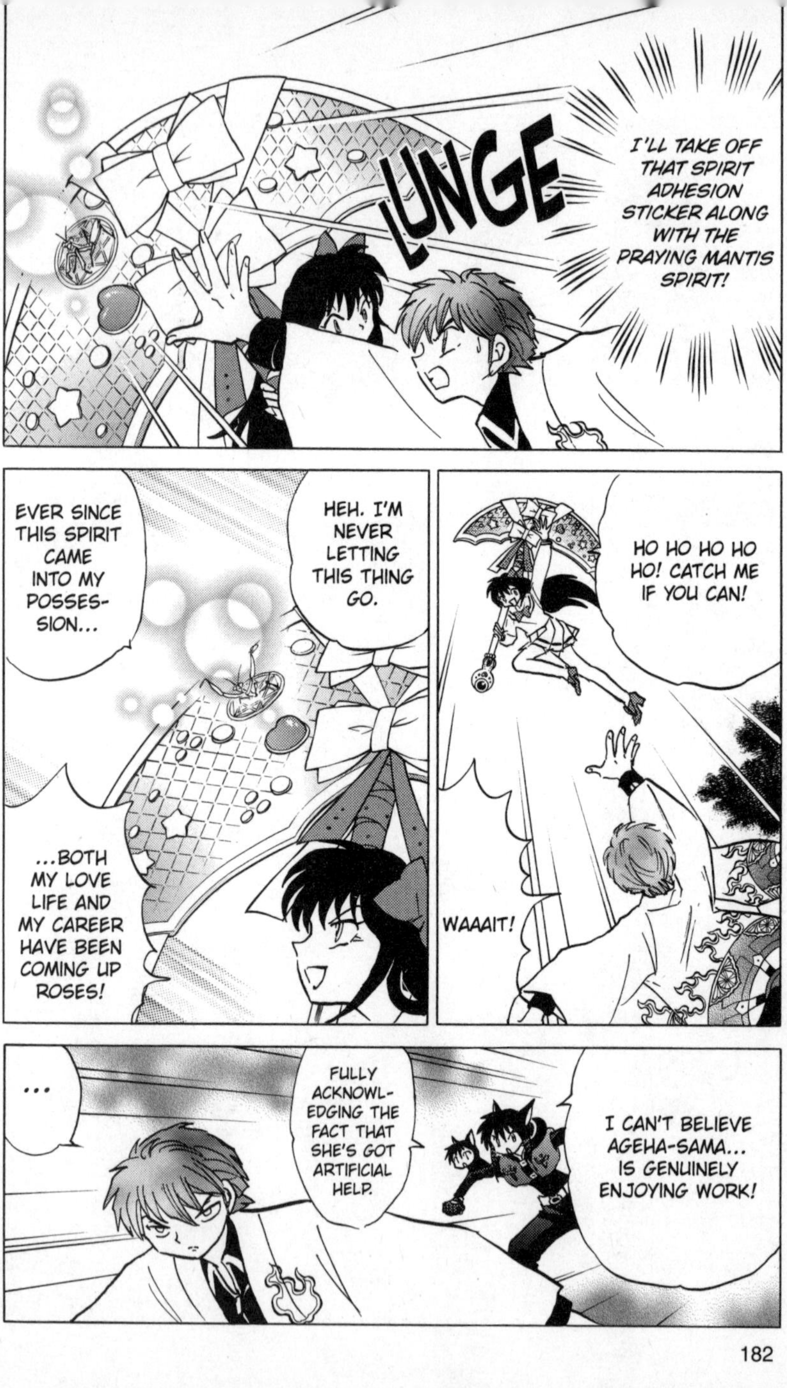
I'LL TAKE OFF THAT SPIRIT ADHESION STICKER ALONG WITH THE PRAYING MANTIS SPIRIT!
LUNGE
HO HO HO HO HO! CATCH ME IF YOU CAN!
WAAAIT!
HEH. I'M NEVER LETTING THIS THING GO.
EVER SINCE THIS SPIRIT CAME INTO MY POSSES-SION...
...BOTH MY LOVE LIFE AND MY CAREER HAVE BEEN COMING UP ROSES!
I CAN'T BELIEVE AGEHA-SAMA... IS GENUINELY ENJOYING WORK!
FULLY ACKNOWL-EDGING THE FACT THAT SHE'S GOT ARTIFICIAL HELP.
...

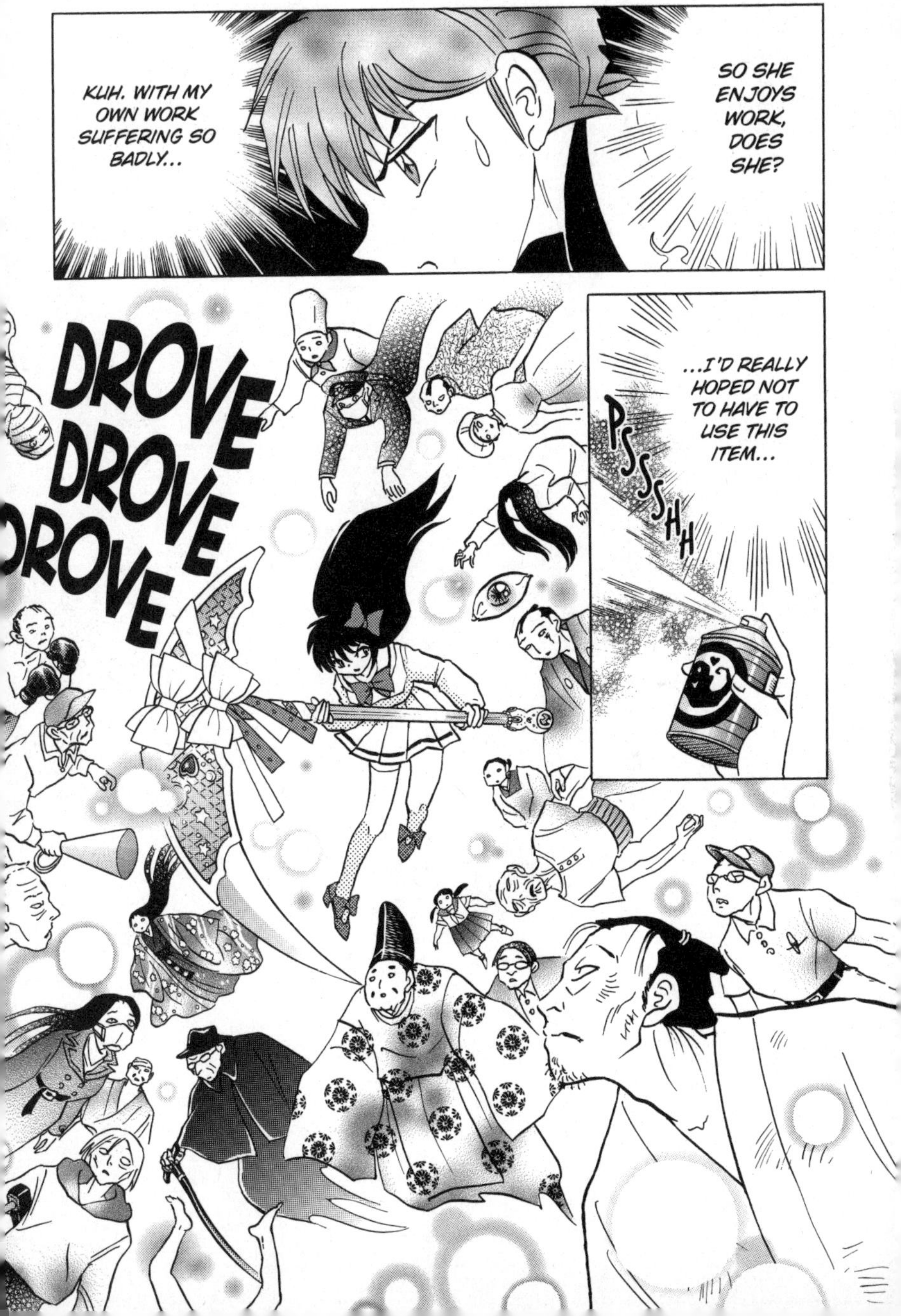
SO SHE ENJOYS WORK, DOES SHE?
KUH. WITH MY OWN WORK SUFFERING SO BADLY...
...I'D REALLY HOPED NOT TO HAVE TO USE THIS ITEM...
PSSSHH
DROVE DROVE DROVE

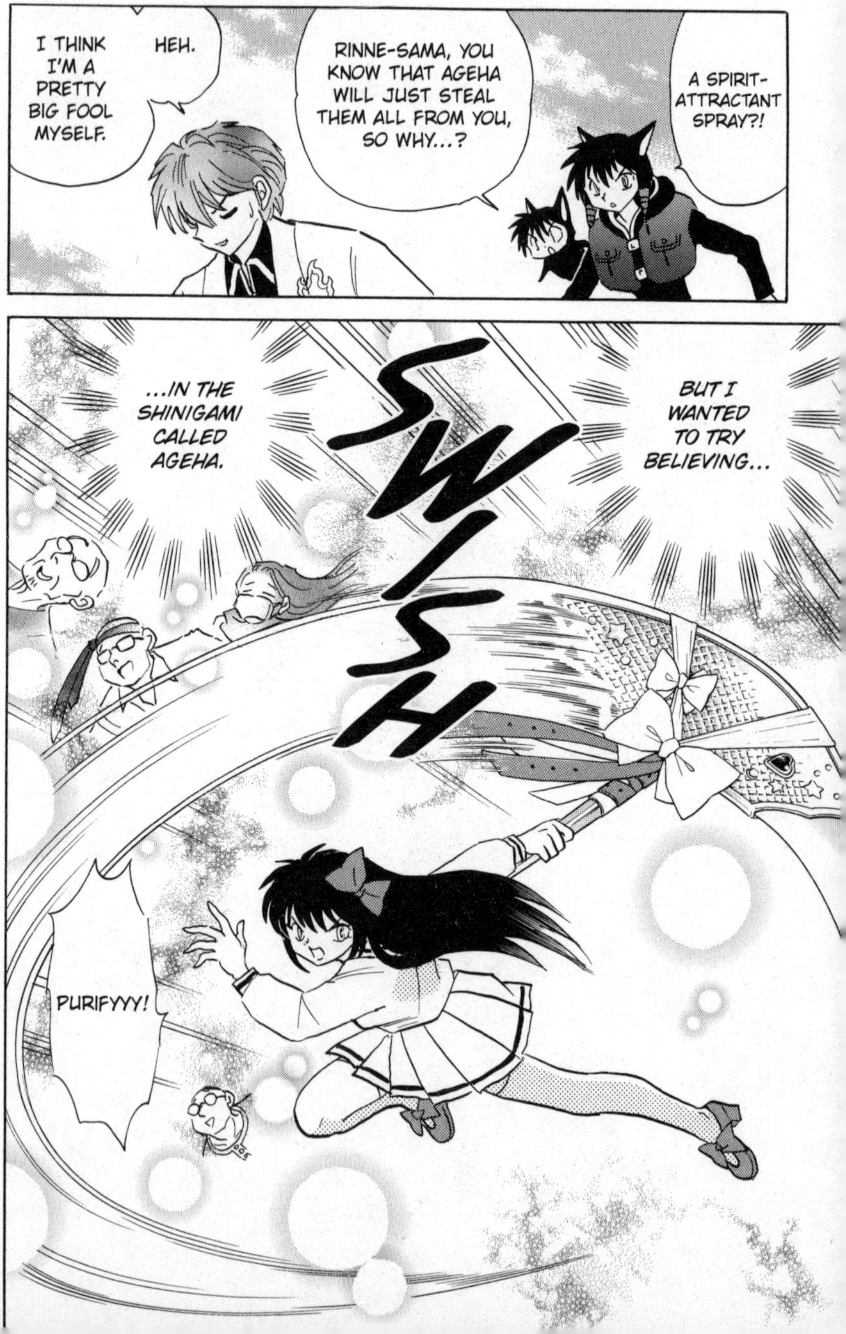
A SPIRIT-ATTRACTANT SPRAY?!
RINNE-SAMA, YOU KNOW THAT AGEHA WILL JUST STEAL THEM ALL FROM YOU, SO WHY...?
HEH.
I THINK I'M A PRETTY BIG FOOL MYSELF.
BUT I WANTED TO TRY BELIEVING...
...IN THE SHINIGAMI CALLED AGEHA.
SWISH
PURIFYYY!

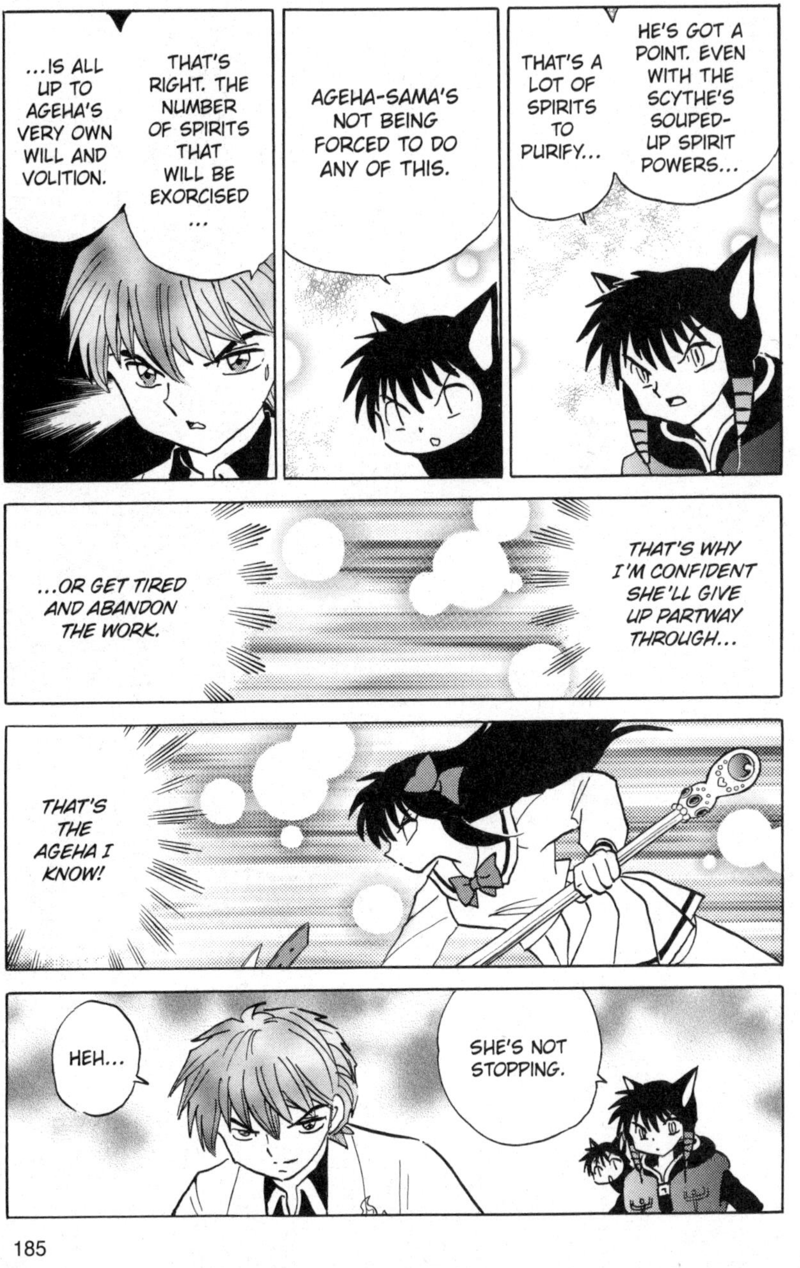
HE'S GOT A POINT. EVEN WITH THE SCYTHE'S SOUPED-UP SPIRIT POWERS...
THAT'S A LOT OF SPIRITS TO PURIFY...
AGEHA-SAMA'S NOT BEING FORCED TO DO ANY OF THIS.
THAT'S RIGHT. THE NUMBER OF SPIRITS THAT WILL BE EXORCISED...
...IS ALL UP TO AGEHA'S VERY OWN WILL AND VOLITION.
THAT'S WHY I'M CONFIDENT SHE'LL GIVE UP PARTWAY THROUGH...
...OR GET TIRED AND ABANDON THE WORK.
THAT'S THE AGEHA I KNOW!
SHE'S NOT STOPPING.
HEH...

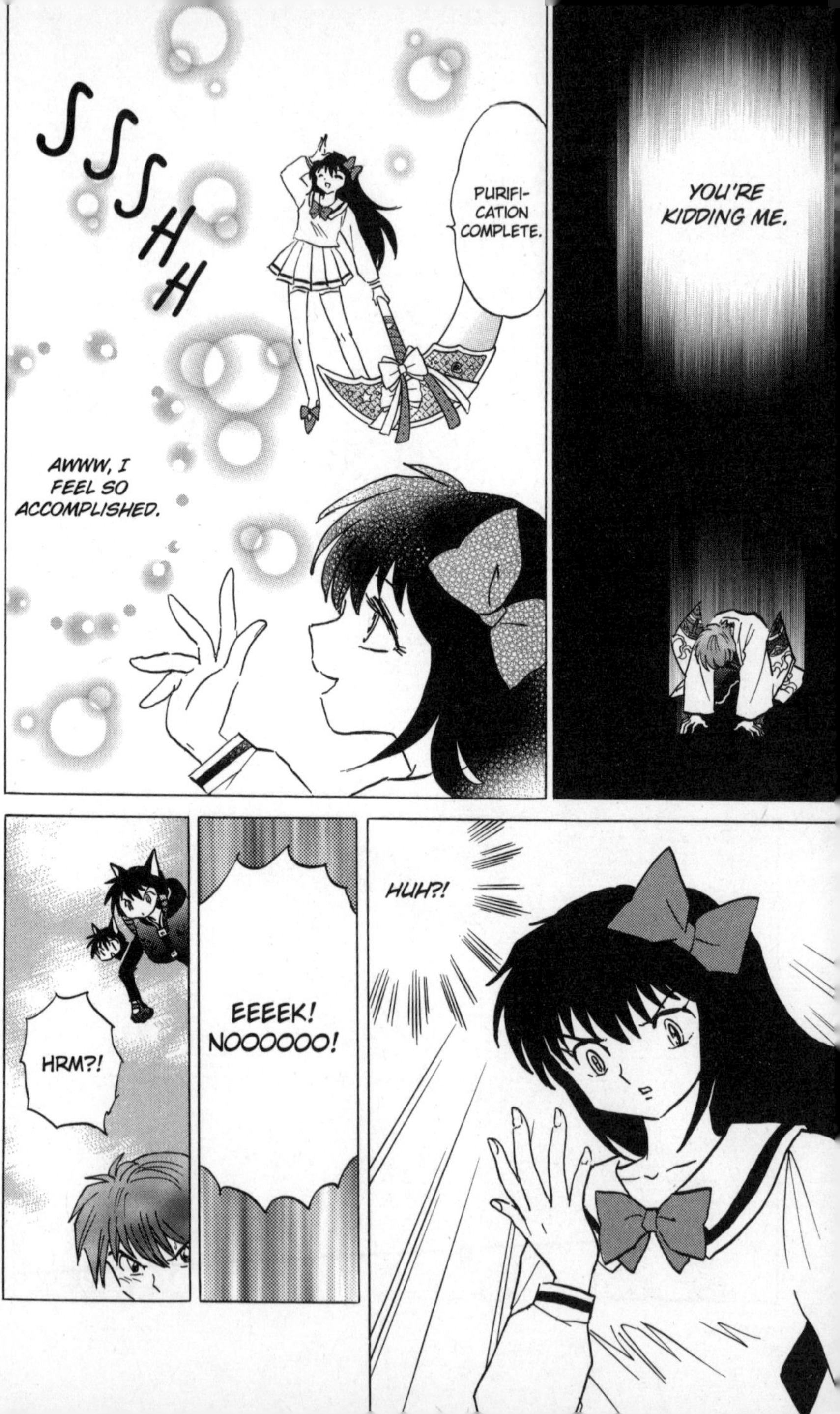
YOU'RE KIDDING ME.
PURIFI-CATION COMPLETE.
SSSHH
AWWW, I FEEL SO ACCOMPLISHED.
HUH?!
EEEEK! NOOOOOO!
HRM?!

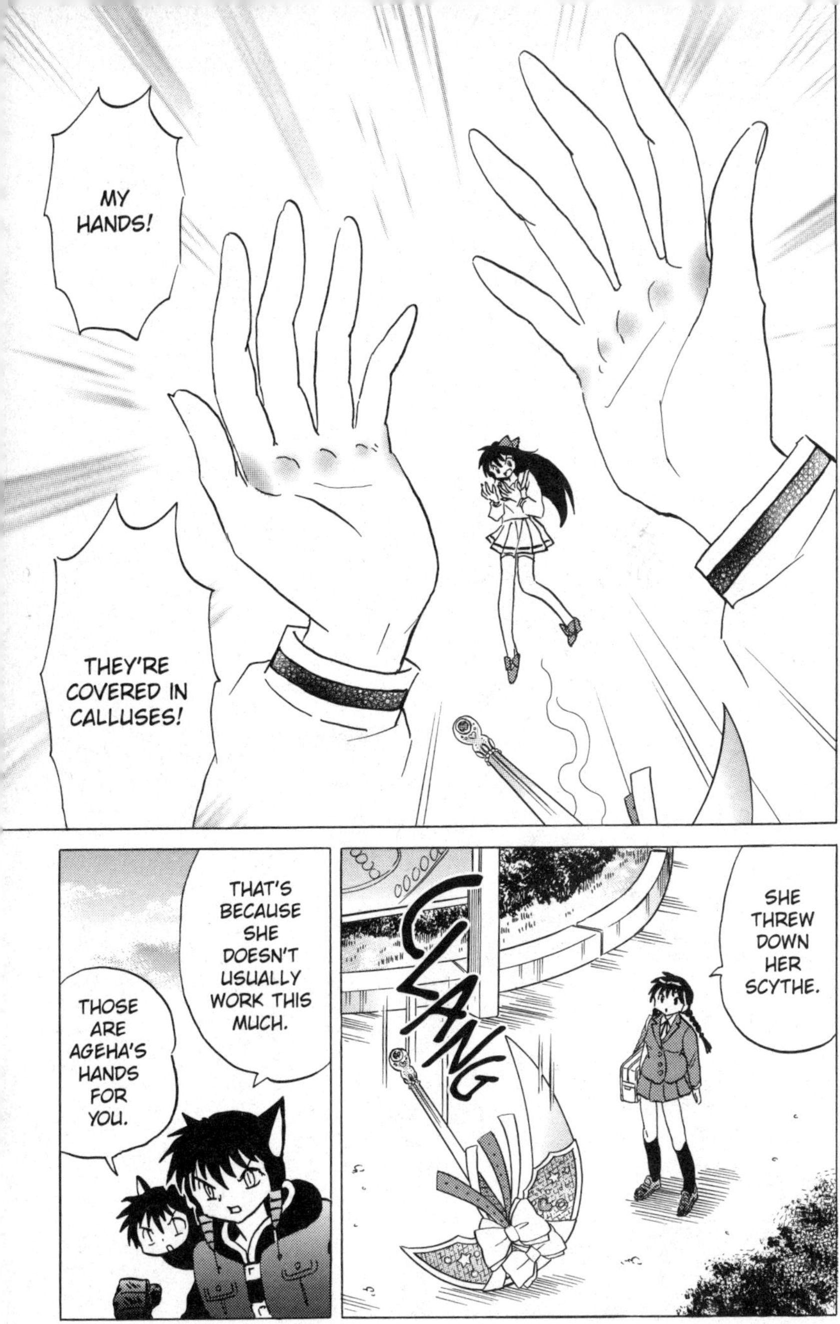
MY HANDS!
THEY'RE COVERED IN CALLUSES!
SHE THREW DOWN HER SCYTHE.
CLANG
THAT'S BECAUSE SHE DOESN'T USUALLY WORK THIS MUCH.
THOSE ARE AGEHA'S HANDS FOR YOU.

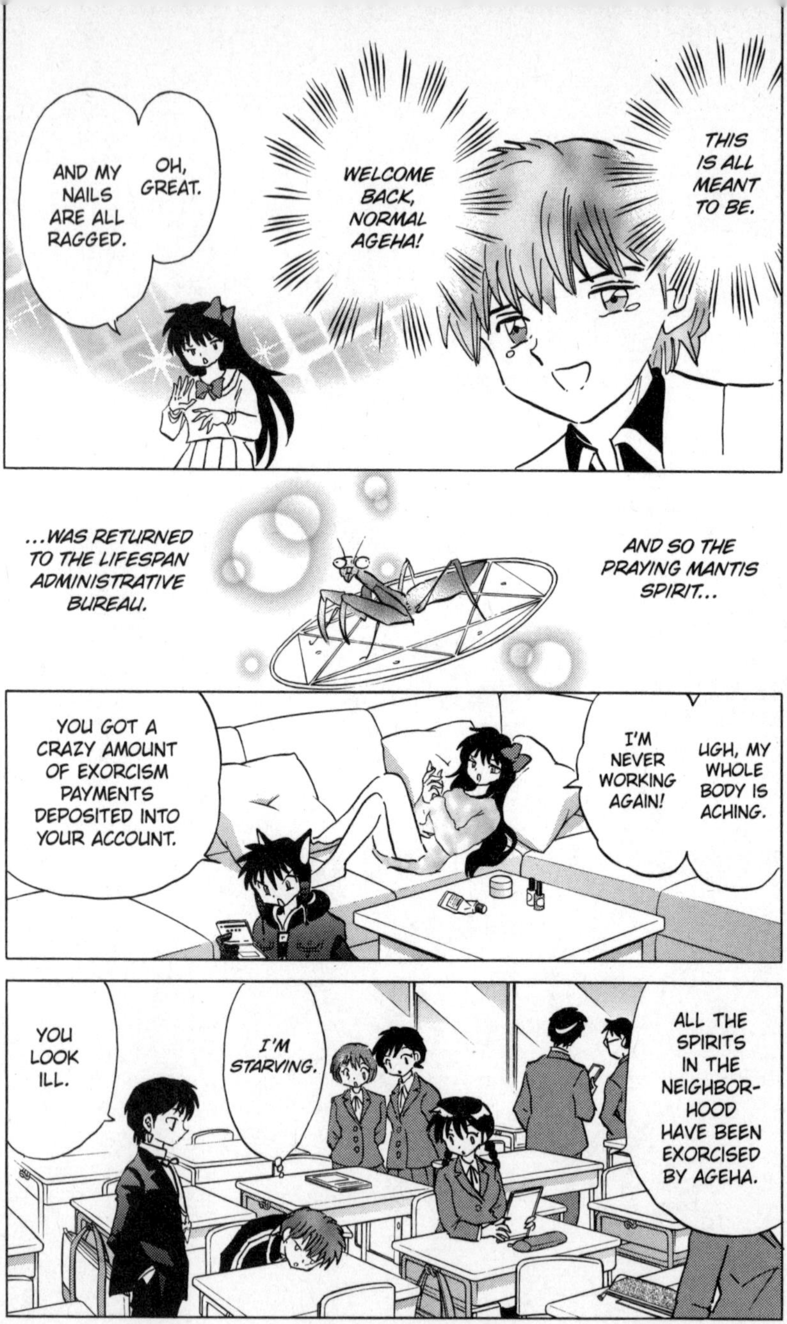
THIS IS ALL MEANT TO BE.
WELCOME BACK, NORMAL AGEHA!
OH, GREAT.
AND MY NAILS ARE ALL RAGGED.
AND SO THE PRAYING MANTIS SPIRIT...
...WAS RETURNED TO THE LIFESPAN ADMINISTRATIVE BUREAU.
UGH, MY WHOLE BODY IS ACHING.
I'M NEVER WORKING AGAIN!
YOU GOT A CRAZY AMOUNT OF EXORCISM PAYMENTS DEPOSITED INTO YOUR ACCOUNT.
ALL THE SPIRITS IN THE NEIGHBOR-HOOD HAVE BEEN EXORCISED BY AGEHA.
I'M STARVING.
YOU LOOK ILL.

RINNE [39] THE END

Rumiko Takahashi

The spotlight on Rumiko Takahashi's career began in 1978 when she won an honorable mention in Shogakukan's prestigious New Comic Artist Contest for *Those Selfish Aliens*. Later that same year, her boy-meets-alien comedy series, *Urusei Yatsura*, was serialized in *Weekly Shonen Sunday*. This phenomenally successful manga series was adapted into anime format and spawned a TV series and half a dozen theatrical-release movies, all incredibly popular in their own right. Takahashi followed up the success of her debut series with one blockbuster hit after another—*Maison Ikkoku* ran from 1980 to 1987, *Ranma ½* from 1987 to 1996, and *Inuyasha* from 1996 to 2008. Other notable works include *Mermaid Saga*, *Rumic Theater*, and *One-Pound Gospel*.

Takahashi was inducted into the Will Eisner Comic Awards Hall of Fame in 2018. She won the prestigious Shogakukan Manga Award twice in her career, once for *Urusei Yatsura* in 1981 and the second time for *Inuyasha* in 2002. A majority of the Takahashi canon has been adapted into other media such as anime, live-action TV series, and film. Takahashi's manga, as well as the other formats her work has been adapted into, have continued to delight generations of fans around the world. Distinguished by her wonderfully endearing characters, Takahashi's work adeptly incorporates a wide variety of elements such as comedy, romance, fantasy, and martial arts. While her series are difficult to pin down into one simple genre, the signature style she has created has come to be known as the "Rumic World." Rumiko Takahashi is an artist who truly represents the very best from the world of manga.

RIN-NE

VOLUME 39
Shonen Sunday Edition

STORY AND ART BY
RUMIKO TAKAHASHI

KYOKAI NO RINNE Vol. 39
by Rumiko TAKAHASHI
© 2009 Rumiko TAKAHASHI
All rights reserved.
Original Japanese edition published by SHOGAKUKAN.
English translation rights in the United States of America,
Canada, the United Kingdom, Ireland, Australia and New
Zealand arranged with SHOGAKUKAN.

Translation/Christine Dashiell
Touch-up Art & Lettering/Evan Waldinger
Design/Yukiko Whitley
Editor/Megan Bates

Printed in the U.S.A.

Published by VIZ Media, LLC
P.O. Box 77010
San Francisco, CA 94107

10 9 8 7 6 5 4 3 2 1
First printing, May 2021

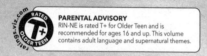

viz.com

shonensunday.com

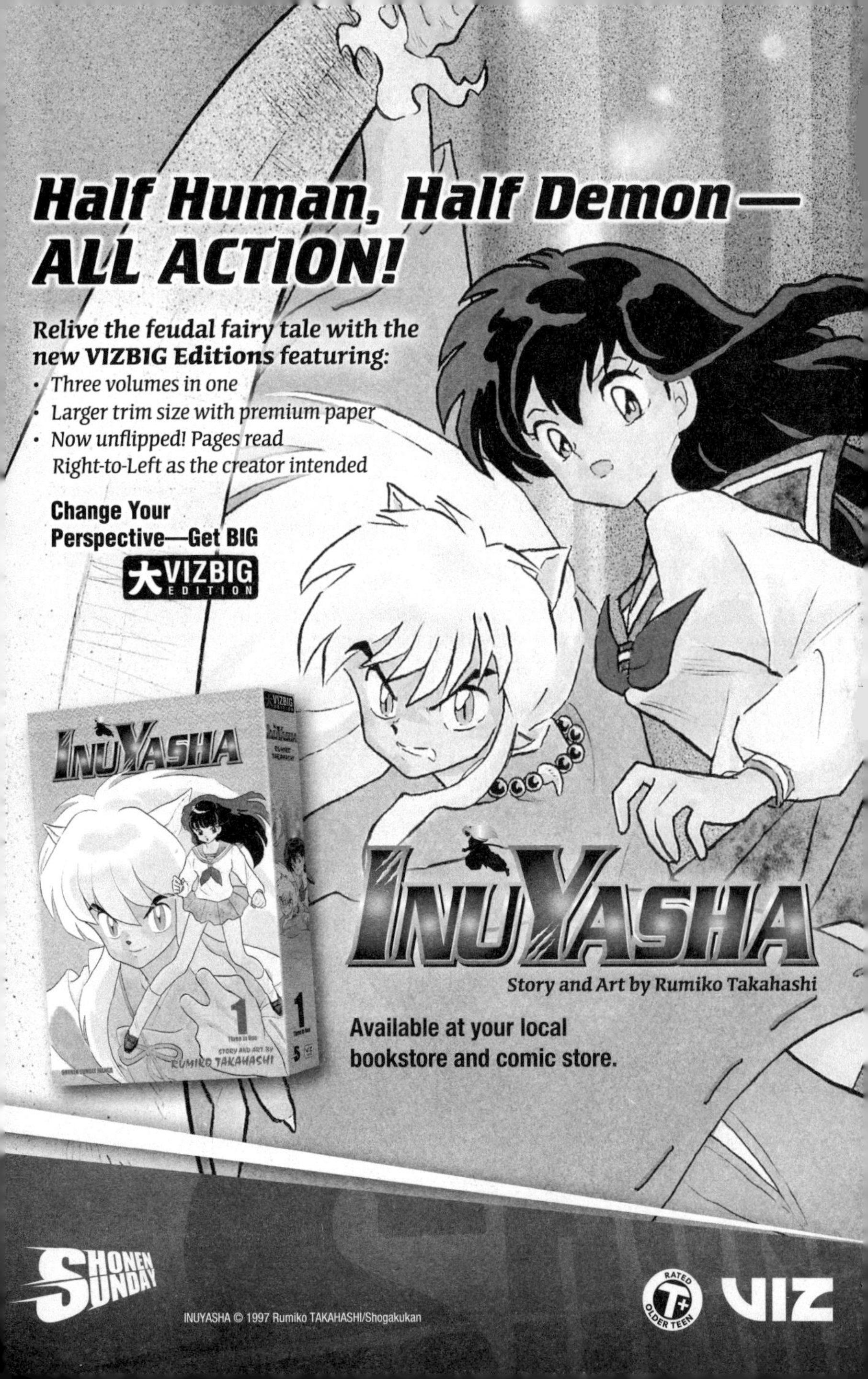
Half Human, Half Demon—
ALL ACTION!
Relive the feudal fairy tale with the new VIZBIG Editions featuring:
• Three volumes in one
• Larger trim size with premium paper
• Now unflipped! Pages read Right-to-Left as the creator intended
Change Your Perspective—Get BIG
大 VIZBIG EDITION
INUYASHA
1
STORY AND ART BY RUMIKO TAKAHASHI
INUYASHA
Story and Art by Rumiko Takahashi
Available at your local bookstore and comic store.
SHONEN SUNDAY
INUYASHA © 1997 Rumiko TAKAHASHI/Shogakukan
RATED T+ OLDER TEEN
VIZ

Hey! You're Reading in the Wrong Direction!

This is the end of this graphic novel!

To properly enjoy this VIZ graphic novel, please turn it around and begin reading from right to left. Unlike English, Japanese is read right to left, so Japanese comics are read in reverse order from the way English comics are typically read.

This book has been printed in the original Japanese format in order to preserve the orientation of the original artwork. Have fun with it!

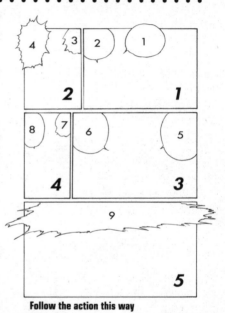

Follow the action this way